PLANETARY LOVES

TRANSDISCIPLINARY THEOLOGICAL COLLOQUIA

Theology has hovered for two millennia between scriptural metaphor and philosophical thinking; it takes flesh in its symbolic, communal, and ethical practices. With the gift of this history and in the spirit of its unrealized potential, the Transdisciplinary Theological Colloquia intensify movement between and beyond the fields of religion. A multivocal discourse of theology takes place in the interstices, at once self-deconstructive in its pluralism and constructive in its affirmations.

Hosted annually by Drew University's Theological School, the colloquia provide a matrix for such conversations, while Fordham University Press serves as the midwife for their publication. Committed to the slow transformation of religiocultural symbolism, the colloquia continue Drew's long history of engaging historical, biblical, and philosophical hermeneutics, practices of social justice, and experiments in theopoetics.

STEERING COMMITTEE

Catherine Keller, *Director*

Virginia Burrus

Stephen D. Moore

PLANETARY LOVES

Spivak, Postcoloniality, and Theology

EDITED BY STEPHEN D. MOORE
AND MAYRA RIVERA

FORDHAM UNIVERSITY PRESS ❧ NEW YORK ❧ 2011

Library of Congress Cataloging-in-Publication Data

Drew Transdisciplinary Theology Colloquium (7th : 2007 : Drew Theological School)
  Planetary loves : Spivak, postcoloniality, and theology / edited by Stephen D. Moore and Mayra Rivera.
    p.   cm.— (Transdisciplinary theological colloquia)
  Includes bibliographical references and index.
  ISBN 978-0-8232-3325-0 (cloth : alk. paper)
  ISBN 978-0-8232-3326-7 (pbk. : alk. paper)
  ISBN 978-0-8232-3327-4 (ebook : alk. paper)
  1. Postcolonial theology—Congresses.
2. Spivak, Gayatri Chakravorty—Congresses.
I. Moore, Stephen D., 1954–   II. Rivera, Mayra.   III. Title.
BT83.593.D74   2011
230—dc22

                                    2010016645

Printed in the United States of America
13 12 11   5 4 3 2 1
First edition

CONTENTS

ACKNOWLEDGMENTS

This volume had its origins in the proceedings of the seventh Transdisciplinary Theological Colloquium, which was held at Drew Theological School in November 2007. There would have been no TTC, however, much less a seventh one, without Catherine Keller, whose inaugural vision birthed the colloquium series and whose indefatigable intellectual energy has nourished it over the years. If the people perish without a vision, the vision itself perishes without material sustenance, and so neither would the colloquium have reached its seventh year without the steadfast support of Maxine Clarke Beach, Dean of Drew Theological School. Helen Tartar, Editorial Director of Fordham University Press, has provided material support of another sort; we continue to be grateful for the opportunity to publish the colloquium proceedings in the series that she created. Several Drew graduate students devoted significant amounts of time and energy to the organization of TTC7, none more than Elaine Padilla. The colloquium program was enriched by a splendid array of respondents, discussants, and student presenters whom we were not able to include in this volume: Virginia Burrus, Anne Daniell, Lynne Darden, Rose Ellen Dunn, Marion Grau, Peter Goodwin Heltzel, Ada María Isasi-Díaz, Melanie Johnson-DeBaufre, Hyo-Dong Lee, Matilde Moros, Mary-Jane Rubenstein, Devin Lin Singh, H. Aram Veeser, Asher Walden, and Traci West. We are also grateful to Lydia York for assuming the daunting task of transcribing the extended public conversations with Gayatri Chakravorty Spivak that constituted the core of the event, and also for compiling the volume's index. Most of all, we are grateful to

Professor Spivak herself—first, for risking a leap into what were, for her, uncharted waters; second, for the extraordinary affability and humility that she brought to the conversation; and third, for editing the transcript of her performance so promptly even while (as she explained in her accompanying missive) she was "on the run across Bangladesh." May she long run and never falter.

PLANETARY LOVES

❧ Introductions

❧ A Tentative Topography of Postcolonial Theology

MAYRA RIVERA AND STEPHEN D. MOORE

As the crow flies, the Theological School at Drew University in Madison, New Jersey, is less than thirty miles from the Department of English and Comparative Literature at Columbia University in New York City. In other respects, of course, the distance between these two institutional spaces is absolute: they occupy two parallel discursive dimensions that, left to their own devices, would extend to infinity without ever intersecting. On the afternoon of November 2, 2007, Gayatri Chakravorty Spivak, Columbia's most distinguished literary scholar, and arguably the most influential literary and cultural critic on the planet (although the term "planet" resists casual usage after Spivak: she has turned it into a complex philosophical concept), stepped through the portal between these parallel dimensions to attend the seventh Drew Transdisciplinary Theological Colloquium (henceforth, TTC7).

This, however, was not her first encounter with the strange tribe of theologians. Peter Goodwin Heltzel, whose office had been contiguous to Spivak's the previous year, had been bold enough to invite her to meet informally with him and certain other theologians with an interest in her work, and Spivak had been bold enough to accept. Thus it was that Peter Heltzel, Mayra Rivera, Lester Edwin J. Ruiz, and Mark Lewis Taylor sat down for a conversation with Spivak in New York Theological Seminary on April 26, 2006. Professor Spivak must not have found the experience entirely disagreeable, because when Catherine Keller and Stephen Moore, organizers of TTC7, got wind of it and invited Spivak to participate in a more formal and more public conversation around her work in its relation to theology, she also readily accepted. Subsequent to TTC7, moreover, she has delivered the William James Lecture on Religious Experience at Harvard Divinity School. Talking to theologians and other religionists is evidently proving habit-forming for Professor Spivak, and many of us could not be more pleased.

BEGINNINGS

These theological conversations with Spivak took place in a space that had gradually opened up within the field of theological studies since the 1990s and that had come, retrospectively, to be named postcolonial theology. This space defies clear demarcation, however, despite its attainment of a name; still in its emergent phase, it overlaps complexly with other, more established areas of theological inquiry, such as liberation, contextual, and political theologies. Even despite—or possibly because of—its blurred boundaries, postcolonial theology has already emerged as a site of intense intellectual and political energy, marked as it is by unprecedented preoccupation with the effects of empires old and new, and productive engagement with the interdisciplinary field of postcolonial studies—including that complex corner of it occupied by Spivak, an iconic figure for postcolonial studies, yet one who appears to be outside the field as much as inside it.

Stephen Moore's essay in this volume explores Spivak's paradoxical relationship to postcolonial studies, the field that has mediated the reception of her work in the theological disciplines. Kwok Pui-lan's essay, meanwhile, explores Spivak's relationship to theological studies in a direct fashion—and in a more systematic fashion, we might add, than any other essay in the volume. As such, Kwok's essay functions as a kind of second introduction to the volume, although it was not written as such. The present introduction, for its part, focuses more broadly on the reception of postcolonial studies as a whole in theology and hence with sketching out the general contours of postcolonial theology.

The task of mapping the reception of postcolonial studies in theology necessarily begins on the always porous boundary between theology and biblical studies, for the Bible was the first focus of explicit postcolonial analysis in the theological fields. Equipped with the tools of liberation and contextual hermeneutics, and/or with the resources of the proliferating interdisciplinary field of postcolonial studies, biblical scholars began in the mid- to late 1990s to examine anew not only the ancient imperial contexts of the biblical texts, reframing those contexts in unprecedented ways, but also to reconsider the fate of those texts in the Western colonial adventures.[1] From these initial explorations emerged a steady stream of contributions to postcolonial biblical hermeneutics, as well as a wide variety of studies in the often convoluted relationships between specific biblical texts and the ancient imperial ideologies and institutions that they reflected, refracted, or resisted; the employment of the Bible, both subtle and explicit, in the modern European colonization of the non-European world; colonialist ideologies and biblical translations; and other related projects too numerous to name.[2]

The emerging interdisciplinary field of postcolonial studies also engendered significant challenges to the histories, methods, and agendas of theological studies and gave rise to novel modes of theological inquiry. The first contributions to what we now term postcolonial theology, however, emerged in close interaction with the seminal postcolonial work being produced in biblical studies, and also had the biblical text and its reception as their focus. Kwok Pui-lan's 1995 monograph, *Discovering the Bible in the Non-Biblical World*, developed from an article with the same title that she contributed to a thematic issue of the biblical studies journal *Semeia* on liberation hermeneutics.[3] Arguably, Kwok has contributed more to the emergence and development of postcolonial theology than any other single figure, even considering that her first postcolonial volumes, her *Discovering the Bible in the Non-Biblical World* and the collection *Postcolonialism, Feminism, and Religious Discourse* (2002) that she coedited with Laura E. Donaldson, were not projects in the field of theology specifically.[4] The first explicitly theological contributions to the nascent subfield of postcolonial theology appeared almost simultaneously. *Postcolonial Theologies: Divinity and Empire* (2004) was a collection of essays in constructive postcolonial theology that emerged out of a 2002 colloquium at Drew Theological School designed to assemble a wide variety of theologians with postcolonial interests and thereby catalyze the further development of postcolonial theology.[5] Kwok's theological monograph *Postcolonial Imagination and Feminist Theology* appeared in 2005.

The range of themes and methodologies represented in these two volumes reflects the diversity of the approaches that have clustered in this still small theological subfield. Whereas the essays in *Postcolonial Theologies* tend to rely on the modes of postcolonial theory and analysis that have been influenced by poststructuralism, *Postcolonial Imagination and Feminist Theology* accords sustained attention to the intricate intersections between colonialism and gender; however, both volumes share and build on many of the established themes of liberation, contextual, and Two-Thirds World theologies. The significant diversity of approaches, however, should not be subsumed too hastily in the common ground. A complex assortment of political influences and theoretical frameworks shapes the themes and informs the debates that characterize the nascent field of postcolonial theology. For purposes of our tentative topography, that multiplicity may, however, be mapped in terms of three primary themes: empire, identity, and the reimagining of Christian doctrines.

EMPIRE

One of the most visible effects of the phenomenon we have been considering is the emergence of *empire* as a critical category for the study of theology. This category has been especially productive of works in historical theology that investigate the mutual imbrications of colonialism, imperialism, and theology. An important subset of works in this cluster analyzes the interplay of theology and ideology in contexts of colonial intervention—for instance, the colonial ideologies of certain Christian missionary enterprises.[6] In terms familiar to readers of Spivak, such works might be described as attempts to trace the "worlding" of the missionized territories,[7] a process not only productive of "other" religions and othered subjects of mission but also transformative of Christianity itself—its ecclesial and political institutions, its cultural practices and enabling metanarratives, and, inevitably, its theology.

Such work is not, however, limited to dealing with the overt, egregious, or explicit investment of Christianity in imperial projects. Other work in this mode treats empire as an ever-present, if often occluded, reality in Christian history, always affecting, whether positively or negatively, theological discourse. This angle of approach is best exemplified by *Empire and the Christian Tradition: New Readings of Classical Theologians* (2007), an imposing collection of more than five hundred pages that seeks to reframe and reread influential Christian theologians, beginning with Paul and ending with late twentieth-century liberationists, in relation to the respective empires that constitute the encompassing material and cultural contexts of their thought.[8] A similar strategy informs Joerg Rieger's *Christ and Empire* (2007), which offers a comprehensive analysis of various Christological models in relation to the imperial formations in which they were articulated, beginning again with Paul and ending with late modernity.[9] A distinguishing trait of both these volumes is their attention to the *ambivalence* of theological discourse—its capacity to be co-opted by empire even when most intent on resisting it—a critical sensibility that differs (in emphasis, at least) from earlier modes of liberationist interpretation. Catherine Keller's *God and Power* (2005) is equally attuned to ambivalence; it focuses, however, not on the long historical sweep but on the contemporary cultural moment. Centering on the post-9/11 reintensification of U.S. imperial ambitions, Keller traces both the overt and occluded effects of apocalyptic eschatology on religiopolitical discourse and foreign policy.[10] Keller's theological theorization of the neocolonial empire brings postcolonial theology into dialogue with transnational cultural studies, impelled in part by Spivak's fundamental contributions to the latter field.[11]

Certain of the essays in the present volume extend this mode of inquiry, using Spivak's theorization of neocolonial empire to investigate the theological dimensions of this complex cultural moment. As these essays map new configurations of empire and their effects on Christian discourses, they are also attentive to the strategies by which its logic might be subverted. Jenna Tiitsman's "Planetary Subjects after the Death of Geography" traces the intriguing intersections between the "death of geography" attributed to communication technologies, on the one hand, and the Christian "imaginary of a universal, immaterial sphere in which we are intimately connected in common God-given humanity," on the other, an imaginary that emerged with the Protestant Reformation, the rise of capitalism, the advent of modern science, and colonialism. Whereas Tiitsman mines Spivak's distinction between globalization and planetarity to highlight the occluded significance of geographical location and materiality for global communications, Sharon Betcher's "Crip/tography" focuses on the impact of globalization on human bodies as they are managed in global cities. In addition to uncovering the integration of colonial computations of difference into the new forms of empire, Betcher proposes a crip/topography: that is, she attempts to think "the crip" as a positionality from which to resist imperial norms. Ellen Armour's "Planetary Sightings?" also traces the legacies of colonial strategies of othering in the contemporary empire, specifically their influence in the cultural wars over the status of sexual minorities, which threaten to divide the Anglican communion in a conflict portrayed as a rift along old colonial lines. Armour suggests "enacting a progressive *planetary* Christian sexual politics" that disturbs theological and political centers and dominant orthodoxies and seeks to undo colonial inscriptions.

Spivak's critiques of empire have always included careful examination of the effects of empire in shaping academic disciplines and scholarship, and Tat-siong Benny Liew's "Lost in Translation?" follows her lead in this regard. Focusing on the complex relations between language and money, Liew explores the complicities of projects of translation and language teaching with the aims of imperialism in readings of biblical, modern, and postmodern narratives. Furthermore, Liew calls attention to the irreducible losses involved in any translation—an unavoidable effect that, however, should not lead to the abandonment of translation and language learning but rather to their supplementation by a love that recognizes the "ethical singularity" of each and every encounter.

IDENTITY

Postcolonial analyses of the responses of marginalized subjects—including resistance and refusal, subversive adaptation, and strategic reinterpretation—overlap most noticeably with contextual and liberation theologies, even when their theoretical frameworks remain distinct. R. S. Sugirtharajah has incisively itemized the principal continuities and disjunctions between liberationist and postcolonial hermeneutics in his *The Bible and the Third World*, arguing that the two approaches share a common vocation "to de-ideologizing dominant interpretation, a commitment to the Other and distrust of totalizing tendencies."[12] Liberation theologies, however, were built on modernist frameworks now challenged by postcolonial sensibilities. For instance, in classic liberationist discourses "salvation history" functioned as a metanarrative focusing exclusively on the God of Israel and moving inexorably toward the Christian kingdom of God as its telos—thereby reproducing the kind of totalizing gesture that postcolonial theory typically seeks to unmask. The liberationist tendency to rely on the Bible as a text that is unequivocally, unvaryingly, and intrinsically emancipatory is also in tension with the characteristic postcolonial attunement to ambivalence—or, in Spivak's terms, to inevitable complicity and hence the necessity of incessant critique.

Yet the differences between liberation and postcolonial theologies should not be overstated. Two-Thirds World philosophies and theologies have often converged with—and at times have anticipated[13]—postcolonial studies in their critiques of Eurocentrism, modernist epistemologies, colonialism and imperialism, global capitalism, and other such interrelated realia.[14] Certain developments in liberation theologies, moreover—mainly but not only those appearing after the 2001 publication of Sugirtharajah's influential appraisal—render the boundaries between liberation and postcolonial theologies still more permeable.[15] An increasing number of self-identified liberation theologians draw on postcolonial studies (names such as Mark Lewis Taylor, Joerg Rieger, and Marcella Althaus-Reid leap readily to mind). Furthermore, liberation theology since the 1980s has regularly been (in)formed by feminism. Due significantly to Kwok's influential role in shaping postcolonial theology, meanwhile, many of the publications it has yielded in the United States to date have also been notably attentive to gender[16]—an approach also modeled by Spivak but largely absent from the work of Edward Said and Homi Bhabha (to name the two other most influential exemplars of postcolonial theory). And the dual feminist preoccupations of liberationist and postcolonial discourses further complexify the liberation/postcolonial dichotomy, by raising fundamental questions about the assumed subject of both discourses.

Many of the contributions to postcolonial theologies that emerge from debates within, or on the edges of, liberation and contextual theologies are marked by intense discussions about cultural identity, occasionally accompanied by critiques of the very notions of identity typically operative in such theologies. Namsoon Kang's "Who/What Is Asian?" exemplifies this brand of postcolonial theology.[17] She draws on Said's concept of Orientalism and on Spivak's critique of the politics of representation to challenge both feminist theology's representation and objectification of Third World women and the self-Orientalizing tendencies evident in certain Asian theologies. Kang, in common with other postcolonial theologians, turns to the concept of hybridity as a constructive alternative to the atomized identities of modernity. Similarly, it is through the notion of hybridity in its relationship with notions of *mestizaje/mulatez* that Latina/o theologies have engaged, sometimes skeptically, with postcolonial discourses.[18] Such engagement with postcolonial concepts and categories, however, has most often entailed not a challenge to constructions of identity in Latina/o theologies but explications of the similarities between hybridity and *mestizaje/mulatez* and expressions of preference for the latter, developed in Latina/o studies outside theology, as a crucial category for describing Latina/o cultural identity.

Hybridity has been a crucial category in discussions by postcolonial theologians not only about cultural identity but also about religious identity (to the extent that the latter can be cleanly distinguished from the former), where it names the fluid boundaries, shifting surfaces, and internal multiplicity of Christian identity. Susan Abraham's *Identity, Ethics, and Nonviolence in Postcolonial Theory* (2007) engages Bhabha's concept of hybridity as well as Spivak's and Ashis Nandy's theorizations of agency to rethink cultural and religious boundaries, as she also challenges postcolonial theory for bracketing religious commitments and discourses.[19] Jeannine Hill Fletcher's *Monopoly on Salvation? A Feminist Approach to Religious Pluralism* (2005) is perhaps the first book in the area of theology of religions to draw substantially from postcolonial theory, specifically from the work of Bhabha.[20] Postcolonial theory raises fundamental questions for the articulation of Christian identity and religious pluralism—questions that theology of religions has yet to address.[21] Religious studies scholars attuned to colonialism argue that the category "religion" itself was a colonial imposition onto cultures and communities for whom the term initially had little meaning. The term "religion"—or perhaps even more so "religions"—regularly operates as a "signifier that allows us to forget [its] 'worlding,'" systematically obscuring the history of its production.[22] For John Thatamanil, the question that still remains unasked might be posed as follows: "Is it possible to imagine a theology of religious pluralism that is not uncritically or unselfconsciously wedded to the category 'religion'?" That is precisely the question that Thatamanil addresses in his essay in this volume.

Spivak's expression "strategic essentialism" is also commonly invoked in these debates about identity and difference, as theologians attempt to carve out a viable epistemological space for assertions of cultural identity in their work.[23] The term "strategic essentialism" is associated with Spivak's early essay "Subaltern Studies: Deconstructing Historiography," in which she provocatively reframes the work of the Indian Subaltern Studies Group, with which she herself was affiliated, as "a strategic use of positivist essentialism in a scrupulously visible political interest."[24] Rather than assuming that action flows naturally from identity, strategic essentialism acknowledges the employment of or appeal to an essentialized concept of identity, however deconstructible, as a sometimes necessary political tactic. Spivak had also used the term to respond to common charges of essentialism leveled against Third World feminisms—which she interpreted as "intellectual posturing" that distracted from the pressing issues being addressed by such feminisms. She warns, however, that strategic essentialism "can turn into an alibi for proselytizing academic essentialisms" when it is presented as a theory rather than as a strategy or tactic fitting a specific situation.[25] Strategic essentialism thus names an important site of possibility and tension for postcolonial theologies engaging questions of cultural identity. At the heart of Spivak's own concern about misuses of the phrase is her assessment of the limitations of identitarianism. As she remarks in a recent interview: "I think identitarianism ignores what is most interesting about being alive, that is to say, being angled towards the other. I therefore found that it was unfortunate that people liked that phrase [strategic essentialism]."[26]

The questions of cultural and religious identity are related but not identical to those of sociopolitical location. Although postcolonial theologies interested in cultural identity have relied heavily on Bhabha's concept of hybridity, those concerned with the possibilities and perils of the politics of representation might find a sturdier ally in Spivak. An arresting example of such attention to the problematics of representation is Marcella Althaus-Reid's critique of Latin American liberation theology. She boldly challenges its construction of "the poor" as a category, drawing on gender and queer studies to unveil the implicit heteronormativity of such construction. A second element in her critique further problematizes the relationship between the liberation theologian and "the poor," arguing that "the poor" have paradoxically enhanced the value of liberation theology as a product of consumption for the global market.[27] Although Althaus-Reid's work is informed by Marxist studies and by the writings of Fanon and Said, there are clear resonances between Althaus-Reid's critique of liberation theology and Spivak's interrogation of the practices through which the woman of the global South is constituted as an object of benevolence that serves the self-construction and upward mobility of migrant intellectuals and First World feminists.

Spivak's controversial essay "Can the Subaltern Speak?" is a further exercise with far-reaching ramifications for identity politics.[28] Its reception within theology has tended to mirror its fate elsewhere: it has provoked multiple accusations of sidelining or even silencing already marginalized constituencies and, as such, has provoked swift dismissals. But there are important exceptions to this often facile reception, where Spivak's essay has led to profound self-critical questioning. Mark Lewis Taylor, for instance, has addressed, critically and constructively, the implications of "Can the Subaltern Speak?" for liberation theology and its commitment to advocacy; while Vítor Westhelle has employed the distinction between the two meanings of "representation" developed in Spivak's essay—representation as "speaking for" in contrast to aesthetic "re-presentation"—to address the problematic tendency to assume a continuity between the two, leading to a focus on re-presentation at the expense of representation.[29] Spivak's essay also provides the hermeneutical lenses for Liew's reading, in this volume, of the widow's offering in Mark 12:41–44.

In this volume, too, questions of identity are addressed in relation to Spivak's planetarity as contributors strive to offer articulations of subjectivity based not on a priori characteristics of common experiences, but on her concept of "ethical singularity" and its implications for interhuman responsi-bility. Erin Runions's "Effects of Grace" deploys a queering, deconstructive strategy. Seeking to unsettle the transcendental differentiations that serve as the foundations for social hierarchies based on identity—especially sexual identity—Runions questions the stability of the difference between the Christ and the sexualized, racialized antichrist through a reading of their common biblical genealogy, tracing the emergence of both figures back to the Son of Man in the book of Daniel. Namsoon Kang's "Toward a Cosmo-politan Theology" pursues a constructive proposal for a cosmopolitanism designed to challenge exclusive notions of identity. Her "cosmopolitanism from below" has as its basic components a "planetary love" practiced as response to "ethical singularity," consonant with Spivak's proposals, and the Christian commandment of radical neighborly love. In contrast to Runions's deconstructive destabilizing of certain identities and Kang's emphasis on the internal multiplicity of categories of identity and "trans-identity" politics, Lydia York makes strong claims for identity in the context of white women seeking to become agents of social change. York contends in "Not Quite Not Agents of Oppression" that anti-oppression work requires learning the real force as well as falsity of binary logics. Spivak's analysis of the soul-making process for colonized and colonizing women is an invaluable tool, York argues, to aid in the liberation of white women from their gendered oppression and addiction to unearned privilege.

REIMAGININGS

The theologies in this third cluster exhibit a more explicit interest in the imaginative rearticulation of Christian doctrines in response to the chal-lenges posed by postcolonial studies. Monographs in this group include Wonhee Anne Joh's *Heart of the Cross: A Postcolonial Christology* (2006), Sharon Betcher's *Spirit and the Politics of Disablement* (2007), and Mayra Rivera's *The Touch of Transcendence: A Postcolonial Theology of God* (2007).[30] These and related theological explorations tend to draw heavily from extratheological postcolonial theory in conversation with other theoretical resources such as psychoanalytic theory, queer theory, deconstruction, and disability studies. The self-conscious commitment to creative reengagement with theological symbols characteristic of these works intersects interestingly with Spivak's complex relationship to her own disciplinary matrix: "The humanities train the imagination to approach the Other. In the contemporary context, and if undertaken seriously, the humanities systematically displace what in the interest of time I will simply call 'the religious transcendental' into the philosophical literary."[31] Postcolonial theologies in the constructive mode accept as their own a commitment to train the imagination to approach the Other and might not even be opposed to the displacement of the religious transcendental into the philosophical literary—which might, after all, turn out to be a richly productive site for theology in the wake of poststructuralism and postcolonialism.

Spivak's agenda is assuredly not religious per se; the public conversations with her transcribed in this volume leave one in no doubt of that. Her unique style of theorizing and trademark strategies of reading, however, are potentially invaluable models for theologians struggling to hold together the deconstructive imperative to engage in the critique of theology and self-critique, on the one hand, and the ethical imperative to engage contemporary sociopolitical contexts, on the other hand. In addition to these lessons in reading, a theologian discovers in Spivak's writing numerous provocations for constructive explorations. Her allusions to the wholly Other in the *Critique of Postcolonial Reason*, for example, constitute an intriguing, perhaps irresistible, trope for theologians seeking to find an intellectually and ethically habitable space in the legacy of Karl Barth. Most feminist theologians have long disclaimed the absolutely distant God most often implied by allusions to the wholly Other, but Spivak's deployment of the phrase as part of a systematic effort to displace transcendence has, paradoxically, profound theological implications. As many of the contributors to the present volume note, Spivak's concept of planetarity is best understood in relation to this detranscendentalizing strategy. Furthermore, this particular figuration of displaced transcendence also disrupts the anthropocentrism that has all too commonly subtended theology.

Susan Abraham's contribution to this volume, "The Pterodactyl in the Margins," advances the elaboration of the theological implications of Spivak's detranscendentalizing moves. Abraham draws connections between a reconfiguration of the relationship between transcendence and immanence and an ethics based on planetarity rather than on identity, an ethics that affirms "the best of our human impulses, which is to be for others." Abraham calls for a planetary theology that detranscendentalizes theism and highlights the entanglements of the mundane and the divine. Mayra Rivera, meanwhile, in her "Ghostly Encounters," searches for the entanglement of the mundane and the divine in the complex zones of historical memory. Inspired by literary images of ghostly presences, and especially by Spivak's interest in haunting as a name for an attempt to relate to the past, Rivera follows the emergence of the Holy Ghost as an elusive agent of memory in the Gospel of John. She proposes a ghostly reading of the Holy Ghost, one that reimagines it as a theological figure for the divine in the faults of history.

Like Abraham, W. Anne Joh in "Love's Multiplicity" receives Spivak's description of the human as "intended toward the other" as an incitement for constructive theological reimagining. Attentive to the challenges of translation that Liew's essay explores in a different register, Joh risks a translation (or transliteration?) of her own: a reading of love that draws from the Korean concept of *jeong*, which, she argues, combines the (already multilingual) concepts of *agape*, *philia*, and *eros*. Challenging the Christian tendency to foreclose particular practices of love, Joh seeks to open spaces for a pluralization of love to ground a politics of planetarity. For Dhawn Martin in *"Pax Terra* and Other Utopias?" a politics of planetarity evokes and potentially inflects the biblical invocation "Thy kingdom come." Implicit in Martin's (de)constructive theological project—and eventually explicit in it—is a theoretical rearticulation of Jesus' parables of the kingdom: "The kingdom of God, therefore, is like a cosmopolis, where the universe and all its universals provide the space, the soil and ground for the various turns and particular expressions of existence lived and loved together, voiced in a cacophony of vernaculars." Martin reimagines the kingdom of God, not as an "originary paradise" or a "monolithic telos," but as an ever-to-come "planetary cosmopolis."

◆ Situating Spivak

STEPHEN D. MOORE

Postcolonialism remained caught in mere nationalism over against colonialism. Today it is planetarity that we are called to imagine.
GAYATRI CHAKRAVORTY SPIVAK, *Death of a Discipline*

When Gayatri Chakravorty Spivak arrived at Drew Theological School on the afternoon of November 2, 2007, she entered a conversation already under way. The immediate conversation had been in progress since the previous evening, the larger conversation for considerably longer. It centered on the challenge of employing Spivak's thought to think theologically. Why Spivak? The facile answer might have been that postcolonial studies, with postcolonial theory tucked under its wing (sometimes uncomfortably), had recently arrived in theological studies,[1] and Spivak was, after all—was she not?—the preeminent living embodiment, the veritable avatar, of postcolonial studies and, above all, postcolonial theory. Thankfully, things were not nearly so simple. The relationship of Spivak's thought to theology is oblique, to say the least. That relationship is the principal subject of the present volume, and the wager of the volume (as of the colloquium from which it sprang) is that the very complexity of the relationship has the potential to stretch theological thinking to its limits and, perhaps, beyond, to deform and reform it in productive ways.

But Spivak's relationship to postcolonial studies is no less convoluted, as it happens, and it is this (more unexpected) complexity that is the principal subject of the present essay. The essay will attempt to situate Spivak not only in relation to the academic field of postcolonial studies but also the field of literary studies in which it first coalesced.[2] As such, our tale begins not with postcolonial studies but with deconstruction.

A STAIN ON DECONSTRUCTION

Between 1974 and 1982, Gayatri Chakravorty Spivak's "Translator's Preface" to Jacques Derrida's *Of Grammatology* was the most detailed and, arguably, most adequate introduction to deconstruction available in any language.[3] Weighing in at eighty pages and dealing meticulously with Derrida's relations to Nietzsche, Freud, Heidegger, and Husserl—and mercilessly with the deconstructive neophyte, to whom it made no concessions whatsoever—it filled the gap formidably until the field-reifying textbooks on deconstruction by Jonathan Culler, Christopher Norris, and Vincent Leitch made their appearance.[4] The English edition of *De la grammatologie*, then, was more than the mere translation of its impenetrable French into equally impenetrable English. The ambitious "Translator's Preface" meant that the English edition was also simultaneously the first systematic installment of the translation of Derridean philosophy into American deconstruction, an effect no less real for the fact that it may have formed no part whatsoever of the translator's own intentions (deconstruction itself, however, leading us to anticipate such effects as inevitable).

Spivak's subsequent relationship to deconstruction, now spanning more than thirty years, has been at once simple and complex. On the one hand, she has remained remarkably "loyal" to deconstruction, has never renounced it, no matter how unfashionable it has become. Consider, for example, the fact that her 1999 magnum opus *A Critique of Postcolonial Reason* needs to devote only one line to "postcolonial discourse" in its index, two lines to "postcoloniality," and none at all to "postcolonial studies" or "postcolonial theory" (an arresting fact to which we shall later return), but more than twenty lines to "deconstruction" and another dozen to "Derrida, Jacques." More than that, the book ends with an appendix titled "The Setting to Work of Deconstruction," which makes deconstruction the object of elementary exposition (more or less; this *is* Spivak, after all) of a kind otherwise absent from the book. "The term 'deconstruction' was coined by the French philosopher Jacques Derrida (1930–)," the appendix dutifully begins.[5] But the book itself also begins with deconstruction. It is dedicated to two people, one of whom is Spivak's doctoral mentor Paul de Man, deceased since 1983, and controversial icon of early American deconstruction. Over the years, Spivak has repeatedly acknowledged de Man's influence on her thought, undeterred, it would seem, by "the de Man affair."[6]

On the other hand, as Spivak explains in the public dialogue transcribed in this book, she has not fully followed in Derrida's footsteps, has never fully been his faithful student, has never felt able to make certain of the signal Derridean moves.[7] But her inability to be a model Derridean disciple made her a model for a different way of doing deconstruction. She tells us that she once told Derrida that she was a *tache*, a "stain," on deconstruction, punning on *Le toucher*, the book Derrida had just devoted to a far less equivocal disciple, Jean-Luc Nancy.[8] In reality, however, her work has not so much stained deconstruction as transformed its fabric. In the 1980s, Spivak's oeuvre, arguably more than any other, was instrumental in realigning, redirecting, and reinventing deconstruction by transforming it into cultural criticism or (borrowing a term from the subtitle of her first essay collection) *cultural politics*.[9] Sangeeta Ray's recent stab at distilling Spivak's methodology suggests simultaneously its intimate yet transformative relationship to "classic" deconstruction:

> A Spivakian methodology hinges on the following: acknowledging complicity, learning to learn from below, unlearning one's privilege as loss, working without guarantees, persistently critiquing the structures that one inhabits intimately and that one cannot say no to, and giving attention to subject formation such that it "produc[es] the reflexive basis for self-conscious social agency."[10]

But let us back up and attempt to situate "early" Spivak more precisely.

First-wave American deconstruction, exemplified by the work of such critics as Paul de Man, J. Hillis Miller, and Barbara Johnson, was characterized by a recurrent insistence on the sublime capacity of the texts of the inherited literary canons always to anticipate or otherwise exceed anything that the critic might think to say about them. This myth of the prescient text ("[T]he text," de Man was the first to insist, "tells the story, the allegory of its misunderstanding")[11] was also the founding myth of deconstruction in America. Deconstruction in this mode, notwithstanding its apparent radicality, was, all told, a remarkably smooth extension of formalist New Critical practice—a New New Criticism, so to speak—as had become readily apparent to many by the early 1980s.[12] Even as "Yale deconstruction" ascended to the apogee of its institutional success, the election in 1986 of J. Hillis Miller to the presidency of the Modern Language Association, poststructuralism elsewhere in North American literary studies had taken a sharp "political" turn, resulting in such field-reorienting phenomena as New Historicism, and, most especially, colonial discourse analysis, later to be relabeled postcolonial theory. Edward Said's *Orientalism* came to be seen retrospectively as the charter document of colonial discourse analysis,[13] a term that effectively implied discontinuity as well as continuity with the pathbreaking analyses of colonialism undertaken by such earlier critics as Frantz Fanon, Aimé Césaire, C. L. R. James, and Albert Memmi. For the "discourse" in colonial discourse analysis, at least in *Orientalism*, was the Foucauldian concept of discourse that Said employed to analyze the construction of the "Orient" by the West ("I have found it useful here to employ Michel Foucault's notion of a discourse. . . . My contention is that without examining Orientalism as a discourse one cannot possibly understand the enormously systematic discipline by which European culture was able to manage—and even produce—the Orient").[14] And what was characteristic of colonial discourse analysis more generally was its (controversial) recourse to European "High Theory," preeminently French (post)structuralist theory, to examine modern European colonialism and its aftermath—ostensibly another element of discontinuity with the precursors (complicated only by Fanon's occasional recourse to Lacan).[15]

The term "colonial discourse analysis" fit Spivak's work less comfortably, however, than Said's, and for two reasons. The less important reason was that Derrida, not Foucault, was Spivak's principal poststructuralist resource.[16] The more important reason was that colonial discourse (whether the term "discourse" was accorded its full Foucauldian freight or used less technically) was not Spivak's main interest—at least if the discourse in question was that of the *colonizer*, as it was for Said. Spivak's main interest was rather the discourse, or, better, the subject positions, of the *colonized*, or, better still, the *subaltern* (a term to which we shall later return). Most of all, Spivak was, and is, interested in the *female* subaltern, and an acute attention to gender pervades her work generally, another feature that distinguishes it from that of Said. In the 1980s, indeed, Spivak was as important a catalyst for an emergent transnational feminism sensitized to issues of class, race, ethnicity, and neocolonialism (in place of a second-wave First World feminism frequently blind to all of these factors), as for a politicized poststructuralist critical practice or the emergent field of postcolonial studies. Tellingly, she reduces *A Critique of Postcolonial Reason*, her most complex and ambitious work to date, to five words: "This is a feminist book."[17] As a deconstructive feminist preoccupied with the systemic omissions and blind spots that enable texts and entire societies to function, Spivak models a literary-critical practice whereby the critic concentrates on those elements of the literary work that either exclude from representation or otherwise conspire to contain "the hyperexploited human subject," most especially women of the global South.[18]

Deconstruction, feminism, Marxism. Although Derrida has loomed large thus far in this brief introduction to Spivak, it should be noted that he has done so at the expense of Marx. The narrative we have been constructing might as easily have begun with Marxism as with deconstruction, and it would have had to begin much earlier. "I didn't actually start with Derrida," she explains elsewhere in this volume. "I come from West Bengal . . . and West Bengal happens to be the longest lasting parliamentarily elected communist government in the world. So I actually started with Marx."[19] Spivak's strategic adaptation and creative retooling ("catachresis," as she herself might say) of "European theory" for engagement with non-European cultures, histories, texts, and politics, then,[20] has by no means been limited to the Parisian brand of theory. As Rashmi Bhatnagar concisely puts it, Spivak "made a conceptual breakthrough in forcing a reading of Marx through Derrida to open up the textuality of the economic."[21] But her deconstructive rereading of Marx has also been a feminist rereading of Marx. Spivak has proposed that "if the nature and history of alienation, labor, and the production of property are re-examined in terms of women's work and childbirth, it can lead us to a reading of Marx beyond Marx."[22]

THE SUBALTERN CANNOT SPEAK,
AND OTHER "INADVISABLE REMARKS"

Essentially an essayist rather than a writer of monographs, Spivak produced a series of essays in the mid-1980s that, more than any other singly authored body of work in that period, served to reorient and resource a literary studies field that was undergoing simultaneous politicization and poststructuralization. The year 1985 alone saw the appearance of such catalytic Spivakian studies as "Scattered Speculations on the Question of Value," "The Rani of Sirmur," "Subaltern Studies: Deconstructing Historiography," "Three Women's Texts and a Critique of Imperialism," and "Can the Subaltern Speak?"[23]

This last essay features prominently in the public dialogues with Spivak contained in the present volume. But there are, of course, other reasons as well for singling it out. It would be difficult to overstate the significance of this essay in the late 1980s and early 1990s for the emergent field of postcolonial studies, epitomized by postcolonial theory. If Said's *Orientalism* widely came to be seen as the field's charter document, "Can the Subaltern Speak?" came to be seen as its most controversial product, but also, arguably, its most representative product.

This much-debated essay, which swelled from ten to forty-two pages between 1985 and 1988,[24] is an uncompromisingly dense, maddeningly subtle, frequently impassioned meditation on the dual impossibility of the privileged ever speaking for the subaltern and the subaltern ever speaking for herself; for the essay notoriously answers its title question in the negative: "the subaltern cannot speak."[25] But who or what, for Spivak, *is* the subaltern? She appropriated the term from the Indian Subaltern Studies group (with which she was affiliated),[26] which in turn had appropriated it from the Italian Marxist Antonio Gramsci, the term changing meaning with each appropriation and geographical relocation. Many of the most irate denunciations of Spivak's essay seem to have stemmed from those who have read no further than the title and assumed that the subaltern is the colonized, the dispossessed, or the marginalized in general. Spivak's own concept of subalternity, however, is so thoroughly theorized, so implacably austere, that even she occasionally has difficulty measuring up to its rigor. For Spivak (or so it seems to me), the subaltern, strictly conceived, is that which is structurally and systemically written out or excluded from any hegemonic ideology, official history, developed economic structure, or political system of representation. The subaltern is the detritus of the system.[27] In *A Critique of Postcolonial Reason* we read: "It is not a mere tautology to say that the colonial or postcolonial subaltern is defined as the being on the other side of difference, or an epistemic fracture, even from other groupings among the colonized."[28] In *Other Asias* she offers a concrete example of such subalternity:

> From an anthropological point of view, groups such as the Sabar and the Dhekaros [two stigmatized Indian tribes] may be seen to have a "closely knit social texture." But I have been urging a different point of view. . . . I am asking readers to shift their perception from the anthropological to the historico-political and see the same knit text-ile

as a torn cultural fabric in terms of its removal from the dominant loom in a historical moment. That is what it means to be a subaltern.[29]

"Subaltern," then, is not a synonym for "oppressed," because not all the oppressed are subaltern. "That word is reserved for the sheer heterogeneity of decolonized space," she insists.[30] Yet she has no desire to glamorize the word, much less the abject subject to whom it refers: "If the subaltern can speak then, thank God, the subaltern is not a subaltern any more."[31]

The specific example of the subaltern, however, whom Spivak fleshes out so memorably in the closing stretch of "Can the Subaltern Speak?" seems, at first blush, to be out of alignment with her strict concept of subalternity; for this seventeen-year-old Bengali woman, Bhubaneswari Bhaduri, dead since 1926 and exhumed from Spivak's own family history,[32] was a member of the middle class. Spivak characteristically remarks: "If, in the context of colonial production, the subaltern has no history and cannot speak, the subaltern as female is even more deeply in shadow."[33] What confers subalternity on Bhaduri specifically, however, on Spivak's reading, is her inability to communicate so as to be heard through a meticulously staged self-immolation redolent with subtle symbolism. Spivak reads Bhaduri's tragic death, suicide by hanging, against the palimpsest of her membership in a group dedicated to the armed struggle for Indian independence, her assignment with a political assassination that she was unable to carry out, and the Indian tradition of *sati* (widow self-immolation), which, Spivak argues, Bhaduri was symbolically rewriting through the details of her death.[34] Of this reading Srinivas Aravamudan has remarked:

> Spivak's bravura interpretation makes Bhubaneswari into a singular figure of absence, silence, and loss. . . . [T]he political content of her defiance remains an enigma until Spivak constructs a complexly positive textual reading of the incident as revealing the surprising agency that could issue from the vilified practice of *sati*. This example, proffered at the end of the essay, is pure poiesis, a supplementary text shuttled out of family anecdotes and multiple rumors of intentions. This brilliant thought experiment of feminist world making uses subalternity catachrestically rather than empirically—in other words as a concept metaphor "for which no historically adequate referent can be advanced from postcolonial space."[35]

PACKAGING POSTCOLONIALISM

Spivak's first essay collection, *In Other Worlds: Essays in Cultural Politics*, appeared in 1987. The book remains one of her most widely read. Yet had the streamlined Spivak of the popular critical imagination who had emerged by the 1990s, the "postcolonial theorist" par excellence, put the collection together, it would surely have looked different than it does. Only partially is it a manifesto, however muted, for "postcolonial studies." The third and final part of the book, to which she gave the title "Entering the Third World," best fits that profile. It includes Spivak's translations of two short stories by the Bengali author Mahasweta Devi, framed by a "Translator's Foreword" by Spivak and a full essay by her on Devi's fiction titled "A Literary Representation of the Subaltern."[36] The influential essay "Subaltern Studies: Deconstructing Historiography" also sits in part 3; and at least one of the earlier essays in the collection, "French Feminism in an International Frame," which elucidates "the inbuilt colonialism of First World feminism toward the Third,"[37] would also prove catalytic for the seismic disciplinary shifts then under way in literary studies. That essay, which dates from 1981, may legitimately be regarded as Spivak's first major published political statement, and as programmatic for much that was to follow. It anticipates "Can the Subaltern Speak?," for instance, in interrogating the European framing of the non-European woman as requiring redemption from the non-European man. In "French Feminism in an International Frame" that woman is the Chinese female subject of foot binding, whereas in "Can the Subaltern Speak?" she is the Indian female subject of *sati*.

Conspicuous in retrospect, however, by their absence from *In Other Worlds* are "Can the Subaltern Speak?," "The Rani of Sirmur," and "Three Women's Texts and a Critique of Imperialism,"[38] all three from 1985, as noted earlier, as well as "Imperialism and Sexual Difference" from 1986.[39] Whatever Spivak conceived *In Other Worlds* to be, it wasn't solely as a showcase for postcolonial theory, apparently, or even for colonial discourse analysis. All four of these essays *do* show up, revised and recontextualized, in her 1999 monograph *A Critique of Postcolonial Reason* as some of its main ingredients, along with "Versions of the Margin," an essay exhibiting profound structural parallels with "Three Women's Texts" and also begging the "colonial discourse analysis" label.[40] Paradoxically, however, neither is the *Critique* a showcase for colonial discourse analysis or postcolonial theory, for reasons elaborated below.

And yet the term "post-colonial" does appear in the first sentence of the brief "Author's Note" that *In Other Worlds* offers in lieu of an introduction: "There would have been no 'other worlds' for me if something now called deconstruction had not come to disrupt the diasporic space of a post-colonial academic. I am, then, in Jacques Derrida's debt."[41] The term crops up more conspicuously, however, in the main title of a 1990 collection of conversations with Spivak: *The Post-Colonial Critic.* The title replicates that of one of the conversations; the idea to recycle it as the volume's main title was presumably that of the volume's editor, Sarah Harasym. The conversation in question is with three other Indian critics, Rashmi Bhatnagar, Lola Chatterjee, and Rajeshwari Sunder Rajan. The title of the published conversation thus refers to the general condition of being a postcolonial critic, with particular reference to the Indian context. By emblazoning the title on the cover, however, next to Spivak's name, tacking on the subtitle *Interviews, Strategies, Dialogues,* and juxtaposing title, subtitle and name with a artist's stylized rendition of an unnamed Indian woman's face ("Spivak herself?" the reader is impelled to wonder), Spivak is not so subtly transformed into *the* prototypical and quintessential postcolonial critic. Small wonder, then, that another Indian critic, Sangeeta Ray, was moved to object to the book as a crass commodification of Spivak and of postcolonial studies in general.[42]

Of course, the beast had barely begun to stir. As the 1990s unfolded and toppled over into the new millennium, Routledge, publisher of *The Post-Colonial Critic,* would bombard the academic market with field-generating textbooks (*The Post-Colonial Studies Reader; Key Concepts in Post-Colonial Studies; Colonialism/Postcolonialism; . . .*); many of the other major academic publishers would be running hard to keep up (*Postcolonialism; Postcolonial Criticism; Postcolonial Theory; Colonial Discourse and Postcolonial Theory; An Introduction to Post-Colonial Theory; Contemporary Postcolonial Theory; . . .*); the beast would be rendered ever less intimidating and confined in ever sturdier cages (*Beginning Postcolonialism; Postcolonialism: A Very Short Introduction; A Companion to Postcolonial Studies; Encyclopedia of Postcolonial Studies; . . .*); every imaginable mix-and-match permutation would gradually and inexorably be worked through (*Post-Colonialism and Post-Modernism; Marxism, Modernity, and Postcolonial Studies; Feminist Postcolonial Theory; Postcolonial Queer; Feminist, Queer and Postcolonial Theory; The Postcolonial Middle Ages; The Postcolonial Bible; . . .*); and small nations and entire continents would be sucked into the vortex one title at a time (*Postcolonial Vietnam; Ireland and Postcolonial Theory; Postcolonial America; Postcolonial Europe in the*

Crucible of Cultures; . . .), all leading inevitably, and with unnerving rapidity, to books in the *Beyond Postcolonial Studies* mode.[43]

Spivak, supposedly, was right at the center of it all, together with Edward Said and Homi Bhabha. In his 1995 book *Colonial Desire*, Robert Young dubbed Said, Bhabha, and Spivak the "Holy Trinity" of postcolonial theory,[44] and the label stuck, becoming an instant academic cliché. Ironically, however, Young himself probably bore more responsibility than anybody for creating the (Un)holy Trinity phenomenon. His earlier book *White Mythologies* had as its climax three substantial chapters on Said, Bhabha, and Spivak that quickly became required reading for anybody wishing to be au fait with postcolonial theory.[45]

"ONE WOMAN TEETERING ON THE *SOCLE MOUVANT* . . ."

Spivak herself, meanwhile, exhibited curiously little enthusiasm for assuming the queenly throne offered to her at the center of the wildly proliferating cross-disciplinary field that now claimed her as one of its founders. When her long-awaited monograph appeared in 1999 (her first since her 1974 study of Yeats),[46] it bore a title that implicitly announced her distance from the field: *A Critique of Postcolonial Reason.*[47] The book's opening paragraph begins:

> Postcolonial studies, unwittingly commemorating a lost object, can become an alibi unless it is placed within a general frame. Colonial Discourse studies, when they concentrate only on the representation of the colonized or the matter of the colonies, can sometimes serve the production of current neocolonial knowledge by placing colonialism/ imperialism securely in the past, and/or by suggesting a continuous line from that past to our present. This situation complicates the fact that postcolonial/colonial discourse studies is becoming a substantial subdisciplinary ghetto.[48]

"Colonialism," Spivak would seem to be implying, has become something of a mana word, even a fetish. Later on in the book she more than implies that a similar fate has befallen the term "postcolonialism"; she writes scathingly of "the aura of identification with . . . distant objects of oppression" that clings to "postcolonial informants" in the Western metropolitan centers where postcolonial studies is flourishing.[49] What, then, is the "general frame" within which colonialism needs to be placed? "Neocolonialism" would seem to be the answer, based on other statements Spivak has made. The real focus of her work, she had remarked some years earlier, was not "colonial discourse" but rather "the contemporary cultural politics of neocolonialism."[50] And in the preface to A Critique of Postcolonial Reason she states that her book "charts a practitioner's progress from colonial discourse studies to transnational cultural studies."[51]

Spivak's relationship to postcolonial studies, then, is instructively oblique. She recognizes its importance, acknowledges her own involvement in it, particularly in the past, but seems to suggest that it is an incomplete project unless it is undertaken in the service of "catch[ing] the vanishing present,"[52] a present that may, perhaps, be summed up with the term "neocolonialism." And what does she mean by neocolonialism? "By neocolonialism I always mean the largely economic rather than the largely territorial enterprise of imperialism."[53] As such, neocolonialism is but another name for late capitalism, or—if yet another overdetermined term be risked for an almost infinitely complex phenomenon—for *globalization*. It is globalization indeed, at once ineffably intricate and ineluctably mundane, ubiquitous yet elusive, that is the object of some of Spivak's most profound reflections in the *Critique of Postcolonial Reason*,[54] her attempt to read the world literarily in a manner that "does not perceive acknowledgment of complicity as an inconvenience."[55] She attempts to read it deconstructively, in other words,[56] and with acute attention to the transnational flow of global capital ("As far as I can understand it, my agenda remains an old-fashioned Marxist one"),[57] and especially to the roles of subaltern women in that incessant flood of exchange ("Feminist issues . . . are the substance of the rest"; "the Woman from the South is a particularly privileged signifier, as object and mediator; as she is, in the market, the favored agent-as-instrument of transnational capital's global reach").[58]

Spivak has, for quite some time, then, been engaged in a project that is only imperfectly captured by the labels "colonial discourse analysis," "postcolonial theory," or "postcolonial studies," even as postcolonial studies and the immense interdisciplinary debate it has generated have wheeled all around her. In recent years, however, postcolonial studies has begun to catch up with her example. Certainly, the term "postcolonialism" is beginning to lose some of its earlier aura and allure. Whatever chance the term had, when first coined, of capturing the geopolitical complexities of the post–World War II era,[59] it has considerably less chance of capturing those of the early twenty-first century. Consequently, there is growing recognition among practitioners of postcolonial studies that globalization now represents the most important analytic challenge for the field and the ultimate test of its continued relevance. Much of the promised "beyond," for example, in the 2005 collection *Postcolonial Studies and Beyond* gains its traction from the turn to globalization.[60] Other commentators modestly eschew the "beyond," settling instead for the "new." Graham Huggan, for instance, writes:

> The wide-ranging cultural effects produced by changing patterns of capitalist globalization have thus arguably become the focal point for a "new" postcolonial studies less obviously concerned with confronting the colonialisms of the past than with negotiating the imperialisms of the present. Examples of the "new" postcolonial studies can be found in a number of crossover cultural studies journals—in the British-based *Interventions* and *Third Text*, for example, or the American-based *Diaspora and Public Culture*, or the Australian-based *Postcolonial Studies*. All of these journals are pointedly inter- or transnational in ambition and interdisciplinary in method; and each, in its different way, offers a useful forum for innovative, politically-committed research in an era of globalization.[61]

"TO THINK OF OURSELVES AS PLANETARY"

What significance is assigned to Spivak in this turn to "the imperialisms of the present"? Symptomatic, perhaps, is the somewhat ambiguous role allotted to her in the first volume to tackle the postcolonialism/globalization debate head-on, the 2008 collection entitled *The Postcolonial and the Global.*[62] On the one hand, she is seldom cited in the essays that make up this volume. On the other hand, the second of the volume's three parts is titled "Planetarity and the Postcolonial," and the editors' introduction to this section credits Spivak's "suggestive contrast" of the global and the planetary with "open[ing] up this division of [the] book."[63]

The contrast in question first surfaces in Spivak's 1999 book *Imperatives to Re-imagine the Planet*, and then again in her 2003 book *Death of a Discipline*[64]— but with a much higher degree of visibility, the latter being her most frequently cited work since *A Critique of Postcolonial Reason.* The primary reason *Death of a Discipline* has drawn so much attention is that it argues for a radical reorientation and restructuring of comparative literature, the discipline whose death knell is sounded in the book's title. What theologians are more likely to cathect with, however (at least the kind liable to pick up a Spivak volume in the first place), are the various profound, faintly lyrical, frequently oblique, ecologically evocative, and—dare I say?—paratheological statements on planetarity that punctuate the latter pages of this brief book.

"I propose the planet to overwrite the globe," Spivak announces. She continues:

> Globalization is the imposition of the same system of exchange every-where. In the gridwork of electronic capital, we achieve that abstract ball covered in latitudes and longitudes, cut by virtual lines. . . . The globe is on our computers. No one lives there. It allows us to think that we can aim to control it. The planet is in the species of alterity, belonging to another system; and yet we inhabit it, on loan.[65]

Yet "responsible stewardship" of the planet (that increasingly tired theological concept), with its implicit presumption of control, is not Spivak's theme, much less an affirmation of the oneness of the planet with its human progeny. Although she is "totally, completely, in favor of ecological justice," this is not about that.[66] Even when she strikes an (oblique) ecological note in her discourse on planetarity, it is not symbiotic human oneness with the planet that is being affirmed but rather the ineluctable alterity of the planet: "To globalize is to think a manageable world. To think of ourselves as planetary is to remember that if we live a hundred years, even a devastated planet lives a billion, without us."[67] Yet neither is the planet simply to be conceived as our constitutive other: "If we imagine ourselves as planetary subjects rather than global agents, planetary creatures rather than global entities, alterity remains underived from us; it is not our dialectical negation, it contains us as much as it flings us away."[68] And so on. The elucidation of these and other related statements is the burden of several of the contributors to the present volume—not least Spivak herself in the public conversation with her transcribed in it. I shall not anticipate that task here, then, but shall attempt instead to situate Spivak's concept of planetarity more broadly.

Postcolonial theory has incubated primarily in literary studies, while globalization theory has incubated primarily in the social sciences.[69] This dichotomy adds further resonance to Spivak's musing question early in *Death of a Discipline*: "How can I, as a reader of literature, supplement the social sciences?"[70] With respect to globalization, the answer the book implicitly (and not unexpectedly) seems to offer is: By reading globalization deconstructively. Reading deconstructively means, among other things, exhuming what the system being analyzed needs to repress in order to feign coherence. As Derrida memorably phrased it in *Glas* (which text was the subject, as it happens, of Spivak's earliest article on Derrida), "what if what cannot be assimilated, the absolute indigestible, played a fundamental role in the system, an abyssal role rather?"[71] Derrida, however, was fixated on what cannot be thought or said, that which exceeds language and eludes representation: the classic poststructuralist problematic (and the primary reason theologians still read him). Spivak is hardly uninterested in the linguistic, but she is no less interested in the economic. Reading globalization means reading late capitalism, and reading it deconstructively might, among other things, mean naming its undigested and indigestible, unassimilated and inassimilable exterior, that which falls outside its monstrously capacious system—even while capitalism itself, ever more insistently, seems to project the specter of ubiquity, the appearance of a globe-girdling "inside" that is essentially and altogether without an "outside." Such naming necessarily verges on the impossible. We should not be surprised, therefore, to hear Spivak say: "In our historical moment, we must try persistently to reverse and displace globalization into planetarity—an impossible figure."[72] And again at greater length:

> [W]hat we learn (to imagine what we know) rather than know in the humanities remains vague, unverifiable, iterable. You don't put it aside in order to be literary critical.
>
> The planetarity of which I have been speaking in these pages is perhaps best imagined from the precapitalist cultures of the planet. In this era of global capital triumphant, to keep responsibility alive in the reading and teaching of the textual is at first sight impractical. It is, however, the right of the textual to be so responsible, responsive, answerable. The "planet" is, here, as perhaps always, a catachresis for inscribing collective responsibility as right. Its alterity, determining experience, is mysterious and discontinuous—an experience of the impossible.[73]

But how would Spivak now name her own (impossible) project? *A Critique of Postcolonial Reason*, as we saw earlier, termed it "transnational cultural studies."[74] *Death of a Discipline* further refines that description. Postcolonial studies is less frequently an object of critique in the latter book, but the critique, when it occurs, is more succinct. "Postcolonialism remained caught in mere nationalism over against colonialism," she remarks. "Today it is planetarity that we are called to imagine."[75] This will also entail a concomitant imagining of the "paranational": "The Earth is a paranational image that can substitute for international and can perhaps provide, today, a displaced site for the imagination of planetarity."[76] Consequently, even "transnational cultural studies," much less "postcolonial studies," will not suffice to name and contain an adequate analytic response to contemporary globalized capitalism. Her annunciation of a "global cultural studies" is accomplished via a brief but scathing dismissal of what it is hard not to read as postcolonial theory in the mode of Homi Bhabha:

> The time for producing historically thin "theory" describing the feeling of migrants in pseudopsychoanalytic vocabulary is over. . . . The old postcolonial model—very much "India" plus the Sartrian "Fanon"—will not serve now as the master model for transnational to global cultural studies on the way to planetarity. We are dealing with heterogeneity on a different scale and related to imperialisms on another model.[77]

In the end, however, Spivak refuses the clean narrative lines that we have been imposing on her intellectual biography. "Global cultural studies" does indeed seem to name what Spivak has been engaged in, or at least has aspired to, for quite some time; but the term is trotted out only in passing in *Death of a Discipline*, not even receiving the muted emphasis accorded the term "transnational cultural studies" in *A Critique of Postcolonial Reason*. The latter book, she tells us, woven mainly from earlier essays, "charts a practitioner's progress from colonial discourse studies to transnational cultural studies."[78] The sum of her books, however—to comment only on the books (a recourse of convenience, admittedly; Spivak is not, as we noted earlier, first and foremost a writer of books)—might be said to chart a practitioner's progress from the first wave of American deconstruction (I have in mind particularly the opening essays of *In Other Worlds*)[79] to global cultural studies.

But Spivak is not one for manifestos. And so the last thing we should expect to see in the book that comes after *Death of a Discipline* is the term "global cultural studies" emblazoned on its cover. And we would not be disappointed. Not only does *Other Asias* (which appeared in 2008) lack a self-locating subtitle of the *Toward a Global Cultural Studies* kind, but the concept of planetarity that glowed so brightly in the latter pages of *Death of a Discipline* and served so brilliantly to illuminate Spivak's global model of cultural studies has dropped below the horizon.[80] At the same time, however, what was mainly confined to the footnotes of *A Critique of Postcolonial Reason* ("my book charts a practitioner's progress . . . to transnational cultural studies. The latter position, a 'moving base' that I stand on as the text seeks to catch the vanishing present, has asserted itself in narrative footnotes")[81] has risen to the main text in *Other Asias* and simultaneously expanded its reach from the "transnational" to the "global."[82] From the very first page of the very first essay of *Other Asias*, and entirely without being named, "global cultural studies" is what is unreservedly being performed.[83] Specifically, "theory" (especially, although not exclusively, of the French variety) is being "tested" (Spivak's own term)—and tested severely—on such improbable and inhospitable terrain as the flood plains of Bangladesh, the Indian megacity, Afghanistan, Armenia, and the subaltern settlements of Bengal.[84] And all of this, her earlier announcement of global cultural studies in *Death of a Discipline* would seem to suggest, is being offered merely "on the way to the planetary."[85] Like any well-turned poststructuralist concept, however, the planetary can be expected to recede from Spivak at precisely the same speed with which she advances toward it, thereby drawing her inexorably onward. And it seems improbable that her continued progress toward this impossible destination will prove any less productive than it has already been. Recklessly disregarding Spivak's own warnings about the perils of ventriloquism, then, I shall presume on her behalf to end this essay with the quote from Lacan with which she herself ended the first essay of her first essay collection: "I ask you to refuse what I offer you because that is not it."[86]

❧ What Has Love to Do with It? Planetarity, Feminism, and Theology

KWOK PUI-LAN

Gayatri Chakravorty Spivak is one of those original thinkers whose work is pregnant with generative ideas that others can "work on" and "work with." Those familiar with my book *Discovering the Bible in the Non-Biblical World*, published in 1995, will know that I have worked with her notion of the native in the master discourse to elucidate the inscription of the Syrophoenician woman in the Christian Gospels of Mark and Matthew.[1] In my 1998 essay "Jesus/The Native," which marked a breakthrough in my thinking on biblical scholarship, I used her concept of "in other worlds" to debunk Eurocentrism in biblical studies and warned against the self-orientalizing tendency of "native" scholars.[2] Her critical formulation of "saving brown women from brown men" enabled me to elucidate in my contribution to *Postcolonialism, Feminism, and Religious Discourse* (2002) the colonial complicity in Mary Daly's *Gyn/Ecology*.[3] As Spivak has become increasingly critical of postcolonial studies and assumed the position of a transnational cultural critic,[4] I found myself working out the preliminaries of a transnational feminist theology in the volume *Off the Menu: Asian and Asian North American Women's Religion and Theology* (2007).[5]

All of these examples demonstrate that Spivak has cast a long shadow on my intellectual trajectory and my theological forays into postcolonialism. Spivak occupies the mind-boggling subject position of a feminist Marxist deconstructivist,[6] and her work pushes each of these theories to its limits to see what each can learn from the others. As a postcolonial feminist theologian, I am situated on the margins of different bodies of thought—postcolonial theorists are skeptical of religion and theology; the cultural dominant of feminism remains white; and mainstream theology is not only white but also androcentric. Being situated on the boundary of more than one margin, though unsettling, can help one cultivate what Toni Morrison has called "a dancing mind"[7] or give one the courage to break rules as Spivak has done in her interdisciplinary work.

A passage in Spivak's work *A Critique of Postcolonial Reason* inspires the theme of this colloquium, "Planetary Loves." Toward the end of the book, Spivak dreams of an animist liberation theology to address the ecological crisis and to mobilize collective political action. She does not think that we can invoke "the so-called great religions of the world because the history of their greatness is too deeply imbricated in the narrative of the ebb and flow of power."[8] Instead, she exhorts us to learn from the "original practical ecological philosophies of the world" and concludes that "[t]his learning can only be attempted through the supplementation of collective effort by love."[9] This sounds a little out of place in her book, since this is not typical Spivakian language, and deconstruction has not been known for offering practical guidelines for praxis or concrete action.

I am going to read Spivak within the contexts of feminist and womanist theologies and theological writings of the Two-Thirds World. My aim is to show that Spivak's work provides some provocative insights into love in postcolonial feminist theology. This could be news to her, because following Derrida, she and other deconstructivists are very allergic to anything that smacks of ontotheology. But it is from Spivak that we have learned to read a text closely in order to identify the strategies of rewriting, recoding, and reframing to trace or plot another itinerary.

The idea of "planetary loves" invites us to join the discussion and partici-pate from many vantage points, because it encourages a capacious imagination that encompasses all the sentient and nonsentient forms of existence. It opens up the margins and the boundaries so that we can encounter or anticipate the unfamiliar and the unexpected. I will elucidate the concept of planetarity, and proceed to discuss planetary love, love "in other worlds," and love for the female subaltern.

PLANETARITY

Spivak proposes "the planet to overwrite the globe."[10]

> The globe is on our computers. No one lives there. It allows us to think that we can aim to control it. The planet is in the species of

alterity, belonging to another system; and yet we inhabit it, on loan. It is not really amenable to a neat contrast with the globe. I cannot say "the planet, on the other hand." When I invoke the planet, I think of the effort required to figure the (im)possibility of this underived intuition.[11]

Spivak's move toward "planetarity" is a self-critique of "postcoloniality," because the old postcolonial model is "very much 'India' plus the Sartrian 'Fanon,'"[12] and cannot help us address globalized neocolonialism. Current imperial designs, such as the European Union, NAFTA, and GATT, are not mapped out according to national and geographical boundaries, and require a new imaginary in order to develop an appropriate ethics of resistance. She exhorts us: "If we imagine ourselves as planetary subjects rather than global agents, planetary creatures rather than global entities, alterity remains underived from us."[13]

Spivak's move toward planetarity attracts the attention of theologians and religious scholars, including Laura E. Donaldson, Catherine Keller, and Mayra Rivera.[14] As a deconstructivist, Spivak says that theology is alien to her thinking, and she is especially suspicious of the dichotomy of nature and supernature, which has undergirded much of religious talk. Yet, planetarity, insofar as it denotes the space of another system, an alterity we cannot fully grasp, provides fertile ground for theologians to probe and engage in dialogue.

Let us first discuss how this concept of "planetarity" works for Spivak. Planetarity functions as a limiting idea, which Gordon Kaufman defines as "the idea of that beyond which we cannot go either in experience, thought or imagination." Furthermore, a limiting idea is "of that which can only be approached but never actually reached, certainly not surpassed."[15] For Kaufman, the concepts of "God" and "world" are such limiting ideas. The use of planetarity allows Spivak to move beyond the discourses of the nation, gender, class, culture, and colonialism to edge toward species talk and an animist liberation theology, to which I shall return below. She invites us to imagine the complexity and pluralization of planetary systems, and not be confined by narrow identity politics or superficial binary thinking. Planetarity signifies an alterity that does not derive from us, a system that is beyond us, and yet we inhabit in it. A planetary ethics thus calls for the experience of the impossible that is radically open-ended and that is "to come." She writes with admirable honesty: "I keep feeling that there are connections to be made that I cannot make, that pluralization may allow the imagining of a necessary yet impossible planetarity in ways that neither my reader nor I know yet."[16]

How might this fertile idea of planetarity inform the way we do theology? I would like to begin by discussing the book *Planetary Theology* by the Catholic theologian Tissa Balasuriya of Sri Lanka.[17] Published in 1984, the book was much ahead of its time, for it criticized the "universal" theology done by Eurocentric, clerical, and male-dominated theologians, as well as contextual theologies, based on gender, race, class, nation, or region, for their partiality and limited scope. Balasuriya boldly proposed a planetary theology, using a world system approach as his guide, seeing the world as an interlocking system exploited by colonialism and capitalism. Writing during the Cold War era, Balasuriya might not have foreseen the ways globalization would change the face of both capitalism and socialism. With too much confidence in the Chinese socialist revolution, he would have been shocked to see how China has become so capitalist and a world economic power in a little more than two decades. Although he highlighted the importance of redistribution of natural resources, he was not primarily concerned with ecotheology.

Balasuriya was still working primarily out of a Latin American liberation theology paradigm that focuses on class and economics, although he also added Asian elements to it. Spivak recognizes the powerful role played by liberation theology, though she does not think the paradigm itself is sufficient. She has not cited any of the liberation theologians, but she cites a chapter in Ofelia Schutte's work,[18] in which Schutte faults Latin American philosophers such as Enrique Dussel for constructing a rather self-righteous discourse based on good and evil, for advocating a total rupture with modernity, and for insufficient attention to women's rights.[19] Unlike Balasuriya, who had a more positive regard for Asian religions and was excommunicated by the Vatican for downplaying the Church and Jesus' revelation,[20] Spivak remains critical of Asian religions, for she must have witnessed how both religious and political pundits have exploited the Hindu tradition.

Marxist thought heavily influences both the Latin American liberation theologians and Spivak, and Spivak's move toward an animist liberation theology deserves close attention. This particular section of *Critique of Postcolonial Reason* originally appeared in the Afterword of her translation of Mahasweta Devi's *Imaginary Maps*, a book of short stories, which depict the plight and struggles of tribals in India.[21] Working with the journalist and activist Devi, Spivak has increasingly written about the plight of the Fourth World and the impact of ecological catastrophe on Indian tribals. Her observation that decolonization has benefited Third World elites but further marginalized the Indian tribals must have contributed to her moving from postcoloniality to planetarity. She asks us to learn from the tribals who are the original practical ecological philosophers, because they retain a sense of sacredness of nature and of life:

> Nature is no longer sacred in this sense for civilizations based on the control of Nature. The result is global devastation due to a failure of ecology. It is noticeable that the less advantaged groups among the Indian tribals still retain this sense as a matter of their cultural conformity, if only because they have been excluded from the mainstream.[22]

Undoubtedly, collective political action, such as the change of law and social policies, and mass public education, will be necessary to address ecological injustice. Yet, Spivak argues that without a change of mind-set, political action will not stick: "What we are dreaming of here is . . . how to construct a sense of sacred Nature which can help mobilize a general ecological mind-set beyond the reasonable and the self-interested grounds of long-term global survival."[23] The change of mind-set is a slow process, as shown by the character Puran in Devi's story "Pterodactyl." This change cannot be coerced, but needs to happen on a one-on-one basis. Thus, collective action must be supplemented by love.

PLANETARY LOVE

Spivak does not seem to be aware that Indian ecofeminist theologians have for some time tapped into the wisdom of indigenous peoples and edged toward an "animist liberation theology." In *Listen to the Women! Listen to the Earth!* Aruna Gnanadason describes the tradition of prudent care among the indigenous peoples of her native India.[24] She notes that the traditions of prudent care dated back to the pre-Aryan period and to the reverence of mother goddesses. Examples of prudent care include the designation of forestland as protected land where the ancestors live, the preservation of sacred groves and particular sacred trees, the restriction of the amount that can be harvested of a given species, and the protection of a variety of plants and animals. The tradition of prudent care aims at providing living resources for the living and for the dead, and for generations to come.

Prudent care as a concrete expression of planetary love is associated with the feminine principle in pre-Aryan thought. Gnanadason points out that the earth was symbolized as the embodiment of feminine *shakthi*, which means energy and power. Female leaders of grassroots movements have been voices of prudence when, out of their care for the earth and for life, they have fought to protect the sacred trees and save the Narmada River. She offers the concept of "brown grace," which points to a God who is not separate from human beings, but works with us to transform the earth with grace. Her suggestion of "brown grace" is meant to counteract the primacy given to "red grace," which emphasizes sin, blood sacrifice, and the atonement accomplished by Jesus.[25] Gnanadason's cosmological consciousness supplements liberation theology's emphasis on human freedom and socio-political struggle: "God in India, from a liberation perspective, is in fact shaped by Indian cosmology, which affirms the interdependence of all forms of life, the dialectical harmony between humanity and the divine, between human beings and the earth and between the male and female principles."[26]

Gnanadason's concept of "brown grace" finds a clear echo in the work of womanist theologian Karen Baker-Fletcher, who has reminded us that we are created as dust and spirit in Genesis 2. We are made of "earth, water, breath, and heat," she states.[27] Jesus, as God incarnate, represents for her a God "who is with us in the very earthliness of our bodies and the dustiness of creation."[28] Since we are made of the same stuff as the trees and rocks, as well as the falling stars, we are all interdependent and interrelated. Such cosmic awareness leads us to see that when one is hurt, all are hurt, and motivates us to expand our love and care for the whole creation and the least among us. In her latest book on the Trinity, Baker-Fletcher discusses how her womanist thought shares similarities with process philosophy.[29]

Gnanadason and Baker-Fletcher have both dwelt on the immanence of God and our affinity with the sacred in an attempt to overcome the vast schism that Western theology has constructed between the Creator and creation. Spivak's concept of planetarity has immanent elements when she says that we inhabit the planet and we are not "specifically discontinuous" with it. Yet, she has focused more on the aspect of alterity and suggested that even "to think of it is already to transgress."[30] We may recall that Spivak constructs "planetarity" as a limiting idea to counteract the global reach of capital and the computerized globe.

In her book *The Touch of Transcendence*, Mayra Rivera builds on Spivak's concepts of "wholly Other," "absolute Other," and "radical alterity" to develop her rich concept of relational transcendence. Rivera places Spivak's work within the philosophical discussion of alterity, the Self and the Other, and responsibility toward the Other found in Emmanuel Levinas and Jacques Derrida. These scholars have suggested that within the Western imaginary, the Self cannot be constituted without the construction of the Other, which the Self negates or excludes. The exclusion of the Other or the appropriation of the Other into the Same has contributed to colonialism, and the Holocaust, as well as other forms of violence. Following these philosophers, Rivera accentuates the alterity of the Other and attempts to spell out a notion of transcendence that is not separate and exclusionary, but relational. She cites as support Spivak's claim that "To be born human *is* to be born angled toward an other and others."[31]

I welcome the radical critique of the construction of the Other in Western thought and consider such efforts indispensable for our common struggle for planetary justice. However, as a non-European who has grown up in the Chinese culture, I do not share the intense anxiety over the Other, whether found in the face of the stranger or in the flesh that we encounter. This is because the Chinese have quite a different construction of the self and a divergent understanding of cosmology and human relationships. Balasuriya captures the difference in this way:

> The Western mind has emphasized this difference [between the Creator and the created] partly because its logic is based on the principle of contradiction, what is, is not what it is not. On the contrary, oriental logic is more analogical, more synthetic. It seeks unity of being more than divergences, it sees continuity as more basic than discontinuity. The West has been preoccupied with avoiding pantheism and has thus drawn a categorical dividing line between God and nature. Oriental thought sees one as emanating from the other, one suffused by the other, even though dependent and transitory.[32]

Some may find Balasuriya's use of "Western" and "Oriental" problematic because of the danger of oversimplifying and homogenizing very complex traditions. Still, he indicates that there are different cultural orientations and approaches to conceptualize the world. Instead of seeing the Self and the Other as if they were mutually exclusive, East Asian philosophy, art, and aesthetics stress intersubjectivity, and the Vietnamese Zen master Thich Nhat Hanh uses the term "interbeing" to describe the reality that we are not separated from each other.[33] In Chinese Daoist philosophy, the ultimate Dao gives rise to one, one gives rise to two, and two give rise to all the myriad things. There is multiplicity, differentiation, and pluralization among all forms of existence and at the same time communion and relationships.

Gnanadason and Baker-Fletcher give voice to this deeply felt suffusion and continuity of all forms of existence. This does not imply that there are no elements of transcendence in their thought. For example, Gnanadason speaks of the brown grace of God, and Baker-Fletcher describes Jesus not only as "dust" but also as "spirit." Yet, they wish to highlight the immanence of God in our midst, that the God incarnate shares the same stuff with the trees, the stars, and our very flesh. I would call this *correlative immanence* based on the logic of correlation suggested by Chinese philosophy. Aristotelian logic is based on the law of identity, such that A is not ~A, and the Self and the Other are seen as dichotomous. Based on such logic, the relation between the Self and the Other becomes an intense ontological as well as ethical issue. Postcolonial critics such as Homi Bhabha have tried to overcome this dichotomy by theorizing the "in-between space" or the "third space."[34] Chinese philosophy provides yet another alternative, which philosopher Chang Tung-sun has called a logic of correlation:

> Chinese thought puts no emphasis on exclusiveness, rather it emphasizes the relational quality between above and below, good and evil, something and nothing. All these relatives are supposed to be interdependent. . . . Chinese thought is not based upon the law of identity, but takes as its starting point relative orientation or rather the relation of the opposites.[35]

I would like to flesh out the idea of planetary love based on this concept of correlative immanence. Following Derrida, Spivak argues that justice and ethics are based on the radical claims of the Other and can be seen as "the experience of the impossible." Although Spivak has talked about love, we are not clear how love is related to justice and upon what love is based. For example, why should a person develop such a love for the Other and why would a person have such impossible obligations toward the Other? A love that is fixated on the alterity of the Other is cut and dried, and love cannot be derived from duty and responsibility alone.

Correlative immanence problematizes the autonomous notion of Self and Other that the Western imaginary has espoused and the straight dividing line that has kept the two separated. In Derridean terms, the trace of the Other is always and already present in the Self and vice versa. The Self is not constructed in relation to the Other in the form of a dyad, but as the center of multiple relations that extend from the immediate family to the nation and ultimately to the universe as a whole. An intuitive understanding of the inseparable relationship between the self and the myriad things under heaven informs Chinese poetry, landscape painting, and aesthetics. W. Anne Joh is correct in pointing out that the East Asians do not speak so much of love and use more often the term *qing* (pronounced as *jeong* in Korean).[36] The Chinese character *qing* has "heart" as its radical. In ancient Chinese view, *qing* is yin energy with desire, while *xing* is yang energy of virtue, and both are seen as part of human nature.[37] Chinese poetics seeks to evoke the poet's sense of *qing* through the minute, detailed description of nature and natural processes. The highest poetic ideal is the suffusion of *qing* and *jing*; the latter means the natural scene and the vista the poet encounters. I would like to cite part of a lyrical poem by the famous poet Li Qingzhao after her husband's death as an example.

> The ground is covered with yellow flowers
> Faded and fallen in showers.
> Who will pick them up now?
> Sitting alone at the window, how
> Could I but quicken
> The pace of darkness which won't thicken?
> On parasol-trees a fine rain drizzles
> As twilight grizzles.
> This time,
> How can a single word "sadness" be enough?[38]

Here Li describes her intense feelings through the images of fallen yellow flowers, the quickening of the hour of darkness, and the rain drizzling through the trees. Through these concrete images, she tries to evoke in her readers the *qing* that she feels, which the words of sadness or grief cannot convey. In this poem, the self is present, and the outside world is seen through the perspective of the self. However, in other Chinese poems, the self is absent and the object in the world is seen though other objects, and the boundary between the self and the object becomes blurred. Without romanticizing East Asian cultures, which have many blind spots, I would say that Chinese poetry and Japanese haiku provide resources for cultivating the sense of correlative immanence and of planetary love or *qing*.

Many Chinese theologians and biblical scholars love John's Gospel, and the Chinese Bible translates verse 1:14 as the Dao became flesh. It is in the specificity of details and in concreteness that the Dao can be understood, as we have learned from Chinese poetry. It is in the immanence of the flesh that the transcendent Word can be fully appreciated. If correlative immanence helps us rewrite the relationship between the Creator and creation, I want to explore how planetary love manifests itself in human relationships across national, cultural, and geographical differences.

LOVE "IN OTHER WORLDS"

The Latino-Jewish writer Francisco Goldman was once interviewed, in the TV series *La Plaza*, by Ilan Stavans, who asked him, "What is the use of the novel today?" Goldman said a novel helps people imagine other people's existence in the world. It is important to remember that Spivak studies, teaches, and translates literature and has to inhabit other cultural worlds and imagine other people's existence all the time. As her critics have said, she has gone "further than any other cultural theorist in engaging with, retelling, and ethically and imaginatively inhabiting other people's narratives."[39] As a deconstructivist whose subject position vacillates between an ethnic in the United States, a racial in Britain, and a postcolonial in the academy,[40] Spivak's literary criticism and philosophical critiques have destabilized both mainstream and feminist readings, and called attention to the hidden voices and marginalized characters.

One of the cultural legacies of imperialism is that the postcolonial or the ex-colonial is overdetermined from outside. Spivak frankly acknowledges that she is a Europeanist by training, and that she draws her theoretical insights from the works of Derrida, Marx, Kant, Hegel, and the French feminists, to name just a few. Some have questioned the "authenticity" of postcolonial theorists because they have relied so much on Western theory, as if these "native" theorists should be limited to their indigenous tradition and return to some culturally pure state. This question shows a remarkable naïveté in relation to imperialism's legacy and the hegemony of Western knowledge throughout the world, as well as Western critical theory's contribution to debunking its own logic.

Spivak asks us to engage in "a persistent critique of what one cannot not want."[41] Although this is important for feminist theologians, it is even more so for postcolonial feminist theologians, who work in a theological tradition deeply embedded in Western philosophical discourses. Spivak's persistent critique not only provides important methodological clues for our own work but also shows an ambivalent love of what she "cannot not want." I want to illustrate this love-and-hate relationship with what she "cannot not want" by discussing her critique of French feminists, though Spivak has certainly not let the male scholars off the hook.

In 1981, she published an important essay titled "French Feminism in an International Frame," which was reprinted in her first book on cultural politics, *In Other Worlds*.[42] That particular essay drew my attention because Spivak was performing a detailed critique of Julia Kristeva's book *About Chinese Women*.[43] Spivak accused Kristeva of imposing her own view onto the Chinese by romanticizing the Chinese past, by conjuring up a matrilineal and matrilocal society, and by misappropriating Chinese literature, including that by Chinese women. For Spivak, Kristeva has naturalized her prejudices as facts, and instead of reporting about the history and present condition of Chinese women, Kristeva is self-fashioning her female subjectivity by using the silent, peasant women in China as her foil.

Toward the end of the essay, Spivak provides some invaluable clues on how to enter "the other worlds." She suggests that we have to reverse our gaze, and ask "not merely who am I? but who is the other woman? How am I naming her? How does she name me? Is this part of the problematic I discuss?"[44] Here as elsewhere, Spivak is concerned about the politics of representation, about being vigilant of the danger of misappropriating the other's story into our own. I will say more about this in the last section on the female subaltern.

But why would we want to be "in other worlds," to risk being undressed and unveiled, to borrow Marcella Althaus-Reid's terminology? Spivak, of course, does not base her argument on some cryptic ontotheology of the human or on the long tradition of Western humanism. I find her negotiation of the space between the I and the Other providing food for thought for a theological anthropology. She provides clues for a new mode of being in the world. This is turning yourself out in order to understand both who you are and who the other person is. Deconstruction asks us not to fetishize the other, and this out-turning to the other is different from turning to the other. Spivak articulates a mode of inhabiting the world that is unsettling, open to the unfamiliar and the unexpected, in a kind of secret longing—I need you.

Spivak writes, "To be human is to be intended toward the other."[45] I would argue that Spivak's understanding of the human is not very far from the Chinese correlative understanding, as I have discussed above. In discussing "the call to the ethical," she uses the phrase "originary relatedness," which she says may just be called the ethical relationship.[46] She challenges the humanist paradigm of ethics, proposed by the Enlightenment philosophers since Kant, which focuses on human freedom, autonomy, and reason. Instead, Spivak expresses a radical relationality and the out-turning of the subject that is foundational for political action and solidarity.

In 1992, she published her essay "French Feminism Revisited," which was a second take on her earlier essay.[47] Here her tone is more dialogical and conciliatory, for she was convinced that in the persistence of patriarchal neocolonialism and fundamentalist nationalisms, the exchange between metropolitan and decolonized feminisms is important. She staged a dialogue between the French feminists and the postcolonial feminists, especially between Hélène Cixous and Marie-Aimée Hélie-Lucas, the Algerian feminist, and showed how the two could supplement each other.[48] Here Spivak demonstrates the possibility of "deconstructive embrace," a gesture of "affirmative deconstruction," in which the Other is embraced, while the differences are affirmed. Such gestures of embrace are crucial today if feminists want to work toward planetary solidarity in a neoliberal economy that increasingly threatens the livelihood of many women and their families.

LOVE FOR THE FEMALE SUBALTERN

Spivak's most significant interventions concern the exclusion of the female subaltern in Eurocentric discourses and organized resistance, on the one hand, and the appropriation of the female subaltern's voice for various liberation projects, on the other. She based her controversial essay "Can the Subaltern Speak?" on a 1983 lecture. She first published it in 1985 and expanded it into a longer version,[49] which she has since revised and included in *A Critique of Postcolonial Reason*. The original essay concluded that the subaltern cannot speak, which spawned many critical discussions. Spivak later explained that if the subaltern can speak, "the subaltern is not a subaltern any more,"[50] for she will have gained access to power. The female subalterns for her are doubly marginalized because of their economic disadvantage and gender subordination. The victims of *sati*, for example, were spoken for by the colonists and by the male elites, but they were not allowed to speak for themselves. However, after mounting criticism, with some critics saying that Spivak would not let the subaltern speak or that she is too elitist to hear the voices and expressions of the subaltern, Spivak has said that the question is not whether the subaltern could speak but whether she could be heard.

I do not want to join the debate about whether the subaltern can speak at the moment but wish to explore what I would call the love for the female subaltern as an expression of planetary love. By retelling the story of a sixteen- or seventeen-year-old young woman Bhubaneswari Bhaduri in her essay "Can the Subaltern Speak?" and by mulling over her story again and again, Spivak demonstrates the kind of love that she has called for. This young woman committed suicide because she had belonged to a militant group during the struggle for Indian national independence and had failed to confront the task of a political assassination. She chose to commit suicide during menstruation so that her suicide would not be considered a consequence of illicit love.

The act of memory is important, for it brings the woman's story alive, and Spivak has refused to forget her. Stories of women who have committed suicide or who have been part of the family secret can be found in Amy Tan's *Joy Luck Club* and Maxine Hong Kingston's *Woman Warrior*. In each case, the stories of these women were taboo; they were not supposed to be told. Each time these stories were told, it was as if a spell had been broken and some truth-telling happened. Miroslav Volf has raised the question of remembering rightly, for our memories are particularly vulnerable to distortion.[51] Spivak explains why the memory of Bhubaneswari Bhaduri is susceptible to epistemic erasure or to distortion. Since the woman's assassination effort failed, she did not quite fit into the study of political movements and national independence in mainstream historiography.[52] The fact that she chose to commit suicide during menstruation—a period that was considered unclean and during which *sati* is forbidden—will have gone unnoticed. The subaltern's insurgence to contest a gender script in her own context will have been lost in masculinist history.

The love of the female subaltern is also demonstrated in Spivak's mourning and lament, which has two dimensions. The first is the lament that even Bhubaneswari's relatives and communities did not remember her death "rightly" after a generation, for they said that hers was a case of illicit love. The second is that the female subaltern has no place to speak—for between being the object of compassion of the West and the victim of male patriarchy, she has no space to speak. Here Spivak asks her readers to hear her comment that the subaltern cannot speak not as a philosophical argument, or an instance of historical description, but as a "passionate lament."[53] And what a difference it makes! Lamentation, as Emilie Townes has shown, has a crucial place in subaltern communities, especially in black religious life, and in Christian ethics.[54]

However, the most radical love displayed is in the form of refusal to fetishize the subaltern so that she can fit into our epistemological framework, whether it is Eurocentric and nationalist historiography or in subaltern studies. Spivak guards against our tendency to rush to retrieve subaltern consciousness or to recover the voice of the subaltern subjects, as if they are "a monolithic collectivity" and their "unfractured subjectivity allows them to speak for themselves."[55] Just like "planetarity," the "subaltern" functions as a delimiting idea for Spivak to signal the limits of our knowledge and representation. I may differ from Spivak in her construal of the alterity of the subaltern and her lack of attention to ways the subaltern do come to voice.[56] Yet I appreciate her vigilance in calling our attention to our complicity in representing the subaltern and allowing her to speak through us, as postcolonial critics, migrant scholars, and enlightened liberals. In theology, we have to heed her caution in our attempt to rediscover the subjugated women in the Bible and tradition and to lift up the voices of "Third World women," indigenous women, and racial and ethnic minority women, so that we will continue to subject our own framework to self-criticism.

Spivak's love as memory, lament, and refusal to fetishize the Other may be helpful for us in looking at the subaltern at the center of the Christian story. For two millennia, Christians have lovingly remembered Jesus and mourned his death during the celebration of the Eucharist. Through the ritualistic enactment, the story of the last supper is retold and Jesus is once again made present in the Eucharistic meal. It may be appropriate to ask, Do we remember him correctly? Have we made a fetish out of him? From Anselm's satisfaction theory of atonement to Girard's scapegoat theory, have we made him fit our paradigms, schemata, and order of things? Have we tried to pin him down through our historical quest or our church doctrines?

I appreciate Laurel Schneider's observation that when Jesus was brought before Pilate for his trial, Jesus "gave him no answer, not even to a single charge" (Mt 27:14a). Schneider writes: "His silence lifts up his own irreducibility—the *irreducibility* of his embodiment—to the charges laid against him."[57] She notes that while Jesus chose to remain silent, others throughout Christian history have rushed to speak for him. He has been variably described as the Son of God, fully divine and fully human, the perfect sacrifice, the hero for the upwardly mobile bourgeoisie, as well as the anti-imperial radical for our time. She raises the crucial question of in what ways we would allow Jesus to speak through the particularity of his incarnation (and I would add through his death), and in what ways we have erased him by our system of exchange, whether it is the divine economy of the Trinity or the substitution theory of atonement.

I began by talking about planetarity and traced Spivak's thought in the discussion of planetary love, love "in other worlds," and love for the female subaltern. I have argued that Spivak offers a love that is tough, nonsentimental, that embodies justice and speaks from a subject position that remembers the blight of colonialism and is mindful of the intersectionality of gender, race, class, sexuality, and so forth. What I had not foreseen when I began is that Spivak's ideas provide many insights into our theological revisioning of creation, anthropology, and even Christology. Spivak's writing has a provisional quality to it, and sometimes you have a sense that it is not quite finished and she is still working out her thoughts. This essay must be seen as provisional as well, not because I have the complexity of her thought process or agility of mind, but because the implications will need much time to work out. I will be interested to know what shape a postcolonial planetary feminist theology might take.

❧ The Love We Cannot Not Want: A Response to Kwok Pui-lan

LAUREL C. SCHNEIDER

I must begin my response to Kwok Pui-lan's introduction with some words of gratitude for the clarity with which she navigates Gayatri Chakravorty Spivak's work on behalf of theology, an extremely challenging feat, especially for those of us, like Kwok, who take seriously Spivak's own suspicions of theological motivations and investments in the detritus of colonial sprawl. One of the difficulties for us is that Spivak does not seem to invest herself in her own insights and claims but rather grounds herself in the world that inspires them, and so as the world changes, so her arguments change. She is as ready is disavow her earlier positions as she is to gesture provocatively toward new ones, as the conditions of globalization and dehumanization and as the possibilities for critique and insight demand. (Her famous discomfort over her own notions of the subaltern and the postcolonial are good examples of this.)

Spivak, in other words, is not wedded to a priori claims about reality beyond a faith in the capacity of literary discourse to critically engage assumptions about that reality. On a purely methodological level this flexibility can spell trouble for some theologians, for whom big words such as "world" and "creation" or "eternity" and "absolute" are meaningful and serve as anchors for additional big words such as "love," "faith," and "truth." For others of us, precisely the fluidity and pragmatism employed by Spivak and thinkers like her, together with her abiding passion for the empowerment of those most marginalized and hurt by totalizing systems of governance, offer some badly needed new ways of thinking big, especially thinking that results from postures of attention to actual relations. The difficulties of this approach for anything approximating an ontotheology are, as Kwok so clearly points out, significant. The ontotheological is in retreat in much of contemporary theology, the reasons for which are too complex and long-winded to rehearse here. But the ontological is still important to the bigger claims that theologians seek to make about divinity and the world (and I dare say "the planetary"). As such, the ontological is still a matter of theological concern even as it (finally!) loses its long-standing footing in Platonic idealism; it haunts every step we take and is an easy target for philosophers and literary critics, like Spivak, who may think that they have succeeded in shaking the ontological off, like an overcoat long out of season. But then such thinkers make suggestions like the one that has motivated this collection of writings, namely that "the planetary" may be a new direction for "original practical ecological philosophies."[1] The theological returns, even in whispers of ontological possibility. It (the ontological) is perhaps one of those things that we "cannot not want," and may even be unable not to need, even as we commit ourselves to its persistent critique.[2]

Kwok focuses on two such theopoetic gestures in Spivak (we'll not call them ontotheological, and I agree with her that it would be erroneous to do so) that Kwok suggests are useful, particularly to postcolonial feminist theologians. Together, both gestures form the main title of the conference for which her essay was written. Each one adds conceptual specificity to pathways that Kwok herself has been charting for feminist postcolonial theologians for over a decade. The first gesture, as we have seen, is "the planetary," and the second is "planetary love." I want to respond briefly to both gestures, both because I think that Kwok's approach to Spivak's cryptic offering of the planetary is indeed very helpful for theological purposes and because I share Kwok's concern that "love" be revisioned appropriately. It is this latter concern that I take up principally in this response.

The "planetary" is a notion that, according to Spivak, stands in opposition to the "global." The global is an abstract notion of the whole in the way that maps are abstract. The planetary, in contrast, is fully embodied and as such cannot be charted except perhaps as the partially submerged monsters who roam the edges of maps (or epistemic systems). Furthermore, the planetary cannot be abstracted from the interlacing multiplicity of bodies (galactic or cellular). Actual bodies compose and decompose the global in ways that always resist or "talk back" to its abstraction by way of the utterly present, irreducible, unrepeatable, and incommensurate local. I wonder if this approach to the planetary functions as an orienting limit idea such as Kwok finds in Kaufman, or whether it functions as an actual end to modernist modes of globalized imagination. It is this challenge to imagination that I believe holds interest for theologians such as Kwok and me (and others in this volume), who have begun to chafe under the heavily policed constraints of Enlightenment rules of the road.

These limits to acceptable rationalization provoked Spivak to her brief proposition of radical planetarity but also clearly worry her. She recognizes the goods that liberalism's globalized abstractions have wrought, such as the notion of universal human rights. And so one of the questions that we must ask is whether the goods that globalized liberal humanism offers (especially to women and, for Spivak, especially to the young women for whom she has founded governmental schools in rural India) can remain intact without the horrible costs that run rampant with liberalism's right hand, namely global capital and its profound disassociation of the planet from the globe. The latter is evident, for example, in globalized capitalism's dehumanization of production and erasure of the incommensurate local into a repetition of franchises.

Kwok is suggesting a way through this dilemma that, perhaps ironically, requires leaving Spivak somewhat to the side. This is because, in the end, Spivak is unable to recognize the possibilities that persist in "the religious." Spivak reverts somewhat disappointingly to a stereotype of religion, as if the world's religions contain nothing of an animist plurality or are not shot through with their own fissures and uncertain edges from which spirits and disreputable angels constantly spill. However, inspired by the cryptic suggestion that the planetary may be based in some "original practical ecological philosophies," Kwok turns to others such as Rivera, Gnanadason, Balasuriya, and Baker-Fletcher, all of whom are less tentative in their various affirmations that just such a planetary imagination is possible, *not* as some kind of backward appropriation or reductive imprisonment of "the native" and not as a disavowal of indigeneity either. The implied result is complex; it is an affirmation of complexity that, as Kwok has written in many places, can perhaps be best navigated by those who already know in their bodies what it means to live in multiple skins, in alternating and co-existent identities, as planetary nomads.

The second gesture that Kwok lifts up in conversation with Spivak, and the notion toward which her essay is driven, is "planetary love." "Love" is a difficult word in theology, just as it is in songwriting; it tends to be overused and often ends up empty. And yet, a great many religious traditions associate their central concept of divinity with love. Love cannot be avoided in theology, and yet theologians must attempt to think love through critically, with proper attention to its vulnerability to abuse, its evacuation of meaning, its saccharine banality, and our relentless desire for it. Given the difficulty even of speaking of love without lapsing into sugary dulcitude, perhaps we should start with the theological assertion that love is one of those things we should include in Spivak's catalogue of what "one cannot not want" and which therefore requires persistent and even painful critique.

Kwok pushes us in the direction of "love" that is grounded in the planetary (rather than in the global, which is where, Spivak points out, no one actually lives). This is the heart of the matter, the *qing* with which, Kwok helpfully reminds us, postcolonial feminist theology should be concerned most of all. But it raises the question, what does *love* mean, what can it possibly mean, in a postcolonial, feminist sense? Both of the modifiers "postcolonial" and "feminist" suggest difficulty for any common understanding of love precisely because the term is relative, requiring relations. Postcolonial and feminist critiques challenge all relations forged in support of patriarchal empires, and so we cannot take for granted loves that are sanctioned therein. But what does that leave us? Forbidden loves? Queer loves? Certainly not loves authorized by colonial powers or patriarchal powers. This means that even, or especially, Christian love is suspect, if only because it has been used so often to suppress dissent, to control bodies against their free and joyful expressions of living, and to deny the planetary. At the same time, as Kwok herself argues, there are strong traces of other loves in Christianity, of lovers who refuse to acquiesce to empire, who refuse to obey the patriarchal rules, who touch women with unclean flows of blood, who break laws to feed hungry neighbors, and who attend to the anointing longings of the body, regardless of propriety. Kwok is arguing that there are principles of planetary love here, available to Christian theologians for creative new ways of imagining planetary love.

Such imagining of planetary love requires a different frame of reference, one perhaps implied in James Baldwin's suggestion that we use the word love "not in the infantile American sense of being made happy but in the tough and universal sense of quest and daring and growth."[3] Kwok focuses on memory, lament, and refusal to fetishize the Other. This is a good start, it seems to me. It offers a bracing, if brave, new world of postcolonial feminist love as courage, work, and a steady regard for the worth of others.

But I believe that there is yet more to be said here about love that accomplishes planetarity, that takes up the irreducibility and multiplicity of bodies. I suggest, following Spivak and Kwok's demand that we engage in persistent critique of that which we cannot not want, that we attend to a latent desire in postcolonial and feminist theologies that bodily desire itself be tamed and disciplined for political purposes. By limiting planetary love for Christian theology to memory, lament, and the refusal to fetishize the Other, we risk serving an austere control of bodies that, as theologians, we may still be unable to not want and so must critique. Kwok warns against this possibility in her development of correlative immanence, illustrated in the concrete evocation of "the minute" in lyrical Chinese poetry.

Could we use more of this correlative immanence? In addition to a theological construction of planetary love based in memory, lament, and refusal to fetishize the Other, do we need to assert a theological quality of love that also runs counter to all three, if only to remind ourselves of the reality of those desires that are indeed grounded in the eventful (and often forgetful) *presence and processes* of bodies? If not, what do we do with the actual desires that flow through and connect bodies against all propriety, including postcolonial and feminist proprieties? What do we do with the strange science of gravity, which seems to have decreed that bodies pull themselves promiscuously toward each other across impossible barriers of distance? Should a planetary concept of love somehow integrate the unruliness of bodies that seem destined to want each other in spite of memory, beyond lament, and with lusty intent? This contrariness might be evoked in a poetics, for example, that forgets to account for the past, that dances in ecstasy, and that seduces against all decency even as it reminds us of God's utter (and utterly indecent) attraction to "the least of these."

Kwok Pui-lan has very helpfully opened the door for dialogue between theologians such as those represented in this volume and Gayatri Chakravorty Spivak by suggesting some points of potential overlap between Spivak's thoughts on planetarity and current possibilities for postcolonial feminist theology. She has demonstrated, as well as argued, the compatibility of some of Spivak's ideas and mode of thinking with the ideas and mode of theologizing by those of us in theology who have been influenced by Kwok. She also, of course, goes much further, sketching out some constructive directions that we might take to further the productive exchange, some of which I have taken up in this response. Both Spivak and Kwok are dedicated to the work of bringing the oppressed and the silenced to voice and to access to power. Both see writing to be a place where some of that work can effectively occur. And both see the importance of bodies, of the actual bodies that hunger and hurt, that feast, work, protest, create, and die as not insignificant for theory. To this end, I encourage increased postcolonial, feminist attention to bodily expressions of love, to heed Kwok's warnings against planetary loves that evade attention to the minute or to the concrete. Rivera's connective notion of horizontal transcendence can also be immensely helpful to this task.[4] Otherwise, we may run the risk of denouncing the contrariness of bodies, which is the bodiliness of bodies, which embody gravitational longings and loves that a lover of justice cannot not want, but which she may, nevertheless, need.

❧ Conversations

❧ Love: A Conversation

GAYATRI CHAKRAVORTY SPIVAK,
WITH SERENE JONES, CATHERINE KELLER,
KWOK PUI-LAN, AND STEPHEN D. MOORE

Catherine Keller: I had mentioned to Professor Spivak that I would rap just a little bit, warming up to a question, while she is settling into our sanctified environment here in the Theological School. We are very grateful for your courage in joining us today. But really, the courage is all ours. [Laughter.]

In the *Critique of Postcolonial Reason*, thinking especially of Bangladesh, you write words that seem to us all the more prophetic now, in the light (the warm light) of global warming. You write that you "have no doubt that we must learn to learn from the original practical ecological philosophies of the world."[1] Insisting that this is no more a romanticism than was liberation theology, you say, "[W]e are talking about using the strongest mobilizing discourse in the world in a certain way for the globe," this globe that you would later prefer to call "planet." You say that "this learning can only be attempted through the supplementation of collective effort by love."[2] And so we are having this event in which, already, this line has become almost scriptural before your advent here this afternoon!

We realize that this conversation, in a theological school, with theologians, biblical scholars, other scholars of religion, may not be part of your normal circuit (if you have one). But many of us do work in schools that actually trained the original missionaries for the triumphalist global Christendom. We have been working, really working rather assiduously for several decades now, to untrain ourselves of the missionary habit; to unlearn for ourselves (and "ourselves" now is partly constituted by the Christian postcolonial) the conversionist presumption. And yet, of course, part of the learning of this unlearning is the continuous discovery of ever new depths of our complicities with the deep history of Christian imperialism. Ellen Armour's talk earlier this morning was unfolding for us, for instance, the incredible wrinkles of sexual politics in the Episcopalian church, vis-à-vis the African church.[3] The tangles of our complicities continue to stun us and keep us lively.

I found that your concept, actually, of complicity itself as a folding together is a beautiful metaphor and an alternative to a certain oppositionalism that is still very much a part of our own unfolding in communities like this—an oppositionalism that provides much of the energy, still, of our critiques of our own traditions. Vigilance as to complicity seems to me to signal a kind of love strategy that for many of us may indeed offer a needed supplement to the identity politics by which we have tried—and continue to try—to free ourselves from the Eurocentric forms of the so-called religion that engulfed ancient Jewish impulses. Among us the very notion of religion is being contested by scholars of religion, indeed, by a theologian such as John Thatamanil, who is with us here today. The concept "religion" may represent a false homogenization accomplished by imperial organization of vastly complex spiritual movements.

Yet we teach in theological schools because we do not or we cannot dismiss these so-called great world religions. For they are "too deeply imbricated," as you say mercilessly, "in the narrative of the ebb and flow of power."[4] We hope we are practicing within these religions what you have called a "decolonization of the mind" by renegotiating root religious structures of violence. We do also find traces within these religions of ours of an underived alterity manifested only in solidarity with the subaltern, the "least of these" of the Jewish Jesus of Matthew 25:40. This is a trace, this old love, among traces almost but not quite erased by the blinding paternal hierarchies of Christian triumphalism. And so we keep negotiating. In perhaps your very sense of "negotiation" as the responsible form of resistance amid our privileged but inevitable complicities.

We are wondering if this form of what you call "critical intimacy" would be recognizable to you—perhaps at least in this time, this millennium, when some internal resistance to Christian globalization may do some handy work, may have some pouvoir savoir that sheer secularism lacks.[5] Your savvy style of negotiation amid complicity and its complexities seems kin to the risky love that you rarely, but importantly, declare there at the edge of your feminist attention to the irreducible alterity, even sacrality, of the planet. And many of us here are very alert to those points, those couple of points, where you draw your minimalist analogy to the work of liberation theologies. You offer some marvelous hints about the globalizing continuity between Christian monotheism and secular monopoly capitalism, suggesting perhaps a new relevance to Weber's Protestant ethic, as maybe now underwritten by Rey Chow's punchy "Protestant ethnic."[6]

So there is a question mark forming here now. I wonder if even theological strategies of deconstruction of that "mono" might mark the sight of a possible collusion, a negotiated complicity, with transnational cultural feminism and with its planetarity. I'm thinking that in our discussion some of these sites of possible collusion, the deconstruction of that double mono, might come out (as perhaps in Laurel Schneider's new theology of multiplicity, with its deconstruction of "the logic of the One."[7] I had in a related way worked at reading the odd grammar of Elohim as a "pluralsingularity," and the tehom of Genesis 1:2 as a chaosmic multiplicity).[8] The strategies for this deconstruction themselves continue to multiply. So I suppose I'm asking if there is not something like what you'd call a "sanctioned ignorance" among hard-core secularists—not only the more vulgar "new atheists"—about the so-called great world religions.

You point out that "assimilated polytheist colonials were taught that European secular imagining of ethics is the only space of critique or dogma." And you note brilliantly that "this ethics never lost touch with its God even in His Death."[9] [Aside to audience:] She properly capitalizes "His" and "Death," along with "God"! We should all be aware that several of the formative Death of God symposia took place at Drew, in this very space, in the 1960s, under the absence of the cross that hangs above us now.[10] These were theological consultations, taking place long before the hip new kind of Christian atheism of someone like Vattimo. Dead or alive, that He-God hovers in some kind of ghostly form, at least within this saturated and sometimes liturgical, space.

Surely these patriarchal deaths complicate the neat line between atheism and theism. So wouldn't a complicitous negotiation with the so-called great world religions perhaps pose a more effective challenge to today's monotheizing, secularizing global narrative than any purportedly pure secularism? And would perhaps the test of that challenge lie not so much in the question of whether we free up the irreducible alterity from the admittedly clunky monosyllable "God," but rather whether we free our planet lovingly and urgently enough from the Eurocentric anthropocentrism and androcentrism of imperial theologies?

Gayatri Chakravorty Spivak: This is hard. You've said such a lot.

CK: I feel triumphant that she thinks it's hard! [Laughter.]

GCS: "It's easy to be hard," and I'm quoting. [Laughter.] I'm predictable, Catherine, in that I would first need to ask who I am, where I come from, to see this task of freeing our planet through love. I am not a religious person in the conventional sense. I am not a believer—so much so that I think even atheism is a religion, always in the conventional sense of course. It seems a little strange to use this word—"religion" (conventionally, what exactly is this convention?—a labyrinth . . .)—in this group. On the other hand, because I am not a believer (in the conventional sense) I have no trouble (hey?) with any religion at all. I am happy to see Christ on his cross right across from me there.[11] When I was active for primary health care in Bangladesh, I had a certain cachet because I was an older woman and I could say anything to the men, and I spoke so strongly to fathers-in-law about birth control, talking about Allah in a certain way, that everyone was convinced I was a Muslim; and for that space I was indeed a Muslim. I was born into a Hindu family, but certainly one of the things that my father said to us again and again was "judge not that ye be not judged," and he wasn't quoting a Hindu text! There was a lot of Sanskrit stuff quoted too; they were not bigoted; it was a sort of ecumenical anti-casteist household.

I gave an interview to the *Chronicle of Higher Education*, and I said that I was not a religious person, but I do have a category which I find is necessary for me to have. An English word that would suffice is "sacred." I said to this woman that the closest thing for me to the sacred is the performance of teaching. I was deeply distressed by what came out. It was reported that Professor Spivak was not a religious person, her only religious experience was teaching. This audience will know that that was exactly what I was not saying. I think, indeed hope, that our shared space is that necessity of something that can be named "sacred" in English—for want of a better word.

These, therefore, are my credentials and I put them before you in a stereotype of myself. Hinduism is a heteropraxy. We are a people without a book, and there is room made for all kinds of positions. I've been told by my very dear friend Bimal Krishna Matilal, who died in 1991, that the kind of person I am would be described within Hinduism as a *karma-kandi* Hindu; that is to say an unbeliever who is culturally produced (to modernize in the idiom of my conventional understanding of myself). I think of religious production also as something inescapable, in a rather profane way.

As you have noted, the opposition between secular and religious has done harm to our world. Within that context, then, I am obliged to ask the question, as a theologically marked utopianism joins with the general feel of utopianism today in the alterglobalist movement. The World Social Forum is one example of alterglobalization, a movement that began in France, went to Brazil, and then slowly spread through the rest of the world. Within the movement, self-selected moral entrepreneurs (with a collective vocation?) choose top-down utopias for the world (a world which is not global, in fact; I will come to the planet in a moment). Some of us old-fashioned people engaged in the kind of activism that does not travel with an NGO global interpreter find ourselves having to say again and again that solutions for a just world are not going to come from Europe or the United States. Is that collective vocation—emphasizing corporate funding and ignoring deep structural change in the system—the new subject of global capital? Love is powerful because it is a dangerous supplement. When that ball, thrown from a feudal concern that cannot earn the right to love, is thrown back, it is difficult to accept. The idea that we who are rich, who are blessed in every possible material way, give to the rest of the world and solve the world's problems top-down— it's very hard to get rid of this. And so my first feeling would be, when I think that I am from New York, the city that holds the UN, and I can save the world by joining with like-minded people, people like me, going through love, to say to myself, "Watch it." I am speaking of myself now, not just to you. I belong with you.

Then love, again. Being what I am—what I think I am—love for me is also a deeply contaminated word. Within gender politics, I'm not someone who works with single-issue feminisms. Of course in a short-term way, a problem-solving way, I'm absolutely for any kind of feminist effort. That too needs to be put on the table. There is no critique there. I would go in almost blind. But in the long term, what seems to me to be much more important is to see how fundamental reproductive heteronormativity is (a term which I will immediately reduce to initials: RHN) as the originary *pharmakon*: medicine as well as poison. It's not so easy just to point the finger at bad gender politics here. I must think of profound complicity here, quite in the way that Catherine has invoked. RHN is the biggest, oldest global institution. Tacit globalization, millennia before the silicon chip. It's all over the world, whether capitalist or anti-capitalist. It's before capitalism. It's before anti-imperialism. The imperialist and anti-imperialist are alike tied in, folded up with RHN. That's how deep it runs. That metapsychological solidarity cannot be broken by what is called today "transnational feminist utopias." It is from RHN that all love is understood. The task is to live that double bind. Love is as dangerous as it is powerful. It is the irreducible supplement.

As for me and the original practical ecologies of the world, I wasn't in fact talking about Bangladesh. Bangladesh is an interesting terrain of the Abrahamic. In that youngest and most intellectual tradition, the pasture is a remote metaphor. I was talking about a small group of Indian aboriginals. I do not romanticize them, and I romanticize them now even less. I will tell you why. The thing about my work is that I learn from my mistakes. [Laughter.] What I said in "Can the Subaltern Speak?" was not a mistake, but the ability for this kind of thinking to survive enough for us to mobilize it, was my mistake because I was still in the armchair. Here is the story, sanitized.

The group that I used to work for—for twenty years, training teachers, living with them—were the ones that I was learning this from. It was the most backward district of West Bengal, and in those kinds of areas the old land owners, ex-zamindars, still flourish because the state functionaries are so corrupt. And this one was a benevolent despot. They mean to keep the aboriginals serf-like, so that they can be helped through litigation and confrontation "on their behalf" rather than be given access to the way to citizenship. A choice between feudalism and left liberalism, not a good choice, but the only choice in this predicament. For twenty years I talked to this guy, and we sat together, but when the first generation of young men—the young women in the schools were robotized by this person's discipline—began questioning authority he closed the schools. Punishing him would have done no good—and anyway the uncomprehending NGOs and the remote metropolitan journals, not to mention the locals, loved him, the only exception being this group of young boys without a base, without training in fighting wars of maneuver. That's often the problem with human rights, because without follow-up, it is the resisters on the ground who suffer. If we want to access and learn from below, we have to have material support. We cannot access their episteme only by way of the imagination. I'm all for the imagination. But fiction is not evidence. We cannot speak in their name.

I may not be a religious person, but I respect good people with faith. This, however, is not going to lead to an animist liberation theology, because in our global emergency, "learning from below" can only be an impatient vanguardism with a winning slogan. To achieve deep epistemic shift into an animist liberation theology is a task that would need a displacement of millennial history and deep language learning of lost languages at once. Our animism is tied to accountability for resources—a reckoning parasitical upon love.

My lecture on planetarity was actually first given to a Swiss philanthropic organization—*Stiftung Dialogik*—that had changed from giving asylum to Holocaust survivors to giving asylum to people from Rwanda, Afghanistan, Bosnia—the list goes on. And they did me the honor of asking me to give the lecture that would theorize the change. What came to me was this idea of how completely undifferentiated, unlistable, it would be if we could think that we lived on the planet. Although I am totally, completely, in favor of ecological justice, it was not about ecological justice. I am happy I used the word planet, but I am also unhappy, because the word planet immediately brings to mind, especially in those of us with this urge to save the world, the idea of using the world's resources well. It's a wonderful idea, but that's not what I was talking about.

In order for planetarity to be used for feminist utopias or ecological justice or whatever, you would have to put it in the value form, and I use the term value form in the original Marxian, not Marxist, sense. Marxists have either given it up or are confused about it, one reason being that the English translation of that simple sentence in Marx describing value has right from the start been wrong. Marx writes that it is *inhaltlos und einfach*, "contentless and simple." Why contentless? Because it allows the use of a form. All the English translations are "slight and simple" or "slight in content." How could they mistranslate a word like *inhaltlos* in which the *-los* is cognate to English "-less"? The only answer is that they didn't understand what Marx was trying to say. Take the example of a bottle of water where you have the ingredients listed and assigned percentages. That is water put in the value form. Because the value form—and this is very simple, many of you already know it, forgive me—is what makes commensurability possible. So by putting a certain percentage on this ingredient you make this water commensurable with roast beef, say. You can compare. That's all it is. If you want planetarity to travel to ecological justice, or utopian feminism, or whatever, you have to put planetarity in the value form, and its unmotivated reminding task—of an epistemological gap—evaporates. Marx was inviting us to understand and use the pharmakontic potential of quantification through an appreciation of the value form. Planetarity is elsewhere, always, from finding a measure.

Now that's not what I was talking about that evening. What I was saying to the Swiss was that the planet is in the species of alterity. It belongs to another system, one that can be scientifically described when it is put in the epistemological and disciplinary value form, but even then its edges are indescribable. A system as beyond our grasp as is the inside of our bodies. I cannot play with my own appendix as I am sitting here, although it's mine. My DNA can be described to death. But the fact remains that the signs I receive from my body like hunger, fatigue, pain, and so on are very simple signs that tell me nothing about the incessant movement of material inside my body. The body is metapsychological. In the same way, the planet that we inhabit belongs to another system, an otherness that we cannot access. We may use that idea in order to stop our corruptions. That's psychological justice; but even that has nothing to do with the fact that if the planet blows out, it blows out. In fact, it doesn't matter if the planet comes to an end. It is within a system that is in the species of alterity.

Now this is what I was trying to tell the Swiss: that if we imagine ourselves as planetary subjects rather than global agents, planetary creatures rather than global entities, alterity remains underived from us. This is as close to the sacred, again, as I can come. If I'm saving the world, it's *my* other. If I'm saving the world, I'm saving it for future generations that are *my* other. Detachment from the obligation to save is hard. It is before all human rights declarations. "Before" even is too logical, too spatial, a concept to put here. That's what I was trying to say. And so I said—it's in a book, by the way[12]—that it's not *our* dialectical negation, that we are good, they are bad, they are screwing up the world, and we will save it. It's not our dialectical negation. The planet flings us away as much as it contains us. It is a harsh thought when a human being thinks it.

By the way, I'm not saying that we should not engage in ecological work. But the invitation from the Swiss organization was for something slightly different. To them I indicated the limits of hospitality by musing that to think planetarity is already to transgress, for in spite of our forays into what we metaphorize differently as outer and inner space, what is above and beyond our reach is not continuous with us, as it is not indeed specifically discontinuous with us. That's the problem. But only by thinking it will we then be able to think the migrant as well as the recipient of foreign aid in the species of alterity—a transgressing planetarity, as it were—and not simply as U.S. persons of the South.

Kwok Pui-lan: Professor Spivak, it is a great honor to have you among us. Many of us sitting in this audience have been studying and learning from your work for many years. And I just want to begin by asking a question about the process of decolonization of the mind, which, of course, is a project that is very important in your work. You have said that you are a Europeanist by training; and those of us who are in Christian theology, we are somehow also Europeanists by training. Even feminist theology has been so deeply embedded in Western philosophical discourse. You began with the work of Derrida and the deconstructionist project, but you have also translated Mahasweta Devi and other such literature into English. And for some time now you have been urging us to learn from below. Some of us are just beginning to do this postcolonial feminist theology. And so I would like to hear, from you who have gone so far ahead before all of us: if you were to do it all over again, imagining yourself as somebody beginning to do postcolonial work in the field of religious studies and theology, what would your advice be? That is, where should we start? In your *Critique of Postcolonial Reason*, you started to unpack Kant, Hegel, and Marx, using the native as your key. Do you think that some kind of similar work should be undertaken vis-à-vis the theologians that are the equivalent of Marx, Hegel, or Kant in our discipline?

GCS: Well, you are also very hard! You can tell me what grade I'm getting at the end. This is like the toughest oral exam. [Laughter.] The thing is, I didn't actually start with Derrida. I come from West Bengal, as you know, and West Bengal happens to be the longest lasting parliamentarily elected communist government in the world. So I actually started with Marx. I didn't read Derrida until I was twenty-five years old and an assistant professor. I didn't know who he was. I ordered *De la grammatologie* out of a catalog, and I was very taken by the fact that, first of all, the word "ethnocentrism" was right in the beginning of the book, and I found that very unusual in a French book in 1967. Also what struck me was that here was somebody who was clearly from somewhere else and who had entered the European system and was trying to undo it with sympathy, that critical intimacy that we talked about earlier.

Although I have been so influenced by him, I have never really been his student. In fact, once I was speaking with him in New York, at a synagogue in the Lower East Side, and I said that even though I had been touched by deconstruction I could no longer claim it, because he had just written a book on his beloved student Jean-Luc Nancy entitled *Le Toucher*.[13] So I said that I was a *tache*, a stain, on deconstruction. He laughed; he knew what I meant. I even often told him that my relationship to him was a bit like Melanie Klein's to Freud, and since Jacques very much liked Melanie Klein, he took the point. Because I am not as worshipful as the big deconstructivists, I was outside. I haven't fully followed them, is what I am trying to say. I can't make all the moves that Derrida made. I can go up to a point, but after that I can't make those moves.

I would say that if I had to do it all over again—and this is a very hard question that you are asking me—the life that we are handed is the best life we could have. So I can't really undo it. One thing I have regretted—but on the other hand I think it was necessary to do—is that in 1981, when I was asked by *Yale French Studies* to write on French feminism and by *Critical Inquiry* to write on deconstruction, I had an identitarian moment and I felt it was strange that in the United States I had become an expert on deconstruction and French feminism, and so I wrote "French Feminism in an International Frame" for *Yale French Studies*,[14] but to *Critical Inquiry* I said that I wanted to translate a Bengali short story and I would write an accompanying essay which would have deconstruction in it, and *Critical Inquiry* took away the commission and said okay, on spec, let's see what you do. And that was the wrong reason for starting to translate Devi.[15] Also, in response to my identitarian impulse, I chose a woman from my own class, my own caste, an upper caste Hindu who had adopted the name Devi, which means "goddess," and all Brahmin women can in fact have that as a surname, although she had also been a communist, a lapsed communist at any rate, an anti-communist of a sort now. I chose from my own class because I was being identitarian, but I also tried to move beyond that. After I translated *Chotti Munda* I stopped translating her because I think that novel was too romantic about the tribals, and it gives them a certain kind of middle-class soul.[16] Isn't that what I was talking about when I spoke of epistemic planetarity? So I just want all that to be said also. What would I do different? I don't know.

I think I would repeat more strongly what I did try to say in *A Critique of Postcolonial Reason*, namely, that the native informant, who was so useful to the anthropologists, is not a real perspective. As far as the anthropologists went, the native informants were produced because anthropology had to be possible. What I tried to say in that book is that the pathos of so-called postcolonial work is that as we grow up and go up in class in metropolitan circumstances or at home, we want to claim the place of the native informant, until the real subalterns become completely unhearable. That's what I was saying there.

The woman who hanged herself in "Can the Subaltern Speak?,"[17] as I was saying to Serene [Jones] earlier today, is my grandmother's sister. I never mentioned this because I knew that if I did, all I would get was unquestioning admiration, so therefore I didn't mention it and all I got was unexamined hostility. Many published on it, because everyone wanted to claim that they were the subaltern. I could give you many examples of the muting of the subaltern, which is very different from their "not speaking." I used rhetorical language that was too difficult for people to read in a culture where humanities education has been trivialized. I would say that the lesson I learned—you are going to be very disappointed with what I say next—was to write more clearly. [Laughter.] I don't defend the fact that sometimes in search of the precise word I feel obliged to write in a way that seems incomprehensible. That's part of my obligation to my readership, but it may be a misplaced feeling. I think I misjudged my readership. I should have written for people who are not looking for precision.

As for postcolonial work, I'm the product of a national liberation movement, so therefore postcolonial work is in one way or another tied to nationalism for me. But I suspect that postcolonial work may be slightly out of step in today's world. I mean it should still be done, I'm not censoring any kind of work, but to look at it as the solution for contemporary problems may be slightly questionable. Even with the worst kind of necessary national liberation today, the case of the Palestinians, say—they know and we know that their case will not find its solution on the postcolonial model.

It's a very hard question that you asked me. Nobody has ever asked me this question before, and so I have never given this answer before. [Laughter.] Thank you. In you I seem to recognize someone else from somewhere else, who is also working from the inside out. As for finding the wedge to swivel—rather than the key to unlock (your metaphor)—the European tradition from this particular interest, it is you who will find it as you move through it, borrowing from it. I have not the required critical intimacy—hence my use of those conventional words in the beginning.

Serene Jones: I have three questions for you. The first has to do with this category "religion," and it's a version of Catherine's much more eloquently stated opening question, and there are two parts to it. The first part is asking for you to reflect generally on the travels of the category "religion" through postcolonial discourse and its shifting status. What Catherine highlighted is the degree to which, within secularism, there was a sanctioned ignorance about religion. Or, as I often think of it, in secularism, particularly within the humanities, religion functioned as the hysterical other: look, we're not them. It's interesting to me now that religion as a discursive site has returned—a moment of revenge, perhaps. But how is it going to function in this new globalizing discourse, in the logic of transnational discourse, in ways that don't, upon its return, simply turn it into no longer the hysterical other but, in fact, the very site of domination itself. So what will be the other of religion in its new form in the global market as the commodity that sells these days?

The second part of that opening question is this: it is very interesting when you say, "I am not religious." I am just curious as to what that word "religious" marks when you say that. What is it that you're not?

My second question is actually two quick observations about some possible collusion between liberationist Christian discourse and many of the themes you were suggesting earlier. It strikes me, first of all, that precisely what you are describing as a reckoning with the abnegation of the claim to save the world sits at the heart of the Christian tradition, the doctrine of justification by faith, in which the very first step of becoming is a step in which one abnegates any claim to accomplishing faith.

GCS: What was it called?

SJ: Justification by faith.

GCS: You know, I don't know anything about that, so I'll take it on faith. [Laughter.]

SJ: And the second observation has to do with reproductive heteronormativity. It is very interesting that also at the heart of the Christian tradition is a figure who was adopted, and how that notion can travel as a moment of resistance in this reproductive heteronormativity.

And then the last question. I am really interested as a theologian in Dalit theology, and this phenomenon, particularly in Tamil Nadu and Kerala, of a Dalit Christian Marxist recuperation of the image of the Suffering Servant. What does it mean to claim this space of abjection as the heart of political action?

GCS: Okay, well, beautiful questions. And I really do feel that I can't give you learned answers because I'm not an expert where you are. It's very hard to answer informed questions with a lack of information, but I will do the best I can.

On the category "religion," when you say that it is a commodity that sells. . . . You will notice right at the beginning of that book where Derrida, Vattimo, and others are gathered on the Isle of Capri, debating together, Derrida begins to talk about the Latin and Roman roots of the word "religion" and how little that word would cover those kinds of impulses that we term "religion" in English or French today.[18] That is a very astute observation. It seems to me that the attention paid to the intuition of the transcendental within deconstruction is rather different from the religion that sells as a commodity in the global marketplace. That object is not what is looked at within the deconstructive enclave.

On the other hand, there is also the deep distrust exhibited by upper-class multiculturalists, which makes Badiou claim universalism in Paul while taking good care to dismiss everything religious in Paul.[19] I find that extremely unnerving, that one is not looking at the religious material, even though I think, of course, that a faith in the resurrection is faith in a fable. Nonetheless, if you mean to go at all, go the whole way, like Derrida reads Marx. Don't try to keep yourself clean.

Again, I'm not a scholar of a religion. I only know the so-called religion within which I was brought up, which was a very different way of thinking about religion. Take the word *dharma*, for example, universally translated as "religion." Christianity is *khristodharma*. In the *Mahabharata* again and again when it is described that Draupadi was brought into the assembly menstruating, the word that is used is *stridharma*—*stri*, "woman," in her "nature,"—*dharma*—her definitive *natural* predication. That's hardly a religion, one might say. So it's therefore that word for nature, for definitive predication, for ethical behavior, for law, for institutionalized religion, etc., where institutionalized religion becomes a moment within a much broader context. It does in fact speak to us in those kinds of inchoate ways. When I am looking at how religion affects deconstructive thinking, or how it is sold in the global marketplace, I am not even thinking about *dharma*. Why? Because I have a horror of identitarianism. I'm not trained here, but I know very well that if I step forward with all the *dharma* stuff, especially since I know some Sanskrit, and can quote it, people will immediately lap it up as some authentic nonsense. [Laughter.] So that's my number one.

Number two, it's a very fine question you have asked, "What am I not?" I tell you, I don't know. This is a stereotype of myself that I am giving here. You know, the definitions come from outside. When I told Pavitrananda in 1963 that I had lost my faith, he says to me, *"Gayatri kothay jabey? Tomar adhhyani tapasya."* "Gayatri, where will you go?" And he says, "Your focused concentration"—which phrase is used colloquially for studying for exams and so on—"is your *tapasya*." Now, what did I know about *tapasya*? Nothing. *Tapasya* is the word used colloquially for penance, meditation. "Lose your faith; as long as you remain a humanities scholar, you won't escape it." Is that what he said?

But then, many years later, I was trying to put together some of the work that Bimal Krishna Matilal and I did together on the *Mahabharata* and I read one of the creation stories in the *Satapathabrahmana*. And in this very interesting creation story, Brhaspati has made all of the creatures, but the creatures are physically stronger, so they run off. And Brhaspati runs after them, but he can't catch up with them, and finally he comes back, sweating away. And his sweat falls in the fire. And that's the first *grhtahuti*, the first offering of clarified butter. "Butter" sounds so awful; *ghrta* is a good word. You know, it's like calling your breakfast egg "the unfertilized ovum of domesticated poultry." [Laughter.] And so what happens? The human being is created. And, because there was clay there, also the first brick. The brick is called *istaka* in Sanskrit. Why does the brick have that name? Because basically it was sweat falling. Why sweat? Because the body is a heating machine. So those first animist-like Hindus really thought that heat was a solid thing, because first of all, all they knew was to make fire with two pieces of wood, can you imagine? Not that easy. And the body does it on its own. And *tāpa,* the root word in *tapasya,* is "heat." So maybe thirty years later, I have discovered that Pavitrananda had said to me my focused concentration was my humanizing labor? Who knows? Bengali lacks a colloquial weak "to be." There is no "is" in the sentence, just an emphasizing suffix. So I don't know what I'm not, but it is curious that I keep insisting, as my old schoolfriend Manjari Ghosh remarked in March '08. I could say more here but will stop for lack of time. I do not want to be called religious in this time of religious violence. Safety in denial?

But I would say to everyone then that I was *adharmik,* which can mean "irreligious." My mother, God love her, took me aside and said, "Gayatri, don't say that. I know many people who are into institutional religion who don't do a hundredth of what you do. You should say instead, 'I am *abiswasi,*'" which means "unbeliever." So at least she gave me the word for one thing that I am not. Yours is a question that cannot be answered. I'm grateful that you asked it.

The abnegation of the claim to save the world. . . . Yes, you can find this, because it's good advice, in many religious traditions. But the problem with reading something and wanting to control it is deciding—and this we can't help—to make it familiar by saying it's something with which we are familiar. I don't think we can let this go, but I think the second step is to question it. My mom, when she first went abroad in 1967, came back and said, "My God, you know London is just like Calcutta!" And I said, "No, mama, it's the other way around." [Laughter.] That's the whole thing, see? So I would say to my students that if you say that Marx is nothing but Freud libidinized, or Derrida is nothing but a poor man's Nietzsche, you lose the thing that escapes your ability to control it. This nothing-but-ism stands in the way of expanding, going forward to new things. So although one can undoubtedly find in many of the great religions an imperative toward abdicating the desire to save the world, we should relearn it as good Americans. My students, in fact, sit in my classroom thinking that history happened in order to produce them so that they could save the world. [Laughter.] We legitimize by reversal in the United States, by taking everything as the fault of the United States. It seems to me that this is a lesson which should certainly be related to older imperatives toward not wanting to save the world, but it should not be seen as nothing but that, because then we don't learn the lesson, we just kind of say, "Look, you see? They said this already long ago." On the other hand, perhaps I get this via Kant's harshness about philosophizing—the transcendental deduction as laundered "justification by faith"? Remember, however, that his analogies come from sense perception.

Your next question concerned reproductive heteronormativity and the fact that the central figure in Christianity is an adopted one. It seems to me that the function of that particular mode of adoption is to cleanse RHN of the embarrassing fact that, to quote Yeats, "Love has pitched his mansion in the place of excrement." And I think there may be a problem with the divine instrumentalizing of the female body as "adoption." "Surrogate mother" for the price of redemption? "Illegitimate" child kindly adopted? Christ's birth is not even conventionally continuous with positive law. It's not really a critique of RHN, it's rather a way of purifying the woman, because woman is already contaminated. I want to give you a parallel example from the *Mahabharata* because I've just been teaching it. According to my very dear friend Romila Thapar, who is arguably the best historian of ancient India alive today, the *Mahabharata* represents a move from, to quote her words, "lineage to state," from blood dynasties to the possibility of some other way of controlling polity. And so in the *Mahabharata*, on the good side, everyone is a bastard, there is not a single legitimate son. And on the bad side, these hundred kings, they were all born so premature, so pre-human, that they were kept in a hundred jars to incubate in order to come out as children. So this was a critique of RHN for sure, but for what? To make it plausible to people that legitimacy was not the only good thing, so that one could move from legitimacy to state. On the other hand, it is also deeply committed to RHN even as it questions it. To deny RHN would almost be like denying the possibility of love, and that's the problem. We are in a deep double bind when it comes to RHN. As I said before, it's medicine as well as poison. That's what makes it such a hard thing to deal with.

Your final question had to do with Dalit theology. I am generally in favor of the Dalit movement, but I am also critical of the fact—and I am not alone in this—that the Dalit movement, as a structured movement, is not always negotiating its access to movement status in ways that are fully sympathetic to the realities of what is termed "Dalit" in our very large country. The word Dalit, as you know, is a Sanskrit word, and it's a word which means "oppressed," "walked upon," "crushed underfoot," etc. What Dalit theology seems to me to show is that in spite of all of

Christianity's triumphalism and universalism, it is also possible to use the text of Christianity well in order to work in the interests of suffering. Of course it is. That is something that needs to be kept alive. Therefore, I am certainly for it. But—and I am always a creature of "buts"—as has been said forever about liberation theology by people like me—cynical, awful, unbelieving people—I wish we could have had the liberation without the theology. [Laughter.] So remember that this is also said.

Stephen D. Moore: I'm a biblical scholar by training, if not always by temperament, so my question is entirely predictable. In essays such as "Three Women's Texts and a Critique of Imperialism" you have brilliantly demonstrated how the civilizing mission of European, and especially British, imperialism was disseminated through the medium of English literature.[20] I imagine that many in this room might be interested to hear you comment on the role of what Homi Bhabha has termed "the English book"—that is, the Bible[21]—in the British colonial enterprise, especially in India.

GCS: I don't think with Homi that the Bible is an English book. I believe it would be bad faith for us to say that Christianity in India comes down to an English book. I think it would be wrong for us—I am not saying for you, I am saying for us—just to wave a flag against it. When I think about the influence of Christianity in my country, I also have to think of the great efforts at semitizing Hinduism in the nineteenth century by reformed thinkers like Vivekananda and the leaders of the Brahmo Samaj, which are clearly not just the English Bible. I think we should rethink how we speak about it. You already have read the interview where I praised my teachers who were converted, Christianized aboriginals.[22] Who was caring for them? No one. And then the great Ulgulan at the end of the nineteenth century, the first big subaltern move against the British, however local—a millenarian Christianity appropriated by aboriginals and stopped by the Indian Hindu officials of the British. So what am I supposed to think?

I will tell you a little story. One year I left my British passport and my green card by mistake on the bright yellow box near the VAT counter in Heathrow Airport. I only realized it when the plane was halfway to New York, so I called the flight attendant and asked him to contact the airport and say that a Third World citizen is coming in without any papers. No passport, no visa. Well, I arrive and I'm taken care of right away. I was flying economy so there was a huge line, but I go right through. And

there's an African American woman at the visa place. I have no identification except an old expired ID from Wesleyan University where I was for
one semester for a fellowship. She looks at it and says, "I waive the
requirement for a passport and visa." And she tells me, "There's a door
there that says 'No Entry'; go through it, and my boss will give you a
temporary green card immediately." And he does. Afterwards I call my
mom, standing there in a phone box. "Mom, I'm in. I had no papers,
nothing." So what did my mother, who is certainly also Hindu, say? She
says, in Bengali, "The Lord is my shepherd, I shall not want." [Laughter.]
So what am I supposed to say? That it's an English book? The English
was also a translation, interminably. What is the language at the origin?

SDM: Let's go from the English book to the Englishman in your book,
then. In the chapter of your *Critique of Postcolonial Reason* entitled "History," you vividly conjure up for us the figure of Captain Geoffrey Birch,
who, as we meet up with him in 1815, is busily riding around the foothills
of the Himalayas, accompanied only by a native guide. You write, and I
quote, that he would be "a slight romantic figure if encountered in the
pages of a novel or on the screen."[23] But the purpose of his ride is anything
but romantic. As he himself represents it in a letter that you cite, he has
undertaken the journey precisely to acquaint the people of the hill country
with whom and with what they are subject to. You parse out his purpose
as follows: "He is actually engaged in consolidating the Self of Europe by
obliging the native to cathect the space of the Other on his home
ground. . . . He is worlding their own world, which is far from mere
uninscribed earth, anew, by obliging them to domesticate the alien as
Master."[24] In so doing he is also obliging them to see themselves as
"other," as you later observe. Finally, and most importantly, perhaps, for
your analysis, "[t]he truth value of the stranger is being established as the
reference point for the true (insertion into) history of these wild
regions."[25] I'm wondering, however, whether you might be willing to
comment on certain other implicit dimensions of the situation that your
analysis leaves unspoken. The aptly named Captain Birch is an agent and
disciplinary arm of the East India Company, and later you note in passing
that the company's board of directors at that time contains members
"whose obsession with the Christianizing of India is too well known
to belabor."[26] Presumably, then, the captain's symbolic intervention is
designed to oblige the inhabitants of the hill country not only to reconceive of themselves as subject, native and other, but also to reconceive of

themselves as non-Christian—or, to adopt a heavily freighted nineteenth-century idiom that is inseparable from what you have termed "the axiomatics of imperialism"—to reconceive of themselves as "heathen." As such, the "true history" into which they are being inserted is also Christian salvation history. How might these considerations be folded into your analysis?

GCS: At the moment when Birch is riding around, the evangelicals were in power in the Company. But the appropriative power of subaltern religions is something that we should not underestimate, whether we are looking at African Christianity, for example, or Black Christianity in this country, or Christians below a certain class demarcation in India. There is a way in which there is a kind of counter-theological appropriation until it is politically mobilized for warfare. I saw this myself. I'm from Calcutta, born in 1942. I saw the Hindu-Muslim riots in 1946, as a child, one of the reasons why I have no faith at all in conventional religion. On the one side, the famine created by the British to feed the soldiers in the Pacific theater, and on the other the religious riots. You realize that the subaltern acceptance of religious discourse, which appropriates and changes, can be very fragile. It can be contaminated and mobilized into opposition. And it lasts. And fake cultural memory can be created on the ground of religion. It's an extremely important question and we mustn't see it as a binary opposition. Which is why Gregory Bateson, when he's writing the essays that form *Steps to an Ecology of Mind*, says that within theories of play what happens is that the subject says "this is play," giving a meta-communicative signal. Except in religion and patriotism.[27] So it seems to me that that is the task of detranscendentalizing, which I understand you spoke about, that I am talking about. "Play" is not a bad word, and it seems to me that that sense, if it could be restored, would be a much better way of understanding how Christianity became one of the Indian religions. I think it would be better to look at it that way than have some metropolitan upper-class migrant writing a book saying "the Bible is an English book."

So that's where I would go, Stephen, with your excellent question. And I would also like to say that showing oneself as Master, and separating the other from its place, still happens now. I could give you many examples, especially in the field of gender, because I do travel into places that are below the radar. Alienating people from their own space by erecting a figure who knows how to transform the landscape is very much the case within the NGOs. And I do not say this because I am against them. I have many students who are in this work, and I love them. But it's necessary to be aware of the connections with the Geoffrey Birches and the nineteenth century. One last reminder, however. Christianity is hardly there in Sirmur today, though Fateh Prakash, the Rani's son, seems to have favored the Brahmo Samaj.

Elaine Padilla (from the audience): Upon considering your comments on exile and origins, I would like to ask how exile with a rejection of a return to origins poses a challenge to feminism and its view of origins in terms of the maternal. Rejection of a pure origin is the acceptance of a homelessness that does not seek a "return to" but rather a remembrance that entails a movement of past, present, and future in reconstructions of home. How would the back-and-forth movement that experiences of exile set forth provide a challenge to origins from a postcolonial feminist point of view? In addition, for some of us who are immigrants, exile has been about dislocation, multilocation, and translocation, and thus a reshaping of the "originary" into multiplicity beyond "home." How would this khoric locality defined by movement and the multiform complicate or problematize even further the notion of the feminine as origin?

GCS: A wonderful question, a very timely question. It seems to me, however, that there are two questions here. One is about losing a connection with one's roots perceived as lodged in the cultural system of the place one left behind. Another is about mothers as origin, as it were. But mothers, of course, still do it alone. So it's a question about parents, reproductive heteronormativity yet again.

People, in fact, have always been on the move. And movement of peoples is what has made human history. That is the broad outline. We are in the belly of the superpower here, so when we talk about exile we are not talking about this general exilic condition of humanity. But what of the narrow outline of my own life, my own group in the metropole, we ask? We are talking about the fact that a group such as the one that I identify broadly as mine is exiled in a very powerful country that has a very peculiar approach toward other kinds of people. So we need to keep that separate. It is not exile as such that we are talking about. I mean, you can go and read the Alexandria Codex, and you will see how the folks there thought of exile as some displeasure of God upon them. And they began to think diaspora in quite another way, rather than in order to reclaim the fact that they could not read the word of God as it was uttered. That is a very different kind of thing. So exile as such is not what we are talking about. We are talking about the condition of our own communities. And even within our own communities, the exilic is quite often someone who has been denied, for political reasons, a return journey. Now that person is a little bit different from someone who for economic reasons is equally not able to undertake a return journey. So let's not do the useless thing that people do when they say, "Oh, well, you know, this one's political, this one came willingly." That is a very unjust and limited definition of the word "willingly." On the other hand, you have to make this distinction—and I hope the Indians here are not going to be upset with me. When in 1965 Lyndon Johnson lifted the quota system and there was a 500 percent increase in Asian immigration, most of the Indian folk who came were disappointed with decolonization, and they were mostly professionals who (as Toni Morrison said to Charlie Rose) were not necessarily identified with the disenfranchised communities of color in this country. So there is a difference. I am not saying that therefore they should go home. But we should see who is speaking for exile, who is making exile the slogan. And we should keep it clear of the broader definition of human beings as exilic, and also keep it clear of the illegitimate accusation that political migrants "wanted to come here." Those are all very complicated issues. Who is speaking for exile?

Now within this exiled situation, I would go back to Du Bois's *Souls of Black Folk*, and I would look at the epigraph in every chapter—I have written about this in *Death of a Discipline* and elsewhere.[28] What does he do? He takes what was called Negro spirituals (he called them "sorrow songs") and he puts them in European notation at the head of every chapter. What does that show? It shows a move from—again I am quoting myself—the performative to performance. I think rather than coding it as looking for my origins, we should code it as moving our own performative into the permission to perform, which is all about racializing class positively. Once one is upwardly mobile and ascends to another class, then one can do as much culture as one wants. I'm sitting here wearing a sari; if I were working in a 7-Eleven I would not be allowed to wear a sari to work. It's a class thing. If we look at it as working to move the subaltern into hegemony—class mobility without the incredible corruption within the upper classes in this country at present, the exacerbation of the difference between the rich and the poor—then we can become at once a force for saving not just our origin, but for the country we have chosen, without being on top. Okay, so who wants to save? Remember, that's where I began. Who's the "we"? What used to make us work, the performative of our culture, was that old culture at home, like the software in the computer that makes the computer work. But since coming here, that has become subculture-fied in our little enclaves so that in fact we have become much more like that culture than the folks there are. That's number one.

And number two is that it is no longer, however, our performative. Have you ever heard the incredible bilingualism of the underclass Hispanics? New York is a Latin American city. When they are speaking in English, they are absolutely speaking American. And when they are speaking to other Hispanics, they are speaking a high-speed Nuyorican type of Spanish, a Spanish that, of course, doesn't exist in Spain. Subculturally, then, it's a partial performative. It's a partial performative even as you translate it into the dominant performative. You know, then, that the time has come for it to become performance, included within curricula, placed in museums, a language that is allowed to be taught and learned and used. Its mark is the button you press for Spanish in telecommunication. All of those things are performance within the dominant culture, which, however, is *changed* by this performance. That is not going back to one's origins. It should be recoded as this other discourse whereby you thicken the civil society that you have chosen to come to. And then nobody can say, "Oh, well, you wanted to come here." No, there is a difference between want and choice.

Your question is an excellent question, and it is a real question, but it has to be thought not in terms of claiming origin in exile, but rather as a task to change, taking Du Bois as the example. Why did he put the spirituals in European notation? So that they could be performed. He did not want to have only double consciousness and going back to Africa; he changed completely until finally at the end of his life he became a citizen of Ghana rather than some imaginary origin, a shadow. My friend, keep this wonderful question in your head but rewrite it another way. Change it. Marx wanted the working class to change their self-concept from victim to agent of production. It has come to nothing because that change never took place; but we can make that change in the field of exile.

John J. Thatamanil (from the audience): It has been a treat listening to you, meeting you, and also, by proxy, your mother. She sounds like a very special person, especially when she corrected you as well she ought, because the term *adharmik* ought to be translated "wicked" . . .

GCS: There you go.

JJT: . . . and you can't go around calling yourself that. So I appreciate that comment because it helps circle us back to the question that was asked about what are you denying when you are denying religion. I also appreciated the *karma-kandi* option, because from a classic perspective, you do the rituals whether the gods exist or not. So in that sense, that too seems like a wise characterization of some of what you are up to. But all this leaves me still unclear about what, precisely, detranscendentalizing means. Because sometimes when I hear you speak, I hear you criticizing kinds of reifications, absolutizations, when, say, a contingent identity, Hindu, etc., gets reified, sanctified, and absolutized, and is used to undergird violence. If detranscendentalizing is undercutting all of that, I'm all for it. But I suspect you mean more, and I suspect you mean something ontological, or at least you could be read as meaning something ontological, dismissing the realm of the gods. Do you mean to do that as well? Would you speak about that?

GCS: This, now, is a question that worries me. [Laughter.] I use the word "detranscendentalizing" because I think I want to undermine—you are right—an ontological commitment. On the other hand, I don't think everybody has an ontological commitment, and I'm fine with them. But I don't want to be a sort of silly rationalist detranscendentalizer. What is the imagination? It is neither reason nor unreason, neither truth nor lie. So what do we do with that?

Martin Luther King spoke "Beyond Vietnam" in 1967. He was talking about the necessity of imagining my enemy as a human being even if I don't endorse his actions. And he says at a certain point, "I speak in the name of someone who so loved his enemies that he gave his life for them." Now what I thought was that for Dr. King this is a transcendental moment. For me it was not. So I would say that yes, it has something to do with ontological commitment. On the other hand, I don't want to reduce religion to culture. That's why I use the word "sacred." And that's why at the end of my talk about "Righting Wrongs,"[29] I quote Orlando Patterson and say that you have to be like the Jesuits; you have to be so committed to teaching this way that you need a licensed lunacy. I use those words. So yes, there is a something-shaped hole there in my work.

Since you acknowledge my mother's presence, I will end with another story about her. Her name was Sivani Chakravorty; she is not a nameless person. She had made herself a considerable Sanskritist, and she had an MA in Bengali literature. And she would tell me, since we had many conversations about me being *adharmik*, "You know, dear, I too don't really *believe* in gods and things" (speaking in Bengali, of course); "it's more like I believe in a force." And I would laugh at her, "Yeah, mom, you believe in a 'force' all right. He's a huge man in the sky with Birkenstocks and a flowing beard, that's your force." And when I would find a parking spot very quickly in New York City, I'd say, "See, mom, the bearded gentleman really does exist." [Laughter.]

That conversation was all about ontological commitment and detranscendentalizing. At the end of the day, I think, the transcendental in my work is like Kant's transcendental deduction—what you have to assume in order for experience to be possible, but you cannot bring forth for any commitment. But that doesn't cut the religious question completely because of this business of the effect of grace, as when in the *Critique of Pure Reason* Kant says that mere reason is too lazy morally, and so in order for morality to be possible there must be an effect of grace, a metaleptic gesture, which is incredibly bold. What you bring up in your question actually seems close to this hope. And I would also want it in my project because it is not only an intellectual one.

Postscript: For the William James lecture at Harvard (April 10, 2008), I used a provisional tripartite distinction: religious, philosophical, and literary transcendentalization. I recall that moment and end on a promise to publish.

The Pterodactyl in the Margins: Detranscendentalizing Postcolonial Theology

SUSAN ABRAHAM

To be human is to be intended toward the other. We provide for ourselves transcendental figurations of what we think is the origin of this animating gift: mother, nation, god, nature. These are the names of alterity, some more radical than others. . . . If we imagine ourselves as planetary subjects rather than global agents, planetary creatures rather than global entities, alterity remains underived from us; it is not our dialectical negation, it contains us as much as it flings us away. And thus to think of it is already to transgress, for, in spite of our forays into what we metaphorize, differently, as outer and inner space, what is above and beyond our own reach is not continuous with us as it is not, indeed, specifically discontinuous. We must specifically educate ourselves into this peculiar mindset.
GAYATRI CHAKRAVORTY SPIVAK, *Death of a Discipline*

PHILOSOPHICAL AND THEOLOGICAL CONCERNS

Gayatri Chakravorty Spivak's idea of "planetarity" is a postcolonial topology for ethics in the wake of the demise of identitarian forms of ethics. Moreover, it is the basis of her call to detranscendentalize[1] all forms of radical alterity (mother, nation, god, nature). How can we stage a conversation between "planetarity" and theology? Instead of the arbitrary cultural and imaginary maps for identity-based ethical models, Spivak suggests that the topographical expanse presented by planetarity will affirm the best of our human impulses, which is to be for others. This is an impulse that can be embraced by theology. However, for Spivak, the taint of the religious as a system of beliefs and its transcendental foundations must be rigorously opposed in view of its continuing co-optation by imperial and nation-building interests. Yet, detranscendentalizing does not mean the erasure of religion entirely. Spivak, it would seem, has reassessed the role of religion for politics. "Detranscendentalizing" refers to the move to counter secular attempts "to privatize the transcendental."[2] Thus, detranscendentalizing as a deconstructive move is not primarily a challenge to religion or theological discourses. It is a challenge to secularist politics that seeks to marginalize religion. This essay consequently stages a conversation between theology and Spivak's detranscendental proposal for ethics in its nonsecular frame.

Spivak's argument is primarily directed to area studies in comparative literatures. For theology, her notion signals the manner in which postcolonial theological thought ought to be attempted. Firstly, theology in view of planetarity must revise its ontotheological framework and reliance on traditional theological metaphysics and belief systems in its presentation of the relationship between transcendence and immanence. The traditional ways of clarifying the relationship between transcendence and immanence shifts to a material and cultural plane while eschewing identitarian cultural conventions. Consequently, theological discourses can be interrogated for their commitment to heterogeneity and plurality that goes beyond a mere "logofratocentric"[3] notion of democracy in view of planetarity. Theology done in the postcolonial moment cannot ignore, postpone, or simply add on the problem of sexual difference. Further, planetarity presents a more complex topographical context for ethics. It is not simply the planet that ought to be at the forefront of ethical inquiry; it is the manner in which we live together as creatures that belong to the planet, "planetary subjects," that is the more urgent frame for ethics.

Spivak's call to "detranscendentalize the sacred" seems to be an attempt to rethink transcendence and immanence on a cultural plane. In this effort, her reading and presentation of religion and theology is self-avowedly "nonspecialist." For Spivak, transcendence as an other-worldly phenomenon is useless for ethics. Yet, as I shall argue, deconstruction need not sound the death knell for theological discourses of transcendence if they are able to consider the cultural contexts in which they are generated. Planetarity challenges theological discourses to speak of transcendence and immanence in a cultural mode. As the epigraph suggests, planetarity is a "peculiar mindset" that challenges the exploitative dualisms of colonial and postcolonial power. The detranscendentalized space of transcendence consequently is "here," not "there" (other-world). This mundane space of transcendence is complemented by the incursion of complex temporality. Space, the here and now, in urgent, immediate, and singular encounter, is complicated by a complex time of past, present, and future *in the present*. Detranscendental postcolonial theology is resistant to those spatial and temporal maneuvers invested in the separation of transcendence and immanence. To this end, Spivak's notion of planetarity will go far in bridging this separation but only when grasped as a disposition to construe the relationship between transcendence and immanence differently.

If planetarity means simply a stance of ecological responsibility in the face of the continuing degradation of the planet's resources, then Spivak would have an ally in none other than Pope Benedict XVI himself. Benedict has commissioned the Vatican's buildings to be fitted out with solar energy panels and has insistently commented on the deleterious effects of climate change. He has written and spoken extensively of human responsibility in maintaining the health of the planet. Such a renewed concern with ecology reflects the need to present viable forms of transcendence of space to the next generation of believers in an ethical frame. The earlier moment of cultural, racial, and gendered calls to ethics is revisioned in the new universalism of planetary health. The contingency for ethics in speaking of the planet's health is also a response to time. Here, Spivak and Benedict's agendas converge in articulating the urgency of the present moment. Transcendence is presented as the going out of the self in response to the need of the other. In both proposals, time transcends the merely present countable and experiential moment. The simultaneous coexisting of past, present, and future is the basis of nonidentitarian ethics in both proposals.

However, Benedict's exhortations stand within a tradition in which the call to protect creation is a caution to safeguard and protect "natural" relationships, the most significant of which is heterosexual marriage.[4] One cannot but notice the cultural and material frame of these concerns. The preoccupation of conservative forms of Christianity seeking to speak of ethics in relation to nature slyly circumvents the (strategic) essentialist arguments of racial and gendered groups routinely marginalized by such conservatism. The move recuperates the steady erosion of assumed elite masculinist privilege while simultaneously advancing ethics in theology. The protection of "nature," then, is in service of a salvage agenda surfeited with heterosexist masculinist logics. "Nature" in other words, becomes part of the ideological battle for control. Nature is to be rescued and to be retrieved to the extent that it affirms particular cultural notions about hegemonic marriage and notions of family. Thus heteropatriarchal norms, hegemonic masculinity, procreative sex, and subordinated femininity are Benedict's answers to postmodern critiques of theology. In the polarized space of postmodern critiques of religion, official theological proposals reinstating traditional arrangements for transcendence have seductive appeal. It is incumbent on postcolonial theological imaginations retrieving Spivak to present viable forms of transcendence to counter official religious attempts at recuperation.

While Benedict mobilizes "nature" as the space of familiarity and the homely, Spivak, in proposing the planet, argues that she will "render our home uncanny."[5] This is postcolonial cultural and detranscendentalized space, where the business of ethics is not business as usual. Planetary thought, by introducing uncanniness into our relationship with space, defamiliarizes space. In an earlier commentary on defamiliarized spaces, Spivak writes:

> In the contemporary context, when the world is broadly divided simply into North and South, the World Bank has no barrier to its division of that world into a map that is as fantastic as it is real. This constantly changing map draws economic rather than national boundaries, as fluid as the spectacular dynamics of international capital. One of the not inconsiderable elements in the drawing up of these papers is the appropriation of the Fourth World's ecology. Here a kinship can be felt through the land grabbing and deforestation practiced against the First Nations of the Americas, the destruction of the reindeer forests of the Suomis of Scandinavia and Russia, and the tree felling and eucalyptus plantations on the land of the original nations, indeed of all the early civilizations that have been pushed back and away to make way for what we call the geographic lineaments of the map of the world today.[6]

Defamiliarizing known space by identifying its fantastic boundaries serves transcendence by deconstructing its bounded nature. The imperial and neo-colonial formations of contemporary cartography draw attention to the manner in which the poorest of the world exist with barely enough space on the margins of these boundaries. In other words, Spivak points to the occlusion of the poorest by nationalist politics insisting on projects of identity, when the true postcolonial project ought to be an ethical one of inclusion and work on behalf of the poor. When the rigid and bounded nature of the boundaries is revealed as porous, the identitarian imperative, that is, the naming and branding of cultural and social identity, dissolves.

Space, our home, is rendered uncanny and unfamiliar, an uncanny space that transcends our grasp and becomes a site of revelation beyond mere cultural particularity. Consequently, all homey spaces become unhomey and uncanny.

Detranscendentalized time is reconceived in Spivak's view of contingency in order to interrupt the faddish and entirely toothless academic "postcolonial" theoretical practices.[7] Uncanny time, like uncanny space, exists on the margins of our experience and consciousness. Uncanny time confounds the demands of some types of postcolonial theory to posit a linear unfolding of historical time and resists being managed and assimilated. Time and space thus configured make our notions of collectivity "undecidable."[8] This is contingency, presented through comparative literature. Her reading of Mahasweta Devi's "Pterodactyl, Puran Sahay and Pirtha," for example, invites us to see in the revelation of the Pterodactyl, a contingency that remains unimaginable to recuperative agendas. The presence of the Pterodactyl signals a time that is prior to the establishing of national identities, geographical regions, indeed, the very creation of the continents. This time before our time cannot be grasped by the terms "primitive" and "aboriginal" of postcolonial contexts. These "historical alibis" simply rearrange space-time in a manner that shores up neocolonial power. Planetarity is a counter to this form of thinking, a "utopian idea as a task for thinking ground"[9] based in utter and absolute contingency. In *Death of a Discipline*, Spivak writes about her initial realization of planetary time:

> The lesson of the impossibility of translation in the general sense, as Toni Morrison shows it, readily points at absolute contingency. Not the sequentiality of time, not even the cycle of seasons, but only weather. . . . If Mahasweta undoes the division between Aboriginal and Indo-European India by the experience of impossible planetarity, Morrison undoes the difference between Africa and African-America by the experience of a planetarity equally inaccessible to human time.[10]

Planetary uncanny time is the urgent time of now, a present time in which ethical response cannot be postponed. In uncanny time and space, planetarity signals the love that must infuse any relationship. Planetarity as the utopian ground is protection from the imperial maps and imperial histories being constructed and controlled by neocolonial interests. Intrinsic to neocolonial and neoimperial interests is the marshaling of religious identity to mark difference and privilege. "Hindu India" and "Christian America" are terms that bespeak neocolonialism. Puran, the protagonist of Devi's novella, in contrast, enters the space and time of Pirtha "responsibly." Spivak points to the aboriginal embrace of Puran to signal the contingency of postcolonial contexts. The people are not objects of benevolence; they are active participants and initiators of ethical action. The pterodactyl in the margins makes our space, time, and ethics uncanny, undecidable, and entirely unassimilable.

Planetarity must be scrupulously protected from the taint of religious power yoked to nationalist politics. Spivak writes:

> Having seen, then, the powerful yet risky role played by Christian liberation theology, some of us have dreamt of an animist liberation theology to girdle perhaps the impossible vision of an ecologically just world. Indeed the name "theology" is alien to this thinking. Nature "is" also super-nature in this way of thinking and knowing. . . . Nature, the sacred other of the human community, is, in this thinking, also bound by the structure of ethical responsibility of which I have spoken in connection with women's justice. The pterodactyl is not only the ungraspable other but also the ghost of our ancestors that haunts our present and our future. We must learn "love" . . . as Puran does in "Pterodactyl," in view of the impossibility of communication. No individual transcendence theology, being just in this world in view of the next—however the next is underplayed—can bring us to this.[11]

Spivak asserts that all Christian theology simplistically presents the ethical stance in view of the "other world" of transcendence. In the passage following this one, she asserts that all the "great" religions of the world are bankrupt in their moral visions since they are "too deeply imbricated in the ebb and flow of power." The sacred vision, which is not the same as a conventional religious vision, ought to be the precise opposite, that of the encounter in love and its mind-changing experience, which can only happen in present, urgent encounters, in their singular and shocking differences.

One does not forget that Spivak is highly allergic to her "affirmative constructions" being co-opted by the liberal academic establishment. Indeed, as she has reminded us many times over, the "persistent critique of what one must inhabit, the persistent consolidation of claims to founding catachresis, involve an incessant recoding of diversified fields of value."[12] "Value" as

Spivak explains, is Marx's notion of the "contentless and simple" thing whereby through mediation and coding, human work becomes more important than the person who does the work. We are to be very vigilant of value codings because were we to uncritically ground our political practices in value-coded positions, we would simply exacerbate the problem of imperialism. Postcoloniality[13] then is a position, not "of the discovery of historical or philosophical grounds, but in terms of reversing, displacing and seizing the apparatus of value coding."[14] Hence from the outset, her affirmative construction undermines the academic ploy of co-opting a concept and positioning it within its framework. In this sense, planetarity is akin to her notion of postcoloniality; it is less about marginal and resistant identity claims and more about demonstrating the "irreducible margin in the center."[15] In other words, planetarity may be deployed rhetorically without seeking a positivist foundation for identity or ethics.

Planetarity is the rhetorical field in which contemporary theologians must speak of transcendence and immanence. Not only is transcendence and immanence an (im)possible theological question in modernity and postmodernity,[16] but speaking of God too seems to be limited to specialist theological discourses. Theism in particular, in the context of critical methodologies, seems to be overly dependent on the pole of transcendence (in particular, on ontotheological forms of transcendence) and thus overly inimical to the concerns of much liberation-oriented thinking concerned with culture and power. Feminist and other critical frameworks seem to overly emphasize the immanence pole and seem to have sacrificed transcendence, reasserting the postmodern separation between transcendence and immanence. Feminist theism, the subject of the next section, artfully struggles to articulate transcendence and immanence with an eye for ethics and justice. The specialized discourse of feminist theism would not find planetarity alien to its method and thinking. Their cultural embeddedness points to ways in which planetarity forms the rhetorical context of feminist theism. A discussion between Spivak's planetary program and contemporary feminist theism is not an arbitrary choice; it signals the way in which theological thinking can proceed beyond postcoloniality.

SPEAKING OF TRANSCENDENCE AND IMMANENCE

Contemporary feminist discourses on theism present a range of options in response to the challenges of modern culture, such as scientific thought and the challenge to supernaturalism. These options are feminist assessments of classical theism, panentheism, and pantheism. Predictably, in response to cultural demands, some feminist theistic thinkers are preoccupied with policing the boundaries of their disciplines. Postcolonial and planetary challenges to such projects reveal the social conditioning and political allegiances of these discourses. Academic and elite white feminism seem to be carrying on a very narrow conversation among themselves with a view to protecting their turf. Consequently, it might seem to many planetary feminists that feminist theistic discourses are irrelevant to their particular space-time concerns. Nevertheless, feminist theistic proposals grapple with the relationship between transcendence and immanence in ways that resonate with planetary feminists.

An early essay by Nancy Frankenberry alerts us to the cultural embedding of feminist theism and the precise relation between the form of God construction and gender constructions.[17] Thus, her concern is to examine the problem of sexual difference in classical theism, a move that would have affinity with planetarity. Classical theism in Frankenberry's opinion is implicated in reinscribing traditional gender stereotypes and positing imperial and patriarchal qualities onto God-talk. For her, the force of classical theism articulated in the language of absolutes describes the divine entity in "unintelligible" terms such as "necessary, eternal, infinite, unchanging, self-sufficient, simple, one, and all-powerful and all-knowing."[18] Frankenberry's major contention is that in an age of science, such terms are mystifying and incoherent. A God that exists "beyond space" and "before time" invites philosophical derision owing to theological dependence on analogies, metaphors, symbols, and paradoxes, because it "forfeits cognitive content to the use of God language."[19] In other words, Frankenberry displays her predilection for scientific terminology and its apparent clear yield of meaning and truth and its affinity with material and immanentist concerns of feminists. Her concern with material space and time however displays the familiar motif of separate spheres for transcendence and immanence since her self-avowed "focus is philosophical rather than theological."[20] Classical theism, consequently, in her view, produces a God who is absolutely transcendent, infantilizes human beings, and retains an authoritarian hold over creation. Such a God "disproportionately inscribes male bias" into theological accounts, rendering them merely discourses on domination. The classical doctrine of God therefore presents us with the image of a patriarchal and monarchical male image of the Divine who stands over and above material space and time. Consequently, genuine "creaturely freedom" is thoroughly compromised, for divine omnipotence is assumed to be the ability of the divine to interfere in human affairs at any moment. Theodicy becomes *the* issue for theology as a consequence, for the claim of the absolutely transcendent and powerful divinity seems to be diminished in the face of evils facing humanity. Frankenberry dismisses classical theism as unintelligible for feminists on philosophical and scientific grounds and the transcendence that it speaks of as inaccessible to feminists.

Others may not agree. Sarah Coakley, for example, a theologian and feminist analytic philosopher, has resurrected a classical theist argument to counter the arguments of evolutionary science and its absolutist claims of how nature came into being by arguing the opposite, that all processes of natural evolution as described by science offer ample evidence of God's immanence.[21] The language of classical theism in this view continues to have vigor because God's transcendence is not to be simplistically opposed to God's immanence. Coakley's definition of "God who is Being itself, creator and sustainer of all that is, eternal (atemporal, omnipresent), omniscient, omnipotent, all loving and indeed the source of all perfection" reflects the dependence on coherence for the integrity of the Christian theological system. She argues that this God who is atemporal and occupying all space is not absolutely contradictory to scientific theories of evolution; precisely within the attempts to describe evolutionary theories we are able to note God's immanent presence. In her attempt to secure theistic frameworks in a post-Darwinian context, she advances a theory of "natural cooperation," which, first, evaporates the Deist argument that "God" must compete as a "(very big) bit player," since God is "that-without-which-there-would-be-no-evolution-at all," the (Augustinian) Being closer to the inner workings of evolution than evolution itself. In other words, the challenge of scientific evolutionary theory to account for God in the theory of evolution is trumped by the assertion of the theologian who insists that God is prior to all thinking or theorizing about creation. Darwin and any theory of evolution is incomplete without taking into account the creator of evolutionary processes. Second, the (secular) philosopher's contention that classical theism compromises creaturely freedom depends on two mistaken notions of the relationship of evolutionary contingency and divine guidance. God, in Coakley's view "timelessly knows" what will transpire since God is the undergirding sustainer of the process. Genuine human freedom is not inimical to divine providence and action since genuine creaturely freedom exists only in the context of "right submission to the graced will and action of God." Evolutionary contingency only appears to be so to us who are creatures that do not possess the fullness of divine knowledge. The philosopher is thus mistaken about the nature of evolutionary contingency as well as the nature of creaturely freedom. Third, the presence of evil in human life is not an automatic deterrent for classical theists. Sin, suffering, death, and evil are all marked in classical Christian theism by God's direct action and participation as evidenced in the theologies of the Incarnation and the Trinity, that is, from a "robustly theological" perspective. Christ's death, suffering, and resurrection are miraculous events precisely because they seem, from a narrowly natural and scientific perspective, "both unaccountable and random." Thus, the question of the presence of evil invites theists to note the many ways in which the divine approaches us in our finitude. Finally, (in my reading), this probing of classical theism is potentially useful to the feminist agenda because the all-perfect goodness of God is capaciously bigendered in the writing (Spivak would dismiss this last move as an example of "pronominal piety"[22]).

It is important to note that in the current North American rhetorical climate of reductionistic science (dogmatic atheism) and reductionistic religious sentimentality ("intelligent design"), Coakley's analysis is a thorough and specifically theological riposte to putative theological unintelligibility in the face of scientific or philosophical cognitive literalism. Frankenberry's bald assertion that theological dependence on categories such as analogies, metaphors, and symbols that possess no cognitive content displays such a reliance on cognitive literalism. Coakley's attempt to draw the philosophical contours of her view of classical theism transgresses the boundaries between theology, philosophy, and "white" (Enlightenment and rationalist) science in a far more radical manner. In regard to the relationship between transcendence and immanence, Frankenberry's major issue with classical theism is that it develops claims that are abstract in relation to the "space" and "time" of creation whereas Coakley contends that classical theism is able to bear a God without whom there would be no space or time at all since this God suffuses the very fabric of creation. Frankenberry's challenge to classical theism rests on her assumption that transcendence as expressed in theological discourses is contradictory to scientific concerns. This is a familiar polarizing move in contemporary cultural discussions regarding science and religion. In contrast, Coakley demonstrates that there is little warrant for such polarization since theistic claims trump scientific ones.

While Coakley's move may be assessed as successful against Frankenberry's particular polarizing strategy in contemporary academic culture, its feminist advances remain paltry. A planetary feminist reading would find Coakley's theological argument too narrowly focused on drawing clear disciplinary boundaries for academic theology and concerned with propounding the coherence theory of truth. There is no reflection on how classical theistic claims function *ethically* in mundane contexts. The rhetorical context of her interpretation of classical theism strategically intervenes in the famed science and religion debate about the nature of truth. However, the strategy to focus the discussion on such a specific cultural issue obscures the move's consolidating attempt to retain the sui generis status of theological language and truth claims. Transcendence in Coakley's proposal is also ultimately separated from immanence except when bridged by divine power.

Does this mean that planetary feminist theologians should stand with Frankenberry and find all classical forms of theism to be hopelessly reliant on masculinist values? Consider the sharper feminist proposal for classical theism as presented by Elizabeth Johnson in *She Who Is: The Mystery of God in Feminist Theological Discourse.*[23] Johnson argues that the insights of classical theism can be used for a feminist agenda since those insights can help to *delimit* the patriarchal dominance of naming God through the patriarchal symbolic and imaginary framework.[24] Three classical insights in particular offer such possibilities to rein in patriarchal dominance. The doctrine of God's hiddenness and incomprehensibility, the play of analogy in speech about the divine, and the resulting need for many names for God—all undo the hold of a masculinist imaginary for classical theism.

For Johnson, abstract speech about God functions in classical theism to restate the relationship between transcendence and immanence. Here, classical theism reimagines the space-time relationship so that creation need not be thought of as a one-time event. Creation, as the ongoing relationality of God, is the ground of transcendence. Creation (and its magnificent plurality) is precisely God's interiority in action; creation is the very indwelling of God. Thus, the "one relational God, precisely in being utterly transcendent, not limited by any finite category, is capable of the most radical immanence, being intimately related to everything that exists."[25] God's "godness" is not destroyed by being in intimate relation to everything that exists; God's very nature is to be in continuous relation. Johnson is attempting to upend the reliance on a particular vision of divine sovereignty and separateness that characterizes classical masculinist theism and transcendence. That separatist model can be reimagined in a planetary way if creation is reinstated as the ground of divine revelation. God's relationality, a notion above reproach for classical theism, can revision divine action as action for liberation and wholeness. In Johnson's view, God is not above space and time; God is in the warp and woof of space-time.

Frankenberry's other concern with language about God is also quickly dispatched by Johnson. For Johnson, the mystery of God "goes beyond all thematizing,"[26] precisely because of the human condition of being creatures. Here is an argument that relies on a notion of transcendence that "cannot be contained in the space of reason,"[27] as Spivak would argue. Johnson's call for restraint in naming God reflects official Roman Catholic injunctions to avoid fideism and rationalism. Consequently, she argues that classical theism's primary goal, to protect the divinity of God, is best met in the experience of faith. Such faith is not merely gullible and suggestible; such faith actively constructs relationship with ineffability without capitulating to modern demands for discrete and countable knowledge. In the mundane experience and activity of faith therefore, the chasm between transcendence and immanence is bridged.

Acknowledging divine mystery and transcendence opens up the way for plurality in Johnson's argument. Symbols for the divine can be shaped by women's reality to destabilize masculinist and hegemonic speech for God. Analogies, which Frankenberry dismisses as "unintelligible," are also retrievable. The "knowing" of God accomplished in the analogical process is a dynamic and relational one: "The creaturely roots of speech about divine reality give assurance that words have a certain measure of meaningfulness, that we are not launching into a black hole so to speak, at the same time as their meaning escapes us. God is darkly surmised while remaining in essence conceptually incomprehensible."[28] Johnson argues that we need to "stringently apply" the critical negation of analogy to male images and conceptualizations of God and continue to spin out emancipatory language about God arising from their participation in the mystery of God. Finally, heterogeneous names for God arise from the experience of being plural and planet-bound creatures: God as creator is "Great Mother, Supreme One, Fashioner, Designer, Father, Distributor, Carver, Molder, Hewer, Excavator, Architect of the World . . . the Great One, the Powerful One, Wise One, Shining One, One who sees all, One who is everywhere, He/She who is Friend, the Greatest of Friends, the One you can confide your troubles to, the One who can turn everything upside down, the One there from ancient times, the One who began the forest, the One who gives to all, the Rain-giver . . . the Queen of Heaven, the Great Spider, Great Spirit, Great One of the Sky, Protector of the Poor."[29] Johnson's list of Many Names begins to capture a planetary basis to speak of the all-encompassing mystery of God. A planetary feminist need not be afraid of classical theism, at least on these three counts, for transcendence is inseparable in this view from immanence.

A planetary feminist need not be afraid of the other two proposals for God-talk either. Panentheism, the second of the three proposals (in Fran-kenberry), is an effort to achieve a cosmological balance between the poles of transcendence and immanence. Panentheism is the notion that God undergirds the whole of the discrete parts without being wholly subsumed by the whole. Frankenberry's presentation of panentheism describes the difference between classical theism and panentheism through the latter's emphasis on both the similarity and the dissimilarity of God through dipolar concepts: "God is *both* necessary and contingent, *both* finite and infinite, *both* temporal and eternal, *both* changing and unchanging, *both* many and one, *both* actual and potential, *both* cause and effect."[30] These dipolarities are articulated by making a (philosophical) distinction between their abstract and concrete aspects. In this view, God's relationship to the created world is emphasized as much as God's absolute difference from it. Thus, creation is a web of interpenetrating and integrating entities in a process of mutual becoming, unifying through a dipolar process. In Frankenberry's assessment, panentheism begins with the transcendent pole and simply argues that all concrete requirements for immanence in God-talk are unified through dipo-larity. Skeptical of this solution as well, she argues that the unifying and organic model falls short of feminist requirements for liberation precisely because dominating and exploitative forms of social relation are all sub-sumed in the "process" of becoming, making this theistic solution an inhospitable one for revisioning exploitative social relations.

Other feminist thinkers critically engaging process philosophy find it to be more hospitable to feminist concerns but not devoid of the problems bedeviling classical masculinist theism. Grace Jantzen, for example, argues that even though the God of panentheism is a different sort of God from the God of traditional classical theism, this God is still presented in an ontotheological framework that prioritizes the epistemological rather than the ethical.[31] She points out that although it is process thought that allows for the possibility of thinking of God as a verb instead of a noun, it operates in terms of an "unproblematized metaphysical realism" in which God is still an entity, albeit a dipolar entity. Such ontological realism is not fertile ground for a feminist symbolic that can interrupt the masculinist concerns of traditional forms of theology. Nevertheless, the possibility for opening up theistic language to present God as Verb, process thought is able to provide the more acceptable symbolic of natality and flourishing in the divine attributes of change and growth. Process thought can provide for a feminist symbolic in which transcendence is the quality of sensible, material reality to change, grow, and become.

Jantzen sharpens the critique of panentheism by raising the question of the relationship of divine becoming to human suffering. The classical theist is comfortable with the assertion that the doctrines of the Incarnation and the Trinity make provision for the space of divine and human action in response to evil. Jantzen opines that the "God of the West"[32] is clearly discernible in such discussions since the "problem" of evil arises only when the "omni" qualities of God come under scrutiny. The valorization of power and control presented in such an image of God is revealed when theology seeks to justify this God in the presence of evil. The location of human suffering—in the actual, concrete lives of human beings—requires us to imagine another God. Such a God is in solidarity with human suffering and such a God comes out of a symbolic of "outrage, imagination and desire, and compassionate action, not the detached and objective intellectual stance which traditional philosophers of religion assume and which they also take to be characteristic of God."[33]

The feminist argument that evil, as experienced by human beings, is generated in particular experiences in particular places becomes critical to the work of imagining the presence and activity of God. Jantzen's impassioned plea for a concept of the divine that can address the places, victims, and perpetrators of evil *mundanely* is precisely the requirement for planetary feminist theology. A mundane theism is articulated not within the horizon of philosophical or theological commitments to abstract reason but within the horizon of praxis to address mundane problems of concrete evil. Divine activity, therefore, is a response to mundane suffering. Both Frankenberry (who dismisses panentheism as "simply pantheism for people with PhDs") and Jantzen argue that a move away from the abstract dipolarities of process thought requires feminist philosophers and theologians to posit continuity between God and the created world far more strongly than even panentheists. Both consequently make the case that pantheism, the third solution, which derives God's transcendence from God's immanence, is the form of theism that can be embraced by feminist theological thinkers. Divinity for Jantzen means mutuality, bodiliness, diversity, and materiality—mundane aspects that point to the radical transcendence of the divine contained by these processes.[34] Creation, nature, space, place, planet—all the names we give to the ground of our becoming are also the instances of the becoming of the divine. It is a leaky, porous boundary that reveals (re-veils?) the divine imprint in the mundane living processes of the biosphere even as this leaky, porous boundary allows the mundane to well up from its mundane occupations to encompass that which is more than itself. Theism must then speak much more of these entanglements of concrete and abstract, the mundane and the heavenly from the (im)possible place of "sensible transcendentals"—a phrase that Jantzen borrows from Luce Irigaray. Planetary theism in such a view speaks of God in the here and now, in this common space-time of becoming divine and becoming human.

MUNDANE TRANSCENDENCE

Spivak's current work continues to make clear what she means by "detranscendentalizing transcendence." She is obviously not interested in expounding religious or theological forms of transcendence, even any form of "sensible transcendence." However, Spivak's intent to subvert the secular academic postcolonial theorists' attempt to marginalize all languages of transcendence reveals her growing acknowledgment of religious experience as a material context for politics. In her latest book, *Other Asias*, she acknowledges that her criticisms of "Abrahamic religions" prevented her from seeing beyond the secular framework for religion. In the introduction to *Other Asias*, she writes that her essay on the Great Goddess called "Moving Devi" is but her counter to aggressive academic postcoloniality and identitarian politics. Her brief here is "to rearrange the desires of the largest sector of the future electorate, break postcolonialism into pluralized (Eur)Asias, train the metropolitan imagination to detranscendentalize the transcendental."[35] Her aim here is to go after the essentialist frameworks for cultural identity. Speaking of religious transcendence thus enables us to grasp the planetary plurality and heterogeneity to counter mere identity politics. We can trace the genesis of such a development in Spivak's thought by comparing "Moving Devi" to her earlier reading of "Pterodactyl, Puran Sahay and Pirtha." In my view, Spivak has come to a realization that religious identities, often based in transcendental claims, have led to the essentialization of cultural identities and the opprobrious identitarian politics thus engendered. Thus, the specifically religious itself need not be erased or muted; the specifically religious needs to be shown to be "detranscendentalized" so that its basis exists in the continued negotiations of identity. At the core of her agenda for planetarity is her insistence that essentialized cultural and religious identities can lead only to moral impoverishment and violence. Planetarity is, consequently, a mode of narrating belonging in which the multiplicities of narratives of cultural and religious belonging coexist as "permissible narratives that constitute material culture."[36]

Planetary plurality as the corrective to identitarian ethics reminds us that the boundaries of disciplines miss the complex interdependent living that comes from sharing a home with many and neglected others. Planetarity thus is the corrective to inward-looking disciplines bewitched by internecine quarrels and requirements to police disciplinary boundaries and enables them to imagine transcendence as a program for ethics. To this end, Spivak presents a reading of Mahasweta Devi's "Pterodactyl, Puran Sahay and Pirtha" in Death of a Discipline as a counter to Joseph Conrad's Heart of Darkness. Puran "responsibly" enters the space of the aboriginal other, but it is the aboriginal other who accepts Puran into the collectivity. Puran has gone to Pirtha, because Bikhia, an aboriginal youth has drawn a pterodactyl. Spivak writes: "The novella is embedded in a critique of the postcolonial state and a declaration of love for the historical other of the entire legal collectivity of the Indian nation. Indeed the figure of the pterodactyl can claim the entire planet as its other. It is prior to our thinking of continents . . . [and] is a figure of the mindset that can make the new Comparative Literature work."[37]

Spivak explains that Devi interrupts "normal" space-time precisely in the light of the ethical imperative. Devi urges an attentive reading of her story for "Pterodactyl" to communicate the agony of the aboriginal people who barely exist on the margins of the imaginary map of the nation called India. The poetry of her words communicates the inexpressible suffering of these people in modern space and time. The story attempts to capture this agony in its wordplay.

[Puran thinking about the Pterodactyl]. Did your eyes give Bikhia a sharply urgent wordsoundless message? The reason why your form was xeroxed on his brain and he could come running and draw that picture with chalk? Did he think then that chalk rubs off too easily, and did he therefore pick up hammer and chisel? Why is Bikhia not speaking? Why is he remaining mute? Was some communication established between your prehistoric eyes and his eyes, so that he (illiterate, never having read a book, with no knowledge of the history of the evolution of the planet) grasps that to keep your affair secret is tremendously urgent. The world of today cannot be informed about you. "Today" does not know the "past," the "ancient." "Today," "the present times," "civilization," becomes almost barbaric by the demands of getting ahead. Yet he doesn't know that "today" desecrates the ancient people's burial grounds by building roads and bridges, cutting down forests. They won't let you go if they know of your existence, this is why he is protecting your visit like the sacred ashes of a funeral pyre or the bones of the dead. He has found some contact. He is a tribal, an aboriginal, you are much more ancient, more originary than his experience, both your existences are greatly endangered.[38]

The story, which, akin to Spivak's writing, has often been characterized as "incomprehensible," produces meaning precisely through the performance. Such performances require a particular disposition—*anushilan* in Bengali, meaning "attention and concentration." Spivak writes: "What Mahasweta asks for is *anushilan*, on our part, of the First Nation, the *Adim Jalti*. I am learning to write on Mahasweta as if an attentive reading of her texts permits us to imagine an impossible undivided world; without which no literature should be possible."[39] Only such attention to the concrete particularity of First Nation peoples and their suffering will create the condition for empathy and ethics in the postcolonial context. Devi calls this "Love, a tremendous, excruciating, explosive love, a first step."[40] For Spivak, such empathy and love through the imagination for the aboriginal will introduce us to the mode of planetarity. The disposition of planetary belonging fosters the empathic attention to the negotiations of the aboriginals whose mobilization of transcendence looks rather different, even incredible, to secularized or academic enterprises. The appearance of the pterodactyl on the margins of such activity challenges the imagination to extend concern beyond the planet to the poorest of the planet. It is also not just benevolent concern for them; it is to enter their narrative of belonging responsibly. To be *human*, therefore, is to be intended toward the other, a mundane transcendence of the self. For Spivak, such transcendence is "de-transcendentalized" because it is a mundane ethical response. In her comments on the story in *Death of a Discipline*, Spivak's attention is resolutely focused on detranscendentalized planetarity. A closer reading of the story sets the stage for Spivak's growing understanding of the economy of transcendence in Devi's stories.

Transcendence *is* to be found in the mundane space called Pirtha. Devi asserts unambiguously that the pterodactyl's revelation necessarily roots the inhabitants of Pirtha in their home space. In binding their past to their present, a suffering people cannot be robbed of its images of transcendence: "How can one rob a people of the supernatural, of myth, what is in their understanding an unwritten history, when the present time has given them nothing? *No one holds that right.*"[41] The pterodactyl's revelation in this space is a reminder of a time when people made their home in nature. Nature was sacred to them and the presence of the pterodactyl in their time now shows that it continues to be sacred. Spivak may want to quibble here with the meaning of the word "sacred," but Devi speaks for herself: "Bikhia brought in bundles of grass. Before heaping grass at the mouth of the shrine-room, Puran had seen flowers, rice, grains of kodo. . . . [Bikhia] puts his palms together, lowers his head and takes one turn. He expresses respect by lying prone." In the space called Pirtha, the shrine to the pterodactyl is a sacred place and ritualized worship in this space is not an alien or strange gesture.

Reading Devi's story with attention reveals this: Puran's father, the Indian "comnis" (communist) named him "Prarthana Puran," the fulfillment of prayer, a name that Devi explains right at the beginning of the story. It is true that Devi also says that Puran was the result of prayer by his grandfather who wanted his son to have a male heir. "Prarthana" is a female name given to the child who is the fruit of prayer. Devi does not provide any more explanation for this name, except that the child was named before its birth. Puran changes his name when he becomes a man, but what manner of man? He refuses to marry after his wife dies in childbirth. This is a perplexing decision. Puran's sisters are confounded by his disavowal of his masculinity: "[T]hey find it hard to understand that Puran, a male of the species, does not make his masculinity felt in harsh words, in manifestations of heat and light."[42] Puran fails to be a man, a responsible family man. His sense of failure hovers throughout the story and is the filter through which he sees the pterodactyl. The lines of the story bob and weave through simplistic gender and heterosexual privileges. Devi's feminist agenda is a complex one, presented in her subtle portrayal of failed masculinist expectations.

Further, postcolonial India is precisely not an irreligious project. Planetarity in fact, demands a rootedness in the religious. The names of actors in the story—Saraswati, Harisharan, Shankar, Bikhia—are names that richly resonate with religious meaning. The secularized project of the nation-state ignores the originary intuition that naming people after divinities recognizes the divine potential in each. These embodied mundane divinities barely exist on the margins of postcolonial India. Meanwhile, religious power, with its usurping of transcendence, ignores the genocide unfolding right in front of its eyes: "A young bride was feeding cooked sweets to a bull sitting in the courtyard of a Shiva temple and all the milk that was being poured on the Shiva phallus was collecting in a stinking pool of sour milk, and the devotees were taking that milk and drinking. Obviously, there's no extreme food scarcity in the district."[43] These are a people in exile from the modern nation-state. Modern India gives them nothing, except "posters for family planning." Yet, they cannot abandon their supernatural and mythical past. Devi writes: "They don't know if that past is legend or history, and no researcher comes to separate the two. . . . If we can get so much history out of the *Ramayana* and the *Mahabharata*, what is the problem with Shankar's nostalgia?"[44] In other words, the religious rhetoric of contemporary India's identitarian politics retrieving sacred texts as "history" is juxtaposed with the aboriginal people's desire to invoke and narrate past time. The incredible story of the appearance of the pterodactyl in the present moment collapses the ordinary requirements of secular time and its neat linear progression. Postcoloniality, whether articulated by the nation-state or academic enterprises, collapses before an apparition that boggles the mind. The people's struggle, symbolized by the incursion of prehistoric time into modern space and time by the pterodactyl, makes sense only in the rhetorical context of Hindu religious sensibility.

The revelatory presence of the pterodactyl creates in Puran a tremendous confusion because he does not understand what he is seeing. Bikhia, the original recipient of the vision, realizes what is being revealed—the soul of his ancestors in his mundane world of destitution, starvation, and desperation. Puran is even more confused when the people call him "god," ostensibly for bringing the rains. Devi is hinting at the transcendence of sight and recognition: in the space of the present time in Pirtha, he "sees" the pterodactyl and is "seen" by the tribals to be divine himself. This economy of transcendence, embedded in the story's use of religious names and languages, confounds the inattentive reader. The very stance that Devi draws for Puran is that of the worshipper of Hindu divine images even though he is a "rootless weed." He arrives at the realization of the pterodactyl only when he "sees" in the darkness. Seeing, of course, is an act surfeited with theological significance in India. One looks into the eyes of the deity in order to be seen by the deity. In this specular transaction, one which most religious people recognize, Puran is awakened to his responsibility. This is revelation in this earthbound time-space: to be *divine* is to be intended toward the other, a mundane transcendence of the divine self, and to be human is to be defined by such transcendence toward the self-revealing divine.

Spivak's comments on gazing in *Moving Devi* demonstrates her growing realization that transcendence and religion are able to operate in the economy of the gaze, distinct from a belief system. A primary concern articulated in *Moving Devi* is the separation of "Hindu" culture and cultural practices from the codified and easily co-opted system of beliefs by Hindu nationalists and fundamentalists. A parallel concern is for subaltern religious experience to remain unventriloquizable by the Western academy. Thus, Spivak makes a clear distinction between gazing and museumizing. The "cultural" Hindu way, that is, the *"dvaita* impulse," which is at the heart of the polytheist imagination—"negotiates with the unanticipatable yet perennial possibility of the metamorphosis of the transcendental as supernatural in the natural."[45] This is planetarity in different words. Planetarity is consequently in a field of rhetorical play that includes religious and theological attempts to address the relationship between transcendence and immanence, within the cultural frame of Hindu *dvaita* practices.

Dvaita practice, in the manner that Spivak narrates it, introduces uncanniness into belief systems. Thus, the *dvaita* episteme controls the logic of *"avatarana"* (to be thoroughly distinguished from the Christian Incarnation as the descent, not the enfleshment) by providing the counter-pull of the *arohana* or ascent. This insight can be read as a theology of *avatarana* within the *dvaita* episteme, but Spivak's iconoclastic nerve asserts that the idea must be grasped not as "truth" but as "fiction." The narrative potential of *dvaita* reveals to us the "future anteriority of every being as potentially, unanticipatably, *avatar* in the general sense."[46] The ability to note the divinity of mundane, embodied, and forgotten beings on the margins of one's consciousness is the work of the active polytheist imagination.

Dvaita is the apprehension of twoness beyond mere duality: "For the *dvaitin* or twoness-minded, radical alterity is in an impossible invagination in every instance of the other."[47] Or, take the clarity of the statement of the epigraph quoted at the beginning of this essay: "[F]or, in spite of our forays into what we metaphorize, differently, as outer and inner space, what is above and beyond our own reach is not continuous with us as it is not, indeed, specifically discontinuous." To think of space and time in such a way as to note their plurality woven within the fabric of one space and one time in intimate relation is uniquely *dvaita*. The *dvaita* disposition, the mode of approaching twoness, without letting it collapse into a rigorous singularity, counters rigid belief systems so easily co-optable into nationalist, identitarian, and racist agendas. It is a disposition that requires attentive discipline: "[W]e must persistently educate ourselves into this peculiar mindset."[48]

For Spivak, such an attentive discipline is best captured by the religious negotiation of *Bhakti*. *Bhakti* in the postcolonial mode is twoness in action, the disposition of *dvaita*. In her reading of the photograph of a young boy attentively gazing at the headless, multilimbed body of a (still-becoming) goddess and her image before its eventual immersion in the river, Spivak articulates the insight that *Bhakti* is the exemplary *dvaita* habit: "It is the *dvaita* habit institutionalized—to see in the obviously transient and ephemeral the possibility of alterity—that conjures up the goddess's absent yet gazing, living head for the boy."[49] This gaze, like the pterodactyl's, is precisely the opposite of the museumizing gaze organizing the disciplinary boundaries of much academic expertise. It escapes the control of all "built spaces" (home, nation, temple, church) as well. The *dvaitin* gaze is not phenomenal but radically material; the negotiating gaze acknowledges that a future time already arrived will demolish the relative permanence of present built space. In this negotiated transaction of space and time, human intending toward the other remains free of the distortion of possessing the other, knowing the other, naming this other and avoiding the temptation to "freeze in the artifice of a forever present."[50] Divine intending for the human also escapes disciplinary and institutional control; the headless still becoming divine being is free to gaze upon the boy. Human and divine intending toward each other is a mundane negotiation of attention.

Spivak's (early) reading of the story intuits the economy of transcendence in the economy of the gaze but does not work it out until *Moving Devi*. Planetarity is positioned between those two narratives and cannot be retrieved as a positive affirmative proposal for feminist theology. But it can, as I have argued, present the complex semantic field in which theistic discourses highlight (or fail to highlight) cultural and material concerns. The rhetorical move permits the argument that Jantzen's "sensible transcendentals" provide an opening for detranscendentalized postcolonial planetary feminist theology. The planetarity of *dvaita* practices makes theology uncanny as a cultural narrative alongside other narratives of identity or relationship. For example, it roots Jantzen's suggestion of sensible transcendentals (appropriated from Irigaray) for pantheism as the preferred strategy of feminist theism. As Jantzen argues, the Western theological symbolic is heavily invested in the polarization of immanence and transcendence. For Irigaray and for Jantzen, the sensible transcendental is "a transcendence which is wholly immanent, not in opposition to the flesh but as the projected horizon for our (embodied becoming)."[51] Thus, planetarity infuses the narrative of pantheism as a way of speaking of the divine using sensible or mundane categories of relation. Elizabeth Johnson, who reached the opposite conclusion of panentheism as the best narrative for speaking of human and divine relationship, is also sharpened by *dvaita* planetarity. As Spivak argues, *dvaita* is precisely the experience of nonduality and not the experience of singularity. For Johnson, pantheism provides us with an image of God that "merges with the finite being of things, thus ceasing to be their creative, transcending ground. Correspondingly, there is no substantial independence or freedom in anything finite, since the divine is the essence of all essences."[52] This leads to a "suffocating deception" for feminist agendas because freedom in Johnson's view needs to always emerge in relation, not simply as an essence. In decrying pantheism, Johnson advocates panentheism, which is the model of "free reciprocal relation, God in the world and the world in God, while each remains radically distinct."[53] In this model, transcendence and immanence are correlative rather than opposed. It is not the dissolution of the boundary between the two that interests Johnson; it is the work at the boundary that can provide key feminist insights. Spivak's exhortation to secular humanists interested in religion to "de-transcendentalize the transcendental," however, comes closer to Johnson's Roman Catholic view of the relationship between transcendence and immanence. Planetarity, in rhetorical play with feminist theist proposals detranscendentalizes theism by engaging transcendence and immanence in their cultural frame.

Cultivating the disposition of nondual twoness seems to me to be the mode in which planetarity animates the postcolonial feminist theological imagination. Planetary feminist postcolonial theology not only "sees" the pterodactyl in the margins, but detranscendentalizes the revelation in the mundane space-time of mutual belonging, trust, and love. Devi writes:

> Only love, a tremendous excruciating, explosive love can still dedicate us to this work when the century's sun is in the western sky, otherwise this aggressive civilization will have to pay a terrible price, look at history, the aggressive civilization has destroyed itself in the name of progress each time.
>
> Love, excruciating love, let that be the first step. Now Puran's amazed heart discovers what love for Pirtha there is in his heart, perhaps he cannot remain a distant spectator anywhere in life.[54]

❧ Lost in Translation? Tracing Linguistic and Economic Transactions in Three Texts

TAT-SIONG BENNY LIEW

With her suggestion of using the term "planetary," Gayatri Chakravorty Spivak talks about an interdependence beyond postcolonial independence and hence "an undivided 'natural' space rather than a differentiated political space."[1] Part of that interdependence involves, for Spivak, the need to learn another language so that one can read its literature—especially its poetry—to experience the impossible.[2] In a delightfully ironic way, Spivak also sees language learning as a way to counteract the temptation to accept and abet the neocolonial status quo behind the pretext that transcultural knowledge is plainly and simply impossible.[3] She is clear, at the same time, that a lot of persons learn languages for a different purpose, namely, for trade.[4]

The lines between linguistic, intellectual, cultural, and financial exchange are, of course, also almost impossible to draw. For Karl Marx, the way ideas in the form of a mother tongue need a foreign language to produce meaning is comparable to how commodities need prices to produce value. These parallel processes enable circulation and exchange; Marx further capitalizes on the foreign quality of language to verbalize, textualize, or transcribe the experience of alienation under capitalist societies. In a section of *Capital* titled "The Fetishism of Commodities and the Secret Thereof," Marx writes, "It is value . . . that converts every product into a social hieroglyphic. Later on, we try to decipher the hieroglyphic, to get behind the secret of our own social products; for to stamp an object of utility as value, is just as much a social product as language."[5] In other words, the change from actual labor to abstract labor is a process of transformation—or translation—that is hard to read, unless you learn how to read the language. Similarly, Ferdinand de

Saussure states that both economics and linguistics "are concerned with a *system for equating things of different orders*—labor and wages in one and a signified and signifier in the other."[6] Transactions of translations—from which language into which language?—are also market-driven and dependent. In 1987, for instance, translations of books from English for Brazilian readers outnumbered translations of Brazilian works into English by a ratio of one hundred to one.[7]

In 1985 Spivak published "Three Women's Texts and a Critique of Imperialism."[8] And twice, she has published a book by translating three different short stories of Mahasweta Devi from Bengali into English.[9] In what follows, I would like to focus on reading three brief texts or stories—all of them concerning loss and translation—to talk about the complicated relations between language and money in the context of imperialism and Spivak's planetary love.

BETWEEN DIVERSITY AND COMPLICITY: A THIN LINE

Let me begin our textual travels with a story of translation that got lost. By getting lost, I mean both how a project of translation turned into something else and how this story has been largely forgotten. I. A. Richards was one of the most prominent literary theorists of the first half of the twentieth century and, as such, possessed of an influence comparable to that of Spivak in her role as a founding figure of postcolonial theory and criticism. Richards was "a founder of the 'Cambridge School' of English in the 1920's."[10] His influence was trans-Pacific as well as trans-Atlantic. He had also famously compared religious statements to poetry, and his theory of rhetoric— particularly that of metaphor—has continued to be used by some in biblical interpretation.[11] Like Spivak, Richards advocates for the power or potential of literary studies. In fact, according to Richards, poetry—notice not only a similar emphasis on poetry by Spivak but also the religious language Richards uses here—"is capable of saving us; it is a perfectly possible means of overcoming [the] chaos" of modernity.[12] Particularly with his practical criticism, Richards believed that a person might learn to respond fully to a poem. By doing so, one might not only train and facilitate the kind of mental operation that was needed to deal with the information overload of modern life but also be able to live a fully human life despite the rise of science and consumerism.[13] Richards's theory of literary criticism, like Spivak's, gradually expanded and extended to focus on pedagogy, especially in his attempt to teach English literature and the English language to Chinese students in China. Richards first went to China to work with a team of Mencius specialists to translate Mencius into English in the 1920s. Within a decade, however, Richards became the tireless advocate of C. K. Ogden's Basic English program to *overcome* transcultural communication by envisioning Basic English as a world language.[14] In addition to taking Basic English to China half a dozen times in the next fifty years of his life, this program of 850 English words that include only eighteen verbs also took Richards from being an adjunct faculty at Magdalene College in Cambridge, England, to a professorship at Harvard University in Cambridge, New England. Rather than lecturing "on approval" and making fifteen shillings for any student who attended his class at least three times as he did at Magdalene,[15] travels, translations, and Basic English turned Richards into an internationally known scholar and a recipient of a Rockefeller endowment that financed or subsidized his work on promoting Basic.

Among the general objectives established under China's Ministry of Education for teaching Basic English in China, which Richards was influential in helping to develop, one had to do with its "vocational and practical uses."[16] This emphasis is undoubtedly consistent with Richards's belief that Ogden's Basic program provided the most *economical* way to learn English. As a biblical scholar, I should also point out that Ogden had also developed a complete New Testament in Basic English. Biblical literature has actually seldom been left out in any kind of linguistic or economic boom. Attempts to have a new Chinese translation of the Bible by Chinese scholars with knowledge of the biblical languages have boiled into a controversy about the sacredness of the almost-century-old Chinese Union Version of the Bible. As many of my colleagues across the Pacific would say, part if not most of this controversy has to do with money rather than theology. Since the Chinese Union Version was not copyrighted, anyone can print it to sell.

Richards's concern with transcultural communication—and hence Basic English—was, however, also related to his politics. Like Ogden, Richards was a pacifist.[17] One can see Richards's politics even more clearly from his books *Nations and Peace*.[18] Richards was wary of nationalism, which could, in his view, bring about a fragmented world. Short of his dream to dissolve all nations, Richards banked on the United States to lead and guide all the other nations into a world organization to establish a world government that could make binding international laws for all nations. Parallel to his trust in literary studies or poetry to provide or make meaning in modernity,

Richards's Basic English program was key to creating a world language to undo the linguistic confusion of Babel and facilitate the workings of this world government for world peace, since he believed that Basic had the capacity to circumvent linguistic ambiguity and cultural misunderstanding. Again, Richards used religious language—in fact, that of Plato's—to describe his purpose as nothing less than "saving society and our souls."[19] It is for this reason that Rodney Koeneke sees Richards's work on Basic as "one of the most significant attempts in the twentieth century to bridge the gap between literature and action."[20] In other words, Richards's teaching, translation, and travel were all tied to his commitment to cultural pluralism and global communication. One may even link this commitment on Richards's part to a kind of postcolonial sensibility through Edward Said's naming of Richards as representative of "a genuine type of pluralism."[21] Koeneke has further characterized Richards's refusal to "essentialize" China as diametrically opposed and inherently inferior to the geopolitical West as having "a strong affinity with the postcolonial notion of the hybrid."[22]

Given Richards's own gains from Basic and his view that it was the most *economical* way to learn English, it is perhaps apt that in 1941 he gave several reasons for focusing on English in the magazine titled *Fortune*. First, as an uninflected language, English was easier to learn; second, English was the language of not only science but also world trade; and third, Richards tellingly acknowledged that the dominance of English rested "on the steel shoulders of the British and American fleets."[23] After all, Basic's founder, Ogden himself, was clear that Basic is an acronym for five English words: "British," "American," "Scientific," "International," and "Commercial."[24] Obviously, Richards was both a good student and a candid teacher. His pluralism or internationalism was—cryptically or not—connected to the power, purposes, and profit of the geopolitical West, and China was his experiment to test or prove his pedagogical and political understandings. This is particularly problematic since Basic allows no hybridization or borrowing from other languages. It basically reifies through language a "British" or an "American" experience as universal by eliminating what is considered "foreign," "non-standard," or "non-foundational."

It is little wonder that Winston Churchill, when receiving an honorary degree from Harvard in 1943, chose to highlight Basic with high praise in his acceptance speech:

The gift of a common tongue is a priceless inheritance and it may well some day become the foundation of a common citizenship. I like to think of British and Americans moving about freely over each other's wide estates with hardly a sense of being foreigners to one another. But I do not see why we should not try to spread our common language even more widely throughout the globe.[25]

For that reason, Churchill, in that same speech, also commended the Harvard Commission on English Language Studies for taking Basic English to Latin America. One will see a clearer trace of what Churchill had in mind about Basic in another speech, when he suggested that the program would help "those who do not have the good *fortune* to know the English language to participate more easily in *our* society."[26]

This almost lost story of Richards's translation and transportation betrays the ambiguous nature of "well-intentioned" academicians, or the inevitably and intricately interested nature of all that we do in and as academics. This ambiguity—and hence risk of complicity—must not be lost on us even or especially as imperialism continues to expand in various forms and disguises. Let us remember too that interest is not only derived from *inter-esse*—"to be among or between"—and thus involved in a network of relations,[27] but that it is also not an economically benign term. My point in tracing Richards's story or text here is not to equate Spivak with Richards. After all, Spivak advocates not a single or universal language but the need not only to learn other languages but also to "suspend [her] own training and *learn from* people with no institutional education."[28] Nor is it my goal to identify or accuse Spivak of being a closeted imperialist. I am only pointing to the need—and this is true in both Richards's and Spivak's time—to be vigilant about not only postcolonial complexity but also one's own complicity, even or especially when one begins with noble intentions for noble causes. As Spivak states so helpfully, there is but a thin line between corporatist or imperialist benevolence and education, and—as shown by Richards's turn from translating Mencius to teaching Basic—cultural relativism can easily turn into cultural absolutism.[29] Even Spivak's emphasis on *her* learning and her alterity-grounded responsibility does not exempt her and her program from this ever-present danger.[30]

Basic English, however, did not quite work out in China the way Richards or Churchill had envisioned. This story of translation is thus lost—or lost its direction—in terms not only of its complicity with empire but also its many unexpected twists and turns. Despite his Rockefeller endowment, Richards's project did not materialize partly because the Chinese had their own version of modernization. Lin Yutang, for example, not only critiqued Basic but also advocated for a pidgin English Lin called "Chinglish."[31] Richards's project also came to a halt because of the outbreak of wars in China, including the Sino-Japanese War and China's own civil war. Both of these reasons can help us transition from Richards's story to our own day. The fact that the Chinese in the 1920s and 1930s had an idea about and a strategy for modernizing *without* Westernizing may help us rethink whether so-called globalization in the singular is an adequate understanding, particularly if it is understood as synonymous with "modernization," "Westernization," and "Americanization." This synonymizing move not only implicitly reinforces "U.S. exceptionalism"[32] but also intriguingly echoes Richards's move from complexity—or, for Richards, chaos—to standardization, whether it is through his promotion of poetry or Basic English. As Stuart Hall has suggested with his theorization of "articulation," one must not forget the presence and function of difference in global capitalism.[33] Capital investment seldom remains the same;[34] it often involves unanticipated gains and losses, especially when it is global. An imperial legacy such as globalization may develop in formulations far different from those of the imperial center,[35] like the practice of feng shui in architectural siting and planning within many so-called global cities in Asia. The assumption of cultural homogenization under globalization has much to do with how "research that is exclusively [done] in English misses much of the story,"[36] or how arguments about globalization are too often made with "easy" generalizations.[37] This assumption is as problematic as "assuming [that] the heritage of the imperialist adventures of Northwestern Europe [has] completely obliterated politico-intellectual culture in its former subjects."[38]

Of course, the isolation of China that first resulted from the conclusion of the civil war in China has itself become a page in history, as China has not only continued to open up to the world since the 1970s but also developed into a powerful economic force. Instead of seeing English as the only international commercial language, those of the geopolitical West, including many in the United States, are investing in learning Mandarin Chinese to achieve "global competence" to stay competitive in the global market.[39] Ironically, while his Basic English program has largely been lost, Richards's dream of a global language and what he once called the "Chinese Renaissance" are simultaneously becoming true.[40] Just as money is no longer tied to gold as "a socially recognized (*gültige*) universal equivalent,"[41] so-called global English or seeing English as the golden standard may also be giving way to a fully floating system of conversion to facilitate movements and transfer of capital around the world. This in itself is not a necessarily hopeful change, for those who are economically interested and powerful will continue to define and measure everything, like linguistic or global competence, by financial gains and losses. Language and culture become, in this understanding, sites or instruments in the global marketplace, as the title of a recent anthology, *World Bank Literature*, alarmingly intimates.[42] The process of translation and transaction between culture and capital is not lost around the globe; it is also continuously being negotiated in various locales to bring about assorted and ambivalent effects.

BETWEEN LINGUISTIC AND CULTURAL TRANSLATION: A BIG GAP

Richards's story confirms Spivak's "belief that a training in a literary habit of reading the world can attempt to put a curb on . . . superpower triumphalism only if it does not perceive acknowledgment of complicity as an inconvenience."[43] The reality and subtlety of complicity alert us to the thought that what we call postcoloniality today is not exactly and should not be solely a celebratory term. Let me go on now to my second story or text to talk about how language facility should not fool one into thinking that one has achieved any level of cross-cultural sensitivity, let alone global competence (whatever that may mean).

As a result of Alexander the Great's military conquest and promotions of hellenization, *koine* or "common" (as opposed to Attic or elite) Greek did become a kind of common language of the Mediterranean basin. I want to focus on a brief episode in Mark's Gospel, which is also written in *koine* Greek. It is a story not only of a subaltern woman or subaltern as woman but also of lost translation and lost transliteration. As interpreters try to make sense of Jesus' remark about the widow's offering in Mark 12:41–44, they have rarely if ever paid attention to the fact that Mark uses a Latin transliteration to communicate the value of the two copper coins (*lepta*) that the widow is bringing to the Temple as her offering: "A poor widow came and put in two small copper coins [*lepta duo*], which are worth a penny" (literally, "which is a *kodrantēs*") (12:42). In other words, what we encounter here is another story in which linguistic and economic transactions are key and integral to each other, although one is not likely to know it on the basis of even standard scholarly readings of the passage.

Spivak has suggested that a subaltern is one who lacks not only access to social mobility but also an infrastructure so her act of resistance becomes unrecognizable even to well-meaning activists.[44] It is well known that in the Greco-Roman world of the first century, widows were marginal people outside of the traditional male-headed households. Worse, their livelihood was often at risk unless they had children who could provide for them. It is significant that the poor widow in Mark 12 occupies a similarly tangential position textually speaking. She utters no speech and is referred to only in one short verse (12:42), besides the two-verse commentary about her given by the Markan Jesus (12:43–44). Partly because of the brevity of the episode, her story has been an unresolved mystery within Markan scholarship. Whereas earlier scholarship tends to read the story solely on the basis of Jesus' words ("Truly I tell you, this poor widow has put in more than all those who are contributing to the treasury. For all of them have contributed out of their abundance; but she out of her poverty has put in everything she had, all she had to live on" [12:43–44]) and hence takes the widow's offering as a positive example of self-sacrifice, more recent scholarship—with the influence of narratological and feminist criticism—has moved to link this episode with Jesus' statement about scribes devouring widows' houses in Mark 12:40 to interpret 12:41–44 as a concrete example that both illustrates such exploitations of widows by the Jewish elites and justifies Jesus' proclamation of the Temple's destruction in 13:1–2.[45] What seems to be a consensus between these two opposing camps is that the widow is basically a mere victim; the camps differ only on whether the exploiter is Jesus or other Jewish elites. One may, of course, add among her victimizers Markan scholars, including, as Spivak suggests, well-meaning activist-interpreters who see Jesus as saving her from the scribes and the Temple system.

Ironically for a discipline that prides itself on its rigorous demands for linguistic competence, interpreters of neither camp seem to pay any attention to the words that Mark uses for the coins that the widow brings as an offering. Neither the Greek *lepta* nor the transliterated Latin *kodrantēs* receives any discussion in, for instance, the *Translator's Guide to the Gospel of Mark* put out by the United Bible Societies.[46] If one goes beyond the lexicons to explore further into culture and history—or, in Spivak's vocabulary, to "facilitate love" between Mark's *koine* Greek text and its readers by "fraying" it[47]—one will find that *lepta* were first minted during the Maccabean period. The Maccabean period was, of course, the time of Israel's revolt against the Seleucid Empire and its achievement of a century-long self-governance before being occupied by the Romans. As if he is afraid that one will not make that distinction, Mark adds the comment to compute the insignificant value of the coins in not only Roman terms but also with a transliteration of Latin (12:42), thus signifying that these copper coins might be unfamiliar to his Roman audience. What then can one make of the differences signified by this brief text, where a ghost-like woman brings with her two transliterated coins to the Temple?

I will argue that Mark shows, in 12:42, that a local offering in the Temple of Jerusalem is also linked to broader currents of Roman capital, and Mark in a way becomes itself a medium of transit between them. Since the Jewish Temple was rededicated as a symbol of and for nationalist independence at the conclusion of the Maccabean revolt (167–164 BCE), one may read this poor widow as making a political statement against imperialism and about her agency with her gift, even if she is silent. Unfortunately, most readers—scholars included—are too happy to move on with their reading on the basis of their knowledge about *koine* Greek syntax, grammar, and vocabulary, especially when they have a chance to make this widow the *object* of their protection.

I am, of course, attempting here to read this subaltern woman or subaltern as woman the way Spivak did years ago with Bhuvaneswari Bhaduri, whose suicide in 1926 to cover up an insurgency for India's independence was generally read as nothing but another tragedy of *sati* by "benevolent" readers eager to "sav[e] brown women from brown men."[48] It makes a difference, of course, which interpretation of transliterations and translations—or, in this case, interpretation via transliteration and translation as interpretation—involving the coins count, gain currency, assume value, and are consumed. At the same time, I must also acknowledge, as Spivak did, that I don't know "how much of this is my transactionality as reader."[49] As we are talking about minting of coins, we should note that just as counterfeits are both "fabrications" and "inventions," translations are also "accurate" and "inaccurate" at the same time. All translations involve gains and losses, and the balance sheet is tough to keep straight. That is basically the point that Walter Benjamin tries to make when he uses the geometrical term "tangent" to talk about the convergence and divergence involved in translation.[50] I will return to this problematic of translation and hence my inability to know the other, especially since, in this case of the Markan widow, her agency does include her choice not to inform,[51] an "articulate silence"[52] or "wordless eloquence"[53] to which white, "benevolent" activist-interpreters are prone to be tone-deaf. But let me use this text now to express two further thoughts.

First, as I have suggested through the history of Markan scholarship, reading knowledge of *koine* Greek does not necessarily lead to any "multiculturally sensitive information-retrieval approach"[54] to read a subaltern more adequately. Instead, reading *koine* may become what Stephen J. Greenblatt calls "appropriative mimesis," or a cross-cultural "imitation . . . [that] need not have entailed any grasp of the cultural reality of the other, only a willingness to make contact and to effect some kind of exchange . . . in the interest of [linguistic] acquisition."[55] Mary Louise Pratt has recently argued that we need, not persons with linguistic skills who do the work of translation, but multilingual persons who live multiple lives.[56] I agree, although I am not sure how I go about translating this noble goal into reality for myself and my students. If planetarity is about a connection between not only the local and nature but also between past and present, then how can one nourish one's teaching of and learning from an ancient past with an animistic notion that a seemingly dead and inanimate past is hidden with life and vitality? If Ludwig Wittgenstein is correct that "[i]n order to get clear about . . . words, you have to describe ways of living,"[57] then do I not have to teach and learn artifacts and the text of—or as—material culture, for example? And how much would doing that cost? In other words, what does teaching and learning literature—especially if one is to magnify rather than metaphorize away the link between the literary and the material—really mean here in terms of practice?

Second—and perhaps this is a partial answer to my own question—transliteration, if not overlooked or lost, may function to announce in some way the reality of diversity or heteroglossia—in the Bakhtinian sense of a social register—within a single language. In "The Aims of Ethnology," Franz Boas writes:

> The analysis of dialects enables us to follow the history of words and of concepts through long periods of time and over distant areas. The introduction of new inventions and migration into distant countries are often indicated by the appearance of new words the origins of which may be ascertained. Thus the history of language reflects the history of culture.[58]

Despite Boas's positivist inclination, we do find in Mark 11:42 two radically different social and economic registers of language being set alongside one another in one short verse. Some have suggested—in a way that echoes

Boas but with a lot more awareness of power differentials—that colonized or displaced people, by transliterating their own languages and dialects into English, and thus making it "rotten"[59] or "weird,"[60] are attempting a rebellion against or subversion of sociopolitical and linguistic tyranny. What do we make, however, of first-century Jews who wrote in the colonial language of Greek with a transliteration of another colonial language, namely, Latin? I suggest this transliteration also points to the cultural dislocation that is embedded in a text and in which a text is embedded. Transliteration is a trace of improvisation, invention, nomadic dispersion, or perhaps even transgression. Of course, one should keep in mind here that such transliterations are more often than not translations of "political trauma into linguistic mourning."[61] That is to say, one must pay attention to power differential and unequal exchange rates, including the probability of economic exploitation. In this text, a colonized Jew uses transliterated Latin rather than transliterated Hebrew in a Greek narrative. Yet, we can still read that transliteration as an ambush of alterity that signals the presence of another in the self, or the transnational in the national. This is, I believe, the heart of "Derrida's haunted aphorism that asks us to consider together two statements: that we always speak only one language; that we never speak only one language."[62] Without denying by any means that translation will also bring about with it a transvaluation, transliteration is nonetheless different. It is, in effect, incomplete or interminable translation. It announces the absence of a straightforward translation, perhaps even an inability to translate, or an untranslatability. It pronounces a deficit in linguistic and/or cultural transaction. There is a frontier—even or especially in a "rhizomatic" world of imperial mixing and grafting[63]—that no amount of translation can overcome.

BETWEEN SELF AND OTHER: AN OPEN QUESTION

If the word *lepta* points to the recognition that linguistic skills may not erase the gap of difference across time and culture, the transliterated Latin *kodrantēs* in Mark provides a trace of the otherness within what looks like a single temporal and cultural zone. This leads me to the third story or text. The title of my paper—as no doubt some of my readers have no difficulty in tracing—is indebted to a recent movie starring Bill Murray and Scarlett Johansson. *Lost in Translation* (2003), written and directed by Sofia Coppola, has brought many happy monetary returns for her and her stars. The movie is about a chance and unconsummated romance in Tokyo between an aging U.S. movie star who goes there to shoot a whisky commercial and a young wife who accompanies her photographer husband in his busy work trip across the Pacific. The backdrop of the movie is then the globalized economy, including the travels and the cultural industries of entertainment and commercials. What is most valuable about this movie for my purposes is that the culture shock that it stages through the experience of U.S. visitors in Tokyo can also be read as a metaphor for differences among people of the United States, even or especially when they seem to belong to the same race and class. Like Scheherazade's stories in *One Thousand and One Nights*, Coppola's movie "take[s] [us] to far away lands to observe foreign ways, so [we] could get closer to the strangeness within [ourselves]."[64] One must not forget that both Murray's and Johansson's characters are already distant from their respective spouses. Seeing each other in the hotel bar on a sleepless night, they strike up a friendship as compatriots often do in a foreign land. As one watches their friendship grow closer into something like a "secret encounter," one also senses that something like a chasm exists between these two persons with similar experiences of marital problems at home and disorientation in Tokyo, not to mention their shared race, class, and language. Whether spoken or unspoken, something is still lost in translation even if both parties have access to the same—shall we say, "original" or "first"?—language. Language, both linguistic and bodily, finds itself at a loss in bridging the gap between Murray and Johansson. White and English-speaking citizens of the United States do not only have trouble communicating with Japanese, but they also struggle in speaking among themselves. Despite their shared use of and fluency in English, their "exchange shows the way in which two people presumably speaking the same language are really not speaking the same language."[65] There seems to be an unknown level of "untranslatability" that renders their communication truly an emotional affair, or an impossible world of (in)fidelity.

"Secret encounter" is, of course, a phrase that Spivak has used to talk about "ethical singularity," or the "sense that something has not gone across" despite honest and earnest attempts on both sides to reveal and tell all.[66] Spivak's emphasis on the active attempt of both partners to learn and reveal—like Jacques Derrida's view of translation as at once both "indispensable" and "impossible"[67]—is significant, otherwise we may be back to the status quo under the pretext of "inability to know." As Emily Apter writes, "false pieties about not wanting to 'mistranslate' the other" can end up sanctioning parochialism.[68] Apter's reference to piety is particularly relevant here, since this idea of a singular untranslatability is associated especially—though by no means exclusively—with realms of religion and divinity, as the recent work by Peter Hallward on rethinking the postcolonial through Buddhism and Islam makes clear.[69] Spivak herself—despite her desire to "de-transcendentalize the sacred" and talk about "imagination" rather than "belief"[70]—connotes if not confesses as much when she lists "mother, nation, *god*, nature" as "names of alterity,"[71] or when she uses the word "sacred" generically to refer to the otherness of human life that cannot be approached by reason or by money alone.[72] There is a "touch of transcendence"[73]—and I am using "transcendence" here without any idealizing, utopian, or otherworldly invocations—in every human being that makes impossible any dreams or desires for telepathy or, god forbid, the intuitive divination of a romantic Schleiermacher that would enable you to understand another better than that person understands himself or herself. Isn't this unknown quality, indefinable horizon, "species of alterity," or plain impossibility what Spivak is after in calling her critical idea "planetarity"?[74] Like a planet or a god—I don't really care what term one uses as terms are inevitably limiting and troubling[75]—a human person cannot be fitted into any set of panoptical reasons or calculations. Tzvetan Todorov puts it well when he asks, "how to name the individual, when the names themselves, as we all know, do not belong to the individual himself [*sic*]? If the absence of difference equals nonexistence, pure difference is unnameable: it is nonexistent for language."[76] There is no straightforward translation or conversion even in a face-to-face encounter. There are but tokens of exchange that remain irreducible and irreducibly hermeneutic. That is why Spivak proposes that learning to read—which she glosses as learning to "dis-figure the undecidable figure into a responsible literality, again and again," or basically, an impossible comprehensibility—is central to planetarity.[77]

Whereas Spivak suggests the need to supplement this type of learning with love,[78] I would suggest that this type of learning is in fact the difficult work of love. I am therefore reading the secret encounter in *Lost in Translation* as not a romantic but a love story; it is a story of love. The word "love" is, of course difficult to utter in the context of talking about postcoloniality and theology, because Christian "love" has often been a smoke screen for the "civilizing mission" of soul-making and economic salvation,[79] where the "pagan natives" are economically resourcing the missionary homes and the home countries of missionaries through a translation of salvation coming the other way.[80] Spivak points to this in her discussion about how Kant's categorical imperative becomes colonialism through the scripture about loving god and neighbor.[81] But if one thinks about the double commandment to love god and neighbor—found in the same chapter in Mark in which we find the widow and her offering (Mark 12:30–31)—in terms of what a not-so-slim strand of theology has talked about loving god as loving a wholly other, love of neighbor will also involve a balance between a desire and an inability, or even an impossibility, to know.[82]

This balance is not completely unlike the balance between the seemingly opposing poles or principles of "nothing is translatable" and "everything is translatable" within translation studies.[83] This is so as translation is, in the final analysis, not only textual and material but also epistemological. Just as one may love the divine in spite or because of a dimension that is always already unknown—for instance, in at least most Christian theologies, god's mysterious multiplication into a trinity that no one can really explain—love entails a recognition of "ethical singularity" and the imperative to make room for multiplicity in the planetary neighbor one encounters. Forcing prescribed identities onto individuals—including identity politics—negates not only the truth of but also love for life, both that of an other and that of one's own. This love, this learning, this loving through learning, must then be distinguished from the masculinist epistemophilic delirium of possession and mastery. Just as Spivak's allusion to Derrida's notion that law is necessary to point to but can never be equated with justice,[84] one may say that knowledge is desirable because it facilitates though cannot ever be equated with love.[85] Of course, when terms or rates of exchange are unsettled, it is easy to translate one's own inability to assign value to the other into the other's lack of value. A love that honors alterity by taking into account traces of multiplicity and impossibility will also prevent the not-yet-fully-known and always-becoming emphasis of Spivak's planetarity from turning into Julia Kristeva's "abject" as a "not-yet-object" that threatens boundaries.[86]

According to Spivak, a postcolonial act of reading should help disclose the reader's own positionality, or what she calls a "new narrativization."[87] What Coppola's movie does—as Mark's transliterated Greek does more subtly—is help prevent the seductive move to read or contact the other by way of race, culture, and/or language to affirm the unity or sameness of the self. This move is, of course, what brings about the no-longer-closeted intimacy among anthropology, area studies, and colonialism. What I am getting at is that the study of an other—whether it is through translation or travel or both—is valuable only if it points back to the otherness within the self, puts one's own epistemological certainties into question, and brings about a new calculation on both sides of the balance sheet. The transliterated Latin in Mark 12:42, for example, could or should alert us to not only the heterglossic but also the diglossic aspects of Mark's language.[88] After all, *koine* or "common" Greek and classical Greek represented two varieties of the Greek language that coexisted in the first century. In the words of Derrida, "We only ever have one language" that is "not at one with itself," as there is "no such thing as *a* language."[89] Linguistic otherness, as Derrida suggests, can also be found within a so-called single language. Although I am not ready to endorse Rey Chow's proposal that it may be "comparative enough" for comparative literature students to attend to the diversity within English, I do agree with her—as we have seen from both Richards and Markan scholarship on the widow's mites—that multilingualism does not necessarily prevent one from being imperialistic or monocultural, and that linguistic and cultural multiplicity already exist within English.[90] In other words, translation takes place and gets lost within a language as well as across languages. "The illusion of transparency," writes Lawrence Venuti, "is an effect of fluent discourse."[91] Intralingual translation may look fluent, but its transparency is no less an illusion.

Once again, an inability to translate spells not only loss but also possibilities of gain, or moments of dynamic creativity. I am referring here not only to the fluidity or intermingling between the self and the other but also a complexity or even unknowability of the self that includes but cannot be subsumed under the popular concept of hybridity, or the transmutation of self that results from cultural contact. Secret encounters speak therefore to the need not only to translate the other but also to retranslate or transform the self. While I agree with Spivak's critique of a navel-gazing investment in "a collection of ourselves" as community,[92] studying only the unknowability of an other can also duplicate the pitfall of anthropological learning. Perhaps I can use Spivak's translation technique of "fraying" here so that one will not be grasping for structures of equivalency between self and other but will enter into one's self-staging to see—or try to see—lovingly what is in one's own shadow. Spivak is certainly correct that W. E. B. Du Bois "undid African American continent-think" and reached to the heterogeneity of and within Africa,[93] but one must not lose sight of Du Bois's emphasis on what Robert Gooding-Williams calls "self-recognition," or a re-cognition of "our views of ourselves," especially our own—and not just the other's—multiplicity and complexity.[94] One must remember that tracing or tracking planetarity involves "making *our* home . . . uncanny," or unfamiliar.[95]

If translation, lost or otherwise, does not lead to a reformulation or transformation of the self, no real political change will result. There is a certain amount of self-interestedness here that should not—and must not—be lost in transition. We do not know and can never fully know the other, but the same is true of ourselves. In contrast to Kant who sees the sublime or alterity of the other as a reminder of one's own limit or finitude,[96] perhaps one should also see the other as a reminder of the possibilities or multiplicity of one's own self. The secret of the self is, to quote the late Derrida's memorable turn of phrase out of context, "a secret that one cannot not keep" after a secret encounter.[97] To go back to Richards's story, traveling translators must return to make English less rather than more basic not only for others but also especially for themselves. Without this, we will just keep on rejecting and projecting affect, or what we do not know about ourselves, onto the other.[98] Without this, no amount of study in language and area studies will counteract the threat of economic and cultural imperialism. Without this, one will not be able to account for the "both-sides" emphasis that is necessary to keep love from deteriorating or regressing back into "benevolence,"[99] or "ethics of alterity chang[ing] into a politics of [one's own] identity."[100]

❧ Ghostly Encounters: Spirits, Memory, and the Holy Ghost

MAYRA RIVERA

I pray . . . to be haunted by her slight ghost.
GAYATRI CHAKRAVORTY SPIVAK, *A Critique of Postcolonial Reason*

And indeed He is the strangest
of the Three Persons,
the most estranged.

For the Holy Ghost is nakedly a ghost.
Father and Son may be masks
compassionately adapted
to our capacities, but
Person is not persona and
The Ghost is a ghost, no fiction.
DONALD DAVIE, *"The Comforter"*

I confess that my interest in haunting has not always been theological. The trope, if not the sense, of being haunted has for me the distinct traces of writers such as Juan Rulfo, Gabriel García Márquez, and Isabel Allende, to name just a few. Their ghostly narratives exemplify modes of witness in which the past is both ungraspable and unavoidable, haunting the imaginations of subjects who do not neutralize this ambiguity.[1] I think, for instance, of Allende's *Of Love and Shadows*—a story set during the days following the coup against Salvador Allende on September 11, 1973, which bears witness to the defeat of democratic accomplishments in Chile, to the systematic assassinations and disappearance of citizens. In the story, the protagonist, like the author, is haunted by the events narrated: by vanished hopes as well as vanished bodies.[2] The memory of these images has something to do with the fact that now, many years later, I'm inspired by Gayatri Chakravorty Spivak's engagement with ghostly narratives and drawn back to the spirits—intrigued not so much by this or that particular ghost, as by the very structure of haunting and its theological reverberations.

Haunted by the twentieth-century legacy of massive unjust deaths, contemporary culture is crowded with narratives of ghostly encounters. Vanished hopes and vanished bodies are invoked in literary pages and memorial stones, in fictional accounts and historical archives, as we try to envision a different, and seemingly impossible, future. As part of this effort to respond to the past, postcolonial studies—whose "post" marks not a simple departure from the colonial past but the space of questioning—explores the intervals in and between history and narration. This cultural practice entails not merely a different reading or appropriation of history but an investigation of the very dynamics of remembrance: the possibilities and limits of a relation to the past and the responsibilities bestowed by an encounter with its ghosts.

One would expect Christian theology to be well equipped to encounter ghosts. Not only does Christianity proclaim the presence of a Galilean Jew, executed millennia ago, but it even names the agent of Christian traditioning the "Holy Ghost."[3] However, spectrality is not what a Christian theologian consciously conjures up when speaking of the Holy Ghost. We cannot claim that mainline Christian theology has been particularly hospitable to the ungraspable and uncontrollable character of haunting. To the contrary, one is likely to be advised against the use of the term Holy Ghost, in order to avoid such spooky associations.[4] Especially since the Reformation, theology has tried to exorcise the presumed lower spirits. In accord with the Reformation's "general devaluation of the numinous" and its banishing of intermediate beings expressed in the attack on and official rejection of the doctrine of purgatory, theology has eloquently claimed that its Holy Ghost is completely unlike other ghosts, of a different substance entirely.[5] The Holy Ghost is now seen simply as the third *person* of a wholly divine trinity. In its most common depictions, where it appears as a coherent, timeless presence, the Holy Ghost seems to share nothing in common with those other spirits that haunt the writers I just mentioned. For those spirits, historical time matters, even as they represent the very disturbance of linear progression. Although the Holy Ghost is depicted in respected theological sources as a figure of relationality[6]—and thus could also be an image of *temporal* relationships—the power of memory has not figured prominently in theological descriptions of the spirit.

This essay reimagines the Holy Ghost in its relation to memories of suppressed pasts as well as unrealized possibilities, inspired by Spivak's discussions of history, ancestors, and memory, in which she invokes the theologically provocative figure of the ghost. After a brief glance at contemporary theoretical debates about the need and viability of remembrance that characterize the cultural moment of the present exploration, we turn to the Bible in search of the Holy Ghost. The Bible offers a diversity of images for the spirit(s)—some of them inspire prophetic boldness, while others are morally ambiguous, or even threatening.[7] To focus on the relationships between the ghosts, memory, and the Holy Ghost, I rely on the Gospel of John's depictions of an almost-dead Jesus in his close connection with the Holy Ghost. Tracing the unique appearances of this Ghost in John reveals the complexity and irreducible multiplicity of its origins and can help us perceive a multitude of other ghosts, ancient and current, whose appearance may teach us something about the future.

HUNGER OF MEMORY

> The dead speak, certainly, who would measure their ambiguity?
>
> ASSIA DJEBAR, *"The Dead Speak"*

Our society is intensely preoccupied with the past, with its preservation and transmission in memory. Vows never to forget, museums and memorials sites, and public apologies for the wrongs of the past are all part of the contemporary cultural scene. A "hunger of memory"[8] and a pronounced interest in memorializing contrast with future-oriented ideals that have sought salvation in a total break with the past—the kind of narrative exemplified by Friedrich Nietzsche's oft-quoted statement, "against time and its 'it was,' that alone I call salvation."[9] Today such gestures against the "it was" are likely to be dismissed as naively ignoring the inescapable weight of the past and its demands. Indeed, the prominence of memory in contemporary culture is often read as a symptom of the uncontrollable return of that which future-obsessed ideologies tended to repress: a troubling, but no longer avoidable, reckoning with the past. The demanding memories of the past—of its horrors and failures—seem to mock the triumphalism of modernity.

The intense concern with memory that we experience can also be understood as a symptom of anxiety affecting a culture that cannot hold on to the present long enough, let alone resist the threat of "socially produced amnesia," as Andreas Huyssen argues.[10] We yearn for the past as we see the present reduced to fleeting moments, instants that turn obsolete at stupefying speed; "finance capital is moving at the speed of mind, at the rate of data," as Spivak remarks.[11] W. G. Sebald notes: "[E]verything is constantly lapsing into oblivion with every extinguished life. . . . [T]he world is, as it were, draining itself, in that the history of countless places and objects which themselves have no power of memory is never heard, never described or passed on."[12] This sense of living in a world of fleeting experiences intensifies the perceived need for memorializing. Alongside the perceptions of a "vanishing present" emerge multiple and conflicting attempts to summon the past, to conjure dead ancestors, as well as countless witnesses claiming to be haunted.

But turning to the past has never been a simple solution. Such efforts are always affected by undeniable loss; the paths are uncertain and the effects ambiguous. The past calls, but we do not know how to respond: What kind of relationship is possible, or desirable? What can bearing witness to the past possibly mean when it is instigated by loss, by absence, marked by uncertainty?

Exhortations to remember and efforts to preserve and transmit memories do not necessarily recognize the problems entailed in dealing with its legacies. All too often disciplinary and cultural claims to retrieve the past tend to consolidate it as an object of knowledge or as a cultural commodity. Spivak's interrogations of such engagements with the past are woven through her explorations of history as well as her readings of literature. In the chapter on history in *A Critique of Postcolonial Reason*, Spivak observes that the discussions in that field regarding the relationship between archive and literature, history and language, represent a needed challenge to the hegemonic historiographies that "designated the archives as a repository of 'facts.'"[13] However, a critical approach to the archival should not imply a mere methodological reversal to privilege literary criticism over historical research. Instead, a careful engagement with "history" should seek to uncover the complicity between literature and the archives, for the production of colonial archives was itself a "construction of a fiction whose task was to produce a whole collection of 'effects of the real.'"[14] The process of narration implicates the narrator: "The colonizer constructs himself as he constructs the colony."[15] This intimate relationship between the narrator and the documented history is colonialism's "open secret," "one that cannot be part of official knowledge."[16] The effects of the real thus created and the pitfalls of its processes of narration still haunt us.

Desire for an intimate relationship with the past seduces contemporary retrievals of history. Assuming that the past can become a "past present" we may imagine history as "a genealogy of the historian" thus repeating the colonial practice of constructing the self by constructing the other.[17] Such stances fail to recognize the past as wholly Other, Spivak argues. We may recognize the tendency, and the temptation, to assume a position of "sanctioned authority" to construct the past as our own genealogy, not only in the production of historical texts, but in the broader appeals to collective memory in identity discourses.

Remembrance is threatened by the tendency to objectify the past or construe history as a foundation of reified identities and hypercertainties. As Spivak warns us, references to "one's own hallucinatory heritage for the sake of the politics of identitarian competition" can lead to claims of authority founded on a stabilized memory or to the privatization of history.[18] Furthermore, when references to the past promote illusions of certainty, the imperative to remember can ensnare subjects or collectivities in histories of violence. The manipulation of collective memories to justify violence is a (regrettably) familiar strategy, manifest, for instance, as invocations of authorized narratives as "memory" to rally political aggression against other states (as in the case of the U.S. government's uses of the tragedies of 9/11) or against sectors of the population blamed for past aggressions (as in so-called "sectarian violence"). In such cases, objectified memories become the justification for the displaced repetition of past violence. The blood of the martyrs is fetishized to fuel the shedding of more blood.

Keenly aware of the unavoidable difficulties and ambiguities of any efforts to relate to the past and to do justice to its legacy, Spivak warns her readers against seeking the sanctioned authority to fully represent the past. She proposes imagining the relation to the past as a "ghostly agency of haunting."[19] Further she invites us to "pray to be haunted" by the other's "slight ghosts."[20] The metaphor of prayer—an unexpected gift for a theological reading—aptly conveys the methodological shift being proposed: prayer locates agency not in the authority of the narrator, but in the relation to the Other. A prayer implies the possibility of a response from the Other—a response that is never within the control of the one who prays. Thus, prayer is not a pure origin, but simultaneously a witness to having been called—haunted—and an expression of hope for something still to come.

The "ghostly agency of haunting" thus defies predictable chronologies, calling attention to the "irreducible 'out-of-jointness' "[21] of time. The distinction between this interruptive structure of haunting and the objectifying allusions to the past described above is represented in fiction as a contrast between "traumatic" and "narrative" memory, as Kathleen Brogan describes them. "While traumatic memory is rigidly inflexible, marked by pure repetition, narrative memory—essentially a social act—can be 'adapted to present circumstances.' "[22] Traumatic memory and the dangers of inadequate relationships with the past—those that seduce the subject into pure repetition—are dramatized in stories of "possession," which, Brogan argues, should be read as "cautionary tales about the proper function of memory."[23] Possession is the result of the failure to acknowledge the necessary distance from and otherness of the past—a past that cannot be fully present.[24] Assia Djebar's "The Dead Speak" expresses this process by asserting that the role of the one who accompanies the dead is to "meticulously reestablish the distances" and "reevaluate the relationships": necessary steps to make possible the emergence of new relationships.[25] Just as the agency of haunting displaces the boundaries of the subject—both haunted and praying to be haunted—the unpredictable apparition of the ghost troubles the stability of the frontiers between the past, present, and future. The "present" is exposed to its others, but not possessed by them.

Although narratives of haunting are often associated with traumatic experiences, memory cannot be reduced to horror and trauma. While facing the traumatic legacy of our history is indispensable to "imagine the future and to regain a strong temporal and spatial grounding of life and imagination," memory discourses are also concerned with the future. Collective practices of remembrance may attempt not only to protect the past from oblivion, but also to provide spaces to allow for "individuals to break off traumatic repetitions"[26] as well as to reencounter past promises. Spivak conjures up not only the spirits of those victimized by violence but also of those ancestors whose visions of the future were impossible in their own times. Moving beyond exploring how the colonial past continues to haunt the present, Spivak's work asks what kinds of relationships with the past may open new possibilities and what kinds of memory practices avoid the reinscription of "mere history," exhorting us to imagine a "counterfactual possible world."[27] Spivak's readings of Virginia Woolf's *A Room of One's Own*, Assia Djebar's *Far from Medina*, and José Martí's *Our America*, among others, exemplify such a mode of reading (and of relating to the past).[28] In these readings, Spivak focuses on the hopes that the authors imagine beyond their own lives. Although such ghostly encounters cannot "'work' as the guarantee of a future present," they might be "the only way to go at moments of crisis; to surrender to undecidability (since the 'agent' is the ancestral ghost, without guarantee) as the condition of possibility of responsible decision, to trans-form religion into militancy."[29] The witness that arises from the experiences of haunting is thus infused with the "humility of the imagination" rather than the certainty of proven facts: witness inspired and always to be supple-mented by scholarship.[30]

There are deep resonances between the anticipatory structure of haunting described in Spivak's readings and the messianic structures of Jewish and Christian thought, as reimagined in Derrida's *Specters of Marx* and further elaborated in readings of that book—including Spivak's own.[31] As a way of reading that seeks to listen and respond to ancestral ghosts—without guaran-tee, but inspired by their insistent challenges and elusive hope—haunting suggests further connections with, and possibilities for, a theology of mem-ory and spirit that responds to the challenges arising from postmodern cultures' hunger of memory. Seeking the ancestral voice of a Christian spirit of memory, I turn—in the anachronistic fashion that suits ghostly encounters—from twenty-first-century concerns to a first-century gospel story that bears witness to its own preoccupations with memory. Rereading that narrative's disturbed chronology and its ghostly presences and promises we reencounter its unique portrayal of the Holy Ghost as spirit of memory and truth.

JOHN'S GHOSTS

The Gospel of John gives a prominent place to remembrance, which it associates closely with the Spirit; it wrestles explicitly with the problems of its legacy, emphasizing its own retrospective perspective more than any of the Synoptics.[32] Completed at some temporal distance from the life of Jesus, and possibly benefiting from other gospel narratives, it is often accused of treating the received traditions with astonishing freedom. Yet its frequent references to memories of the past and its allusions to remembrances that will only become possible in the future, attest to the gospel's interest in the power of recollection (*anamnesis*). All of this adds significance to the fact that the gospel introduces a distinctive characterization of the Spirit as a facilitator of memory. John's Spirit is divine companionship experienced as a kind of remembrance, indeed, as the very possibility of relating to the past. In Jesus' absence, the Holy Ghost—tellingly named also "the spirit of truth"—will be present among a collectivity-to-come, and will help its members recall what they have heard and seen (John 14:26). Of course, the readers of the gospel have not themselves heard or seen Jesus in the flesh, but they may still be haunted by the events narrated, even when others do not seem to recognize the ghost.

The gospel's allusions to memory are not limited to the catastrophic event of Jesus' death, as we shall see. Yet the colonial realities that affected the text's author(s) and first readers may have influenced the prominence given to death in the story. Such is Tat-siong Benny Liew's reading of the role of death in John.[33] He observes that in colonial contexts, the colonized might be reduced to what he calls, following Giorgio Agamben, "bare life." Under such circumstances, the possibility of death becomes an ever-present aspect of life. Liew theorizes that John's gospel both reflects and attempts to subvert the economy of death that affected its community. Read through the lenses of the real, imminent threats to John's community, the story's recurrent references to death suggest links with cultural narratives of haunting such as characterized above, where groups wrestle with their "inheritance of loss."[34] In the case of John, the stark realities of bare life, as Liew describes them, may serve as warnings against the temptation to swiftly absorb the gospel's spectral images into a domesticated, ahistorical Spirit—even if that tendency were found in the gospel itself.

The Greek word that John uses for the spirit is *parakletos*. Although there has been a lot of speculation about the genealogy of this peculiar word, its origin remains uncertain. *Parakletos* was originally understood as "comforter" or "advocate," but the term is not used in any of the other gospels, and was simply transliterated in early translations of the New Testament as "Paraclete."[35] In other words, we don't really know where this "ghost" came from! We do know, however, that the Paraclete/Spirit is closely related to Jesus: it descended upon Jesus at his baptism (and "remained on him"—1:32) and will be "among" Jesus' followers and "in" them. The Paraclete resembles Jesus, who even refers to it as the "other Paraclete" (14:16), presumably implying that Jesus is also a Paraclete. But the Paraclete is also not Jesus and will not come until Jesus' death. The close identification between Jesus and this peculiarly fluid Paraclete character offers a key to interpreting John's image of the Holy Ghost.

The Fourth Gospel's "postresurrection" narratives are irresistible sites for a reading of ghostly encounters.[36] Yet, even before those ghostly scenes, the gospel exhibits symptoms of haunting; temporal disjuncture is one of those symptoms. Biblical scholars have often observed that throughout the farewell discourse of John's gospel "the temporal focus seems to shift constantly." Indeed, "the whole farewell discourse is out of place in the progression of narrative time." It is, in fact, "an 'anachrony.'"[37] It is possible to perceive signs of temporal disjuncture even before that point in the narrative, where the gospel is strangely inhabited by moments that do not belong to its time, perhaps belong to no time at all, subverting the linear progression of the story. The gospel famously begins by narrating another beginning, beyond the confines of the Fourth Gospel itself: "In the beginning was the Word, and the Word was with God, and the Word was God" (1:1). It begins by alluding to other creation stories (those of Genesis and Proverbs). The beginning of the story—a story that is already a community's remembrance—is a repetition of other beginnings and of other scriptural proclamations of beginning, of fall into darkness, of the failures of creation as it was expected to be.[38] The beginning also anticipates the gospel's story and that which the story proclaims is still to come.

If the temporal dislocations of the Johannine prologue leave the reader perplexed, this effect is only intensified by subsequent scenes, including those in which the very characters of the story seem unable to keep the boundaries between past and present straight. John the Baptist had been sent by God. John was preparing the way for someone who would come after him, but who was nonetheless before him (1:30). John had been waiting, preparing, anticipating the coming of another. John did not know who that other was (1:26), but he did know that the Spirit would rest upon him: the Spirit of wisdom, the Spirit of truth. In other words, John preceded Jesus and followed him. John himself was confused with another one, with Elijah (1:21), who had come before and was expected to return. Jesus is met with similar puzzlement: Is he a prophet who has returned? Or is he the one who had been calling from the future, the one who would come? *Revenant? Arrivant?* How can we tell the difference?

The temporal complexity of the Fourth Gospel is not settled after the first part of the gospel clarifies (puzzlingly) Jesus' identity as the one who would come. The disciples keep failing to understand. However, after Jesus is gone, they will remember and finally understand, the gospel repeats (2:22, 12:16, 14:26). Presumably, the words of Jesus, perhaps Jesus himself, will come to haunt them. But will they not be puzzled again, uncertain about whether he comes from the past or the future? Are such uncertainties in the face of the past not intrinsic to what remembering means and will mean?

Despite the uncertainties dramatized in the disciples' struggles to understand the relationship between their present and past experiences, Jesus reassures them (and the readers) that remembering is sustained by the Holy Ghost. Yet the (other) Paraclete will not come until Jesus dies (John 15:26, 16:7, 8, 13). And as the narrative approaches the point of transition, when the spirit of memory comes to live among them, a ghostly aura sets in. Not that such a narrative quality is completely unexpected; Jesus had already made some spooky remarks, such as: "I will come to you. Before long, the world will not see me anymore, but you will see me. . . . On that day you will realize that I am in my Father, and you are in me, and I am in you" (14:19). The statement "you in me and I in you," repeated throughout the gospel, is hardly a straightforward piece of information. Its disseminative force can unsettle the seemingly solid boundaries of identity set by the Johannine Jesus' "I am" sayings just as the scenes of Jesus' postresurrection apparitions unsettle the boundaries of identity between Jesus and the "other Paraclete." Indeed, the "I am" shall be interpreted in the light of "you are in me and I am in you."

The Jesus that appears to the disciples in the "postresurrection" scenes has distinctively ghostly features: he appears (or reappears) as the one who departed. Jesus had been unjustly executed. After he gave up his spirit, his friends diligently procured the body, wrapped it with spices in linen cloths, and placed it in a nearby tomb.[39] Jesus' friends had thus taken the first steps toward distancing themselves from the living Jesus and from a past shared with him: burying him, remembering him in a way made possible only by death. However, that which had made that distance appear as an absolute separation—the stone closing off the tomb—would not be in place for too long.

It is Mary Magdalene who first comes to Jesus. But her work of mourning is interrupted. For mourning is tied, Jacques Derrida observes, to attempts to "ontologize remains, to make them present, in the first place by identifying the bodily remains and by localizing the dead."[40] And Jesus' body had not stayed in place. And "nothing could be worse, for the work of mourning, than confusion or doubt."[41] Mary sees that Jesus is no longer there; in fact, both the stone and the body of Jesus are no longer in place: a negative apparition, as it were. But with the separating stone removed, Jesus is unrecognizably "there," elsewhere and otherwise; their relationship has changed.

Summoned by Mary Magdalene to the empty tomb, John and Peter saw and believed—even though we cannot be sure just what they believed, because we are told that they still "did not understand the scripture" (20:8). Meanwhile, Mary wept. I am tempted to imagine the disciples' apparent ease of "belief" as a forward-moving attitude (as if following the advice to move swiftly "against time and its 'it was'"[42]), impatient with Mary's slowness and her need for a time for mourning. It is perhaps hard to conclude, as Ernest Renan did, that Mary's tears were able to effect Jesus' resurrection, but they at least seem to have brought about a transformed vision.[43] The fact is that it is only after Mary's mournful tears that she is able to recognize Jesus, whom she had previously mistaken for a gardener. Thus the story seems to confirm Fredric Jameson's observation, that "only mourning, and its particular failures and dissatisfactions . . . opens a vulnerable space and entry-point through which ghosts make their appearance."[44]

This gardener-looking Jesus—a body conspicuously linked to the earth, to dust[45]—is evidently not quite the same person that they had known and followed. "There is something disappeared, departed in the apparition itself, as reapparition of the departed."[46] As Jesus' relationship with his disciples is reconfigured, the absolute separation marked by the stone is replaced by a more intimate, if elusive, boundary: Jesus' own body. Jesus cannot be grabbed: "Do not hold on to me," he says, "because I have not yet ascended to the Father" (20:17). The relationship between Mary and Jesus has changed, and Jesus' body exhibits the ungraspable nature of his now spectral presence. Mary's witness will not translate into solid evidence.

Jesus' ghostly body appears again, this time to the other disciples. While the disciples are locked inside a house, Jesus, presumably walking through the wall, appears in their midst. "Peace be with you," he simply says. But this time he directs their attention to the marks of the trauma that preceded the encounter: he shows them "his hands and his side" (20:20). The wounds in Jesus' body are traced on the pages of a text that, as Liew suggests, is in turn responding to life in the death zone of colonialism by inscribing and describing it. The surprisingly fluid materiality of a body that is undeterred by closed doors is nonetheless indelibly marked by history—and so are the readers haunted by his story. In this scene, it is only after revealing the wounds in his admittedly strange body that his disciples are able to recognize him. Jesus' wounds, like Mary's tears, open a "vulnerable space" for the apparition.

The not-quite-solidly-embodied Jesus breathes the Holy Ghost on the disciples and they are sent forth. From this point onward the Spirit of truth will help future followers remember. The Spirit will further allow the disciples to forgive and to refuse to forgive—a power inextricable from that of memory. Yet this is hardly a simple narrative ending. There are other appearances: another recorded walk through walls not only to show the wounds but to have them *touched* by the still doubtful Thomas; and many other unrecorded ones, according to John (20:30; 21:25). The encounters spill over the limits of the canonical memory—necessarily and unpredictably.

The qualities of the promised comforter, the *other* Paraclete, are not unlike those of a ghost—or a spectral Jesus. It is experienced "lightly, yet in the most tangible of ways, given and known as the lightest possible touch, the movement of air by the body."[47] Karmen MacKendrick's reading of this text's subtle image of inspiration, suggests a delicate balance between freedom and will, where each of the (ghostly) encounters affords the follower just what she or he needs to sustain her or him. "Each of the faithful is drawn into a curious combination of presence and absence. . . . No one comprehends Christ, no one has proof; each has exactly enough to sustain faith." The disciples find "faith rather than proof, the memory of contact rather than the grasp of vision."[48] Revelations of empty tombs, an ungrasp-able earthy body recognizable through teary eyes and felt in its woundedness: these do not add up to material evidence. Yet the mysterious quality of a ghostly body is too often replaced by straight arguments for hyperpresence predicated on both Jesus and the knowledge gained through the agency of the Holy Ghost—solid knowledge that replaces spectral memory. Still, despite its admittedly triumphant tone, and the subsequent exorcism to which it has been subjected, the gospel's witness is marked by a vital prohibition: "Do not hold on to me."

John's Jesus is not the Holy Ghost, yet his self-representation as the other Paraclete reminds the reader of the continuity between the process of remembering Jesus and the agency of the Holy Ghost. In the stories of postresurrection encounters, when Jesus inhabits the "seam between past and present,"[49] between life and death, he appears like a specter: "a phenomenal and carnal form of the spirit."[50] As a specter, Jesus materializes the disciples' past. Or perhaps the ghostly Jesus is "just the sign, or the empirical evidence if you like, that tells you a haunting is taking place."[51] The apparitions reveal a way of remembrance. Recalling the apparitions, committing the stories to writing, the gospel also points to other encounters, unrecorded, beyond the text. I imagine these encounters as sharing with the ones recorded a structure of remembrance: resisting the temptation to objectify the past or bypass the work of mourning, transgressing strict boundaries between the present and the past, reconfiguring relationships while remaining faithful to the marks of history, even to those that do not translate into solid evidence.

The Spirit of truth comes forth from a wounded body—a Spirit that is also said, at the beginning of the gospel, to have rested upon this man. A Spirit flows from the returning departed to send forth the disciples. Thus the narrative ends with another beginning, a repetition that is also a first time. Other singularly wounded bodies witness spectral visitations, from multitudes of wounded, departed ones. As Liew suggests, "John ends by foregrounding his corpus as but traces of the departed. . . . Our attention is turned away from the corpus back to . . . the corpses."[52] Or perhaps our attention turns not simply to the lifeless body, but to the ghosts and their hopes—from a departed one to multitudes of ghosts, to bear witness, to be witnesses who, still refusing to see gravestones as markers of absolute separation, are called and sent forth.

INCALCULABLE VISITATIONS FROM THE PAST

There is no inheritance without a call to responsibility.

JACQUES DERRIDA, *Specters of Marx*

Millennia later, inheritors of the gospels continue to be haunted, to pray to be haunted by the spirit that rested upon Jesus. The Spirit? Spirits? Apparitions recorded and unrecorded. Among the inheritors of the gospel, and of their calls to responsibility, we place "political theologians" who, challenged to respond to the monstrous death and unbearable disappointments that marked the twentieth century, returned to the narrative of the crucified one in an attempt to remember toward a different future. Seeking the memory of Jesus, political theologians tried to open a space in Christian theology for other memories and other ancestors, to listen to the forgotten dead and be haunted by their witness. Although they were not invoking the figure of the Holy Ghost, these theologies located memory, suffering, and narration at the very heart of Christian theology.[53] Their work, like a work of mourning, opened vulnerable spaces for apparitions, conjuring memories of the departed one, inviting ghosts to show their wounds and proclaim messianic hopes.

The term "dangerous memories," coined by Johann Baptist Metz and adopted by many liberation theologians, is emblematic of theologies that sought to articulate the relationship between the memory of the crucified Jesus, a *"particular memoria passionis,"* and the "memory of suffering accumulated through history.[54] Such memories are perceived as much more than reminders of victimization; they make demands on us: "they flare up and unleash new dangerous insights for the present," breaking through prevailing structures of plausibility.[55] Dangerous memories are sources of power to sustain a political imagination that can resist absorption into the restrictive grasp of economic-technological controls.[56]

Memory appears as "dangerous and *incalculable visitations from the past"* with a "future content"[57]—suggesting a temporality consonant with the anachronism of haunting described above. As Metz describes it, Christian memory resists the presumed linear progression from the past to a predictable future. Indeed, the history of human suffering is not a preamble to a history of freedom, but an inner aspect of it.[58] Time is here not teleological, but eschatological.[59] The call to respond to both "the sufferings and hopes of the past and the challenge of the dead" entails "not only a revolution that will change the things of tomorrow for future generations, but a revolution that will decide anew the meaning of our dead and their hopes," Metz asserts.[60] This would be a transformation of the imaginary not unlike what Spivak calls, following Derrida, a "teleiopoetic imagination"—a relation to past witnesses that bears a messianic structure, "affecting the distant other," "future companions," "unknowingly, with no guarantees."[61] In contrast to attempts to invoke biblical narratives in order to set limits to theological memory, Metz's statement suggests an inherent openness of both the past and the future which call for new decisions.[62] Theology thus conceived entails "creative remembering" grounded in a re-understanding of history in which "vanquished and forgotten *possibilities* of human existence—to which we give the name 'death'—will neither be revoked nor sublated by the course of future history."[63] The "contra-factual" faith of a theology stirred by the past into creative remembering toward a future is necessarily open-ended. Its goal is "opening up of a liminary time into a counterfactual possible world"—Spivak's description of haunting.[64]

Theological appeals to "dangerous memories" may, however, be tempted to lose sight of the unrealized hopes and the agency implicit in "creative remembering" by focusing exclusively on suffering and victimization.[65] An exclusive emphasis on victimization may objectify the remembered past as facts obsessively repeated—a danger that may have affected even John's uses of memory. In Liew's reading, the Gospel of John ultimately fails to escape the colonial logic of death in and against which it struggled.[66] The text's obsession with death and its sacrificial logic, he argues, was locked in destructive repetitions—not unlike that described by narratives of possession I referred to above. To avoid falling into the regressive patterns that affect so many appeals to memory, theology needs to recognize that it "acts contra-factually," as Metz observes. An ethical relationship with history avoids attempting to assimilate the past as an "object of knowledge" or to shield it from time. As Kwok Pui-lan argues, "The historical imagination"— out of which postcolonial theologies are constructed—"aims not only to reconstitute the past, but also to release it so that the present is livable."[67] Distance is necessary in order for new relationships to emerge. Spivak offers an enticing image: in the process of narration a "fissure can open in what is merely 'history,' and the ghost can dance in the fault."[68] The ghost dance describes the movement of that relationship with the past that does not objectify it as "mere history," but opens it to that which is yet to come.

Read through the lenses of the haunting, what Metz describes as "incalculable visitations from the past"[69] can assume the image of ghostly appearances that may "say something about what to do with the future."[70] Haunting, as Spivak uses the trope, resonates with Metz's interest in conjuring vanquished possibilities, interpreted as "an attempt to establish ethical relationships with history as such."[71] Yet haunting evokes a less determining structure than Metz's phrase "future content" suggests, thus avoiding the positivist implications of predictions that have at times shadowed liberation theology's appeal to the reign of God. Even in its indeterminacy as a structure, however, haunting shares the anticipatory aim of political theologies. Haunting further highlights how such relationships with dead ancestors or forgotten possibilities overflow the boundaries of strictly rationalistic explanations.[72]

Haunting necessarily exceeds the conventional boundaries of theological discourse, as the specters thus conjured cannot be kept inside or outside dogmatic walls. Indeed, as Marcella Althaus-Reid suggests, popular discourses in Latin America have often seen the transgressive appearances of spectral visitations from the past. The "sense of displacement and destruction" in Latin America has "produced a ghostly conviviality of simultaneous religious and economic signs," Althaus-Reid observes. "Basically in Latin America people die hard. There is a political tradition of rebellious bodies in the popular discourse of justice that . . . displaces death and life alongside issues of justice. In Argentina, for instance, our dead usually refuse to die. Instead of resting in peace they struggle to resurrect at any inconvenient time, either completely or partially."[73] The chaotic and disruptive character of this ghostly multitude cannot be gathered neatly as a body of evidence to found reified identities and hypercertainties—religious or political. Thus, while I have referred to the Gospel of John to trace the emergence of a memory-facilitating Holy Ghost, I try to resist the temptation to gather all suffering, all memory, and every single spirit under one event (or one figure) in isolation from others. Remaining faithful to "dangerous memories" entails acknowledging their plurality and irreducible ambiguity. Theology must not obliterate the uncertainties of the constructive theological process—or its risks. Witness, we must ever remind ourselves, is the result of being haunted by spirits, rather than possessing them.

SPIRIT DANCING IN THE FAULT

So you are my witnesses, declares the Lord. And I am God [Isaiah 43.12]. That is, if you are my witness, I am God, and if you are not my witness, I am, as it were, not God.

SIFRE DEUTERONOMY 346, Finkelstein edition

The spectral memory that I have tried to summon up in this short exploration of the Gospel of John is necessarily hybrid, not appearing independently from the well-known metaphysical statements of the gospel, but contaminating them. Its witness is thus marked by the uncertainties of remembrance even as it continues to be stirred by a longing to relate to the past, calling on the Spirit for help to remember the events narrated. The gospel's depictions of the Holy Ghost, like its witnesses, are unfinished. Being inextricably linked to the memories of the departed, the Holy Ghost bears the marks of its relations to death and loss. This Holy Ghost appears as a figure of the divine at the fissures of history, conjured up to comfort or advise those visited by ghosts. It is a spirit among worldly ghosts.[74]

In this theology, the Holy Ghost names the divine in the relationships with the past, with ancestors, and with their ever multiple inheritances. It is not a thing that can be determined by ontological definitions or abstracted from the complexities of history, but we can nevertheless call it divine, inasmuch as it saves possibilities of the past. This image of the divine at the interstices of history is not a figure of synthesis that reduces the alterity and plurality of the past or of ancestral memory. According to the biblical witness, the arrival of the Holy Ghost sparks multiple, dissonant voices to speak in tongues. Thus the Holy Ghost would not replace cacophony with univocity, for it is not a figure of presence, but of the quickening that continues to infuse divine breath in what may otherwise be mere history, only dust. We may indeed call it the Spirit of truth that blows from the past, appearing occasionally as/in spectral bodies to incite memory and enliven hope.

Animating ghosts to dance in the faults of history, or of ontology, the Holy Ghost incites those still alive to become witnesses. Without such witnesses there is no dance—and, as it were, no God. It is perhaps the lure of the ghost dance that draws readers to texts, to the rhythmic motions of reading and the never-ending task of interpretation. Indeed, Christian theologies have, throughout the centuries, claimed that any reading of scripture must happen "in the Spirit." Inheriting the gospels, as well as the practices of reading of Jewish, Christian, and pagan ancestors, biblical exegetes credit the Holy Ghost not only as the agent that makes possible interpretation—consistent with its role as agent of memory—but also as the one who lures them into that role. In the practice of reading, through calling on the Holy Ghost, texts become sites of multiple meanings, beyond the purview of the author. The reader enters the dance. As Liew describes the task, "In memory of John's memory of Jesus, we must not only recall but also rework what John has written."[75] Spivak's assertion that hauntology is a name for reading resonates with the narrative text(tile) of Christian interpretation.[76]

The possibility of establishing relationships with the past assumes a cosmology that exceeds postmodern culture's vision of a world constantly draining itself as its objects lapse into oblivion, for in this theology the past is not simply nothing. An inspirited cosmology, where the incalculable past may still visit the present and the dead may speak, implies a nonreductionist view of history and of worldly life. Such a world must be conceived beyond the limits of reason alone, and beyond the calculation of global capital. This is perhaps a theological translation of Spivak's planetarity. This theology of the Holy Ghost conceives the cosmos, like planetarity, as open toward a space of detranscendentalized alterity. While resisting the idealistic dreams of otherworldly existence, this view also seeks to avoid the objectifying and totalizing tendencies of rationalism; it finds alterity in history, agency in the quite Other. Imagining this world without literalizing ghostly figures in closed metaphysical systems would be the risky but unavoidable task of theology.[77]

As we conjure dreams of planetary love and justice, the Holy Ghost might become a theological figure of that relationship with the past that embraces in humility memory's irreducible uncertainties. This theology of the Holy Ghost affirms the divine implicated in the possibility and the processes of remembrance. Such an image would need to remember the multiplicity of spirits and the "specific corporeality of the ghost[s] . . . in the current global conjuncture," to quote Spivak once more.[78] Attuned to the voices of particular ancestors, it would also recognize the cosmic web in which history and memory are inscribed. Resisting the homogenizing force of the single ontological persona and moving beyond its anthropocentric images, the relationality of the Holy Ghost extends to a plurality of ancestors, some of whom do not bear human forms. The Holy Ghost also dances among the nonhuman victims of ecological genocide; their ghosts may visit us as we seek to imagine a different future for this planet. The Holy Ghost inhabits the fissures of a planetary past that cannot be reduced to human history. May we pray to be haunted.

❧ Extempore Response to Susan Abraham, Tat-siong Benny Liew, and Mayra Rivera

GAYATRI CHAKRAVORTY SPIVAK

The papers are very different, all three of them; and, I would bet, also suggest new possibilities for "Can the Subaltern Speak?" The Nicaraguans wrote at a certain point a piece which came out in *The Socialist Review* called "Can the Subaltern Vote?" and, you know, I really felt that they were not taking my little essay in very well. [Laughter.] I was telling Serene [Jones] earlier that I actually sent that paper back to the editors saying, "It's too long, it's too confusing, it needs to be cut. I can't cut it, please help me." They just published it as it was, so . . . I've suffered. [Laughter.] So I am most grateful, not only to the three presenters, but also to the colleagues who invited me here. Such careful thought went into the questions, and also a great show of confidence and support in actually reading my stuff with such care. I'm not a very popular person within my own field, the literary critical field; you hardly ever see people who actually teach literary criticism come to talks I give, and so it is very good to find this kind of confidence. It helps in the survival game. So I thank you all. I will not say everything that I want to say—you should be most grateful for that— because each paper has given me much more than I am going to be able to put in my response.

I would say to start with that I am in general agreement with all three papers. In general, a response of this kind—if I may say this—is expected to cut the other person to shreds, I think. Also in the French tradition—within which I also sometimes speak, signifying myself as a French person, not even just as white—the high tradition is to agree to agree, to agree, to agree, *absolument d'accord*, and then to hit with *néanmoins*, which is "none-theless," and then always blood. So I can't produce that one.

[Addressing Susan Abraham:] I want to begin with the idea of the uncanny and also the idea that planetarity secures a rhetorical space. When I said earlier this afternoon that planetarity has to be put in the value form in order for it to become something that we can use, I was also saying that what I said to my Swiss interlocutors was simply an invitation to consider what Laurie Anderson said when she was asked, "Why did you want to be the artist in residence for NASA?" She said, "I like the space people because it makes us realize that human beings are worms." Now, I wouldn't want to put it quite that way because to say human beings are worms is also like saying human beings are God. But that is what I was telling the Swiss, that it doesn't matter in the long run if one planet disappears as the system keeps on going, and we can't even talk about the planet in a system. That's a kind of astringent reminder; that is not something that one actually uses to do anything. But, on the other hand, it can't hang out by itself because we are persons. Everything seems to indicate that justice should be reflected in laws, that every unconditioned ethics comes uncannily—to take yours and Freud's word (although it's not Freud's word, actually: *unheimlich* means something else)—paired with a politics. Not the single politics—that was Derrida's judgment of Levinas, wasn't it? Therefore, when I take planetarity to be that, I myself dive into a certain value form. You were correct to point it out.

[Addressing Tat-siong Benny Liew:] You chose Marx's and Saussure's quotes—I myself turn it into an invocation not just to learn languages, but deep language learning. Yes. ([Aside to Susan Abraham:] Therefore, I am happy that you used that adjective "rhetorical." That you call planetarity a rhetorical space I find very enabling.) You have noticed that I tied the idea of multiplicity to the imperative to imagine the planet. So the idea of deep language learning and acknowledgment of multiplicity—am I misrepresenting you by using these terms?—can also be tied. I, given my politics, am obliged to be able to imagine a *good* globalization. It failed, of course; and there were real ethical reasons why international socialism failed, but it was supposed to be *good* globalization. It failed already in 1914 when the German Social Democrats voted in war credits. It failed on the altar of nationalism. So one must be able to imagine that there can be an equality of rights, an equality of the goods of the world divided through, shared through, a socialist rather than a capitalist globalization. I am not saying it *can* be imagined, however: we are talking about the "to come." Nonetheless, even if there were no globalization, we would need uniformization. You see, once again, a binary opposition doesn't always do it. We would need uniformization, we would need a few languages. Even Ngugi wa Thiong'o, in his book *Decolonizing the Mind*,[1] accepted that for certain kinds of purposes—the structures of the state, for example—you have to appropriate these big, powerful, unitary languages. That's as it may be.

But this globalization puts us in a double bind. That is to say, we are within a set of contradictory instructions and we must learn to play with a set of contradictions, which is the description of *all* action. (Anybody who has brought up children knows this!) And the double bind is that in such a uniform world—"the globe"—we lose the *world* in order to provide a world. We have to supplement even a just globe with linguistic diversity. I am not saying cultural diversity—"culture" is a bad word—but linguistic diversity. Whereas in globalization, because finance capital is moving at the speed of mind, at the rate of data (the new substance of value form), the work of restoring a world by supplementing is slow. Our unexamined love of the digital—the idea that the Internet will bring salvation and revolution—should be deeply questioned. I am not a technophobe, but it seems to me that that supplementation also goes along with what you are talking about. I agree with you totally that the necessary impossibility of translation exists within one's own language. You teach in a class where you're trying to construct a collectivity for a whole semester, as carefully as possible, and yet everybody in the room is not receiving exactly what you mean to say. And you yourself are not able to say what you mean to say. And you are in fact not saying what you think you are saying. [Laughter.] So this is, of course, a commonsense fact that we tend to forget. I would never, ever say that this is not the case. The reason why I asked for the learning of languages, and especially indigenous languages these days, is because these less-taught languages are defective for capitalism. I take seriously Alton Becker's idea of lingual memory. We were discussing Marx, and, of course, Marx's most memorable phrase about foreign languages is in *The 18th Brumaire*, where he says that the revolutionary practice is like when you have learned a foreign language so well that while you are producing in it, you do not refer it back to the language *rooted in you*—a phrase which is always mistranslated in English. You know my English is good, but I can assure you it is not a substitute for my first language. That first language that I learned as an infant is the only one that activates the metapsychological channels. It's not a mother tongue, let's not get into those kinds of romanticizations, but there is only one language that we learn which activates those kinds of channels. Nonetheless, I know English so well that, as Marx might say, while I am producing in it, I do not refer it back to the language *rooted in me*.

This practice will also cut identitarianism. The UN's efforts are very good, but they are tied to identity politics. And, finally, what is also very important, again here and now, in every university in the country where I teach, is this: there is a total lack of parity between teachers of language and teachers of literature. And when it comes to indigenous languages, there is no quality control of the languages, only "I need Wolof because I got a job in Dakar." From that point of view, if you just emphasize the incredible and irreducible within any communication, what will happen is, people will say, "Look, I am doing comparative literature," and do it in nothing but English or Chinese, which is the problem of my department. It calls itself "English and Comparative Literature," although it has been asked by upper administration not to do so, and somebody writing a dissertation on nothing but Wordsworth gets a PhD in English and Comparative Literature. I think it's a scandal. So it seems to me that even as we acknowledge the idea that any communication is full of the necessary impossibility of translation, as Derrida suggested in his very powerful book *Politics of Friendship*,[2] you cannot do politics if you take this irreducible *courbure* of communication as the last word. He calls acting in the political "that madness," because one must do it—but that's not the reasonable, that's the mad, because it has to base itself on a grounding error which is simply neglecting a commonsense fact that we all know: that I am not saying exactly what I mean, I am not saying exactly what I think I am saying, that each one of you is not getting exactly what I am saying. We know this to be common sense. Nonetheless, we have to ignore it, ground ourselves in an error; which is why politics is corrigible. Laws are revisable. It's when we think that that's the be-all and end-all that we deny the rhetorical space.

So, going back to what I was saying, the idea of planetarity came to me in a flash when I had to confront the Swiss. Planetarity, as I said, was not for performance. On the other hand, it must be put in value form. I put it in a language form; you put it in the feminist rhetorical space. Both of us, both you and I, put it together in terms of multiplicity and supplementing and so on. You pointed to something that can otherwise be taken wrong: Does this then just ignore the fact that one's language is also marked by the discontinuities of language and languages? No. Thank you for that.

And let me say that I don't know if I made myself unclear in that afterword to *Imaginary Maps* (it's been a long time; the book came out, I think, in '95),[3] but I was saying that you can't just go on loving. That word "love" is not for me the name of the phenomenal affect. Like "planet," it's a risky name; it's a name for the effort to call forth a response. And for that you really have to acquaint yourself in humility with the pattern of desire of the other. That takes time and it does not resemble love. That is Shakespeare's point in *Henry IV*, where Glendower says, "I can call the spirits from the vasty deep." The answer is, "But when you do call, do they come?"[4] And do they answer you? So yes, I completely agree with you, it's not just being benevolent; that's a newer problem. In fact I took my cousin as a recruit for these schools. And he was so nice that they just loved him. I told him, "If you want to come again, hold back that ruling class attitude of being nice to these people and them loving you. That is destructive, because what can they do but love you superficially in return. Hold back your love, because it's not love."

I just want to give two examples. In the beginning when I went to Birbhum, they saw me—as these are not "uncontaminated" aboriginals that can be kept aboriginals by the landowner and author, no. The Communist Party of India (Marxist) was ruling there. They had talked these people into being thieves and so on. (I remain a socialist, but this has to be recognized.) The people from this district obviously thought of me as, you know, some stupid rich person who has come from Calcutta and can be taken advantage of. Many of them had no idea of Calcutta as a place. But they liked me, of course they liked me, and so did I like them—big deal! When I walked, they would say, "It looks like you are stingy, what will people say, why aren't we renting cars?" And they were also stealing. It was a long complicated story. Then I told them I was behaving like a foreigner thinking I could do business with them directly; no, it doesn't work that way, I'm going to give it to the big NGO. Okay, I am coming to my point, I'm not Bill Cosby. [Laughter.]

So I am not hugging them and kissing them and being benevolent, believe you me. No. I am not being caustic either, but nonetheless. . . . Anyway, this time, suddenly, they say to me, "Didi, save your money." And I realized there has been a huge epistemic transformation. Huge! This is what I am talking about. Not hugging and kissing and loving and being benevolent. It's coming from the other side. So I am riding in buses. This is a sign of what I am calling love succeeding. It comes from the other side. I don't even call it love to myself, I call it "crossing a bridge." I have crossed a bridge; it is coming from the other side. For hundreds of years we have oppressed them. So this was a completely unexpected change, and I never even thought of this one as an example. The example is unexpected. It's a nothing example, but you cannot imagine the epistemic change. And now they have complained to a small landowner that I am "rude" to them. I'm parsing that one.

The other example is that Medgar Evers College is honoring me on Monday. And the reason why I mention it is because you know very well that in general African Americans and the postcolonial don't mix. I've crossed a bridge; here is a response.[5]

See, those are the kinds of humble examples that I'm talking about, some response coming from the other side. So that's really not at all like being benevolent, and if it didn't come through in that afterword, I am glad you brought it up. Can I absolve myself from that one? I have gone on record so many times, which is why I began by saying "who are we to save the world?" Love is contaminated as a word, an undeserved word for phenomenal affect top-down. Because, of course, the subaltern may be happy; they say, "Oh please come back"—that's what breaks one's heart. How many times have you heard the Women's World Banking and such organizations quoting that as some kind of evidence! It's evidence of nothing but neglect from the top.

[Addressing Mayra Rivera:] Now let's come to hauntology. That was also very interesting because what you were doing was reading. Hauntology is, of course, a name for reading. And it was Derrida who gave us that idea, but then I talked about the Ghost Dance because Derrida had acted in a little film called *Ghost Dance,* but I got the idea of Ghost Dance from James Mooney and the Sioux. So I find no fault with your reading. I think of the reading strategy of going toward a past in order to cope with an unthinkable cataclysmic future as the Ghost Dance. This is indeed what I think Derrida was thinking about; and Derrida was reading Marx by speaking to Marx's ghost, as it were. Derrida is Hamlet, and Marx is Hamlet's father, you know. What a beautiful quote Derrida has in *Hamlet,* and that's how he ends, in English, the French book.[6] To speak to the ghost it's not just enough to emote. "Thou art a scholar; speak to it, Horatio."[7] Thou art a scholar. Takes scholarship in order to be able to speak to it, although it is *my* father. That, I think, is just an unimaginable kind of reading of *Hamlet.* I find fault with Derrida's reading of Marx but not with the idea of reading as prayer to be haunted. That's why I was talking about prayer as a pure performative. Just as you promise by promising, not by necessarily performing the promise, so it is with prayer. In the truth commissions, confession has been made a performative, and so prayer in that sense is also a performative, in the Austinian sense, and a prayer to be haunted. What you said in the end, that it doesn't have to be just one story—that, of course, has to be absolutely so in my understanding. That's how you learn to read and that's why it is different from rational choice. That's why we've been discussing academic freedom in my university, and it is all law and science, etc. I am now doing a colloquium which I am planning very carefully which is called "Academic Freedom and the Decline of the Humanities." The role of the imagination is this prayer to be haunted by whatever it is that one is reading.

I would like to read to you because the translation is not exactly right there. (Peggy [Kamuf] is an unbelievable translator, but the word *hantise*, which is not a French word really, could not be translated by Peggy as anything but "haunting.") Derrida is putting haunting against ontology, just as you are placing it with the Holy Ghost and the one-man theology. So the ontology notion will serve you better than just Spivak. And here it is: "Haunting does not mean being present. And *hantise*"—literally, "haunts stuff"—"must be introduced into the very construction of a concept"—in this case, Marxism. "Of all concepts we have to begin with the concepts of being and of time. Now, see, this is what we will call a hauntology."[8] In French, *hauntologie* sounds exactly like ontology, right? In the English we pronounce the "h." Hauntology, ontology. But in the English, of course, the homonym is gone. You see, Derrida was completely wedded to speech, as well as to writing. (This is a secret that I will reveal some other day.) So, between *ontologie* and *hauntologie*, the difference is nothing but a silent "h," which itself is something that we could talk about. "So between ontology and hauntologie, the only thing that opposes itself is an exorcism," in other words, the existential impoverishment of the philosophical—as the custodian of truth—as it brings ontology by reducing, reducing, reducing. Therefore, Derrida says, and I ask you to find out which *h/ontologie* he is speaking about, "*L'ontologie* encourages liberation." It's acculturation. He is speaking about ontology, the philosophical one. So to an extent, even doing conceptual philosophy, unless you allow yourself to be haunted by your subject, you cannot be as good. "Ontology is a conjuration," an exorcism to put hauntology aside, discounting the role of this prayer to be haunted in the radiation of truth. So indeed, I will not only go with you, but I will take it this far and say that this idea of hauntology is reading. I agree with what you said in the end, because collective memory is also a way of privatizing history; everything good is also dangerous. If it's powerful, it's also dangerous. So I think we really need to keep that in mind.

I will add something from my own religious tradition—but also not mine, as I have explained—about the misunderstanding of the word *bhakti*. The word *bhakti*, which carries within it the Sanskrit for "division," is always understood on the model of the Reformation. But it is not an attempt to make the individual relate to the divine in an unmediated, personal way. No. It is in fact allowing the individual to get into a discursive practice with divinity, and therefore it is a very strong critique starting from the fifteenth century of High Hinduism, but what it does give is affective inscriptions within which the individual then inscribes herself or himself. The names of the affective inscriptions are taken from popularized Sanskrit aesthetic theory—*rasa*—so that *bhakti* has in fact all of these different affective inscriptions, by which the devotee prays to be haunted, as it were, and thereby transformed.

I feel I could talk for another couple of hours right now [laughter], but this is where I am going to make an unwilling ending. So now you can do what you like with my response, and thank you.

[Applause.]

Stephen D. Moore: When we had lunch with Professor Spivak earlier, her only question about how the afternoon might unfold was, "What time are they going to kick us out of the room?" So from the moment of her arrival she made it clear that she was here just as long as we wanted her to be—and even before she knew what an easy audience we were going to be. So we are staggered at your generosity, your warmth, and . . . your utter comprehensibility. [Laughter.]

GCS: That's the best part!

Namsoon Kang (from the audience): I have some pressing questions that have been on my mind for a long time. They are about your controversial essay "Can the Subaltern Speak?" The first question that I have is personal: I am wondering whether you have thought that you should have given it a different title? And my second question concerns the fact that in an interview you said that when the subaltern speaks, that person is no longer a subaltern.[9] And then you didn't give much explanation about what is this speaking that you are mentioning.

GCS: Thank you. These are important questions; you haven't asked questions that could just be cast aside. I think that I might have given it a different title, but I'm glad also that I gave it this title because it provoked a lot of reaction that has been very instructive for me. As I said earlier today, the woman in the essay who hanged herself is my grandmother's sister, and was a friend of my mother. In 1926 she was seventeen and my mother was thirteen, so there were just four years of difference between them. When I found out, through my mother, that in fact she had left a letter I did some research. (I say that I learnt it in the family, so the question of veridicality comes in there too.) Other women in the family said, "Oh well, why worry about her, she was a scandal, she just killed herself over a man"—even though she had taken such good care, and at age seventeen, to wait until she menstruated to kill herself; this is not an easy thing. So I felt then that when the subaltern attempts to speak, she is not heard, and I was full of rage. (It's possible that this story will come out in the published proceedings of a symposium at Columbia titled "Reflections on the History of an Idea," which was on the twentieth anniversary of the essay itself.) What I was trying to do there was to get out of the Foucault-Deleuze thing, into affirming this woman in my own background, right? As I said before, I moved from that; I didn't remain in my own class.

But, to a certain extent, that rage is preserved in the rhetoricity of that question; I felt that later. This also shows how badly people read, because if they read carefully, then they would have known. But as I said, there is a cultural death in this country and elsewhere because the humanities are not taught carefully. Therefore, one doesn't recognize rhetoric any-more. Therefore when I came to this statement "the subaltern cannot speak," it should have been clear that I was speaking to this abominable example. It isn't a postcolonial essay; it's not against the British. I do say that the British criminalization of *sati* is an unquestioned good, but it is against Hinduism, and it is against class mobility for women. You know, people never read it like that because they just want to read it as postcolo-nial. The woman who gave me this answer, "Why worry about her, she was a scandal," is a woman with the same education that I have. We can still talk to each other in terms of ideas, and we do. In fact, if I succeed in giving that William James Lecture on Religious Experience at Harvard, it will be because she has helped me. Therefore, a woman of almost exactly the same education as me could not read what the woman who hanged herself was trying to say. Out of that rage came the rhetorical statement "the subaltern cannot speak." I'm happy that it provokes, generally speaking, speech from people who claim to be subalterns, to say "I'm speaking, so therefore the subaltern *can* speak," and I have nothing but contempt for that and also understanding.

But anyway, then comes another problem, which is that remark that you quoted, that when the subaltern speaks, he or she is no longer a subaltern. The postcolonial critic's sentimental use of the subaltern I find extremely unnerving. That word "subaltern" I get from Gramsci, right? When the subaltern is first defined, it's actually a military word. Gramsci was using it at first for reasons of censorship, but then it began to describe something which became a critique of capitalist encounters. So when the subaltern is able to be heard collectively by others, the subaltern has already entered a simulacrum, at least, of the public sphere. The subaltern is on the path of the Gramscian concept of hegemony. I'm not referring to the colloquial English word, which is all bad, but to the Gramscian concept of hegemony, which is like a *pharmakon*, medicine as well as poison. It is something good that can become, in the hand of the dominant, something bad. This is why Gramsci is quite different from Lenin. Therefore, it was a question of definitions. By definition, if the person is somehow heard collectively, then the subalternity is not. We don't want subalternity to last in the world. That's our work, to create infrastructures so that the subaltern becomes inserted into circuits of hegemony. That's why I said that. And obviously if all I said was that if the subaltern speaks, he or she is not a subaltern, I didn't give sufficient explanation.

When I was in one of the tribal areas, there was a man who was dragging a woman by the hair and beating her, and the woman was screaming. I was alone. No Hindu had ever overnighted in those places. I had sent my assistant home because it was *Vijaya*. I said to this guy, "Come on, it's a big festival, go back to your family." This is a Hindu guy and it is the high holiday. I was completely alone in this subaltern place. A man was beating a woman, and his mother comes to me and she says that I am her friend. That is suspicious to me, but she tells me: "Can't you do something about this? That's my son, he's done that to three women in succession, can't you just go complain to the *panchayat* and can't he be punished? Nothing is done here," and so on. She said *panchayat*, which is the smallest unit of local self-government, not some good-hearted NGOs coming in and changing things. And as a citizen, not a subaltern, I absolutely can talk to the *panchayat*, and so I did. So the subaltern tried to speak, to engage the public sphere, by speaking to me. This old woman collected seeds left by mice in holes and fields in order to have food to eat (a common practice). This is subalternity. She told me. She tried to speak. So I went to the *panchayat*, and I said, "Look here, you know, I am bringing news of some egregious stuff going on in Jonara, and in fact it is one of the women there who asked me to bring it before you, you should do something about it." And what was I told? (It was even a female *panchayat pradhan*, and she was treating me almost like a foreigner; she didn't know that I had been around for twenty years.) She said: "You know that domestic violence is really not an issue for the tribals. Domestic violence is not something to worry about at that level. There is so much other stuff to be done." (Domestic violence is a Hindu issue once you enter the middle class.) The subaltern cannot speak. This was just four or five years ago. You see what I am saying? So that's why I said that if she speaks, then she is no longer subaltern; this woman tried. So that's why it was understood to be such an absurdly stupid thing, Gayatri Spivak suggesting that the oppressed and dispossessed of the world are mute! Didn't they credit me with some intelligence? I mean I would at least be ashamed to say that even if I thought it. [Laughter.]

And so I close with the invocation of Meaghan Morris who acted as a real friend and said to Dipesh Chakrabarty: "Most people who criticize Gayatri's essay think the essay is entitled 'Can the Subaltern Talk?'" On that note, I thank you again.

❧ Appropriations

Planetary Subjects after the Death of Geography

JENNA TIITSMAN

I.

Ankur Jaiswal, a Bangalore call-center employee whose phone name is "Mike," regularly claims that he lives in America when questioned by suspicious U.S. callers. "They ask, 'Where in America?' I tell them I cannot disclose my location. But they are still suspicious and start asking about the weather."[1] Like most of his colleagues in South Asia, "Mike" is able to respond with the weather report, recent sports scores, and tidbits of American popular culture that are displayed on a large television screen posted in many call centers to aid employees feign a U.S. location. Why worry about location when the transatlantic call from the United States to India is a "local" one? Why does distance matter when the globe itself has been proclaimed a village? We live in an age that has proclaimed the death of geography. The world is said to be united into a singular universal community that lives in the abstraction of cyberspace. Real location no longer matters; so promise the internet, digital cable, and satellites. In fact, on its very first transatlantic exchange, even the telegraph was hailed as "an instrument destined by Divine Providence to diffuse religion, civilization, liberty, and law throughout the world."[2] Then, as now, communications technology was celebrated as the means to realize the promise of a singular global people united by the ideals of Protestantism, capitalism, and democracy. If our postmodern era does not accommodate the blatant religious missionizing of the ambitious Christian call of President Buchanan, the aspiration to unity in a nonmaterial realm still bleeds from Protestant history into contemporary American renditions of the power of communications technology to unite the globe and bury geography. However, in the frantic make-believe of South Asian call-center employees, one can hear the reminder that geography has not been successfully interred. The imaginary of the disembodied globe is still haunted by geographies that refuse to be absorbed into the ether and by the histories of colonialism, missionizing, and modern capitalism that these geographies reveal. Buried beneath such universalism is the persistent matter of local particularity.

The way we live in the world is bound to what we imagine the world to be. The imaginary of a universal, immaterial sphere in which we are intimately connected in common God-given humanity emerges in the West from a confluence of events—the Protestant Reformation, the rise of capitalism, the advent of modern science, and colonialism—that mark the beginning of the modern era. As colonial explorers and missionaries crossed oceans, the illusion of universal sameness, derived from Christianity and divorced from materiality and geography, promised to override local differences. However, the illusion of universal, disembodied sameness thrived only when geography and difference were adamantly ignored and simultaneously exploited. For example, the "natives" of South Asia shared a common religious origin with Europe, according to the European religious thinkers of the seventeenth through the twentieth centuries, but required firm rule from the advanced northern continent to guide them toward developed civilization.[3] This universalizing imaginary did not die with the move toward postmodernism in the Jamesonian sense, that is, as the cultural logic of late capitalism; it was merely transposed onto the disembodied, fluid plane of cyberspace.[4] Today, the assurance that communications technology has overridden geography and difference in an immaterial sphere to which everyone has equal access fuels notions that globalization will eradicate poverty and that the internet will spread democracy while, at the same time, multinational corporations fatten the wallets of their executives and Euro-American governments coerce regime changes in the Middle East and Africa. At the beginning of modernity religion became the structure for universal homogeneity; today the structure is cyberspace. In both forms, this imaginary of a global village is an insidious and dangerous illusion. The geography such an illusion disavows and on which such an illusion relies tells a different story, one in which alterity is not coerced into assimilation nor forged as a foil for the dominant subject.

Gayatri Chakravorty Spivak offers two imaginaries of the earth: globalization—the disembodied everywhere of information networks in which everything is accessible, simultaneous, and subsumed into an imagined same "system of exchange"—and planetarity—which offers infinite possibilities for difference in the refusal to assume the existence of a self-same subject against which an other must be posited. To dislodge the illusion of disembodied universality, we must first examine the matter and difference that sustain such an imaginary. In this essay I trace one trajectory of globalization back to the beginning of Western modernity in which Protestant ideals of a spiritualized kingdom exalted universalism, incorporeality, and unity. This imaginary has shifted terms; now we herald the promise of a disembodied network of communication and economic exchange in which democracy governs the unity of a wireless community. Under globalization's promise of the death of geography lies a religiously conceived, geographically bound system on which globalization depends. I will unearth a geography of cyberspace that illustrates how the disembodied sphere was built on a material network of undersea cables that follows the routes of early colonial voyages. I will further argue that the movement Spivak proposes from globalization to planetarity requires more than merely *thinking* the earth differently. Imaginaries of the earth provide a field of relationships that permits only certain social and economic realities, and these imaginaries are sustained by practices that construct such realities. Beneath the mythologies of universalism lie concrete and material practices of difference and domination upon which such universalized networks operate. If planetarity is to "overwrite the globe,"[5] as Spivak desires, we must shift our *practice* of living in the imaginary of globalization. I will show how our telecommunication practices affirm the imaginary of globalization. Only when we develop new practices can we truly live in the imaginary of the planet to which Spivak urges us.

II.

Spivak roots her distinction between planet and globe in the notion that "to be human is also to be an occasional and discontinuous animator of what we call timing and spacing."[6] Part of our humanity is the way in which we make "transcendental figurations" of the universe come to life.[7] Spivak relies on the conception that we cannot access space and time as unmediated realities separate from us but, rather, that we construct, order, and embody them. Geographies, I contend, cannot be established without interpretive work that calls into question the ideas of self and other. They are not fixed and steady ground, transparently mediated by our linguistic and graphical descriptors. Rather, geographies are lived renderings of space that always entwine with our understandings of where or even who we are and what we understand to be separate or different places. The notion of the "West," with its loose tie to a hemispheric designation that adamantly ignores the presence of most of its southern half illustrates this well. In Thomas Tweed's study of the tropes of space and time in religion, he understands geographies to be "autocentric framings that survey space in terms of the binary *here* and *there*, with *here* understood as the boundaries of the body, the home, or the homeland."[8] Geographies, then, always first reference their author. Even the bird's-eye view of satellite photography, which promised the end of subjective sight, was, I would argue, always already domestic. From the beginning, the satellite's distant cosmic perch was articulated in terms of national and military interests.

At the same time that an imaginary articulates the self, Spivak asserts, our labor as the animators of time and space always calls forth the possibility of alterity. How much difference is acknowledged and allowed to thrive depends on the imaginary. In planetarity, difference is inexhaustible.[9] It is neither subsumed into the same nor seen as a derived wholly other. In globalization, differentiation is a threat to the goal of universal continuity. The globe is ruled by refusal of alterity in the drive to think of the whole world as "nothing but neighbors."[10] Spivak claims that the logic of "love thy neighbor," when supplied with an imperial bent, can render alterity impossible. In the globe, there are no different bodies; there are no different places. The Christian logic here reduces the planet to a global village in which every other is nothing but a neighbor. The promise of such global familiarity is empowered by modern Western universalisms.

Western imaginaries of the universal were birthed in the thick of what is known as the modern era. While modernity itself is the subject of much controversy regarding its sources, definitions, and boundaries, what is thought of as Western modernity arose in the confluence of colonial movement, the Protestant Reformation, the rise of capitalism and the nation-state, and the birth of modern science. While modernity pretended to a certain coherence, many scholars have argued that modernity was never really seamless. Randall Styers, in *Making Magic: Religion, Magic, and Science in the Modern World,* traces the development of religion and magic as categories produced as part of the rise of modernity. By examining magic as a category shaped as a nonmodern foil for the adamantly modern categories of religion and science, Styers illuminates the labor of making modernity. In his words, "modernity itself has always been fractured, contested, and ultimately illusory."[11] In fact, as thinkers such as Bruno Latour have argued, modernity is perhaps best understood as a system of illusions that demand allegiance to intentional ignorance of the decidedly unmodern elements that sustain this system.[12] In this essay I am addressing the illusion of universal intimacy and likeness. Like much of the illusory nature of modernity's promises, universal sameness and the shrinking globe were sustained by the very real differences and distances they masked. The mythological sameness of the residents of the now-neighborly globe thrived on the Western exploitation of the colonial "other." In this way, the myth of sameness is sustained by the recognition of a sort of difference that always relies first on the presupposition of the universality of the Western, modern subject. In the same way, modernity's promise to overcome geography in a world made intimate by technologies of travel and communication was sustained by the very distances such technologies crossed. Converting the globe into a village relied on routes of travel for people and communication that reaffirmed these ideas of modern Western exceptionalism.

Religion played the original role of the modern unifier of global difference. In its earliest articulations as a category by Western thinkers, as traced by Jonathan Z. Smith, religion was thought of as a "ubiquitous human phenomenon."[13] When religious difference reared its ugly head during colonialism, quick moves were made to retrieve some primary sameness. Before the sixteenth century, the term "religion" designated obligatory ritual practice. From the sixteenth century to the eighteenth, religion was applied to colonial reports as a pancultural phenomenon that was increasingly divorced from specific ritual practice in order to point to a shared human characteristic. Smith links this particularly to the Protestant Reformation and colonialism: "It is the question of the plural *religions* (both Christian and non-Christian) that forced a new interest in the singular, generic *religion*."[14] By the eighteenth century, religion was an internal process of belief and thought and was understood to be properly human and definitively universal. This shift in definition reflects broader themes of the Western era that came to be known as modernity; in fact, many scholars argue that the claim of a universal, singular religion is a product of the Protestant-inflected modernity of the West.[15]

One significant, early leaning toward comparative religion rests with Lord Edward Herbert of Cherbury, who, in 1625, issued the imperative to look at "empirical data" in the study of religion. In such data, he believed, evidence would be found for "Common Notions" of religion that could be used as a defining set of essential truths.[16] Herbert wrote in the thick of Protestant and Catholic conflict in his native England and at the time that the first reports of "Eastern India" and its religions entered the scholastic field. He radically suggests that there is a sameness among these emphatically disparate peoples that can be recovered through an examination of "data" that is then translated into abstract categories. In fact, it is this very sameness that absolves the "Common Notions" from further interrogation: "The system of Notions . . . has been clearly accepted at all times by every normal person, and does not require any further justification."[17] At its most basic, asserts Herbert, religion is simply that which is universal to all humanity.

David Hume picks up this theme when criticizing the development of "Natural Religion" that followed Lord Herbert's writing. Hume argues that religion is neither an innate capacity of humankind nor one so unified as to pretend any sort of universality. The universals that seem to appear at religion's roots are merely a human response to domesticate inscrutable human origins or the absolute divine alterity to which those origins point:

> There is an universal tendency among mankind to conceive all beings like themselves, and to transfer to every object, those qualities, with which they are familiarly acquainted, and of which they are intimately conscious. . . . No wonder, then, that mankind, being placed in such an absolute ignorance of causes, and being at the same time so anxious concerning their future fortune, should immediately acknowledge a dependence on invisible powers, possessed of sentiment and intelligence. The *unknown causes* which continually employ their thought, appearing always in the same aspect, are all apprehended to be of the same kind or species. Nor is it long before we ascribe to them thought and reason and passion, and sometimes even the limbs and figures of men, in order to bring them nearer to a resemblance with ourselves.[18]

Hume makes the connection between the modern desire for universality and its emergence from an untenable confrontation with difference. His critique of modern universalism shares an anachronistic similarity to Spivak's critique of postmodern universalism, issued nearly 250 years later. Both disdain the process by which intolerance of the unknown is manifested in the project to make the strange familiar and both link the unknown to the search for human origins. For Spivak and Hume, the search for human origins by its nature must confront something other than itself; as such, it is the primary site of confrontation with alterity and a telling illustration of responses to difference in these two eras. The vertical alterity that is posited at the source of life must also be folded back into the determined sameness on which these modern and postmodern mythologies of the universal rely. Moreover, the manner in which original difference is reincorporated into Western sameness reveals the crucial roles of religion and communications technology in both the modern and postmodern mythologies of the universal.

In modernity, both vertical and horizontal alterity are posited against and then subsumed into a European religious universal that is enforced by coercive religious and military power. This is perhaps best illustrated by the development of the trajectory Lord Herbert launched that found a new manifestation in the introduction of ethnography to the study of religion two hundred years later. At the turn of the twentieth century, religious scholars developed a fascination with "pre-literate" cultures as a mythologized origin of civilization, both valued and denigrated as such. This is clearly seen in the work of the early anthropologist of religion, Edward Tylor, who, in 1871, developed the notion of *animism*, the attribution of a soul to objects by preliterate peoples.[19] He was followed by his students, Marcel Mauss and R. R. Marett, who sought a preanimistic phase of *mana*, or awe.[20] Marett posited mana as a more original phase that preceded animism's attributive activity with a feeling of veneration. Notably, like Herbert of Cherbury, Tylor, Mauss, and Marett explicitly employed their study of religion in the service of manufacturing a sameness (here in the form of a shared origin) across apparent difference. Notably, all four also constructed a conception of material reality as a natural site of empirical data that can be translated through discourse into unifying abstractions. In this way, local differences are manufactured into universals when translated from matter to thought. The silence of the constructed origins proposed by Tylor and Marett point to the invested valuation of discourse as a property of the civilized West. The scholarly production of texts functioned as an integral foil to the preliterate origin of religion the texts describe. Discourse as a disembodied practice that removes itself from material reality became the avenue to universalism.

The association of discourse with Western universalism and religion as the source of universal origins are carried into the current era. The secularism commonly associated with modernity and postmodernity does not break

from these earlier traditions of spiritualizing religion. Rather, the spiritualiza-
tion of religion ultimately birthed secularization. Randall Styers traces this
development through the emergent categories of magic, science, and religion.[21] The widening gap imposed between religion and magic ensured that
mundane, concrete, and local practices were relegated to magic while religion took its place in the ether as a disembodied unifier of humanity. From
the anthropologist Bronislaw Malinowski to the sociologist Max Weber,
magic was conceived of as pragmatic and religion as abstract. However,
positioning religion as a disenchanted, dislocated realm ultimately renders
religion apparently moot. Religion, it seems, got caught in its own net.
Styers turns to Bryan Wilson, considered the father of British sociology of
religion, who draws the line clearly from the universalization of religion as
the transcendent to the resulting secularization. Explaining these developments of religion as "gestures in the direction of secularization," Wilson
writes:

> Immanentism gives way to transcendentalism, which leads to a further
> removal of supernatural power from the lives of ordinary men in every-
> day situations. The world is disenchanted. . . . Local religion—now
> designated by urban man as the religion of the heath (heathen) or the
> village (pagan), and as "superstition"—demanded that wherever official
> religion existed, it should compromise and temporize with local need.
> When, however, men ceased to live in communities, when their lives,
> or the lives of the vast majority, were lived out in impersonal and
> functionally specialized contexts, so the locale in which religion had
> flourished best ceased to provide it with hospitality. However contemp-
> tuous the priestly or intellectual classes might become about the
> religion of local communities, it was in these communities that the
> demand for religion had been most sustained, no matter that they were
> disposed to eclecticism, syncretism, and superstition. It is to the passing
> of natural communities, in which people lived virtually all their lives
> and undertook most of their activities, that we may look for a significant
> part of the explanation of secularization, when that term is used to
> refer to the transformation of religious consciousness.[22]

The transcendentalism ascribed to religion ultimately renders it so distanced
from daily life that it fades from usefulness. As Styers points out, Wilson
frames this process in particularly geographic terms.[23] Religion lived best in

the heath and village; once it was evicted from these local homes, it became abstracted and then moot. The migration from life lived in the hometown to the notion of life lived "in impersonal and functionally specialized contexts" marks a defining sphere for human habitation in the modern age that depends on disregard for corporeality, location, and the constraints of geography.

In the place of universalism previously held by religion now stands its massive echo—the promise of a singular globe united not by our Common Notions but by capitalism, cyberspace, and democracy. In two of the recent popular texts on the benefits of global information networks, there are ample illustrations of the shift from religion to communications technology—particularly in its role as the transcendentalized setting for global economic exchange—as the maker of neighbors out of the globe. Jeffrey Sachs begins his landmark plan to eradicate poverty worldwide in *The End of Poverty: Economic Possibilities for Our Time* with a "global family portrait" that tells four stories set in Malawi, Bangladesh, India, and China.[24] In these stories, Sachs describes devastating global poverty and urges readers toward his plan to eradicate poverty—a plan in which the invention and dissemination of technologies and technological know-how play a crucial role.[25] The globe is no longer a village but a single family. Sachs promises, "The colonial era is truly finished. Even geographical obstacles can be overcome with new technologies."[26] This rhetoric of a technologically empowered global intimacy is articulated even more emphatically in the national bestseller hailing the blessings of globalization, *The World Is Flat: A Brief History of the Twenty-First Century*, in which Thomas Friedman argues that as of the year 2000, we have entered the era of Globalization 3.0.

> Globalization 3.0 is shrinking the world from a size small to a size tiny and flattening the playing field at the same time. And while the dynamic force in Globalization 1.0 was countries globalizing and the dynamic force in Globalization 2.0 was companies globalizing, the dynamic force in Globalization 3.0—the thing that gives it its unique character—is the newfound power for *individuals* to collaborate and compete globally. And the lever that is enabling individuals and groups to go global so easily and so seamlessly is not horsepower, and not hardware, but software—all sorts of new applications—in conjunction with the creation of a global fiber-optic network that has made us all next-door neighbors.[27]

In this text, brimming with enthusiasm for the promise of global intimacy wrought through the majesty of the communications network and the geo-political support of the spread of Western capitalism, the universalizing thread rooted in religious origins is alive and well in an age many consider secular.

Spivak addresses these conceptions of a unified, intimate globe in a post-modern context. According to her, these imaginaries are tools of our current geopolitical situation that ensure the illusion of disembodied intimacy while masking the real difference upon which such a global economic network relies. Globalization, as she posits it, is by definition immaterial: "The globe is on our computers. No one lives there."[28] Notably, the very immateriality of globalization is determined, for Spivak, by communications technology. The illusion of a technological no-space functions as religion did: it is a realm of purified abstraction in which difference is subsumed into a disembodied sameness without any apparent possibility for geographical distance.

> Globalization is the imposition of the same system of exchange every-where. In the gridwork of electronic capital, we achieve that abstract ball covered in latitudes and longitudes, cut by virtual lines, once the equator and the tropics and so on, now drawn by the requirements of Geographical Information Systems.[29]

Here the abstract divisions written onto physical space, for example, the equator, are pushed into virtual space thereby inaugurating an era in which spatial differences are overwritten by the illusion of a universally accessible system. Of course, just as in modernity, difference does matter. Like its religious predecessor, the universalism of the globe relies on difference as a foil to reinforce the coherence of the global self. Globalization presumes a self-same reality against which others are dichotomously positioned.

Spivak proposes "the planet to overwrite the globe."[30] Planetarity refuses the universalized sameness of globalization and offers instead difference not as perfectly different from me. The other in planetarity is not derived from the self-same subject:

> If we imagine ourselves as planetary subjects rather than global agents, planetary creatures rather than global entities, alterity remains unde-rived from us, it is not our dialectical negation, it contains us as much as it flings us away—and thus to think of it is already to transgress, for,

in spite of our forays into what we metaphorize, differently, as outer and inner space, what is above and beyond our own reach is not continuous with us as it is not, indeed, specifically discontinuous.[31]

Rather than function as the defining foil to the self, the other of planetarity is "indefinite."[32] Borders between the self and its outside fold into themselves and then split again in a dynamic refusal to separate with clear difference or sameness. The globalized "same system of exchange" is no longer a possible imaginary, nor is an other "a neat and commensurate opposite of the self."[33]

The planet does not recover "matter" or "nature" for a technologically saturated age; the idea of matter as opposed to technology itself is reconsidered in Spivak's articulation. In globalization, the immaterial subject of disembodied global communications is barely hindered by the geography it supersedes. The agent of globalization disregards the earth. Planetarity, however, does not offer the coherence of "natural" space; such an "unexamined environmentalism" serves the interests of globalization, invested as it is in the abstractions of the earth as a palatable concept ready for control.[34] Rather, planetarity refuses a clean break from the inhabiting subject and from the globalization it is intended to overwrite: "The planet is in the species of alterity, belonging to another system; and yet we inhabit it, on loan. It is not really amenable to a neat contrast with the globe. I cannot say 'the planet, on the other hand.' When I invoke the planet, I think of the effort required to figure the (im)possibility of this underived intuition."[35]

By recognizing these folding boundaries between the imaginaries of globalization and planetarity, Spivak allows for movement to the ethical planet without feigning the apocalyptic end of globalized encounter. However, in Spivak's avoidance of positing a materiality opposed to abstraction, she almost avoids materiality altogether. I propose that to actually overwrite the globe with the planet, we must recognize that the geographical information systems are not shaping a globe "cut by *virtual* lines" but one simultaneously cut and bound by the material lines on which our practice of these imaginaries of the earth depend. Materiality here cannot enter as the unspoken given. Our very forgetfulness of the technologies that constitute the globe Spivak decries is one of its most vital ideological weapons. The fiber optic cables on which the globe runs betray the histories of imperialism and colonialism that the globe works so desperately to obscure. These material fiber optic cables are an avenue to undermining the globe's powerful insistence on the disembodied universal and its dangerously empty promises of equality, democracy, and intimacy.

The imaginary of the earth as a universalized sphere of like neighbors—what Spivak calls the globe—was radically shaped by the history of Western colonialism in which innovations in transportation facilitated an understanding of the far corners of the earth as sites of difference to be conquered and assimilated. The colonial movement that participated in the birth of the universalisms of modernity gave rise to the global information networks of postmodernism and their universalisms. In the fifteenth through eighteenth centuries, the possibilities for sea voyage opened new worlds of "discovery" and became the stated motivation of an industry surrounding oceanic travel that produced explorers, scientists, inventors, manufacturers of navigational equipment, and traders. Most important, this industry also produced texts about the world discovered across the waters. The La Condamine expedition of 1735, for example, was intended to establish the shape of the earth but became a new instance of international scientific exploration. According to Mary Louise Pratt in *Imperial Eyes*, "There is one respect in which the La Condamine expedition was a real success, namely, as writing. The tales and texts it occasioned circulated round and round Europe for decades, on oral circuits and written."[36] The technologies of transportation were from the beginning embedded with technologies of communication.

These technologies of transportation and the discursive practices they enabled were never neutral. As discussed above, modern religion was deeply involved in a process of coercive assimilation of difference. The abstraction of concrete practices into articulations of sameness entwined the projects of universalism and disembodiment. However, as histories of colonialism have repeatedly shown, the existent differences were exploited as much as they were denied.[37] The particular was a necessary foundation for a discourse of universality. Today our discursive field relies on the technologies of the satellite, television, and internet. Each has been greeted with promises of a new possibility for a universal community and each has been historically developed, produced, and organized by national militaries and used for practices of monitoring (both military and scientific), education, and communication.[38] These technologies, like the technologies of colonialism, are employed to create both an imaginary of an immaterial globe of sameness and a material means of affirming the distances of the earth and the differences found on it.

It is to this tension between the particular and universal that I would like to turn now by examining the fiber optic cables on which cyberspace runs. Our world is crisscrossed by a net of cables that run underground and underwater, and make current discursive practice possible. Cables began as the first means of the transatlantic telegraph. With the advent of fiber optics, these old pathways have become the physical network that we think of as virtual reality. In 1858, the first successful transatlantic cable was laid. The first public message was sent on August 16 of that year, from Queen Victoria of England to U.S. President James Buchanan. His response via the new technology makes the links between colonial enterprise and these pathways of communication clear:

> It is a triumph more glorious, because far more useful to mankind, than was ever won by conqueror on the field of battle. May the Atlantic telegraph, under the blessing of heaven, prove to be a bond of perpetual peace and friendship between the kindred nations, and an instrument destined by Divine Providence to diffuse religion, civilization, liberty, and law throughout the world.[39]

In this way, the telegraphic pathways are an explicit continuation of colonial movement and already embedded in the project of Western universalism. The promise that communications technology would serve the universal came from the mythology that these technologies would overcome particularity by diminishing the need to travel from one location to a distant other. As James Carey announced in his study of the telegraph, "[T]he telegraph freed communication from the constraints of geography."[40] The dream of making everyone a neighbor seemed to be realized.

Fiber optic internet cables follow the same marine pathways as the telegraph and colonial exploration while more fully (dis)embodying the notion of a communications system detached from geographical space. The connection between colonial marine movement and contemporary technologies of communication comes to startlingly explicit expression in the website for a fiber optic cable system stretching 28,000 km of cable around Europe, the Middle East, Africa, and Asia.

> History tells us that in the space of twelve years, three Portuguese sailors unlocked the secret routes of Africa by finding a sea passage to the East via the Cape of Good Hope. . . . Vasco da Gama finally reached

India from Lisbon in 1498 . . . giving the Portuguese an alternative spice route and a monopoly on eastern trade. Today in the space of just over ten years, submarine fiber optic cables have become the modern vessels for trade and communications between international markets and the African continent. Now, five hundred years after Da Gama's trail-blazing journey, a new submarine cable system has been established which closely follows the navigator's route from Portugal, down the West Coast of Africa, around the Fairest Cape and finally landing in the East at India and Malaysia.[41]

Cyberspace explicitly promises a disembodied global village as the apex of Western colonial geographical expansion.

The most recent surge in cable laying, such as the linked South Atlantic Telecommunications cable no. 3, the West African Submarine cable, and the South Africa Far East cable described above, has been undertaken to support the explosion of outsourcing (call centers and Business Process Outsourcing [BPO]) now moving rapidly through the Asian subcontinent. India has been a primary early choice for outsourcing companies because, as BPO and call-center owners claim, out of the colonial past emerged a population that speaks English and is familiar with or able to learn British and American customs and work habits. India's success in the industry is also the result of postcolonial investments in higher education, including advanced training in information technologies (IT) at the eminent Indian Institutes of Technology.[42]

In many ways, India's successful claim on IT outsourcing seems to be the realization of the globe's promise. According to Sachs, because of the IT boom and concurrent economic reforms, India has risen from colonial occupation to become an eminent player in the global IT-based industry and has significantly reduced the national poverty rate.[43] However, this story reveals a globe that does not eradicate geography and difference into a neighborly universal but makes such distance and difference invisible while exploiting them. As Ankur Jaiswal's response to the suspicious American caller cited at the beginning of this paper illustrated, geographical difference is still very much alive. Jaiswal sidestepped the demand to disclose his location by virtue of the very technologies that facilitated the "local" call to India in the first place. Call centers and BPO teach us that the need for geography is satisfied by the appearance of geography as it is relayed over the technologies that promised the death of geography in the first place. The globe demands as much difference as it disavows. The illusion of a universally accessible economic and communications system in cyberspace depends on difference but demands that this difference be made invisible. Notably, the invisible hub of the internet coincides with the contemporary hub of empire; most internet activity passes through ten root servers located in the United States.

This same demand for invisible difference is echoed by the satellite, another technology that facilitates the imaginary of the globe. Indeed, it is only through the satellite that we have access to constantly updated pictures of the whole earth as one unit. Satellite practices shape the discursive/economic activities "that constitute what we know as 'the global.'"[44] Part of the promise embedded in tools such as Google Maps is the eradication of the need to translate the disjointed fragments of cartographical representations of the globe into a three-dimensional whole.[45] Suddenly, global representation seems transparent and seamless. In 1989, ABC became the first network to televise a satellite image with its use of a *SPOT* photo of a Libyan chemical weapons facility. At the time, ABC executives proudly announced that they could now "use satellite images to 'fly' viewers directly through battle zones during evening news reports."[46] Such flight promises transparent mediation of real events, but the illusion of global transparency is terribly misleading. It gives the effect of simultaneity while constantly offering distance and difference either through the geographical lengths of the submarine cables or the transcendent gaze of the orbiting satellites. We may be metaphorically flown to Libya by ABC, but we will constantly be aware that we have to "fly" to arrive at this foreign place to watch their distant events. The satellite promises the eradication of distance while affirming the distance that requires a "flight" in the first place.

III.

The imaginaries of the globe and planet are enmeshed with electronic communication technologies, but it is not my intention to offer technology a determining role in constructing these conceptions of the earth. Rather, these imaginaries must be understood as systems of practices by which we inhabit the globe or planet. Understanding more about material discursive practice from September 11, 2001, through our current "war on terror" can remind us that we are not consumers of a network laid down without our consent. We participate in these communications systems in ways that affirm the difference and distance between the self and the other while lauding the death of geography. Raymond Williams, in his landmark text on television, coins the term "mobile privatization" to name the paradoxical conditions that shaped the birthing ground of modern industrial communications technology. These conditions are "characterised by the two apparently paradoxical yet deeply connected tendencies of modern industrial living: on the one hand, mobility, on the other hand the more apparently self-sufficient family home."[47] Williams points to the latter decades of the nineteenth century as the origin of this model, which is particularly evident in the dramatic work of Ibsen and Chekhov—the "centre of dramatic interest was now for the first time the family home, but men and women stared from its windows, or waited anxiously for messages, to learn about forces, 'out there,' which would determine the conditions of their lives."[48] This system offers the apparent eradication of distance since everywhere can be reached from within the home while affirming the boundaries of that home as a secure, domestic space safe from the lurking dangers of difference.

Sitting still in my home is a practice of distance and safety. Particularly after September 11, 2001, the fantasy of a self-sufficient cyber home has been the focus of scientific and industrial investment that marks the advent of a new phase in domesticity and communications technology—what Lynn Spigel calls the "smart house." In such a house, the division of inside/outside and work/home are erased as the home becomes a "sentient space" that integrates media into a naturalized domestic sphere and makes physical travel unnecessary. Lynn Spigel begins her discussion of the cyberhouse with a quotation from the 2002 premiere issue of *Broadband House*. The editor, Scott DeGarmo, went to photograph a penthouse in New York City for an article on "High Tech Havens" just a few days after September 11. He describes the evening in his editorial: "On that evening . . . we felt the sadness hanging over New York—and the nation. And yet, atop the residential building . . . we also felt another powerful emotion—the sense of being safely at home. . . . The home is a refuge to which we head when trouble strikes. The country was reminded of that on September 11."[49]

In Spigel's analysis, September 11, 2001, marked the end of a time in which First World men realized their power in their freedom to move through and colonize space. Now the home has become the new domain of power as danger restricts travel.[50] What has developed instead of unrestricted movement is the cosmopolitanism of the hybrid home—a site of work and leisure, brick and silicon, inanimate and "thinking" technologies, and "here and there." This last phase seems to promise the death of geography, but, however obscured, geography remains indelibly part of our apparently dislocated media communications. Spigel reminds us that "even as [the smart house] goes global it uses technology to police its boundaries and purify the perceived dangers of far-off places."[51] I would add that the smart house is an integral part of our discursive practice of establishing distance and difference, now from the safety of our sofas. Recently, of course, domestic communications technology takes a new form as increasingly mobile: now there are smartphone apps and an industry of technology to facilitate mobility such as GPS systems. Now we may leave the home, but we bring our practices of dividing space between home and the dangerous outside with us. These technologies function as ways to negotiate a threatening external space by remaining "linked up" to the safety of the domestic sphere.

Such an understanding of the material practice of media refuses the innocence of the "consumer" and complicates notions of planetarity as an alternative to globalization. The very fact that we cannot conceive of the planet without the technologies of electronic communication and the satellite makes achieving planetarity dependent on globalization. This is not simply a fatalism rooted in the colonial, neocolonial, and global history enmeshed in any planetarity we can imagine now or in the future. Rather, it is a determined recognition that the planet will be built on the globe. Refusing to acknowledge the ways in which the globe will still be practiced by the planetary subject threatens to engage the same process of obscuring relationships of dependence on which the globe thrives. Moreover, such a refusal risks the loss of tremendous possibilities for realizing the planet.

An excellent example of what a planetary practice might be comes from Lisa Parks's study of satellites. In *Cultures in Orbit: Satellites and the Televisual*, Parks offers an analysis of the Australian aboriginal television station, *Imparja TV*.[52] By using satellite broadcasting, Australian aboriginals are able to import shows from around the globe, such as *The X-Files*, *Star Trek*, and, years ago, *Dallas*.[53] These shows are integrated in the broadcast schedule with content produced by and for aboriginals such as *Nganampa Anwernekenehe*, a program that features stories about Aboriginal cosmologies, community-produced stories on traditional lifestyles, and discussion of social issues.[54] Satellite has proved particularly useful for a community that desires contact with the outside world but has also suffered the cultural exploitation wrought by global voyeurism. *Imparja TV* uses the global reach and yet limited footprint of satellite broadcasting to produce television that can be seen only locally but is able to show international programs.[55] "Imparja" means footprints in the Aboriginal Arrernte language.[56] In satellite speak, a footprint is a region that can receive a certain satellite signal. Parks, however, understands this geographically bound space as part of the project of *Imparja TV* to use the satellite "as a means of territorial reclamation and cultural survival in postcolonial Australia."[57] As such, the satellite footprint is not merely a disembodied telecommunications signal, nor is it simply a geographic designation. Rather, the footprint is a "cultural territory shaped by the process of downlinking and uplinking television signals."[58] The conception of geography is here written through satellite activity, and the satellite reach is in turn determined by the geography in which it has meaning. Alterity is recovered here in a matrix of geo-techno-cultural self-inscriptions. Parks introduces the concept of the footprint as a "cultural topography in which spatial and temporal imaginaries accumulate, mix, sediment, and stir."[59] The planetary subject Spivak desires would understand that while the landscape is never purely physical, the global reach of ethereal satellite signals is never divorced from the ground the signals shape and on which they depend.

There is no access to a planet not already carved into territories of difference and marked by new strategies of domesticity. The terrifying truth of our postcolonial condition is that if there is a planetary salvation on the horizon, it is one built by the militaries and economic might of the so-called First World. However, this is not a new or unique condition—recourse to social change is always already enmeshed in a complicated relationship that determines its dependence on the very structures it wishes to dismantle. It is impossible, then, to forget that the very technologies that inscribe our difference on the physical face of the earth do so by connecting us for the purposes of communication. Recent developments in subversive techno-communications (like *Imparja TV*) hold open the possibilities of new modes of speech and new means of connection, identification, and relationship. Postcolonial discursive practice demands a concrete engagement with the material conditions on which it depends so that we can refuse the detachment of discourse from embodied reality and find methods of participation in subversive techno-communications strategies that will shape a planet and facilitate such planetary subjects. Here I find the opening possibility, if not postcolonial mandate, of imagining an electro-communications future of planetarity. As Lynn Spigel notes, "if we do not imagine the future, then Panasonic, IBM and Microsoft most certainly will."[60]

To take Spivak seriously, we cannot enter planetarity while maintaining a sense of materiality as a derived other to our rarefied discourse. The practice of abstracting discourse from its very material movement serves only to bolster the sort of difference on which globalization depends even while denying it. Just as discourse must be remembered as a situated practice, so must the communications technologies that facilitate it. Likewise, religion cannot be revered as an ethereal sphere discontinuous with the local and mundane. Religion in modernity may have been separated from the material and pragmatic, but, as Randall Styers notes and as we have seen in colonial histories, religion in every imaginary has depended on and shaped the cultural topography in which it lives. The planetary subject must recover a valuation of geographic particularity and the spinning network that cables it together. The notion that media moves outside of space and in a plane that has long forsaken geography is reinforced by the practice of refusing to recognize the productive participation of the so-called consumer in accessing, relaying, and constructing media and communication. Unearthing the materiality of discourse as a geographically situated practice may be what allows us to hold ourselves accountable for the purported death of geography and its weighted history. The cultural topography we author as planetary subjects may provide an earth that facilitates the flourishing of local relationships as constitutive of the network of global connection in which they participate.

❧ Love's Multiplicity: *Jeong* and Spivak's Notes toward Planetary Love

W. ANNE JOH

What deserves the name love is an effort—over which one has no control yet at which one must not strain—which is slow, attentive on both sides—how does one win the attention of the subaltern without coercion or crisis?—mind-changing on both sides, at the possibility of an unascertainable ethical singularity that is not ever a sustainable condition. . . . Without the mind-changing one-on-one responsible contact, nothing will stick.
GAYATRI CHAKRAVORTY SPIVAK, *A Critique of Postcolonial Reason*

Is there a way that we might struggle for autonomy in many spheres, yet also consider the demands that are imposed upon us by living in a world of beings, who are, by definition, physically dependent on one another, physically vulnerable to one another? For violence is, always, an exploitation of that primary tie, that primary way in which we are, as bodies, outside ourselves and for one another.
JUDITH BUTLER, *Precarious Life*

Because I am an academic with modest intentions, who is driven by desire for theory in a theory-driven context, that I want to write about love conjures up all kinds of images and insecurities. One wonders if it is even possible to write about love without sounding trite, sappy, sentimental, and soft. Does love free us or enslave us? Perhaps it does both? Somehow writing about and on love seems not such an edgy endeavor after all. Residues of both disdain and desperate search for love have left their imprint.[1] Battling with resurgence of disdain if not outright suspicion coupled with secret guilt, I am drawn again to the possibility of what Gayatri Chakravorty

Spivak refers to as the "uncoercive rearrangement of desire."[2] Perhaps this rearrangement of desire without coercion is something akin to what Christians often experience as love that is the fruit of *metanoia*—change of heart. Such a change of heart allows one to realize that our being is always positioned/directed toward the other. I offer perspectives on love using the Korean concept of *jeong*. While Spivak is not writing explicitly about *jeong*, I want to suggest that *jeong* can be employed for philosophy, theology, and ethics in ways similar to which the French neologism *différance* has been employed. In our efforts to learn from the other, ways of living by, with and through *jeong*, I contend, is an ethical response to suture our torn selves with one another. It is an ethical practice of responding to the other that resonates with Spivak's observation that "To be human is to be intended toward the other."[3]

Since writing on this concept elsewhere, I have had time to think what this concept adds or does not add to love.[4] *Jeong* combines agape, philia, and eros—all three interweaving to form a kind of love that is difficult to define and conceptualize, but often practiced in the everyday relations with the other. *Jeong* is a signifier peculiar to the Korean language and worldview, and it is an untranslatable signifier, but it nonetheless names a phenomenon that exceeds that language and operates on a fundamental level in other cultures. As such, it is the object of philosophical and ethical reflection in those cultures—for example, in the work of Spivak. *Jeong* is not something unique to Koreans; a form of it is practiced by many cultures, and those forms are often not identical to the dominant discourses on love. By bringing *jeong* into our particular conversation, I am arguing that it will serve us well to learn the different languages of love that have been foreclosed in the past. I am asking that we enter into the epistemic structure of many ordinary people, while fully aware of the limits to what can be known in full transparency. There's something about *jeong* that keeps its opacity.[5]

Jeong is that which cannot be wholly repressed or easily dissected into parts, for its fluidity defies any attempts to define its boundaries. Experience of *jeong* between the self and the other opens a space in which we begin our journey of awakening to the other and to the self. *Jeong* makes difficult our easy and often tempting impulse to enclose the other into retricted binary constructs by resisting the self-other binary. Years ago, I remember thinking that *liking someone* was even more serious than *loving someone*.[6] Perhaps this was so because of my familiarity with *jeong* more than love.

Somehow, love always seemed very clear-cut whereas *jeong* was much scarier because experience of *jeong* allows one to recognize the complexity, vulnerability, and fragility of the other. While *jeong* makes sense to me, I have wondered if I should cease foregrounding *jeong* and make the best of love.[7] There are various reasons for this but primarily it is because *jeong* is a new and foreign concept. I have wondered how long it would take before it makes its way into the larger theological context. Even as I want to infuse our talk on planetarity with this concept/practice, there are persistent questions and suspicions. I ask myself: Is there a danger that *jeong* could aid and abet new forms of financialization of the globe where the Native Informant is violently shuttled back and forth, and also either complicit or foreclosed? Is it possible to become a subject without foreclosure of others? Yet can love really do the hard work of emancipation? In a world where a "litany, a prayer of pure sorrow and pure loss . . . falls from the lips of millions of refugees every day: whether they be deportees, people besieged, those who are mutilated, people who starve, who are raped, ostracized, excluded, exiled, expelled,"[8] is it still possible to have hope in love? We have no choice but unreservedly to have hope.

Through various readings of Spivak's works I have been encouraged to stay with *jeong* because her complex notion of love opens toward *jeong*. Spivak's thoughts on the need to learn other languages, in order to facilitate a kind of one-to-one, student-by-student learning, compels me to keep writing about *jeong*. My translation of *jeong* "risks fraying at the edges," but since it is "done in love," I hope this fraying will be minimal.[9] Rather than aiming for accuracy in translating *jeong*, I offer my interpretation of *jeong* while knowing that it's not a question of mastery or nonmastery but "gradations" of interpretation. I'm also encouraged by Trinh Minh-ha, who argues that a good translation is one that takes off and departs from literal meaning such that in taking off "it creates for itself another space." Translation then can remain loyal to the letter but also to the spirit or the "lived quality of that experience. . . . This process is a re-creation . . . rather than mere illustration, imitation, or transfer of meaning."[10] Translation, then, is always an act of love but also one of disruption. *Jeong* is not English, and so it will be slowgoing. Nonetheless, because it adds another dimension to our talk about love, in this essay, I want to explore this notion even further as we engage in our "planet-talk," this provisional "open field plan work," with unanticipated results. My work at an uncoercive rearrangement of desire in this particular academic context, by and through *jeong*, will be slowgoing, and as Spivak so rightly observes, this learning is as mysterious as learning to ride a bicycle or learning to swim. During this learning period one falls off the bicycle constantly or constantly sinks to the bottom of the pool (and sucks in water—of which our own bodies are made) until suddenly, one is swimming or riding a bike. Soon, I hope, *jeong* becomes as familiar to those of us in the Anglophone academy as certain German or French words, such as *unheimlich* or *jouissance!*

The essay begins by examining Julia Kristeva's notion of abjection. Abjection describes a dimension of violence in our primary ties that constitute the making of the self. Spivak is right to note that the aim of psychoanalysis is to access the subject to strengthen the agent "to restore social viability."[11] While abjection reflects the state of our psyche, Spivak's use of foreclosure adds a critical postcolonial sociopolitical dimension to abjection. I will use Kristeva's notion of abjection in conjunction with Spivak's foreclosure to foreground relational dynamics lacking in the dominant understanding of love. Foreclosure and abjection are ways by which exclusion and expulsion take place on many levels. The second part of the essay addresses the failure and inadequacy of love to account for abjection and foreclosure. In the spirit of pluralization of love that would give birth to a sustained collective effort toward planetarity,[12] I examine *jeong* as one possible dimension or form of love as a viable option for bettering our planet-talk. As we begin to speak in many tongues and from different places, I argue that *jeong,* in its own unique way, helps us to be open to the pluralization of practices of love/s. By bringing *jeong* into conversations about love, my goal is not to replace love with *jeong* or to imagine that it is superior to love, but to propose that *jeong* is one specific dimension of love among many different modes of love in the world. Christianity has foreclosed many practices and interpretations of love. One of the common metaphors for *jeong,* which I have often heard, is that *jeong* is "sticky" (about which I shall have more to say below). Perhaps it is *jeong* that will make Spivak's one-on-one contact adhere, or "stick."

The argument of this essay is threefold. I argue, first, that the dominant Western discourse on love is too limited and continues in its failure to understand love in its practices; second, that dominant Western liberal understandings of love work often only to reinforce the civilizing mission of the West and of Christianity, thus foreclosing other practices of love; and third, that our most fruitful move toward planetary loves requires a widening and deepening of the notion of love through learning other languages of and for love. In this regard, I examine *jeong* as one multiplicity, an attempt at pluralization of love.[13] So, here we go with my love notes toward planetarity . . . notes seeking ever-widening and deepening "planet-think," as Spivak comments, cultivating "the mind-set where you imagine that you're on this moving thing in outer space. . . . [W]hat the hell is over against you? What is the other side of this little planet?"[14] I remain in my obstinacy that *jeong*, ever imperfect as love, will add to the pluralization of love, for it might allow "the imagining of a necessary yet impossible planetarity in ways that neither my reader nor I know yet."[15]

SETTING THE PROBLEM: ABJECTION AND FORECLOSURE

> Abject peoples are those whom industrial imperialism rejects but cannot do without: slaves, prostitutes, the colonized, domestic workers, the insane, the unemployed. . . . Inhabiting the cusp of domesticity as its constitutive, inner repudiation: the rejected from which one does not part. . . . Abjection is that liminal state that hovers on the threshold of body and body politic—and thus the boundary between psychoanalysis and material history.
>
> ANNE MCCLINTOCK, *Imperial Leather*

The practice of *jeong* might be understood to be especially difficult for "abject peoples," precisely because they have been abjected. What is interesting to note is that it is also within cultures of abjection that *jeong* often emerges, and so the notion of abjection needs to be examined closely in that context. Abjection, subjectivity, agency, difference, and the relationship between the self and other are all intricately connected. What is important to keep in mind is the presence of *jeong* in the midst of abjection and that this presence is precisely what in the final analysis contests the logics of domination and oppression.

Abjection is a helpful notion, complexly examined by Julia Kristeva, the French psychoanalyst of self and society. "Abjection" can be loosely defined as an operation of the psyche that requires the expulsion and exclusion of that which threatens the formation of one's identity. This process assumes that identity, especially the subject of the dominant West, is shaped and formed in opposition and as antagonistic to the other. However, the abjected is never fully extinguished. In times of crisis, the abject becomes usable and necessary for reassuring and shoring up the disintegrating yet dominating self. The abject is understood as that which the self perceives as unclean, foreign, and improper. Kristeva argues that the psyche needs the other as object in order to become a speaking subject. The abject is everything that the subject feels it needs to expel in order to create its own subjectivity. The abject, once expelled, marks the boundaries and the borders of the self as both deeply repressed inside and expelled outward by the psyche. The subject understands the abject as threatening the fabric of her social order. The abject continues, however, to defy the subject's comfort in clear and absolute lines of demarcation and must constantly be jettisoned from the self. Inasmuch as the abject is jettisoned, it is experienced as "garbage." In short, the abject is the "refused refuse."[16]

The abject haunts the subject as its outwardly projected boundary. Yet it is a boundary that unwillingly is transgressed: the subject cannot divorce herself from that which she abjects. The abject is "something rejected from which one does not part." Having fabricated an anxious border between subject and other, abjection reveals a society's precarious hold over the fluid and disorderly interplay of individual and collective psyches. Abjection is thus not something to be overcome but that which must be acknowledged and embodied as irreparably part of our very selves. All people, Kristeva seems to claim, engage in the process of abjection and foreclosure of another in this process of becoming. Moreover, this process as part of the inner psychic world often materializes in the social, historical, and collective work of dominant groups, namely, acts of foreclosure and abjection of another group.

Psychoanalytic theories of abjection tend to presuppose the givenness of this process of abjection in human development and that the relationship between the subject and the other is antagonistic.[17] I would argue that our understanding of the process of becoming a separated self is at its core not only violent but also produces an ongoing cycle of violence stemming from the individual and moving to the collective psyche. However, abjection and its attending violence need not be part of our subject formation. I am proposing an alternative way to understand self as distinct from others without antagonism—a way in which the subject recognizes its intimate connection with other differentiated subjects as subjects, without the abjecting violence that is so widespread. In order to dismantle our impulse to kill or erase the other in order to feel we exist, we must first learn to become subjects without the oppositional other. When I use the pronoun "we," I have in mind a largely Western audience but one in whom speakers and agents like myself can only "fit" with some discomfort. It is a we that presumes a shared audience, but the sharing is problematic.[18] Since the cycle of abjection occurs in most all of us, all of us are in need of learning new ways of becoming subjects. Violence is indeed a violation of our most primary ties to others and to the collective. I want to be clear that Kristeva's understanding of abjection is valuable to understanding the self, but one does wonder if she assumes that the process of abjection is normalized in her understanding of how the self becomes. Might it be possible to envision the becoming of a self without abjection and foreclosure? The mending of such a process of abjection, for Kristeva and perhaps for Christian tradition as well, can be said to reside in understanding the love of the other as inextricably tied with the love of the self.

Similarly, taking from Lacan, Spivak observes that foreclosure is a "form of psychic defense . . . which involves the 'rejection of affect.' . . . [R]epression cannot purely and simply disappear . . . it can only be gone beyond."[19] For Spivak, foreclosure is that which is expelled from the Symbolic, yet reappears in the Real which "carries the mark of that expulsion."[20] However, Spivak's foreclosure is not just psychic but involves geopolitical differentiation of the ethical subject of the European Enlightenment tradition, and in this regard the Native Informant is the "mark of expulsion."[21] The Native Informant, similar to the abject, functions as the mark of undecidability that is neither completely excluded from Western reason as its grounding condition of possibility nor is merely a subject of Western rationality. The foreclosured Native Informant is not erased, but occupies an (im)possible space of double inscription. The Native Informant is "foreclosed but the marks of that foreclosure remain legible. It is this legibility that persistently interrupts."[22] Like the abjected body, the Native Informant as the foreclosed is often used to shore up the construction of a particular dominant understanding of the self. Abjection and especially foreclosure, as Spivak discusses it, in connection with the Native Informant, is much more aligned with the Freudian notion of disavowal, which plays on the dynamic of refusal/ exclusion, and at times retrieval/inclusion, when necessary. One can go further and say that the foreclosed, like the abject, is necessary for the formation of the psychic and social self in the dominant episteme.

Judith Butler's work on foreclosure is also helpful here. For Butler, the subjugation and subordination of the subject begins with the foreclosure of certain types of desire. Like Kristeva, Butler assumes that both foreclosure and abjection constitute a necessary part of the subject's becoming. The logic of exclusion and expulsion is built into their understanding of the formation of the subject. I interpret their lack of questioning the process of abjection in the first instance as inadvertently normalizing violence as part of the becoming of the subject. In *Excitable Speech,* Butler argues that the foreclosed is shut out completely while simultaneously the idea of foreclosure is continuously invoked. This creates a context in which subjects are always pitted against one another in a constant war to exist.[23]

Again, I find both Butler's and Kristeva's reading of abjection to be useful, yet not fully satisfactory, in understanding the psychic life of the subject. They both accept that abjection is inevitable. In fact, Butler accepts this as the "inaugural trauma" and proceeds, as Kristeva does, from that point to seek ways to find restoration. Again, it is possible to argue that abjection does not have to be part of the formation of the subject, or if it is, perhaps we need to explore how deepening our understanding of love in all its variations might work to mend the torn fabric of the self.

If our collective identities are formed in antagonistic relationship to others and if our collective or individual identities rely on rejecting what is different, then it seems unavoidable that violence will always be present. The alternative I suggest is for us to find ways of becoming subjects that are not opposed to another by abjecting the other.[24] Abjection and foreclosure are forms of psychic, discursive, social, economic violence against the other. It seems that this also has a direct implication for how we interpret theological anthropology. Abjection and foreclosure are in violation of our belief and promise of the *imago Dei.* In face of Spivak's excavation of the new Hollander and the man from Tierra del Fuego, who are needfully retrieved and at times necessarily foreclosed and abjected, how do we respond to the singular position of the Native Informant, the abjected, without blindly falling prey to that foreclosure? Vacillating from being the "lost object" to falling prey to the more sophisticated method of being named the "vanguard," are there ways that one could be opened up by that which faces possible indeterminate and indefinite foreclosure and abjection? Spivak reminds us to "not accuse ourselves" but to make a place for logic as not only a property of Europe so that we "grant the subaltern, the foreclosed, the abjected, possibility of their own logic."[25]

How might we overcome violence? How can we practice an ethics of respect for irreconcilable differences? Is it possible to seek justice and mutuality without erasing all our particularities into a form of universalisation?[26] Perhaps, just perhaps, if we engage in the kind of "planet think" and "planet feel," "our other . . . cannot be the self-consolidating other, an other that is a neat and commensurate opposite of the self."[27] It is only when we recognize the abject as a profound part of our psyche that it becomes possible to overcome violence and to love our neighbor as ourselves.

INTRODUCING JEONG

To be human is to be intended toward the other. . . . If we imagine ourselves as planetary subjects rather than global agents, planetary creatures rather than global entities, alterity remains underived from us; it is not our dialectical negation, it contains us as much as it flings us away.

GAYATRI CHAKRAVORTY SPIVAK, *Death of a Discipline*

So, what's love got to do with all this? Most of the time, as Tina Turner so rightly laments, "it's only a secondhand emotion. . . . A sweet old-fashioned notion." Before we speak of any kind of love or its various formations, my dormant sense of guilt for even writing on what seems to have become a sappy, seemingly unemancipatory concept compels me to at least offer a preliminary critique of love—a very provisional and preliminary critique at that.

The notion of love is deeply problematic for having been so readily valorized by the civilizing-Christianizing mission and Enlightenment ethics. Love's discourse should be closely examined for its contribution to colonialism. Those who have been abjected cannot ignore the connections between love, reason, benevolence, and imperialism. For scholars such as Dawn Rae Davis, love is a "problem for feminist postcolonial theory and philosophy" precisely because the discourses of love and benevolence were used to disguise imperialism's violence.[28] Rather than the often assumed transparency of love, Davis proposes what she terms as "the ability of not knowing" as a revolutionizing possibility of love "to feminist practices freed from the humanist/imperialist impulse that is dangerous."[29] In this "ability to not know"—similar to Spivak's recognition of "contrived collectivities" and "limits to what can be known"[30]—Davis concludes that transparency is not possible.

In her book *The Empire of Love,* Elizabeth Povinelli links the navigation between thick kinship, face-to-face socialities and what she terms "stranger sociality"—seemingly incommensurate contexts. Drawing from her own personal navigation of these two contexts—that of "radical fairies," those deeply involved in queer counterpublics, and as one who also lives and moves within the Australian indigenes—Povinelli offers insights on the connections between liberal governance and forms of love. How is love understood in these different contexts? How is love practiced and embodied in these communities and in the formation of "empire"? Central to Povinelli's work is her critique of Enlightenment liberalism. For Povinelli, the problem with this liberalism is the assumption that discourses were the agents of social life, that there is such a thing as the sovereign subject, a genealogical society, individual freedom, that our choices are only derived from binary oppositions and, most important, that any and all other potential and possible positions and practices of love and sociality "were impractical, politically perverse, or socially aberrant."[31]

Povinelli's book is an examination of intimacy as a form of "immanent dependencies among indigenous and queer people."[32] After examining what she argues has become "normative love," she declares that "love is a political event."[33] For Povinelli, love, intimacy, and sexuality are not about desire, pleasure, or sex per se, "but about things like geography, history, culpability, and obligation; the extraction of wealth and the distribution of life and death; hope and despair; and the seemingly self-evident fact and value of freedom."[34] In her scathing critique of love as a form of empire, and as practiced in the language of empire, she finds that such liberal love opposes other ways of living and practicing love. Other loves are foreclosed. Love, within Enlightenment liberalism, argues Povinelli, is understood as a higher civilizational form, even though it happens only between two people. It is claimed that "love changes history even though its own history stretches no further than its own performative duration and even though it has no social anchor beyond its own self-positing."[35] She observes that any other forms of love that might possibly be based on lust, tribalism, race, kinship, or religion are considered not "true love." At the same time, love is also often described in the Western liberal paradigm as a loss of self in another, even as such love is "often opposed to lust because in lust the self dissolves into the body and yet without a little lust, love may be nothing more than friendship."[36] With saying things like, "she is not simply my sister, she is more: she is my best friend," European history gets inserted into the indigenous social imaginary. This local kind of intimacy is, from the perspective of the indigene, an intensification of kinship rather than its negation. Furthermore, she notes that her Aboriginal friends indicate their closeness by intensifying social relation. They say, "sister-sister."[37]

Let us turn now to the notion of *jeong*. In Korean contexts, *jeong* saturates daily living and all forms of relationship. Often I am caught off guard when I hear everyday folk using the concept in creative phrases with one another—phrases like "oh you are so stingy, you have no *jeong*"; "That is not generous at all! There's no *jeong* in you"; "She has such a good heart. She has so much *jeong*"; "There's an overflow of *jeong* in that person." If one sits at a hair salon and eavesdrops, one can be guaranteed of hearing a reference to *jeong*. I in no way want to give in to binary thinking, but let me note that where one sees much individualism, one also hear less talk of *jeong*. On the contrary, those who are abjected or the gendered subaltern often seem more at ease on calling upon the power of *jeong* in sustaining their relationships. *Jeong* is bodily and physical as well. It is in touching, and in the doing of sustaining relationality. As a cultural concept and practice, *jeong* encompasses, but is not limited to, notions of compassion, affection, solidarity, vulnerability, and forgiveness. Here, let me just say few things in passing regarding each of these elements.

Compassion is not pity but rather, as Jean-Luc Nancy observes, "a contagion, the contact of being with one another in this turmoil. . . . [I]t is the disturbance of violent relatedness."[38] As a significant component of *jeong*, compassion has a way of making difficult our desire for easy boundary-making. The concept that comes to mind as I articulate more on *jeong* is the Hebrew notion of *hesed*. I will not develop this connection here, but I do believe that there is a deep connection between the practice of *jeong* and the practice of *hesed* that can deepen our understanding of ontic dimensions of theological anthropology and Christology.[39] *Jeong* is first of all affection, but it is not at all a cuddling feeling of affection; rather, it constitutes the affective part of our psyche and our relatedness with one another through a deeper kind of adhering. *Jeong* is affective and as such contests dominant Western tendencies of univocality, where love is told only in one way. *Jeong* as affect is not a derivative modality in relation to rationality, for "one cannot access another directly and with a guarantee."[40] Solidarity is also a part of *jeong*. When we realize that who we are is always constituted through and in relation to the other, and when we begin to really "see" and "hear" the other, we cannot help but become aware that the other's well-being is my well-being, the other's pain becomes my pain. And this leads us to vulnerability, or more aptly to what Catherine Keller writes as "mutually assured vulnerability,"[41] as the risk factor that makes the blossoming of *jeong* possible. Without this risk, this openness to the other, this reception and drawing proximate to the other, there's no possibility for *jeong* to emerge.

Jeong assumes a robust imagination that undoes prevalent binary oppositions. It is Spivak's use of *teleopoiesis* that articulates this dimension of *jeong*. For the work of teleopoiesis is in the imaginative exercise "in experiencing the impossible—stepping into the space of the other—without which political solutions come drearily undone into the continuation of violence."[42] Of this openness and indeterminacy in teleopoiesis, Spivak says, "This is really imagining yourself, really letting yourself be imagined (experience that impossibility) without guarantees, by and in another culture," and the failure of teleopoiesis, which engages in "bottomless responsibility," is "not knowing how to learn to learn from below."[43] Teleopoiesis is a collaborative coming together as Spivak notes, "a reaching toward the distant other by the patient power of imagination, a curious kind of identity politics, where one crosses identity, as a result of migration or exile." Like teleopoiesis, *jeong* generates possibilities for "touching the distant other with imaginative effort."[44]

Many Koreans often feel that *jeong* is more powerful, lasting, and transformative than love. *Jeong* makes relationships "sticky" but also recognizes the complex and dynamic nature of all relationalism. While *jeong* works to resist oppression and suffering, it does not have elements of retaliatory vengefulness. When *jeong* is present among sufferers and the oppressed who do not forget justice, they preserve an element of forgiveness even for those who participate in structures of oppression.

The presence of *jeong* in Korean cultural contexts does not mean that there is no oppression or violence among Koreans. Korea, like most other contexts, has, of course, covert and overt forms of sexism, racism, and classism, among other forms of individual and systemic structures of violence. Let me share an example.

As in many other patriarchal cultures, sexism and violence against women are rampant. The presence and practice of *jeong* does not mean that violence against women is completely eradicated. However, *jeong,* as practiced by and between women who are victims of patriarchy, helps them to form networks not only to survive such brutal victimization but also to form movements to confront and resist various manifestations of violence against women. Participants of these movements and networks are both men and women. Although all Koreans may not always practice my understanding of *jeong*, I am inviting us to examine what I understand to be liberative about *jeong*.

Jeong is difficult to categorize in relation to the notions of agape, eros, and philia. Like eros, *jeong* is an intense and vital mode of bonding, but unlike eros, it is less susceptible to the romanticization of love as "erotic/ sexual" attraction. Again, the most common description of *jeong* is that it is "sticky." This stickiness is not fusion without distinctions but the kind of stickiness that understands that we are, whether we want to admit it or not, always connected to one another. Because we are constituted in and through relationality with all others, *jeong* recognizes that we are indebted to others as well. Like philia or friendship, *jeong* has a strong sense of relationality, but unlike philia, it does not depend on equal regard and mutuality in order to flourish. Finally, like agape, *jeong* often involves dramatic sacrifices in relation to others, even vis-à-vis an oppressing other, but unlike many renderings of agape, *jeong* is not self-emptying self-sacrifice. It is certainly not self-abnegation. In contrast to self-sacrifice, *jeong* is an intentional, wise, and knowing decision to relinquish, which recognizes not only the dignity and worth of oneself but also that of others. In this context, agency is not relinquished.

For those who argue that liberation can be achieved only through dismantling oppression, *jeong* perpetuates passivity and powerlessness; this, though, is to misunderstand the kind of relation that *jeong* inhabits. Allow me to describe more precisely the kind of relation that *jeong* seeks, with some references, again, to Spivak's work. A practice of *jeong*, in Spivak's terms, is about a love that is, or includes, a "learning to learn from below . . . toward imagining planetarity that builds solidarity with the subaltern."[45] This solidarity, Spivak is cautious to emphasize, is always "without guarantees." Choosing to live by and through *jeong* is to claim one's agency and power in a situation of powerlessness. Again, though many will see this as passivity, it is not. The praxis of *jeong* is precisely what allows for a practice of agency by those who have been stripped of it. At times, sacrifice enters as a form of agency, such that *jeong* works to restore life in the face of forces that destroy life. Practices of *jeong* in the spirit of Spivak's notion of teleopoiesis are an attempt to "mend the torn fabric of subaltern ethics," and, as Kristeva writes, a poiesis that is "the putting into form of relationships between humiliated and offended individuals: the outline of connections."[46] In short, I would say that *jeong* is an agent's enactment and assurance of agency through an intentional relinquishment (that is simultaneously an assertion) that aims at and creates a restorative dignity.

How might *jeong* be understood in these ways be related to justice? Practice of *jeong* in the praxis of liberation holds love and justice together with a fierce commitment that also embraces an art of playfulness. Oppression is a serious business. However, to say that those who are oppressed do not have an interior life of love, joy, beauty, generosity, and play is to further render them powerless. It is especially within the everyday living-ness of those considered the "subaltern" that one also can witness the powerful presence of *jeong*. Everyday practices of *jeong*, especially by those who have been marginalized, can be interpreted as a tactic in that it "insinuates itself into the other's place, fragmentarily, without taking it over in its entirety, without being able to keep it at a distance," and thus everyday practices of *jeong* are "many ways of operating as victories of the weak over the 'strong' . . . polymorphic simulations, joyful discoveries, poetic."[47] What we need then is to imagine a *jeong* that is beyond domination. *Jeong* operates on both the psychic and social levels by restoring the agency necessary to imagine oneself as an ethical and political subject. *Jeong* thus is a concept that opens out into many directions of interpersonal and sociopolitical living. *Jeong* manifests itself in unique combinations of the different dimensions of love, justice, and restorative dignity, transgressing boundaries between oppressor and the oppressed, finding ways to mix resistance and embrace amid oppressive relations, and giving birth to new forms of love and justice. *Jeong* does not compromise with those who perpetuate violence and oppression. Rather, the power of *jeong* allows us to recognize the seriousness of the suffering of the oppressors even as we resist their oppressing practices. *Jeong*, in other words, emerges in the interstitial space between the self and the other, between the oppressors and the oppressed, but it does so through *jeong*'s fostering what Spivak refers to as that "one-on-one" epistemic change with no guarantees.

There are dimensions to love prevalent in many communities that, I think, resemble *jeong*. There are other communities that recognize interdependence as primary, rather than independence, thus enabling life to flourish. For instance, the African notions of *Umbuntu* and Indian concepts like *Ahimsa* ("largest love/love force") recognize that a communal and relational way of being in the world benefits not only humanity but also all of creation. This may be the key to our social and planetary recovery and survival. Many of the peoples and cultures who daily practice that which is similar to *jeong* also have been exploited historically and know suffering and violence in their bones.

For example, many people who have experienced the violence of poverty, emigration, war, genocide, racism, sexism, homophobia, forced labor, and state-sanctioned torture, to name just a few examples, often seem to hold onto what resembles *jeong* because that is what ultimately gives them dignity in the face of such inhumanity. A woman who experiences domestic violence does not *love* her abuser, but she might hold on to *jeong* for that abusing other and not only because it is about holding onto the kernel of the abuser's humanity; more important, *jeong* preserves her in that situation from the abyss of inhumanity and restores to her a certain valuable dignity and agency. *Jeong* does not discourage separation and autonomy, but *jeong* works to help us be mindful that we are always in relation to the other.

In returning to Spivak, we can note her comments about "female individualism" in the age of imperialism. Spivak notes that "as the female individualist, not-quite-male, articulates herself in shifting relationship to what is at stake, the 'native subaltern female' . . . is excluded from any share in this emerging norm."[48] I am aware that there could be an argument against *jeong* as yet another way in which the gendered subaltern's practice of relationality can easily become an opportunity for more exploitation. However, this is based on a problematic binarism in which the "West" is associated with the liberating form of autonomy, freedom, and individualization and the "rest" with the bondage of collectivity, self-loss to the point of "sacrifice," and lack of authority and agency.

It is often the case that is easier to love only where reciprocity and mutuality are present. That is an ideal state, and one would wish that for all relationships. However, we know that frequently that is not the case. *Jeong,* in contrast, is not conditional, nor is it restrictive, because one cannot will or determine when, where, or with whom one can experience *jeong.* *Jeong* is then a powerful force that is experienced, exercised, received, and works to uncoercively rearrange our desires.

Sometimes, even in relationships of animosity, as in the case between the colonizer and the colonized, *jeong* emerges despite our best efforts to block it out because we cannot prevent glimpsing the image of oneself mirrored in the other. When one sees one's very self mirrored in the face of the other, one knows in the deepest recess of one's heart that complete severing is not the solution. In this way, *jeong* is even more expansive and generous than love even in the context of relational complexity, for it inherently believes in the possibility of the impossible.

SPIVAK'S *JEONG*: "NONCOERCIVE REARRANGEMENT OF DESIRE"

Love is a wager on rebirth.

JULIA KRISTEVA, *Tales of Love*

Love is what makes of thought a power, which is why love alone, and not faith, bears the force of salvation.

ALAIN BADIOU, *Saint Paul: The Foundation of Universalism*

Something like the Korean notion of *jeong* can be discerned in a number of academic discourses, especially those by intellectuals who reflect on historical oppression, such as postcolonial theorists who have recently made a surprising turn by calling for love. Spivak, for example, dares to hope in a "postcolonial love" as a supplement that will allow for different peoples and movements to develop and maintain strength and duration, to stick, we might say, as "the strongest mobilizing discourse in the world . . . the supplementation of collective effort by *love*."[49]

Although I agree with them, I still find that "love" often does not seem to convey the breadth, depth, and complexity of all our ways of being with one another. When we speak of love, it often seems conditional, unilateral, and restrictive, the flip side, as it were, of love's romanticized sappiness. This kind of conditional love easily morphs into some familiar binarism: either I love the other or I don't, either you are with me or not, friend or foe, evil or good, abused or abuser, familiar or stranger.

Jeong is a practice of openness to the other without foreclosure or abjection, similar to Spivak's "ethics of singularity." It renders the love of the Western liberal paradigm more complex, breaking it free from both its straitjacket of calculation (which Spivak notes with irony) and its romanticist "idealisms." It is a way to pluralize love. *Jeong* widens and deepens how we understand love. Wagering in the possibility of continuous rebirth, and looking for ways to keep love ever birthing new forms, I want to suggest that *jeong* is a movement that stretches toward possible pluralization of love. Surely love cannot be monolingual?

Jeong reveals its multidimensional characteristics. Its multiple shades of meaning derive mainly from the notion of heart. *Jeong* emerges within connectedness to unravel abjection/foreclosure, within abjecting and abjected subjects, and thus enhances the process of becoming a self in relation to the other. The possibilities for *jeong* reside in the contact zone, the interstitial space between the self and the other. This interstitial space where *jeong* emerges is made possible when we see the other with our heart. In the Korean context, "heart" often refers not to the organ in our body but to that which in our being constitutes both the emotive heart and the mind. There is no split or privileging of either the affective use of "heart" over the mind of "reason" as often seems to be the case in the West. When I speak of "heart," I am pointing toward a disposition of the subject toward the other.

Jeong is a form of relationality that is more than interdependence. It is a mode of interdependence that is fostered when agents of love embrace even a form of sacrifice, but this is not the *self*-sacrifice that feminists so rightly criticize. By challenging absolute lines of demarcation between the self and the other, *jeong* does require, in certain instances, the decision to put the other before ourselves. This kind of relationality, however, is based on an ethics of mutual recognition and resonance that counters violence in a distinctive way, because violence is understood in a new way, that is, as the oppositional and individually oriented process of subject formation and abjection examined above. A wonderful example of this comes from the martial arts film *Fearless*. At the beginning of this film, the main character, played by Jet Li, believes that martial arts are about fighting and winning over your opponent. The context of his film is in China, then overrun with British and Japanese imperialism. Jet Li's character goes through a transformation during the middle part of the film. In the scene of his last fight where his character dies, we discover that his transformation brought him to a new awareness of his relation to his opponent. His opponent is Japanese. In this last scene, Jet Li's character dies, not because he cannot "win" over his opponent, but because he values his opponent's life. In his last fight, the main character's self-sacrificing of mere conquering power achieves dignity and agency in a colonized situation of struggle by reshaping viewers' awareness that martial art is not about fighting within the binaries of win/lose, conquer/conquered, but winning through a strength that creates peace. Jet Li's character refuses to use his power to take out his British-backed Japanese opponent. Just as he challenges the lines that oppressive British imperialists in China drew between themselves and their subjects, so *jeong* also challenges absolute demarcations between the self and the other and seeks victory along strange paths. It is a resistance to colonialism, but as a reworking of and a working-beyond the colonized/colonizer binary, it is a postcolonial love that *jeong* affects in the oppressive situation.

In *jeong*, one knows that asserting one's subjectivity by rejecting the other is brutal. This does not mean that *jeong* is not confrontational or that it reifies relations of domination and powerlessness. In Korean culture, I have experienced relationships between people who do not give up on the other in their relationship of *jeong*, but who have a sense of obligation to preface even the most confrontational of challenges with "because I have *jeong* for you, I need to be honest and say this to you." *Jeong* allows us to have hope in the capacity of the oppressor to be transformed. *Jeong* is both an agency and a pathway to both individual and collective transformation. However, it does not mean that we languish in a kind of hope that waits for change to take place. Rather, it is because of *jeong* that we are compelled to move continuously to demand change and justice. *Jeong* recognizes not only our connectedness but also the dignity and worth of both self and other.

This *jeong*, if imagined and practiced, is able to wedge itself into the smallest gaps between the oppressed and the oppressor. *Jeong* is powerful precisely because it is an emancipatory and healing power, even in relationships that have been reduced to simple binarism, as is often the case between the oppressor and the oppressed. *Jeong* contests the very existence of and pronouncement of binarism. In this regard, the notion or experience of *jeong* has gradations and levels of "thinness and thickness," that is, it exhibits weaker and stronger forms of relationality.

Jeong replaces dichotomies with more inclusive frameworks for understanding self and other. While systemic oppressions must be critically analyzed and resisted, *jeong* also recognizes the brokenness and pain of the oppressors. *Jeong*, and here again I resonate with what might be called Spivak's notes toward a planetary love, is to "listen to the other as if it were a self," yet not erasing difference or making us "the same," "neither to punish nor to acquit."[50] Ultimately it is this intimate existential recognition of the self, mirrored in the other, that leads to transformation of the heart. It is, as Spivak notes, a "mind changing on both sides." This recognition can occur for each one, at different times, or simultaneously. Unbeknown to her, perhaps, Spivak provided an example of *jeong* when she describes the risk and openness to the other thus: "[T]he toughest task is to imagine myself a Hindu, when everything in me resists, to understand what in us can respond so bestially, rather than merely to show cause, or to impose rules . . . unless prepared for by a sustained and uncoercive rearrangement of desires with moves learned from the offending culture."[51] In this regard interdependence as practiced with *jeong* is not figured as violent, alienating, subjugating, and dominating. These ways of understanding interdependence arise when we begin with the ideal of the self-possessed autonomous subject. However, if we were to operate in a world with an interrelational conception of subjectivity, "subjectivity without subjects," then interdependence is seen as a "force of life."[52]

Jeong emerges in the in-between space created by the juxtaposition of suffering, injustice, and the need for justice, between death and life. Because *jeong* is so difficult to define yet so concretely known in everyday practice, Koreans have attempted to analyze the many forms of *jeong*. One of the common distinctions made about *jeong* is the one between *mi-eun jeong* and *go-eun jeong*. Many Koreans share the notion that the former is a form of *jeong* that emerges even when one is in an antagonistic relationship with the other while the latter emerges in relationships of mutuality and reciprocity. A popular saying in Korea precisely embodies this collective solidarity that might be uncomfortable for the Western individualistic sensibility: "You die—I die; you live—I live," or, alternatively, "I am because we are." These sayings embody the form of *jeong* that emerges within relationality and community, connectivity and collectivity.[53] Perhaps they also embody something similar to what Spivak terms "collectivities"—a concept that embraces communities, collaborations, cooperatives, coalitions, and networks real and imagined so that we might learn and practice "love" otherwise. For as Spivak intuits, this work of teaching, learning, and loving "otherwise" is a "necessary but impossible task—like taking care of health although it is impossible to be immortal; or continuing to listen, read, write, talk and teach although it is impossible that everything be communicated"—that leads "to *renewed and persistent effort*."[54] At this point, let me allow Spivak's ethics of love, which seem very much to me not-quite-love, to intersect with what I have been describing as *jeong*. What am I referring to as Spivak's "not-quite-love"?

Perhaps, like me, Spivak also senses problems and failures of Western foreclosure within the ways love is practiced across and in different contexts. As a person who is constantly made aware of her own foreclosure and absence in the Name of Man, yet at the same time possibly part of that very structure that induces, ensures, and invokes the foreclosure of the Native Informant, how and where does she find love? While Spivak's embodiment of *jeong* works as a kind of undergirding love—her globe-girding project—it is interesting that nowhere in the indices of her books does one find an entry for "love." Perhaps the word isn't mentioned with enough frequency to make the indexes, but it is telling that her own encounters seem profoundly dependent on, and animated by, the infrequently mentioned "love," so manifest in her building relationships and in her learning to read the world, whether in the classrooms of Columbia University or the rural schools of India. Taking on extra lectures to cover expenses for her work in rural schools and teaching and learning "student by student," she does not seem to miss a step or miss her classes. Love and loves seem at work in her devotion, commitment, risk, her openness to an effortful task of undoing asymmetry, and learning from the subaltern. Moving and moved by imagination for planetary consciousness, Spivak embodies practices of *jeong* without any guarantees—without indexing.

Spivak notes the difference between the "doing" and the "thinking" and the differences between both in regarding the "how" of the doing or the thinking. And the difference here concerns how much we are able to examine our liberal alibi and the effort it takes to do the hands-on undertaking "with the subaltern, to undo this asymmetry," which would require an "effortful task of 'doing.' "[55] For Spivak, who interjects herself in engagement with the liberal project of Martha Nussbaum and her critique of postmodern theorist Judith Butler, constructive counterglobalizing work begins with learning to learn from below,[56] learning to learn from the subaltern. As Spivak declares, "My teacher is the subaltern."[57] The subaltern does speak when we open up to learning to learn from the subaltern.

According to Spivak, in still other words that are yet pointers to *jeong,* the space between the self and the other is where the *noncoercive rearrangement of desire* can take place. This noncoercive rearrangement of desire is a "suspending of oneself into the text of the other. . . . It is not the loss of will . . . but a training to learn from the singular and the unverifiable . . . striving for a response from the distant other *without guarantees.*"[58] For those who live through the practice and embodiment of *jeong,* they do so fully knowing there are no guarantees. However, the practice of building relationality through *jeong* is like Spivak's call for literary training in learning to read the world. It is a dynamic that is "a slow mind-changing process . . . used to open the imagination," for when this dynamic works, the agency of the responsibility is in that "outside of the self that is also in the self, half archived and therefore not directly accessible."[59] Yet, we are bound to the other because the ethical subject is marked by an experience of affectivity such that the "core of my subjectivity is exposed to otherness."[60]

As I indicated in the first section, *jeong* is not unique to Koreans. Whenever the communal is emphasized and honored, and when this communal sense is allowed to temper and transform the lines of power in violent encounter, I have found the presence of *jeong*. Although it might have a different name and may be stressed in different ways, *jeong's* notion of relinquishment creates dignified restoration. Lack of *jeong* is most noticeable in cultures that have adopted capitalist individualist notions of the self and the violent foreclosures that are necessary to sustaining that sense of self in opposition to the other. "Rational economic man" is a site that rarely exhibits the humanity and planetarity of *jeong*. *Jeong* threatens a culture that values individualism and separation while devaluing communal interdependence and the interconnectedness of all.

Born in movements of justice and compassion, *jeong* addresses and redresses that whole process of abjection and foreclosure at the heart of and disseminated throughout the violent financialization of the globe, a problem so often addressed by Spivak.[61] *Jeong* requires two, the self and the other, and perhaps dare we say even othered others, a multiplicity of selves and ever more complex unities of selves, which allow the subject to cross the boundaries of the self and "be" other. Unless we are trained into imagining the other, as observed by Spivak, "a necessary, impossible and interminable task, nothing we do through politico-legal calculation will last, even with the chanciness of the future anterior."[62] This form of *jeong* provides identification through difference without abolishing or assimilating differences. It respects and lives the call of Edouard Glissant that "We clamor for the right to opacity for everyone."[63] Because the power of *jeong* is not confined within particular boundaries, divisions, and dichotomies, justice can come through its reconciling work. For Spivak, even political agency is grounded in the "restricted and accountable model of the person that bears a discontinuous and fractured relationship with the subject. . . . [T]he most difficult part is in the opening myself to be 'othered' by the subaltern, it is this more mysterious arena of the subject that the self hopes to enter."[64] To risk being "othered by the subaltern" is to risk being abjected, foreclosed. Are we prepared to take that chance without guarantees of any positive outcome?

Jeong lives in saying both a Yes and a No in relation to the suffering it bears: No to violence and abjection and a simultaneous Yes to the power of *jeong* to seek ways beyond that violence and abjection. One is able to recognize the vulnerability of the other by looking beyond the hardened heart of the other. *Jeong* exists even within—especially within—relationships not based on mutuality. At the heart of the transgressive power of *jeong* is its presence, its emergence, even within the terrain of confrontational and oppositional relationships and often in the absence of mutuality and equality. Spivak pushes this with an example that might be difficult for many of us but one which resonates with *jeong,* in a lecture at the University of California at Santa Barbara, when she strongly states, "[W]e would rather have a relationship with a rogue state than no relationship at all."[65]

Many of us live in a culture that privileges the mind over the heart and that poses heart over and against mind. When we live with heart, we cannot stay immune to the other. When we open ourselves to the other, it is less easy to rationalize suffering. The suffering of the other becomes my suffering; his/her joy, my joy in a relationship that is often but not necessarily that of reciprocity. If we do not have heart, we do not have life. *Jeong* emerges within relationships, with contact. It is important to keep in mind that ordinary relations, the matrix for practicing *jeong,* are crucial for both personal and corporate life. Such praxis of *jeong* entailing fidelity, courage, and justice cannot help but be prophetic witness and resistance to powers of death as it manifests itself in domestic and international spheres. The logic of love and the logic of justice, often pitted against each other, must be held together, for the bifurcation between subject and abject is false just as the binary between oppressor and oppressed fails to imagine the possibility that we are co-victims in the long run. *Jeong* and justice must work together to overcome violence. In fact, *jeong's* multiplicity builds in a relationship to justice that makes the traditional binary of "love and justice" questionable. The agency of oppressed peoples, I would argue, springs from their awareness of how vital *jeong* is for their survival, for our survival. Some may wonder if here I am privileging *jeong* over love. More accurately, I am presenting *jeong* as a dimension of love, or perhaps better, as a paradigm of what love is—one that often has been erased or repressed, especially, in the dominant Western culture's understanding of love. For any fruitful "planet-talk" to take place, each of us must be open to learning new paradigms, new modes of being in the world, new ways of loving.

I hope to recover a vigorous and vibrant prophetic love in the work of emancipatory movements by seeing them infused with practices of *jeong* that most effectively work by way of a *noncoercive rearrangement of desire.* Perhaps, *jeong* already works out of what Spivak refers to as "planet-feeling" that reminds us that to be "human is to be intended toward exteriority. And, if we can get to planet-feeling, the outsider or other is indefinite."[66] Drawing from her way of conceiving "invagination," I'm hoping that *jeong* creates enough space for the multiplicity of love's expressions. It is in the work of openness to and in the imagining and the "doing" of "teleopoietic delicacy" that one sees an excess of *jeong* that might provide access to the other—reaching and reached, caressing and caressed (of course without any guarantees). Nonetheless, we might realize that learning *jeong*, and its complexity and suppleness, might be a way to participate in the suturing of our own torn selves. It would be, finally, to live out in full bloom that which Spivak values even above transcendence—a wild "licensed lunacy."[67]

✒ Not Quite Not Agents of Oppression: Liberative Praxis for North American White Women

LYDIA YORK

[I]f one simply understands [difference] as a division between culture, between people, between entities, one can't go very far with it. But when that difference between entities is being worked out as a difference also within, things start opening up. Inside and outside are both expanded. Within each entity, there is a vast field and within each self is a multiplicity.
TRINH T. MINH-HA, *"Inappropriate/d Artificiality"*

Agents of Oppression are members of the dominant social groups in the United States, privileged by birth or acquisition, who knowingly or unknowingly exploit and reap unfair advantage over members of groups that are targets of oppression. Agents of oppression are also trapped by the system of institutionalized oppression that benefits them, and are confined to roles and prescribed behaviors. In United States culture, agents have the power to define the "norm" for what is reality, they see themselves as normal or proper, whereas targets are likely to be labeled as deviant, evil, abnormal, substandard, or defective.
MELANIE MORRISON, ELEANOR S. MORRISON, AND ANN FLESCHER, *Doing Our Own Work Training Handbook*

IN DEFENSE OF BINARY LOGICS

One of the crucial methodological starting places in anti-oppression work is the presentation of strictly oppositional understandings of who is oppressed and who is oppressor. This is an either/or logic in the rawest sense. There is no gray area or third zone: either you are a "target of oppression" or an "agent of oppression."[1] The language intentionally forces participants to identify as one or the other. The idea is to make clear which way oppression flows, to hold the dominant class in the hot seat. The language of agency is key to this framing; it highlights the idea that there are no innocent bystanders to the structure and process of oppression. Someone (most likely someone who is reading this essay) is actually *doing* it.

This kind of bifurcated identity instruction is surely incompatible with Trinh Minh-ha's vast field of multiplicity within a self.[2] It certainly seems out of step with the fluidity, multiplicity, and hybridity of postcolonial theory, and dampens any dream of postracial politics. And so my next move ought to be the deconstruction or at least denunciation of this rigid binary, but this is not my intention. For it is the confrontation with the binary that produces a necessary crisis in meaning for people of dominant groups: for example, white women seeking racial consciousness. The tension between the postcolonialism of Trinh and the identity politics of anti-oppression work is exactly my theoretical and ethical concern.

Explaining to the oppressor what it means to be the oppressor necessitates the use of a binary explanation of the conditions of colonization. This is not only a teaching strategy; it is reflective of the actual power dynamics at work around and through us in neocoloniality. The logic of empire is binary, producing and defending structural inequity. Poststructuralism teaches us that this logic ultimately cannot stand, collapsing under its own weight as opposites deconstruct into each other, mirrors and fragments all. Postcolonialism teaches us about the politics of the binaries and their breaches, doing so in alignment with liberation struggles around the planet and drawing from the positionality of those who don't fit neatly into the either/or of empire. But in the excitement over the possibilities of interstitiality and hybridity, we must not forget that these third spaces are contact zones of *oppositional* logic and power. And isn't this always already the postcolonial position? Where Marxisms and poststructuralisms collide as colonized and colonizer rub elbows and more, combining chromosomes in the cosmopolis—that is where liberation theology and postcolonial theology must come to terms.

Liberating the oppressor from the structures and practices of domination requires a few transdisciplinary moves. Psychoanalytic and philosophical theories of subject formation, explored through postcolonial and feminist theory will be indispensable. As Trinh remarks, difference between is also difference within. U.S. and postcolonial whiteness and critical race studies theorize internal structures of the subject in conjunction with historical or literary narrative. To learn how whiteness itself is disordered requires intimate and big-picture work in tandem. Indeed, this is the practical inherited wisdom of antiracist teachers who attempt nothing less than the reconstitution of otherwise well-intentioned whites into agents of institutional change. For theology and ethics, the white colonizer's addiction to violence and unearned privilege is a matter of systems and a matter of soul, a reflection of the interconnection of all life and the mutual captivity of oppressor and oppressed. The liberation of the oppressor from his situation of oppressing is a project of soul recovery and re-creation. But what about the liberation of the oppressor from *her* situation of oppressing?

GENDER, AGENCY, AND WHITENESS

Women as colonizing subjects occupy mixed-status positions, dominating as to race and subordinated as to gender. In a very slight reference from which the title of this essay derives, Spivak gestures toward the North American woman who publishes as occupying the place of the native informant; not quite native, not quite *not* native.[3] The liminality of women as *not quite* or *not quite not* is consonant with feminist theory, but in relation to the second epigraph for this essay, a definition of *agent of oppression*, the conjunction jars. For women, agency is that elusive, almost impossible, longed-for quality (or is it a commodity?) of true subjecthood, the *pouvoir* without which we cannot do. How can women interact in any sensible way with an identity like "agent of oppression?"

For Spivak, the metropolitan feminist project of subject constitution is not unlike colonial racial subject constitution: it is solipsistic and individualistic, its own form of fetish. In contrast to this feminist obsession, one should try to "wrench oneself away from the mesmerizing focus of the 'subject-constitution' of the female individualist."[4] She likens this and other feminine efforts of "soul-making" to the imperial project of civilizing: making something (not someone) from the nothing of raw material. Of course, the name *soul-making* has an ironic inflection; it isn't the making of other selves, but rather the making of *my*-self that happens in the civilizing mission.

What this crisis unveils are the co-constitutive properties of race and gender in the subject constitution of a white woman. The discursive polarities white/other and man/other constitute one another in slippery mimicries that are nonetheless not quite parallel. When the colonizer is a woman, who or what is the subject? How does the mistress's whiteness shore up, replace, stand in for her feminine lack of subjectivity? White racism is the subjectivity operative in a white woman in whom empowerment slumbers. The master needs the mistress to shore up his racial as well as gendered superiority.

Does *white* oppose *woman* sufficiently for *white* to stand in for *not-woman?* And if so, how do we account for the ways whiteness lurks in a universal category of woman, as in Gloria Smith Hull and Patricia Bell-Scott's observation that "all the women are white."[5] As Laurel Schneider, Anne McClintock and others theorize, race is never not gendered, as gender is never not raced.[6] Race and gender always occur in actual bodies, and necessarily together—in myriad variations. Is what I am suggesting in danger of undoing this critical work, and re-separating rather than thinking race and gender together?

In old-fashioned and cutting-edge critical theory, dominant attributes such as white, male, and able-bodied line up opposite subordinated attributes such as not-white (black), not-man (woman), and disabled. Against this grid Laurel Schneider chiasmically asks, "What race is your sex?" and "What sex is your race?"[7] In this inappropriate crossing-over, Schneider invokes a crisis beyond the intersection of identities to their co-constitution, whereby "they cannot meaningfully be separated *except* in support of racist and sexist goals."[8] And yet, Schneider's catachresis would not be meaningful without the rough parallel that categories of race and gender can assume with each other based on their respective hierarchical binaries. It is via this parallel that "the white race is thus gendered male by virtue of its dominance, and the non-white races are gendered female, indicating their need for supervision."[9] So it is that analyses of race, class, gender, and sexuality— precisely through the oppositionality of domination and subordination—will produce observations of separable parallelism alongside (and enmeshed with) mutual imbrication.

Unraveling the warp and the weft of the race/gender of white women, we will need to search the many morphing faces of whiteness, pernicious in their instability. Yet if whiteness were not such a fluid construct, it could never gather the nations at its feet. So white women need to look around corners, at the edges of mirrors to catch whiteness in a glance. (Not so, of course, for those for whom whiteness means hypervisible violence.)[10] Within the liberal ambitions of neocolonialism, whites have needed to develop new forms of blindness to white violence in order to make the whole project a success. During times of marked economic or imperial insecurity, symbolic and literal white violence shows itself more crudely as a means of soothing white anxiety. But whether conditions call for whiteness to act above or below white consciousness, white women have a crucial role in its deployment. White feminists become propagators of *patriarchy* by performing whiteness uncritically; and whether we feel innocent or unmarked, being racially unconscious makes us better instruments of empire.

WHITENESS IS . . . BUT IT IS NOT

One of the cultural residues left in the wake of empire is precisely [the] ideal of or aspiration to whiteness, what we might call a postcolonial "will to whiteness" that lurks in the burgeoning state's national racial unconscious, as an unacknowledged, because unexamined, national aesthetic.

ALFRED J. LÓPEZ, *Posts and Pasts: A Theory of Postcolonialism*

Alfred J. López argues that the conditions after colonialism produce a whiteness in crisis in three forms: as a returning of repressed cultural history; as aspirations or cultural ideals operating via contempt or nostalgia, whereby whiteness is synonymous with material success for the colonized; and third, in the daily encounters of whiteness with its others on the street.[11] In the colony that has become a nation, whiteness remains in the form of white colonizers turned citizens, in structural institutions, and in ideological and cultural forms of national language, religion, and education.[12] Whiteness has an "aspirational" structure, representing the best of human beauty and virtue, Richard Dyer claims. As such, it is simultaneously identified with physical bodies of white-skinned people, and moves past embodiment toward a luminous transcendence of no-thing-ness or absence. Dyer astutely draws out the religious dimensions of this, as a spiritual pinnacle or transcendence translates into absence or negation: whiteness as the height of civilization is also the absence of liveliness and sexuality, approaching negation via death. As Dyer notes, "[B]eing nothing at all may readily be felt as being nothing in particular, the representative human, the subject without properties."[13] Thus he embarks on a project he identifies as "making whiteness strange."[14] Dyer identifies three ways in which white is a color: as a hue or tint among others; as a category of skin color, varied as to gender and class; and as a symbol of virtue, beauty, and civilization.[15] He suggests that each of these discourses is unstable, yet that instability strengthens rather than weakens the power of whiteness.

Showing the instability of whiteness as a performance or as a property that can be negotiated does not negate observations of its entrenched fixity, either as an attribute or as a concept. Fixity and instability are not incommensurate aspects of hegemony, as deconstructionists have demonstrated. For example, whiteness can define itself by what it is not—historically in the case of the United States, for example, as uncontaminated by black or Indian blood—while standing in for humanity or normativity in general.[16]

As Mayra Rivera observes, while imperialism depends on a logic that produces opposites, reducing individuals and differences to strict oppositional categories, it has to work overtime to cover (and selectively reveal, I would add) its tracks. To make those tracks is to run roughshod over groups and individuals who belong on neither side or on both sides of the categories. The heterogeneity of those subjects exceeds the distinctions of colonizer and colonized.

> Because these oppositions are neither natural, stable, nor essential, imperial discourses perform long, repetitive attempts to cover over the links between the colonizer and the colonized, which, simultaneously, exceed the boundaries of each of the terms. In other words, colonialism must obliterate the relations between colonizers and colonized and deny heterogeneity and the singularity of subjects, arresting them under fixed categories like those of colonizer and colonized.[17]

The boldness of the imperial logic is a sleight of hand. For all its conceptual violence, it distracts us from embodied links between colonizer and colonized, relations characterized by definitively brutal violence and tender ambiguity. Whether the conceptual simplification enforces the categories by hypervisible terror, romanticism, or the appearance of normalcy, the real relations between colonized and colonizer are much more complex. Families and cultures are created in and through such relations.

The editors of the 2001 anthology *The Making and Unmaking of Whiteness* compile and appraise various theories of whiteness, offering strongest support for definitions of whiteness as structural privilege, as violence and terror, and as the institutionalization of European colonialism.[18] They further question the tendency to represent whiteness as invisible and unmarked, defined only by what it is not, as well as the assumption that whiteness studies are inherently antiracist. In a similar vein, López in *Posts and Pasts* describes the postcolonial project as it relates to whiteness as less about abolishing whiteness or plunging into "multiculturalism" and more about developing a "postmastery whiteness, a whiteness that can enter into a relation of mutual recognition with its others without admonitions, without fear, without shame."[19]

Whereas theorists such as David Roediger and even Thandeka build arguments for antiracist white mobilization via recognition of economic self-interest,[20] Mab Segrest appeals to white spiritual and emotional self-interest, the healing of what Segrest calls the "wounding psychic perversion" of domination.[21] She calls for a politicization of therapeutic processes that would recognize the historical basis of personal and familial psychic suffering, and the relationship of addiction to capitalism and colonialism. Segrest explores the history of contemporary addictions and the fetishism of commodities involved in the Atlantic slave trade: black bodies for labor to produce and be exchanged for tobacco, sugar, rum. She associates these addictive substances with the pain of soul splitting that must happen to whites who, whether directly or indirectly, commit violence.

Segrest explores the implications of the psychic splitting she calls anesthetization via the story of a white slave mistress who watches an enslaved African woman on the slave block. Mary Boykin Chesnut records in her diary a scene that brings her contradictory identities of woman and mistress into high relief. This scene could have been a doorway to conscientization; the reader recognizes the tragedy that it did not.

> A mad woman taken from her husband and child. Of course she was mad, or she would not have given her grief words in that public place. Her keepers were along. What she said was rational enough, pathetic, at times heart-rending. It excited me so I quietly took opium. It enables me to retain every particle of mind or sense or brains I have, and so quiets my nerves that I can calmly reason and take rational views of things otherwise quite maddening.[22]

What is otherwise quite maddening is the window of empathy that opened in Chesnut as she heard the words of the enslaved woman, and felt her humanness: specifically the womanness—the wifeness and motherness—of the otherwise not-quite-human. This momentary awareness—a stew of precognitions and feelings—signals the return of the repressed: the humanity of an enslaved other and Mary Chesnut's own participation in and dependence on the violence that created the scene. Segrest remarks that this diary entry could have gone another way, the way of the Grimké sisters, white southern women of Chesnut's generation who chose abolitionism.[23] Instead, unable or unwilling to tolerate the threat of rising emotion, Chesnut chose a substance to fill the abyss. The commercial enterprise that brought her drug of choice to her across the ocean, perhaps in a vessel of the triangle slave trade, persists in various ways into the present. Colonial appetites haven't changed much in 150 years; in a moment of emotional discomfort we still reach for chocolate, a cigarette, a cup of tea.

Ever wary of projects that involve saving others, Spivak would lend a critical eye to the actions and motivations of abolitionists, then and now, who might be motivated by a benevolence that reinscribes domination and dependence. Thus, mere action is not a sufficient answer. bell hooks proposes that whites are capable of acting in solidarity with the oppressed through a rejection of domination.[24] I suggest that whites cannot reject domination unless we engage in a process of psychic healing. And we cannot engage in a process of healing without acknowledging our own pain. So it is that whites need to find ways of remembering and telling our personal and familial stories of the wages and costs of whiteness.

INTIMATE EMPIRE

> Relations between the individual unconscious and political life are, I argue, neither separable from each other nor reducible to each other. Instead, they comprise crisscrossing and dynamic mediations, reciprocally and untidily transforming each other, rather than duplicating a relation of structural analogy.
>
> ANNE MCCLINTOCK, "'No Longer in a Future Heaven':
> Gender, Race and Nationalism"

In *A Critique of Postcolonial Reason*, Spivak works through Jean Rhys's retelling of the story of *Jane Eyre*'s Bertha in *Wide Sargasso Sea*.[25] Rhys writes into the foreground what had been foreclosed by the colonial concerns and assumptions of the Brontë version: the life story of the "mad" woman in the attic, the first wife from Jamaica whom Rhys lovingly renames Antoinette. A white Creole already ambiguously white in the context of her colonial community, Antoinette suffers unrequited love and marriage to a thoroughly English man. Called "white cockroach" by emancipated slaves and "white nigger" by English women, she wonders, "Who I am and where is my country and where do I belong and why was I ever born at all."[26] Spivak describes Rhys's characterization of Antoinette as a suggestion that "so intimate a thing as a personal and human identity might be determined by the politics of imperialism."[27] Spivak interprets the novel's recurring dream and mirror images via the Narcissus myth as "the place of encounter with Love."[28] In a reflective pool amid the lush gardens of her childhood, Antoinette had to learn to see herself as white over against Tia, her black girlhood friend; now as a married woman in England, Antoinette finally must come to see herself as the racialized Other to everything and everyone around her. In a dream that prepares her to complete her destiny, Antoinette sees her face reflected as the mad wife of the Brontë novel, as the Other of the white man's house and his feminist heroine. In distress, she calls out for Tia.

What Spivak says about this is important and puzzling, bordering on the mystical: "The gilt frame [in the dream] encloses a mirror: as Narcissus's pool reflects the *selfed other*, so this 'pool' reflects the *othered self*. Here the dream sequence ends, with an invocation of none other than Tia, the *other* that could not be *selfed*, because the fracture of imperialism rather than the Ovidian pool intervened."[29] In Spivak's words, Narcissus's "madness is disclosed when he recognizes his other as his self: 'Iste ego sum,'" *I am that*.[30] Elsewhere, she quotes Ovid's Narcissus more fully: "I am that. . . . I now know my image. . . . I have what I desire. Strange prayer for a lover, I would that what I love were absent. . . . Death is not serious for me, for in death I will leave my sorrow."[31]

What madness is this? Spivak calls it mortiferous self-knowledge, whereby Narcissus can live only as long as he does not know himself.[32] Hence the impossibility of self-knowledge, for "[i]f I make disappear what I cannot not desire, I disappear too."[33] So the "that" of "I am that" is the selfed other—the other that discloses itself as merely a reflection of the self—what one longs for and yet can never attain because one has it already, in a form unpossessable. Instead of the selfed Other, what Antoinette sees in the dream mirror is herself in the eyes of the colonizer, a character in someone else's story, a creature somewhere between human and animal. This self is both other to her and the Other of the colonizer.

In the confounding profusion of "selfing" and "othering" it is significant that Spivak presents her insights about the crisis of knowledge within a broader conversation about the epistemological failures that are projection and foreclosure. And as I will observe later, it is crucial that within a conversation about foreclosure, revelation haunts. At this point in the Jean Rhys analysis, however, Spivak uses the phrases *selfed other* and *othered self* to refer to specific epistemological moments, processes in time. If it were not for this nuance, the reader might easily construe these same phrases to mean the condition wherein a colonizer appropriates the other into herself, a condition characterized by a *lack* of understanding of her own and an Other's personhood. Indeed, the words "foreclosure" and "projection," intimate processes that are anterior to knowledge—not quite conscious, if not utterly unconscious. In such circumstances, revelation would be of a Levinasian kind—of the other as transcendent to oneself. But this is not what Spivak means here with the crisis that happens when the other is *selfed* in the Ovidian pool and when the self is *othered* in a dream. These are revelations, not of Other, but of self. For both Narcissus and Antoinette these moments have the shock, the horror of recognition that belongs to the worst nightmares. And for both, this knowledge is quickly understood as death.

If I were to pursue Spivak's direction, it would seem that Antoinette and Narcissus both become themselves at the moment they must undo themselves, or perhaps become undone. The white/not-quite-white Antoinette constitutes herself and is undone by white violence as it manifests in her own self-gaze. In a region Spivak doesn't explore explicitly, Antoinette isn't merely the other of her other, she is the other of herself. And this is a clue for white women who would be other than white mistresses: the possibility that, gazing in the pool in pursuit of the beloved, we will find the fractured other of ourselves. The fragility of whiteness is such that most of us are passing already in some form or other, and when internal inconsistencies reveal themselves, when the fog of unitary whiteness is disturbed to reveal already active contestations within a formerly untroubled white self, that self can no longer see herself as absolutely always, originally, or inevitably white. She is therefore more creole than not, not native to be sure, but then not quite not native either.

Spivak concludes her reading of *Wide Sargasso Sea* with a critical gesture toward Rhys's white Creole position as more white than native, in a statement that well encapsulates the problem of any liberal attempt at benevolence: "No perspective critical of imperialism can turn the other into a self, because the project of imperialism has always historically refracted what might have been an incommensurable and discontinuous other into a

domesticated other that consolidates the imperialist self."[34] How dishearten-
ing (and what a challenge) to hear confirmation of the impossibility of one's
project. How meaningful—according to Spivak's own understanding of the
role of crisis in meaning making. For I hope to do exactly this: to create
within the former colonizer the space for a discontinuous other, allowing
within the imagination of the imperialist self the possibility of an independent other, another self. According to Spivak's logic, this attempt would be
threatened by the tendency to domesticate otherness for the consolidation
of the imperialist self. In other words, to heal the narcissistic fragmentation
of the imperial self, to consolidate it, the colonizer must find a way to do
it without consuming a disadvantaged other. Indeed, there is a more hopeful
interpretation of Ovid than that which Spivak presents, of the (im)possibility
of self-knowledge at the Ovidian and the Imperial pool. In a moment of
recognition, a self can be at once subject and object, self and other. The
crisis of the gaze can result in knowledge, understanding, insight; and death
can be the symbol of transformation.

WHITE/WESTERN? COLLUSIONS OF COLONIALITY

An opportunity for clearer insight resides in the ambiguous treatment of
whiteness in the field of postcolonial studies. A confusion of terms (intentionally provoked by Spivak and others for their own strategic reasons)
results in an odd collusion, not quite conflation, of whiteness and the repre-
sentatives of empire in postcolonial studies. Whiteness tends to stand in for
empire, sometimes explicitly, but often ambiguously or assumed under that
shadow, as in the Bhabha logism "almost the same but not white."[35] Certainly any one-to-one correspondence between white and colonial subject
or colonizer forecloses the importance of native informants and hybrid
peoples; and yet whiteness is notorious for slipping out of view in discourses
that are overdetermined by whiteness. W. Anne Joh suggests that the postcolonial emphasis on hybridity may bring about a conflation of race with
ethnicity, so that critical racial analysis becomes difficult.[36] So, in accord
with Alfred López in Postcolonial Whiteness, I am suspicious of any unnamed
whitenesses or anything like a race-blindness in a discourse that simultaneously seems to depend on the givenness of racial difference and oppression.
And then I will ask—somewhat glibly, perhaps, if he is right—whether an
inhibitor to ongoing interrogation of the category of race within postcolonial
theory might be that poststructuralist-informed postcoloniality finds race to

be an especially oppositional logic, or perhaps as Joh suggests, too essential-ist? Intended to give conceptual room for the tension and incom-mensurability of multiple identities, hybridity-talk sometimes seems reducible to what Spivak might call a Hegelian compromise, instead of a magnetized, tension-taught space of contestation. The importance in the hyphens of hybridity is a recognition of the tensions and splitting that must come—sometimes in pitched battles within the self—as a catachresis embod-ied, oppressor and oppressed within one flesh.

BINARY BLACKNESS

When people ask about my project and I say it has to do with race, they almost always hear this to mean African American. When I clarify that I am interested in whiteness, they hear this as interracial black-white relations. This obtains across the board: my mother, my bank teller, even my academic colleagues of various racial identities. Even in my own head when I say the word race I sometimes catch a specter of blackness. Theorists such as Linda Martín Alcoff and Lorraine O'Grady recognize the prototypicality of black-ness when signifying nonwhiteness.[37] Without launching a full analysis, I would like to venture a couple of guesses about race and postcolonial stud-ies—that it is the geographical concentration of the academy in the north Atlantic that inflects the field with the particularities of U.S. racial history, which confesses and forecloses its relationship to black bodies first. Of course, this habit itself forecloses many other histories of not-black-not-whites, including the radical genocide of First Nations people on this conti-nent. So race remains a haunted category in postcolonial discourse not only because it is the site of unresolved conflict, unintegrated rage, shame, and melancholia in the United States, but because the foreclosure of not-quite-black others from U.S. imagination has created an aporia of academic iden-tity theorizing that postcoloniality seems to fill. And for this we are grateful—not for dependence on any kind of foreclosure, but for the carving out of any and all footholds by, say, Latina, Korean, or Indian scholars. That said, the danger of an unexamined whiteness in postcolonial theory is an unexamined Orientalism; and this is a caution I bring forth with trepida-tion—that U.S. whites, having failed at multiculturalism at home, have outsourced diversity. Feeling stuck in what Susan Friedman calls discourses of accusation and confession,[38] mostly in black/white encounters, liberal whites welcome postcolonial subjects whom we hope may provide the kind of mirroring we wish for ourselves, as good multicultural global subjects.

THE *DOING OUR OWN WORK* SEMINAR

Since 1994 at the Leaven Center in mid-Michigan, white women have gathered to "do their own work" on racism in small group settings. "Educating themselves, confronting racism, holding each other accountable, and demonstrating good faith as they seek to build genuine and lasting coalitions with people of color," these women acquire skills and tools necessary to "work with people of color to dismantle institutional and cultural racism, as well as personal and interpersonal manifestations of racism."[39] Participants travel from the state of Michigan and from all over the United States and Canada seeking a context where they can form in-depth relationships over time with other anti-racist allies. They seek more than what is typically found in diversity training experiences. They are hoping to be challenged and corrected as they struggle to meet the goals of the program—to become agents of structural change among other such agents, to nurture personal and social transformation, and to build ongoing communities of accountability with people of color and with other white antiracist allies.[40]

Doing Our Own Work: A Seminar for Anti-Racist White Women, as developed by Melanie Morrison in conjunction with Eleanor Morrison and Ann Flescher, is an intensive seminar with more than forty hours of in-class time, relying on an action/reflection pedagogical model and a "sphere of influence" each participant locates in the fabric of her life. Each participant catalogues the particular manifestations of racism in the places of her everyday life—with her family, job, worship, and learning settings; then, in conversation with other seminar participants, she discerns specific and achievable actions that include finding and nurturing allies already present in those setting. Participants are assigned a partner within the seminar to check in with about feelings, experiences, and encounters in between weekends, and are assigned articles and book chapters and encouraged to keep a daily journal of reflections about what they are learning and doing with regard to racism and antiracism.[41]

When participants gather, typically for three extended weekends over a period of four to six months, they utilize a variety of pedagogical strategies and workshop techniques that attempt to foster resources for sustained commitment over the long haul. The program understands that such a commitment requires "an infusion of spirit and courage."[42] Racism is understood as a spiritual disorder, requiring spiritual and material responses.[43] Poetry, essays, speeches, and songs of artists from diverse spiritual and cultural traditions, who are committed to the work of dismantling oppression, become increasingly important as spiritual resources, as participants grow in insight and activism. The seminar makes a space for white people to express remorse, grief, and shame at what our ancestors have done and what we ourselves have done or failed to do. And in the crucial work of grieving and uncovering shame, we offer each other mutual self-criticism, challenge, and support. This support and challenge lead us beyond what Nancy Richardson calls "a vague sense of dis-ease," or beyond the stuck place identified by Susan Friedman, of which an activist of color has noted, "Just when I think we are getting somewhere, she [the white woman] starts to cry."[44] We learn to toughen up, to "buck up," and find healing that comes with collaborative transformation.

Doing Our Own Work evolved in a context where feminism, spirituality, and social justice are normatively intertwined, and where a disproportionately high percentage of constituents identify as queer or lesbian. Hence the seminar uses a multi-oppression approach that both relies on and unpacks the simple binaries of oppressor/oppressed, informally informed by insights of queer theory and postcolonial theory about the co-constitution of race, gender, sexuality, class, nation, and ability. We encounter and hold the tension of the not-quite opposites "white" and "woman."

Relying on the "not-quite-not-native informants" among us—those not quite women who are lesbian or trans, or not quite white enough because Jewish, poor, or disabled—we peel back the layers of privilege and oppression in a living deconstruction that aims toward reconstruction of a self with enough power to be an agent of change. The remade (or first-made for some of us) self includes and surpasses the individualist subject of white feminism in both communal and soul-making dimensions. Through a recasting of the colonial subject-making process, we *other* our selves to uncover the ways we have *selfed* others. By twinning and mirroring our white sisters, we come to see ourselves in Narcissus's pool, as well as in the fractured frame of the colonial gaze. Learning ourselves through one another, we learn self-love through love of one another. The seminar asks, poignantly and pointedly, "What would it mean to do this work from a place of self-love?"[45]

WHITE LOVE

[T]he final and most damaging obstacle to the psychic maturation of a postcolonial whiteness remains its own will-to-mastery—the lasting legacy, in short, of a colonialism that has left its ineffaceable mark on the postcolonial world.

ALFRED J. LÓPEZ, *Posts and Pasts: A Theory of Postcolonialism*

How do whites unlearn will-to-mastery? Of course the colonizer "loves" the native; he created it—or rather the idea of it. But the process of conscientization requires more than the recognition of will to power in this kind of love; it also requires recognizing *love* in the will to power. Understanding the colonizer qua rapist must not reduce to the (yet important) feminist maxim that rape is about power and not about love. White violence (and perhaps rape in general) is also about love—love lost, distorted, and violated. The white subject produced by the consumption of an other is an empty self, desperate for love. This kind of *soul-making* is anything but, as the self that results is a shell, propped up in ways that eat away at my insides, like a hungry ghost. I am inhabited by the alien other whom I have swallowed in my neediness, devoured in my ravenousness, who now ravishes me from the inside. Alongside or underneath sublimated layers of shame (per Thandeka), rage, and nausea (Fanon) is melancholy, an inability to grieve the lost object, per Anne Anlin Cheng.[46] Sealing over the surface of the whole thing, keeping the infection in, is the "social construction of heartlessness" that, according to Rebecca Parker and Paul Rasor, numbs white subjects.[47] The narcotic powers of imperial commodity fetishism forestall any kind of catachresis or crisis of recognition. And so the suppression of shame becomes a return to melancholic avoidance that manifests today as white liberal guilt and suppressed (or active) rage.

The complicity of white women in structures of racism can be addressed by something that we already know something about: the elusive struggle of subject constitution. Feminist consciousness is a process of recognition—a framing, perhaps a harboring, of meaning in which a person can locate her experience, finding that she is not alone or crazy. By tracking the names "woman," "patriarchy," and "compulsory heterosexuality," a person can map her life. I suggest the same is true of racial consciousness for whites, and that by placing these almost but not quite paradoxical identities together can something like liberation come to white female subjects.

FROM FORECLOSURE TO INVAGINATION

Spivak's invocation of a process of invagination, wherein others truly can be themselves and not me, "participat[ing] without belonging—taking part in without being a part of,"[48] can be lodged within me in a spaciousness larger on the inside than the out. This lodging is a visitation, a housing of aliens—monsters or angels or just people without papers—wherein a self has enough self to offer hospitality, a hospitality that values the freedom and selfhood of an other as much as the freedom and selfhood of itself. Somehow, the process of being folded in, again and again to alterity, must repeat with a difference the taking in of a lost or rejected object. Perhaps the repetition is a key. It requires practice, in every sense.

What is the difference between the fetishized foreclosure of the other and the opened embrace of invagination? In foreclosure, the colonial self takes in the colonized other in order to constitute herself. This "embrace" of the other is the vampiric addiction of the colonizer upon the personhood and power of the colonized. This feeding upon the lost object is the condition Cheng identifies as melancholia.[49]

Hybridities are themselves a form of invagination—envelopes in which contrasting identities can be housed and shielded either from one another or from external invasion. Where singular identities have been accepted, these envelopes are largely unintegrated into consciousness; where contentious, perhaps sublimated from consciousness. Coming into consciousness requires making a bigger envelope—made up of loving relationships that include self-love—within which to open the sequestered contents of the repressed awareness. Invagination has already happened, is already keeping us alive, surviving amid the contradictoriness of multiple identities. To heal from the splits requires a conscious invagination within which to restructure identity. This is not possible within a closed system; there must be a beyond, a difference that can also open a space within.

> An intersubjective theology of the embodied self affirms life in its fullness as the primordial experience and ever present moment of release from the constraints of human bondage. . . . Human beings are not unpardoned sinners. Rather, they have committed unpardonable sins that result in a shutdown of our inner spaces. There always remains, however, a tributary of life, some aspect of an "undestroyed capacity for love."[50]

The theology of this is quite simple. It is that loving an other is bound up with loving oneself, in reciprocal intersubjective ways. To successfully allow an other to be a self requires making, somehow—allowing others to make—a subject of myself. This is a shift in the Levinasian direction of others making an object of myself.

In the remarkable différance of fetishization and invagination, the repetition of selfing is what matters. The presence of a container, a bigger envelope—made up of community or good-enough self objects, and my own deep desire—tends to the alien within, keeping it fed and clothed and warmed and loved, over time, making a self.

The chasm between colonizer and colonized, man and not-man, white and not-white is not especially deep, as theorists have been demonstrating for decades via gender, race, and postcolonial theories. And yet without the pull of opposites that resolves at an imaginary magnetic north, the hybrid places would not be. When identity politics or anti-oppression work deploy oppositional stances or seem to force the issues, it is because the issues are otherwise *en*forced. And as we each depend daily on the structures that pulse domination dynamics like electricity into every aspect our lives, it doesn't seem likely that race or gender will be going away any time soon. Nor perhaps, should we wish them to. Without the witness they can bear to the violence that created them, we might cease to be haunted by what we need.

In the game of life in the everyday empire, you are either a target or an agent of oppression. One or the other. Stick with it for one minute past the point of discomfort and you will be that much closer to a capacity for difference. Stick with the telling of the terrors of empire without enjoying the satisfaction or the denial of shame. Refusing to buy into the logic of binaries doesn't mean avoiding their oppositionality, it means abiding with the deep vulnerability that a crisis of knowledge produces.

Working out the theoretical space between oppositional and fluid logics is like keeping time to two different meters simultaneously. Keeping time to the binary with one hand and the multiple with the other makes it possible to notice *when* the categories slide around in order to maintain their rigidity; *when* the up/down of man/woman becomes woman/not woman, or white/black slides across to white/not-white. The effort to keep true to the multiple without collapsing into the either/or of the logic of dominance requires learning to clearly hear the binary beat of the imperial drum that orders us below conscious hearing. It is yet possible to hear both, move between meters with a change in emphasis, and integrate them every now and again, as in the musical form of the hemiola. In part this is because the vast field of multiplicity within each self does not exist in spite of, but because of and through, the logic of empire.

In a psychological theory that takes the history of empire seriously, those who identify with the category White will learn to hear the beat that controls us and puts us in charge. A postmastery whiteness of mutual recognition will involve healing the psychic splitting that white souls suffer in the denial and perpetuation of white violence. Being white in neocoloniality means holding lightly the impossibility of self-knowledge along with the promise; doing justice with the multiplicities means attending to the binaries capaciously. Those of us who may not be all the way white, all the way subjects, or even all the way women may have a better shot at living out a deconstruction of privilege. If, that is, we can bear the tension.

✧ Planetary Sightings? Negotiating Sexual Differences in Globalization's Shadow

ELLEN T. ARMOUR

In *The Death of a Discipline*, Gayatri Chakravorty Spivak critically evaluates her discipline, comparative literature, exposing through the mundane (the book opens with a set of academic memos) and the sublime (Spivak's usual combination of literary analysis and theoretical counterpunch) this discipline's imbrication in not only academic but global politics. Born in response to an emergent postcolonial sensibility and emblematic of that movement's own political aims of attending to "the other" on "the other's" own terms, it nonetheless finds itself caught in the gravitational pull of nationalisms evident in its mapping of literary traditions according to nation-states and in its own Americanism: privileging "America" as a haven for the multicultural. As a mechanism for the circulation of cultural capital, comp lit participates—unwittingly and perhaps unwillingly—in the dynamics of globalization, which Spivak describes as a grid-like mapping of the world as nothing more or less than a network for the circulation of capital (of all kinds, including cultural). She hopes that planetarity will broaden comp lit's perspective beyond its capitulation to these dynamics. Specifically, she calls for continued attention to those populations whose literary traditions launched postcolonial studies (Africans, Asians, Hispanics) but also to newer postcolonial locales (the former Soviet bloc, for example) and to Islam's emergent importance on the world scene.

As an alternative (though not a direct opposite) to globalization, Spivak proposes planetarity. If the globe is exhaustively mapped via an economy of sameness subject to the desire for ownership, the planet is an (im)possible alterity that we inhabit on loan, she says. Thus, it renders our home, the

Earth, *unheimlich*—literally, unhomelike (though usually translated as "uncanny"). Behind the place we take for granted lies a (non)place that gives place: a planet that both makes possible and undoes our mappings of its surface into a globe.[1] Thus, planetarity offers no secure and well-known terrain across which we can stride confidently, but an unstable landscape of shifting ground, at once familiar and unfamiliar, with fissures opening beneath our feet as we attempt to navigate it.

This evocative and troubling landscape seems an apt backdrop for an inquiry into the global reach of what we call in the United States the "culture wars" currently being fought over the status of sexual minorities, primarily gay and lesbian people. The battle lines are drawn right through Christian denominations and communities—locally, nationally, and globally. Nowhere is the global dimension of this war more clearly and painfully visible than in the threatened schism of the worldwide Anglican communion. The 2003 consecration by the American Episcopal Church of the Reverend R. Gene Robinson, an openly gay man living in a committed partnership, as bishop of New Hampshire has become a central catalyst for the conflict.[2] In its aftermath, rifts have appeared within local parishes, between parishes and their home dioceses, and between and among the provincial churches.[3] The controversy is fracturing the map of the worldwide Anglican communion, which, at eighty million members distributed among forty-four provincial churches across the globe, is the third largest Protestant body in the world.[4] Often portrayed as a conflict between the (generally more liberal) "global North " and the (generally more conservative) "global South," the controversy within the Communion has spawned powerful alliances between Episcopalians opposed to Robinson's consecration and African Anglicans that suggest this map—itself redolent of colonialism—is on its way toward obsolescence. Though largely operating under the radar screen of mainstream media, at least, alliances between Northern and Southern sexual minorities have also taken shape. How far these kinds of remapping will go remains to be seen.

In this essay, I want to use Spivak's concept of planetarity to analyze some of the central features of this controversy. I begin at home with a critical look at the tendency in the United States to seek a resolution by locating "the cause" of homosexuality. This route is problematic in a number of ways, I suggest, for a progressive Christian sexual politics. In particular, it fails to contest or even acknowledge the racist underpinnings and colonialist legacies of our current sexual economy—necessary vectors of analysis if we are to face up to the global dimensions of this issue, as manifest in the Anglican communion. Deploying Spivak's critique of comp lit and her notion of planetarity, I suggest, can help us see differently both problems and possibilities inherent in this controversy.

"ADAM AND EVE, NOT ADAM AND STEVE"

If the headlines pertaining to the contemporary debate over homosexuality in the United States are any indication, the unsettled terrain on which it is fought is that where religion and science meet. Central to this controversy is the question of the origin of homosexuality, typically framed as a question of nature versus choice. Take the infamous slogan of opponents to the so-called homosexual agenda on the religious right: "God created Adam and Eve, not Adam and Steve." Heterosexuality, the slogan asserts, is grounded in divinely ordained nature while homosexuality violates the natural order and thus the will of its Author. Against the claim that homosexuality is a (sinful) "lifestyle choice," many Christian lesbians and gay men (and their allies) assert their conviction—based, for many, on the experience of coming out—that being gay is not a choice. Coming out is a matter of coming to terms with who they are and always have been—at a very deep level. Being gay or lesbian is, they would argue, every bit as natural as being heterosexual.

On this question, religion can, for once, draw on science as an ally. In recent years and months, news outlets have reported various claims by scientists to have established a biological basis for differentiating between gay and straight that promise a natural cause for sexual orientation. In recent years, the popular press has announced that scientists were on the trail of "the gay gene." In 2008 it was reported that scientists in Sweden have conducted studies that appear to establish differences in brain function between homosexuals and heterosexuals, differences that the scientists say cannot be explained by postpartum environmental differences (more on this below).[5]

In many quarters of U.S. Christendom, the claim to a natural cause for homosexuality seems to draw in straight allies—and understandably so. If homosexuality is natural, then, like heterosexuality, it can claim to be part of God's good creation. Yet I am wary of latching on to the nature band-wagon. I resist not because I think being gay or lesbian is, after all, a simple "lifestyle choice." Nor would I claim that "nature" plays *no* role in same-sex desire (or opposite-sex desire, for that matter). I resist, rather because on theoretical, historical, and pragmatic grounds, I think framing the debate in terms of "nature" versus "choice" is unsustainable and myopic as well as ethically and theologically problematic. Finding a "cause" in nature is hardly the panacea that it seems, I shall argue. At the same time, describing homosexuality as a "lifestyle choice" obscures the deep imbrication of contemporary sexual identities in a regime of knowledge and power whose origins lie in the nexus of sex, gender, race/ethnicity, religion, and imperial ambition that we have come to call colonialism. Buying into the nature/nurture schema leaves a Christian progressive sexual politics at either a literal dead end, I will suggest, or mired in an unacknowledged yet powerful history, a history whose effects are all too legible in the Anglican controversy.

There are deep and long-standing theological limits to the efficacy of the argument from nature. Just because something is natural—especially something sexual—doesn't make it good, not in a Christian theological framework shaped as it is by the concept of original sin. In its classical Augustinian formulation (which claims biblical warrant in the Genesis narrative referenced by "Eve not Steve"), the first human beings violated the proper order of creation by turning away from God and toward themselves. This *was* a choice, according to Augustine—and it had serious repercussions for, among other things, human sexuality. Because human beings used their free wills to disobey God, God punished them by turning them over to the disobedience of their bodies. The primary symptoms of this punishment show up in and around sexuality, now activated by inordinate desire rather than, as God intended it, by the rationally directed will. The actions of the primordial pair corrupted human nature, and that corrupt nature is itself passed down from generation to generation—through procreation. (Though the smug tone of the slogan conveniently obscures this fact, even procreative heterosexuality is hardly untainted.)[6]

The assertion that Christians should love the sinner but hate the sin, a principle often invoked by opponents of homosexuality who resist being tagged as homophobic, echoes this theological vision. Same-sex desire, it suggests, may indeed originate in our nature, but that doesn't excuse acting on it. We carry the source of sin in our bodies, and the Christian life involves struggling with sinful nature in one form or another. Homosexual tendencies are no more—and no less—than some people's particular cross to bear. The "promise" of scientific research and therapies offers little help for the progressive cause. Consider, for example, the viewpoint articulated by Dr. Albert Mohler, the president of Southern Baptist Theological Seminary. If a genetic cause for homosexuality is discovered, he said, Christians should support the pursuit of a prenatal "cure." He imagines a hormonal "patch" that the mother might wear to eliminate the orientation altogether[7]—a particularly frightening prospect in the light of the latest research on brain differences. As the reporter for *Slate* put it, "If the idea of chemically suppressing homosexuality in the womb horrifies you, I have bad news: You won't be in the room when it happens. . . . The reduction of homosexuality to neurobiology doesn't mean your sexual orientation can't be controlled. It just means the person controlling it won't be you."[8] Routing progressive Christian sexual politics down nature's road, then, is likely a literal dead end for minoritized sexualities.

But there are also good historical and theoretical reasons for moving away from nature versus choice. As theorists such as Michel Foucault have argued, "heterosexuality" and "homosexuality"—both as terms and as lived identities—may be normative, but they are not (simply) natural. Rather, they are of relatively recent *and culturally specific* vintage.[9] Let's be clear: this is not a claim about sexual *desire* or *acts*; human beings have, as far as we can determine, always and in every corner of the globe engaged in same-sex sex (homo-sex) and opposite- sex sex (hetero-sex). This is true of the global South as well as the global North, despite claims by some clerics that any presence of same-sex practice in the South is attributable to Western corruption.[10] But only within the last two hundred years or so have some human beings come to understand those sexual acts as expressions of who they *are* at their deepest core. That those human beings happened to live in the West—dominated as it has been by Christianity—is not entirely coincidental, according to these theorists. Premodern Christianity sets the stage for sexuality's emergence as the centerpiece of Western identities. And the concept of sin plays a central role. The shift in monastic penitential practices from bodily performances of fleshly chastisement to verbal confessions, and then from confession of acts to confession of thoughts literally constitutes the soul as the site of the self. We are some distance from the modern ideal of the self-contained and self-interested individual. The ideal monastic self is other-directed (toward the community and ultimately toward God), but pursuing other-directedness required ever deeper inquiry into the self's own contours. In this context, sexual acts and desires—note the parallel with flesh and spirit—served as an index of one's closeness to God.

A central development in medieval Christian thought and practice, Mark Jordan demonstrates, is the creation of a new sexual identity, "the sodomite," who, while markedly different from our contemporary notion of "the homosexual," provides fallow ground in which the creation and pathologization of "the homosexual" takes root.[11] The sodomite (a monk who engages in, or thinks about engaging in, certain kinds of sex acts with other monks), Jordan notes, is a creation of medieval penitential manuals crafted originally to maintain disciplinary order within monasteries. Jordan describes sodomy's move from one among a list of sexual sins (and a vaguely defined one, at that) to "a brand that burns condemnation into certain acts. It burns into them as well the presumption of a stable essence, a sameness found wherever the acts are performed."[12] In other words, that a man engages in "sodomy" is a result of who he is, a "sodomite." But the sodomite is not fundamentally a *sexual* identity; it is rather a religious identity. Being a sodomite indexes one's distance from the divine and proximity to the demonic.

In modernity, science and history replace religious authorities as arbiters of truth, and the West develops a science of sexuality that aims at both identifying and determining the cause of sexual behavior—particularly aberrant sexual behavior, including "homosexuality," a term that emerged in medical parlance in the late nineteenth century. The science of sexuality reflects these Christian antecedents. Confession—now to doctors rather than to priests and framed by the demand that *sexuality* tell its truth—continues as the mechanism through which the so-called perversions are not only named and catalogued but ultimately attributed to their source in the deepest recesses of the person who engages in such acts. To paraphrase (and "Jordanize") Foucault, if sodomy began as "an aberration," by the early twentieth century, "the homosexual [had become] a species."[13]

And there is more. Homosexuality and heterosexuality themselves rest on other identities we take to be natural: being a man or a woman. Just as our slogan assumes a clear distinction between Adam and Eve, so do we. We expect maleness or femaleness to be legible in clear anatomical differences. Those differences ground appropriate gender behavior and sexual desire. Males (naturally) act masculine and desire women while females (naturally) act feminine and desire men. By this schema, desiring otherwise cannot but appear "unnatural," undoing the entire linear chain. Thus, we expect all gay men to be effeminate and all lesbians mannish.[14] Indeed, a number of scholars have suggested that folks get worked up about homosexuality in large part because it challenges the presumed naturalness of our hierarchical sex/gender system that places men above women. Note that the slogan speaks of Adam and Steve, not Anne and Eve. Note as well that a specific form of "homosexual *behavior*" (anal sex between men) seems to arouse particular anxiety.

Human beings—even in the West—have not always mapped sexual behavior and gender in this way, however. Our modern notion of sexual identity has no precise correlate in the ancient world, as a number of scholars have argued. In the Greco-Roman culture in which Christianity came into being, for example, one's legitimate sexual partners—and one's proper role in sex acts—were determined by one's place in a social hierarchy. An elite man, for example, could have licit sex not only with his wife but also with his male and female slaves. Having homo-sex posed no challenge to his masculinity—as long as he was the penetrating partner, not the receiving partner. While ancient Greeks and Romans associated certain sexual practices/positions (males who are penetrated, females who penetrate) with gender transgression, they did not expect to see such practices necessarily reflected in one's everyday manner and style of dress. Moreover, they associated certain male same-sex bonds with virility and warned men against the effeminizing effects of too much sex with women.[15]

Further challenges to the presumed naturalness of our sex/gender schema come from the realm of contemporary theory. "One is not born a woman, but, rather, becomes one," the philosopher Simone de Beauvoir argued in her classic text, *The Second Sex*.[16] More recently, feminist and queer theorist Judith Butler has undone our presumption of a linear link between sex, gender, and desire. Noting that biological sex is ambiguous at all bodily levels (the chromosomal, the genital, and the morphological) more often than we suspect,[17] she goes on to argue that our binary sex/gender system is social not natural in origin. Our heteronormative system requires desire to channel itself via gendered identities that invoke bodily markers as their signature and guarantee. Masculinity and femininity are not the natural expressions of bodily sex; they are identities we come to inhabit through bodily practices that conform to cultural standards. And sexuality is embedded in this process, too. Taking up one's place in this binary system requires becoming not only a specific gender/sex, but taking on a specific sexual identity, as well. The process of coming out is arguably precisely that process—with the labor involved rendered visible and tangible because, in the case of LGBTQ folk, the identity taken on is nonnormative. Indeed, most of the labor involved centers on coming to terms with that nonnormativity and its real or potential consequences. And that, I submit, is a problem created not by nature, but by history and culture. Put theologically, it is a problem created by Adam and Eve, not by Steve, and not by God.

Furthermore, the shape and emergence of these particular sexual identities is bound up not only with gender, but with race and ethnicity—that is to say, with sexism and racism, and thus, in turn, with the imperialist project we know as colonialism, globalization's predecessor. Recall Spivak's description of globalization as a map of the world as simply a network through which capital circulates. While the two maps are not identical, one could describe colonialism that way, as well. Colonialism involved relatively centralized movements of economic, cultural, and human capital from South to North largely via nation-states and their surrogates. While these categories of capital moved in both directions, the specific forms capital took differed considerably. The North took from the South raw material, exotic curiosities, and unskilled labor to the North's benefit. In an asymmetrical exchange, the North exported financial capital, "civilization," and managers—also resources turned to the North's benefit. Globalization is colonialism's decentralized heir. Capital of all sorts moves in both directions, but the entities that primarily manage and benefit, while still predominately Northern and Western, are more diffuse. Non-state actors are more significant (multinational corporations and/or terrorist networks, for example). Wealth still concentrates—for now, at least—primarily in the North, but globalization creates scarcity and excess in both regions at the micro- as well as macroeconomic levels.[18]

Colonial expansion was a system of exploitation justified as a divinely ordained method for civilizing the barely human and aided and abetted by Christianity. Indeed, Anglicanism is a global faith because of its connection to the British Empire. Under colonialism, sexuality demarcated the line between civilized and savage. In colonial contexts, including much of the global South, the project of civilizing the savage other included reorienting their sexual and familial practices toward Western (often Victorian) mores. Although we may never have a fully accurate picture of sexual practices in the global South before colonialism, there is evidence of a range that doesn't fit neatly into the West's binary system of sex, gender, and sexuality.[19] The historian and Anglican missionary Kevin Ward notes that, while same-sex relationships have always existed in African societies (in various forms and with varying degrees of acceptance or rejection), they have not been understood within the framework of sexual essence, as they have in the West. Nor do they replicate the associations we make in the West between same-sex orientation and gender deviance.[20] Though he cautions against taking this research as definitive in all times and places in Africa, Ward cites David Greenberg's taxonomy of African sexualities. Greenberg distinguishes at least three forms of same-sex relationships: transgenerational, transgenderal (one partner adopts the dress or habits of the opposite sex), and egalitarian (similar age, similar gender identity).[21] However, the colonizers clearly did their best to encourage greater conformity to Western/Northern models. The British colonial powers made homosexual conduct illegal in Nigeria in the nineteenth century.[22] Practices like polygamy were deemed deviant and strongly discouraged across Africa, at least officially (though in practice the Church was and remains more tolerant, according to Kevin Ward).[23] The Ugandan Church authorities withheld access to the sacraments in order to enforce Western sexual mores. Today, only a small minority of participants in the Ugandan Anglican church are communicants. This is so because, until 1973, the Church would only baptize children born to parents who had been married in the church.[24]

But accusations of sexual deviance could work another way, as well. The sexual exploitation of slaves was justified by attributing to Africans a deviant sexual nature characterized by voracious appetite (a sign of particular deviance in women) and inappropriate object choices (African men desiring white women, for example). Not only theorists, but theologians such as Kelly Brown Douglas and Marcella Althaus-Reid have documented various ways in which these legacies continue to affect descendants of formerly enslaved and colonized peoples.[25] Indeed, there is strong evidence for considering the current conflict within Anglicanism as a reflection of a colonialist legacy. The conflict reminds white Christians from the global North that, although we don't usually think of ourselves that way, we, too, are heirs of this legacy.

PLANETARY SIGHTINGS

Spivak's planet is space we occupy on loan that transcends all of our maps and the material practices they articulate and sustain. As (non)place that gives place, the planet has given place to the distribution of property that was colonization, to its redistribution under globalization, and to the fractures and fissures therein. Using planetarity as a lens to analyze the controversy over homosexuality in the Anglican communion, then, will allow us to take account of the effects of colonialism and globalization while remaining alert to gaps in those systems.

The standard depiction of the controversy in the Anglican communion assumes a map that divides the planet into two relatively monolithic regions, the "global South" and the "global North." Human, financial, political, and theological capital is distributed asymmetrically between these regions. The South is wealthiest in human capital. Of the forty-four provinces of the Anglican communion, just twenty are located in the global South, but those twenty house a substantial majority of the Anglican Church's population. Insofar as the controversy pits essentially two Northern provinces (the American and Canadian churches) against most of the provinces of the global South, the conflict resembles the struggle between David and Goliath. Consider the small size (2.5 million members) of the Episcopal church in comparison to that of the Anglican Church of Nigeria (claims range from 15 to 20 million members),[26] and the asymmetry looms larger.

Consider financial capital, however, and the asymmetry cuts differently. Economic resources continue to move primarily from North to South via Northern (indeed, Episcopal) largesse, as they have since colonial times. No surprise, then, that the specter of colonialism hangs over this controversy. In an official document, the most Reverend Peter J. Akinola, the archbishop of the Nigerian church, who has emerged as a primary spokesperson on behalf of Southern churches, speaks of "unilateral actions taken without consulting the wider Communion"; he refers to actions taken by materially advantaged Northern churches without regard for their impact on the materially disadvantaged as just the latest evidence of "a new imperialism."[27] For some Southern Anglican bishops, then, resistance to greater openness toward gays and lesbians is an anti-imperialist and anticolonialist stance. Although the Episcopal church has continued to provide financial support to the larger communion and its missions, some primates in the global South have refused Episcopal financial support in the wake of Bishop Robinson's consecration.[28]

At the heart of the controversy are charges of theological imperialism. The Northern churches stand accused of imposing a new theology on the Southern churches. That charge is made, however, in the name of the original imperial theology as a recent interview with Archbishop Akinola by Ruth Gledhill, religion correspondent for the U.K. *Times*, demonstrates.

Gledhill writes, "The irony is not lost on [Akinola] that he is attempting to preach a gospel back to England that was brought to his country by English missionaries in the mid-nineteenth century." She quotes Akinola: "The missionaries brought the word of God here and showed us the way of life. We have seen the way of life and we rejoice in it. Now you are telling me this way of life is not right. I have to do something else."[29]

Theology also appears to be providing common ground for the emergence of powerful alliances between dissident Episcopalians and the provincial churches of the global South, particularly Africa. Many of the Episcopal parishes that want no truck with the Episcopal Church in the United States sought episcopal oversight from primates in the global South. In 2006, they banded together to form the Convocation of Anglicans in North America (CANA), headed by Martin Minns of Fairfax, Virginia, consecrated as bishop by Archbishop Akinola.[30] The schismatic Episcopalians report finding common cause with Akinola's assertion that a progressive stance on homosexuality is not in itself the problem but that it indexes deeper theological differences over biblical authority and church tradition.

The activist role taken by Southern—particularly African—primates in the controversy is often seen as evidence of the shift of theological and political capital from the North to the South following the changing demographics of Christianity.[31] Many on both sides of the Anglican divide see in these dynamics evidence of Philip Jenkins's claim that we are witnessing the inevitable rise of a "next Christendom," a "global Christianity" headquartered in the South this time rather than the North or West. Like Southern Anglicanism, we can expect this new Christendom to be more theologically conservative on the whole than Northern Christianity, a reality to which Northerners will have to accommodate.[32]

The standard account of the controversy is certainly troubling for Northerners who want to promote a progressive Christian sexual politics. This account decenters us and renders our globe *unheimlich*, an unpleasant sensation for those of us long used to a comfortable place of relative privilege and power because of our socioeconomic location. The tenuous footing LGBTQ Northerners thought we had found seems to be shifting under our feet. I think there is value, though, in being thrown off-center. A progressive Christian sexual politics cannot succeed by ignoring the realities on the ground, as painful as they may be. Doing so is not only dangerous but also may mean that we miss signs of promise as well as peril.

Both appear in and around the alliance that has formed between dissident Episcopalians and Southern traditionalists. The sociologist Melinda Hassett finds Jenkins's thesis (or, at least, the use to which Anglicans tend to put it) rather too facile. Rather than the inevitable and natural consequences of emerging global realities, the alliance between Southern and Northern traditionalists is the product of a significant expenditure of capital by dissident Episcopalians. At the decennial conference of bishops at Lambeth in 1998, the controversy over homosexuality moved from backstage to center stage in the Anglican communion. This was no accident. A series of conferences held in advance of Lambeth by Episcopal dissidents with local bishops and primates in the global South laid the groundwork for it.[33] In these settings, theological, political, and financial capital came together to forge new alliances across lines of geography, race, and class. Progressive Northerners have frequently denounced these efforts as something just short of bribery on the part of Episcopal dissidents, a depiction both Southerners and their Northern allies reject—and with good reason, according to Hassett's account. Though hardly unaffected by the legacies of colonialism, these alliances are genuine and serve the interests of both sides (which are not necessarily the same). Moreover, their effects—at least in some cases— challenge Northern expectations of conservative and liberal political and theological alignments. At least one dissident Episcopal congregation, called "St. Timothy's" in Hassett's account, has taken its new provincial affiliation with Rwanda quite seriously. Led by lay members who have visited Rwanda, many in the congregation have become advocates for issues like ending poverty in Africa that Rwandans define as critical. A closer affiliation with Africa has also yielded emergent practices of self-criticism around anti-African racism (what connections are made to anti-African *American* racism is not clear, according to Hassett). These are surely moves that progressive Christians would welcome. Yet they come at the expense of a progressive stance on sexuality.

A deeper look at the historical and social context of Southern Christianity belies a presumed theological uniformity between Northern dissidents and their Southern allies—even by Jenkins's account. Like fellow scholar of global Christianity Lamin Sanneh, Jenkins argues that substantive differences in social and historical context give Southern Christianity—especially in Africa—a distinctive theological shape. If, to use Sanneh's terminology, Northern Christianity must reckon with a context that is largely post-Christian if not postreligious, African Christianity confronts the complex realities of a postcolonial context that is much more akin to the worlds of the biblical writers. Tyrannical or corrupt governments that offer few reliable services for their constituents, economic struggles, the need to establish one's place among a variety of religious traditions—all are everyday realities for many African Christians. Elements of biblical thought (supernaturalism, martyrdom, apocalypticism) that modernist Northerners have come to regard as historical curiosities are living modes of faithfulness for Southerners. Thus, to Northern eyes, Southerners appear more "conservative," at least in theological and sexual matters, though "liberal" on issues of poverty, racism, and national politics. Yet both Jenkins and Sanneh stress that Southern Christianities are becoming truly indigenous creations that do not conform neatly to Northern political and/or theological alignments.[34]

Almost completely obscured by the standard account of the controversy in the Anglican communion are potential alliances for progressives across geographical lines. Hassett and other scholars provide evidence that complicate monolithic portraits of the global South. Terry Brown, Bishop of Malaita (of the Province of Micronesia), an openly gay man living in celibacy, has edited an anthology of essays by Anglicans from across the global South—several of them of sexual minorities themselves—that belie any claim that Southern Anglicans speak with one voice on this issue.[35] Africans' views on sexuality issues range far more widely than the standard depiction suggests, even within the Anglican communion. Archbishop Njongonkulu Nkungane of the Province of the Church in Southern Africa welcomed Bishop Robinson's consecration with prayers of support and congratulations. Christopher Ssenyonjo, a retired Ugandan bishop, also saw the event as "God's way of making the church come to terms with homosexuality."[36] In 2001, with Ssenyonjo's support, a Ugandan Anglican priest and his wife (whose ministry with youth led them to get involved) founded a local chapter of Integrity, the EC(USA) organization for LGBT Anglicans.[37] It seems likely that the realities on the ground are more complex than we Northerners can see from a distance—and perhaps than traditionalists would like us to believe.

FINDING NEW FOOTING

It is critical that the LGBT faithful, who have seen their lives and vocations reduced to bargaining chips in a decade-long game of Anglican politics, speak out together and give voice to the hope and the faith and their witness to the Anglican Communion.

INTEGRITY USA

What lessons are present in this admittedly all too brief sketch of the Anglican controversy for those who want to promote a progressive Christian sexual politics on such an unstable landscape? We do no one any favors if we allow the South to become the site of a proxy war between Northern factions. Those most likely to pay the highest cost in the short term, at least, in this controversy are not Northern gays and lesbians but sexual minorities in the global South.[38] Archbishop Akinola has lent his support to draconian legislation moving through the Nigerian legislature that would criminalize public association of Nigerian gays and lesbians. Activists in Nigerian AIDS organizations and gay and lesbian organizations have been outspoken in their opposition to that legislation—often at considerable cost to themselves. Their cause has been taken up by such secular organizations as the United Nations and Human Rights Watch and the International Gay and Lesbian Human Rights Commission.[39] Gay and lesbian Anglicans in England have joined with their counterparts in Nigeria to speak out against acts of violence against Nigerian gays and lesbians.[40] How exactly these alliances are playing out between Southerners and Northerners on the ground I am certainly not in a position to say, but allow me to offer some suggestions for going forward.

To succeed, progressive Christians will have to not only acknowledge but contend with the specters of colonialization and globalization that lend legitimacy to the claim that the global North is, once again, dictating theology to the global South. First of all, we have to recognize that Christianity is itself a network for the circulation of capital (financial, cultural, and human). It is embedded in political and social entities (nation states, faith-based NGOs, etc.) that are themselves nodes in the larger network of the global economy. The controversy over homosexuality will necessarily reflect these realities, and progressive activists are just as vulnerable to them as traditionalist activists.[41] The temptation, of course, is toward paralysis or withdrawal from engagement lest we further contaminate the field. Willis Jenkins notes that progressive Anglicans responded to colonialist critiques largely by withdrawing from mission activity in Africa and elsewhere. What mission activity persists takes the form of sending money rather than people, thus enabling ignorance about the lived experience of African Anglicans and leaving the field of human missions labor largely to those Anglicans of a more evangelistic and theologically conservative bent.[42] Progressives could learn something from the dissident Episcopalians: there is no substitute for face-to-face contact, as risky as it may be.

In her groundbreaking essay "Can the Subaltern Speak?" Spivak famously coined a sentence that has become emblematic of postcolonial critique: "[W]hite men are saving brown women from brown men."[43] Although one can attach it to particular historical events (Spivak links it to the outlawing of *sati* by the British in India), Spivak intends it to name a fantasmatic position that comes to life from time to time in the form of certain imperial subjects. Though motivated by a desire to rescue those subjected to injustice, the attempt at rescue or redress becomes an asymmetrical exchange with the indigenous oppressor that produces a defensive response ("they want to die this way," Hindu men responded, in the case of *sati*). In the process, the supposed object of rescue is consigned to being spoken about or spoken for.[44] The history of colonialist and postcolonialist interventions by Northerners—including progressives (even feminists)—is rife with evidence of the collateral damage caused by these kinds of interventions.

In the first part of this essay, I argued against grounding advocacy for U.S. gays and lesbians in the claim that homosexuality is "caused" by nature. I made the argument based primarily on the problems inherent in arguments from nature. Perhaps now, though, we can see a positive argument for abandoning that sinking ship. It might be tempting to reach back to arguments from nature and see therein terra firma on which progressives might build alliances with sexual minorities in the South. Evidence that Southerners are latching onto Northern sexual categories as sources of self-naming would seem to further bolster the cause. However, they do so against significantly different historical backdrops and sexual economies—inflected, to be sure, by our binary system, but not exhausted by or merely coextensive with it. Here again, lessons from past interventions in Africa document the damage wrought when Northerners—no matter how well-intentioned— import assumptions from their own sex/gender system into African contexts.[45] Just as there is nothing natural and inevitable about the alliance between Northern and Southern traditionalists, the same is true for alliances among progressives. Alliances must be carefully crafted in and through genuine engagement with differences as well as similarities, not in spite of them. Starting with the assumption that there is nothing (merely) natural about those sexual identities we take for granted creates an open space—a planetary gap within a global system—in which differences in context and experience might more easily register.[46]

Miranda Hassett describes the conflict in the Anglican communion as featuring competing visions of a truly global communion: progressives seek unity in honoring diversity, traditionalists in enforcing conformity with the global majority. Neither, in my view, provides solid footing for a progressive Christian sexual politics, as both tend to leave theological and political centers and dominant orthodoxies (local or global) undisturbed. But solid footing on a planetary landscape is impossible. Enacting a progressive *planetary* Christian sexual politics will require a light and careful step out of our comfort zones into places of peril and promise, and likely with results we cannot anticipate.

❧ "Effects of Grace":
Detranscendentalizing

ERIN RUNIONS

Gayatri Chakravorty Spivak's writing is nothing if not challenging. Somewhat daunted, I console myself with the fact that every reading is necessarily, and sometimes deliberately, a misreading, and proceed on those grounds. Perhaps the most important thing to grasp when reading Spivak on religion is her insistence on detranscendentalizing. She insists on it as the secular work of the humanities. I would like to explore this insistence on detranscendentalizing, as it relates to a much larger theme in her work: that is, ethical singularity. In other terms, the theory compressed into the phrase *detranscendentalizing alterity* helps us think about what she means by *love*. I would like to take up these ideas by reading one instance of alterity—the myth of the antichrist—in order to trouble the political calculations that are made in the name of Christ. This troubling is a kind of *queering*.

DETRANSCENDENTALIZING

In the published version of a talk on terror that Spivak gave at Columbia University not long after 9/11, she uses the tools of deconstruction on Kant's *Religion within the Boundaries of Mere Reason*, in order to imagine how religion might be used to interrupt political calculation.[1] In particular, she is concerned with questioning the kinds of calculations posing as ethical action that have taken over in the U.S. war on terror. She gives as an example the U.S.'s self-proclaimed role of world police, "ethically" enforcing human rights and at the same time condoning the right to kill.[2] In looking at religion, she does not want to think about transcendent truths (higher powers, moral wills) as much as about the possibilities that religious metaphors open up for the ethical interruption of calculation. She wants to "work for a world where religion can shrink to [the] mundane normality" of "the weave of permissible narratives."[3] In this world, religion would be understood as "idiom rather than ground of belief."[4]

Such an insight is familiar to scholars of religion thinking within a Foucauldian paradigm of discursive construction, or thinking beyond a sui generis view of religion.[5] What is theoretically challenging about Spivak's work, however, is the precise way in which she reconceptualizes the transcendent, as radical alterity, and then proceeds to detranscendentalize it. She writes: "Radical alterity, an otherness that reason needs but which reason cannot grasp, can be given many names. God in many languages is its most recognizable name."[6] Kant, she notes, gave it the name of the transcendental.[7] Some might call it terror. Spivak insists on the need to detranscendentalize radical alterity in order to interrupt the calculative.[8] I take her to mean that she wishes to criticize the notion of radical alterity (in its guise of either terror or transcendence) as a kind of self-contained goodness or evil that acts as a kind of independent a priori. She wants to move away from any conception of radical alterity as a kind of causeless cause that grounds reason within a given culture.[9] Spivak seems to play with the slippage in the way that radical alterity is sometimes understood as an omniscient power outside of knowledge (the transcendent), and sometimes as the condition of possibility for knowledge (Kant's transcendental).[10] Indeed, it is in this elision between the transcendent and the transcendental that religion (as belief in the transcendent, or God) can come to provide the terms, or create a condition of possibility, in which a "cultural imaginary produc[es] reason."[11]

To help her conceptualize a detranscendentalized radical alterity, she turns to a very dense and compact deconstructive reading of *Religion within the Boundaries of Mere Reason*—perhaps because Kant explores the question of human goodness and evil in this text, or perhaps because Kant acts, to some degree, as a model for her own insistence on reason, secularity, and ethics. She borrows from his attempt to think through the relation of reason, morality, the transcendental, and secularity. In her words, "Because Kant was deeply aware of the limits of reason, he asked himself if it was possible to forge a species of what we might as well call secularism, which would incorporate intuitions of the transcendental. Let us see how he solved his problem and what we, who must be fair to our debt to Kant and yet must undo him, can learn from him."[12]

She goes on to explain that, for Kant, mere reason is not able actually to *produce* moral action. As she puts it, "mere reason . . . merely likes to patch a minus with a plus, push legally good actions with no attention to the mind's corrupt attitudes." If morality is to be possible, therefore, pure reason requires some help from elsewhere to produce moral capacity. In Kant's terms, "Reason, conscious of its impotence to satisfy its moral needs, extends itself to extravagant ideas which might make up for this lack." One might expect, perhaps, that such help would come from transcendental intuitions, but instead it requires what he calls "effects of grace." As Spivak notes, Kant calls the "effects of grace" one of four *secondary elements* of religion within the bounds of pure reason (the others being miracles, mysteries, and means of grace). In Kant's words, "these are, as it were, *parerga* to religion within the boundaries of pure reason; they do not belong within it yet border on it." They, like the transcendent for Kant, are not available to cognition, and so cannot be theoretically useful, but they are made available to the will, though incomprehensible and unbidden, and are therefore able "to make up for [reason's] 'moral impotence.'" Spivak seizes on the phrase "effects of grace" and rereads it in a way that hangs on to the radical alterity of grace, but detranscendentalizes it.[13]

It should be noted that understanding "effects of grace" as parergon, is central to Spivak's deconstructive reading. A footnote tells her reader that she is engaging with Derrida's reading of Kant's *Religion within the Boundaries of Mere Reason*, which talks, among other things, about the dangers of misrecognizing these parerga as religious knowledge or religious experience that can found a moral program.[14] But she also clearly has in mind Derrida's earlier analysis of Kant's discussion of parerga with respect to aesthetics, where he shows how difficult it is in analyzing works of art to separate out parerga—secondary or framing elements—from primary elements in a work of art, as for instance, in his example of "the drapery on statues which simultaneously adorns and veils their nudity . . . clinging to the work's edges . . . but not a part of the representative whole."[15] Along these lines, Spivak suggests that radical alterity or effects of grace, as parerga, are difficult to determine as either fully internal, or fully external, to the system of reason, or the secular. This bordering function for radical alterity can best be seen if it is detranscendentalized. She performs this deconstructive operation on "effects of grace," by taking the word "effect" out of the realm of the theological and into that of the aesthetic—which she understands here as the literary.[16]

Two things happen if "effect" (in the phrase "effects of grace") is understood as something to do with aesthetics. First, when effect is understood
in the realm of aesthetics, it disrupts calculation. Because Spivak calls the
aesthetic (again following Kant) "purposiveness without purpose,"[17] it is not
goal-oriented, it is not calculative. Although the aesthetic will have an effect,
it is not one that can be computed in advance. Second, if "effect" is moved
into the aesthetic, or literary, then "grace," or radical alterity, must also be
understood as related to that realm. It is no longer the transcendent(al)
causeless cause as much as something like a semantic possibility that is
opened up by the aesthetic. "Grace" becomes an "unverifiable effect of an
effect." Grace operates, she suggests, something like the figure of speech,
metalepsis.[18] To spell it out, metalepsis works through an occluded chain of
cause and effect—the metaphor is successful because this chain of cause and
effect works without being readily visible. Grace, or radical alterity, looks
like the work of the transcendent, but is the result of this hidden chain of
cause and effect. If we were to spatialize her move into the aesthetic, I think
we could say that it is a move from the vertical to the horizontal, from a
theological spatialization of heaven and earth to a Derridean spatialization
of signifying chains and the possibilities opened up therein. She makes it
clear that this move is different from literalizing religious metaphor (which
would maintain a notion of verticality), as she claims liberation theology
and suicide bombing both do.[19] She is not interested in operationalizing
religious tropes on earth—for example, martyrdom or the kingdom of
heaven—but rather she moves *into* metaphor, or into the signifying chain—
into the literary and its effects.

This move is an important one in the current debates about the relation
of the secular to the religious because it makes room for both, but in a way
that one cannot trump the other. Belief (or lack of belief) is irrelevant to
this kind of analysis—indeed, Spivak is trying to move away from what she
calls "belief as faith,"[20] which could be applied both to religious and atheistic
belief structures. Belief as faith does not acknowledge that there are perhaps
unverifiable operations of signification, and dependence on existing structures, that produce a notion of radical alterity.

But if alterity is a space within signification, it is a place of impossibility.
It is something like the constitutive outside to rational possibility within
discourse. Reason requires radical alterity for morality, but cannot grasp it;
reason requires effects of grace from radical alterity to induce ethical action,
but cannot apprehend them through cognition. How can this happen? And

how can it happen in a way that is not simply the appropriation of alterity by reason?

ETHICAL IMPOSSIBILITY

I would like now to connect the notion of detranscendentalized alterity to Spivak's discussions of radical alterity, ethics, and religion elsewhere in her writing. For instance, in her essay "Moving Devi" (on the Hindu goddess Maha-Devi), Spivak theorizes the relation of radical alterity to the religious, using the literary term "permanent parabasis," a phrase she borrows from Paul de Man, which refers to the persistent interruption in Greek comedy whereby the chorus appears to comment on something apparently unrelated.[21] In deconstructive terms, she describes permanent parabasis as "*invagination*," borrowing from Derrida. Invagination is "a participation without belonging—a taking part in without being part . . . the boundary of the set comes to form, by invagination, an internal pocket larger than the whole."[22] It functions as a permanent ironic interruption, a "nonpassage" to the other side.[23] In "Moving Devi," Spivak reads the supernatural in Hinduism in the way that she advocates religion should be understood: as the weave of permissible narrative. Her description of the way she understands the supernatural to function in Hinduism—in the principle of *dvaita*, or twoness, where divinity appears in a natural phenomenon—helps us see how she understands radical alterity to function as "an impossible invagination in every instance of the other."[24] She suggests that this conception of the supernatural that resides in (invaginates) the natural can counter and disrupt another tendency within Hinduism, *advaita*, that is, a nondual notion of the supernatural that is less open to negotiation with the profane, wherein "a cathected god or goddess occupies the entire godspace."[25] The possibility of the "unanticipatable emergence of the supernatural in the natural" acts as an ironic interruption, or permanent parabasis, to *advaita*.[26]

In terms of her reading of Kant and ethics, invagination might be understood as the nonpassage between radical alterity and reason. In *Critique of Postcolonial Reason*, Spivak calls this nonpassage "the impossible boundary marking off the wholly other" that, insofar as it "may be figured, has an unpredictable relationship to our ethical rules." Because invagination is "impossible," it cannot be predicted. It cannot, therefore, be put to work in calculative fashion.[27] This point can be better understood through her discussion of ethics.

This notion of the permanent parabasis of radical alterity *sounds very much like* the impossible experience of ethical singularity that Spivak describes both in her translator's commentary on Mahasweta Devi's *Imaginary Maps* and in *Critique of Postcolonial Reason*. Ethical singularity is the famous way in which Spivak envisions love.[28] Taking her example from one of Devi's stories, Spivak draws the conclusion that "We must learn 'love' (a simple name for ethical responsibility-in-singularity) . . . in view of the impossibility of communication. No individual transcendence theology . . . can bring us to this."[29] Ethical singularity is the communication between two people in which "slow attentive mind changing (on both sides)" can take place.[30] It is produced in acts of true exchange (not charity), and with the recognition that even in this exchange something is always lost in the attempt at communication.[31] An engagement with ethical singularity recognizes that in any dialogue with the other, something does not get through; thus it can never ground a *program* of ethics. Ethics is an impossible single encounter. As Dawn Rae Davis glosses it in her essay on ethical singularity, "[F]rom this perspective, love is the impossible experience of knowing across radical difference, and simultaneously, that which requires ethical choice and action even in the face of the impossible."[32] Davis calls this kind of love a "not knowing." Such impossibility and not-knowing interrupt the colonial power relations that are predicated on knowing the Other.[33] They also interrupt the kinds of calculation that are often made in the name of ethics, much in the way that radical alterity operates as a kind of invagination or permanent parabasis in the house of ethical reasoning.

Yet Spivak stresses in *Critique* that ethical singularity is *not* an experience of radical alterity.[34] She clarifies this point in her foreword to the Blackwell *Companion to Postcolonial Studies*. She writes: "The subaltern [the Other with whom one might have an encounter of ethical singularity] is not the absolute other. (Nothing) (is) the absolute other."[35] At the same time, Spivak's vision of the ethical and singular encounter with the Other clearly seems to mimic the relation of radical alterity to reason. Indeed, once radical alterity has been detranscendentalized and moved onto this horizontal literary plane, it seems that we cannot help but move from speaking of the absolute Other, to the Other. I am suggesting that her move to detranscendentalize is a move toward the (im)possibility of ethical encounter.

Spivak's consideration of the relation of the transcendent(al) to ethics is crucial in a world that is increasingly run along Schmittian lines, whereby leadership is characterized by calculations on the strong moral decision, that is, the decision on truth and on the enemy. The calculative decision on the enemy is, as ever, justified for many people through recourse to the supernatural, to judgments about good and evil. Transcendence in certain worldviews is not only about God; it is also about the realm of evil—which we see well dramatized in the speeches of former president George W. Bush. His Schmittian focus on the strong decision appeals both to neoconservatives with their focus on moral virtue and to conservative Christians concerned with combating evil.[36] It also appeals to those who are working to remasculinize Christianity, because, as they argue, the strong man is the one who can make decisions. In the words of theonomist Phil Vollman, senior pastor of Shiloh Christian Church in Ohio, strong and moral Christian men do not have "PTA (permanent testicular atrophy)."[37] These and many other kinds of calculations about action and ethics are made through recourse to the transcendent. Kant might call the appeal to the transcendent in such calculations to be "the dogmatic faith which announces itself to be a knowledge."[38] The question is whether the transcendent as radical alterity can disrupt those calculations (without calculating, of course).

RADICAL ALTERITY AS EVIL: THE ANTICHRIST

Spivak's move to detranscendentalize is focused on critiquing any politics that guarantees its authority by imagining itself as "the proper shadow of the transcendental,"[39] as having some kind of calculated access to radical alterity. But I would like to think about the flip side of this kind of calculation and consider what is named "evil" as a form of radical alterity. Evil, just like God, or the transcendental, is sometimes understood to exist outside of natural or rational processes of cause and effect. I would like to attempt to detranscendentalize at least one discursive instance of evil of this type, which is the invocation of the antichrist. I am thinking about those discourses in which the spiritual enemy behind terrorist threats is the antichrist. I would like to play with the notion that the antichrist invaginates the Christ. One might also think of this move as queering the Christ figure, in that it transgresses the lines of cultural and even gender identity for the Christ—it blurs the lines of certainty on which calculation might be based.

As Catherine Keller and others have pointed out, the apocalyptic thought that has long been central to U.S. history and culture has once again come to the fore in matters of U.S. politics.[40] As in the past, the antichrist once again stands in for anything or anyone who appears to be hindering the prevalent set of nationalist and capitalist desires. A predominantly voiced fear is that the antichrist will establish a one-world order, thus doing away with nations (and U.S. hegemony).[41] In one common scenario, the antichrist "will take over the reins of world government and establish Jerusalem as his capital."[42] The worry is that if Christians do not fight against the work of the antichrist, the whole world might be lost.

The tradition of reading the political enemy as antichrist has also produced a racialized Middle Eastern Muslim antichrist. It is in this vein that Saddam Hussein and Osama bin Laden have been designated as possible candidates for antichrist by conservative Christian and otherwise spiritually interested Internet sites.[43] The political enemy as "Islamo-fascist" antichrist also appears in coded fashion in U.S. national politics. For instance, in one speech on the war on terror (October 6, 2005), without ever mentioning the antichrist, George W. Bush was able to paint a picture of "the enemy" that is truly apocalyptic and inhuman, posing a "mortal danger to all humanity." The speech began with an apocalyptically drawn recollection of 9.11: "a great evil . . . a proud city covered in smoke and ashes, a fire across the Potomac, and passengers who spent their final moments on Earth fighting the enemy." It ended with the assurance that the war on terror "is also the current expression of an ancient struggle," and the promise that "the cause of freedom will once again prevail." Within this apocalyptic frame, the enemy was described as "Evil men, obsessed with ambition and unburdened by conscience," who in "their cold-blooded contempt for human life" were "the enemies of humanity." As a sure sign of their antichristic intent, these men were said to be "part of global, borderless terrorist organizations." The president ingeniously both named this evil Islam and disavowed that he did so: "Some call this evil Islamic radicalism; others, militant Jihadism; still others, Islamo-fascism. Whatever it's called, this ideology is very different from the religion of Islam." The fear—made particularly manifest in the term Islamo-fascism and in its alleged global, borderless organization—was, and continues to be, of world dominance in the wrong key.[44]

So a strong decision against the enemy is needed, and this was, of course, how the Bush administration tried to gain support for its decisions. Such statements as "[W]e face a global terrorist movement and must confront the radical ideology that justifies the use of violence against innocents in the name of religion,"[45] clearly played on the fear of an antichrist in order to motivate action. Indeed, it appeared that the Bush administration used the term "transnational" when it wanted to signify borderless (as antichristic). The administration applied this terminology not only to terrorists but also to drug traffickers (in a speech on Guatemalan immigration and trade), pirates (in a statement on maritime security), and international crime and corruption (at the E.U./U.S. Peace Summit).[46]

In another line of apocalyptic thought, the antichrist has been interpreted as a homosexual or "sodomite" (two preferred terms of the homophobic).[47] The antichrist's probable homosexual orientation is derived from a particular way of translating Daniel 11:37. Some translations render the middle part of the verse as follows, "He will show no regard for the gods of his fathers or for the desire of women" (New American Standard Bible). The arrogant king's apparent lack of interest in women allows for the suggestion that the antichrist may be homosexual. As TV and Internet preacher David R. Reagan expounds, "Daniel indicates that he will be a sexual pervert, most likely a homosexual. As Daniel puts it, the Antichrist will show no regard 'for the desire of women' (Daniel 11:37)."[48]

This translation is technically possible from the Hebrew phrase ḥmdt nšym (desire of women), because the noun ḥmdh could mean "desire"; it also could mean "treasure" or "desirable thing," and so be rendered "the treasure of women." Many mainstream twentieth-century translations, therefore, translate this text as "He [the self-promoting king], will show no regard for the gods of his fathers or for *the one desired by women*, nor will he regard any god but will exalt himself above them all" (New International Version). Such translations follow biblical scholarship in understanding the entirety of this verse to be about the deceitful king's attitude toward other empires' gods. As biblical scholar C. L. Seow points out, within this context, "the one desired by women" is thought to be a god, possibly Tammuz (the Mesopotamian version of Adonis), whose worship the Ptolemies took up in Egypt. John Goldingay suggests that this god would have been "slighted by Antiochus," in his aggressive interactions with the Ptolemies.[49] But the apocalyptic translation allows for a steamier reading.

Not surprisingly, given the contemporary configuration of the ongoing culture wars, some commentators extrapolate from their understanding of the antichrist's sexual orientation a diagnosis of the problems facing marriage in the twenty-first century. So, for instance, Joseph Chambers of Paw Creek Ministries suggests in pamphlet and video that the spiritual prototype of heterosexual marriage, described in Revelation as the marriage of the Lamb (i.e., the marriage between Christ and the church), is under threat from "sodomites." He lays the blame at the feet of the antichrist.

Satan is on a rampage to defile the family of humankind and the future family of the redeemed. . . . I do not believe that there is any question but that the Antichrist will be a homosexual. The world is literally hell-bent on making the sodomite lifestyle the order of the day. . . . Sodomites are thrilled to destroy any institution that stands in their way. Their motives and methods cannot be called anything but demonic.[50]

Other sites call gay marriage the work of the beast, and of Satan, without necessarily citing Daniel. So for instance, the Watchmen Bible Study Group finds the acceptance of homosexuality and gay marriage to be a sign of the first beast: the emergence of a "one-world political/religious system . . . which will make it possible for the antichrist to step in, take the reins, and assume control of most every soul on the planet." Within that one-world system, "Satan's false teachers" try to convince people of unbiblical truths, including acceptance of gay Christians and gay marriage.[51]

It is easy to see how religious discourse is operating here on the horizontal level, as Spivak describes, to open up certain possibilities and foreclose others. The antichrist as political and homosexual enemy must be fought. Exhortations for strong political decisions are motivated by the need to fend off evil both on international and domestic fronts, in the war on terror and against gay marriage.

INVAGINATING CHRIST

The tactic of demonizing same-sex marriage by affiliating it with the work of the antichrist more or less hits us over the head in explaining what it means for calculative reason to require alterity—though here without the effects of grace. One of the central affiliations this discourse opens up—and I barely need to say this except to set myself up for the next point—is of the United States with the force that fights the antichrist, that is the Christ. It is no longer necessary to elaborate on the sense of messianism with which the United States justifies its action, as it has become somewhat commonplace in the discourse justifying the war on terror.

Yet if we stay on the horizontal chain of signification, we have to look at the textual relations between Christ and antichrist. In at least one of the texts commonly used to fill out the form of the antichrist, Daniel 7:1–14, we can also see that an alterity usually associated with the antichrist comes to invaginate the Christ figure. Let me trace the chain of significations that produce and occlude these relations. Daniel 7:1–14 is thought by many apocalyptic interpreters to describe the antichrist. As readers of this text well know, the writer of Daniel uses the imagery of beasts to allegorize the political threat posed to the Jews by their various colonizers, culminating in the Hellenizing project of Antiochus Epiphanes IV. Yet for dispensationalists and other apocalyptically oriented readers, the text tends not to be read as only, or primarily, about any ancient situation. Rather, the famous dream image of the boastful little horn rising to power through deceit—out of the head of other beasts—lends itself well to descriptions of the impending arrival of the deceptive antichrist. Though the threat of the antichrist is understood to be imminent, it is not considered to be permanent, since in Daniel 7, this figure is defeated by the Ancient of Days, who then appoints the one who comes on the clouds, "the Son of Man," to reign forever.

Scholars of apocalyptic literature have spent some time trying to determine the historical background and mythic antecedents to Daniel 7, both for the succession of beasts and for the Son of Man. Scholars have argued over whether it borrows from Babylonian or Canaanite myths of creation.[52] In both Babylonian and Canaanite myths, the favored god defeats the chaotic sea god, or sea monster, in order to establish order, creation, or sovereignty. In the Canaanite myth, the rain god Baal, rider of the clouds, defeats the god of the sea (Yamm) and the god of death (Mot). Baal is much like the Son of Man who comes upon the clouds, to defeat the arrogant and deceitful little horn. John J. Collins argues that in Daniel Baal becomes the Son of Man.[53] He also reminds the reader that the Christian tradition, specifically Mark 13:26, clearly reinterprets Daniel's Son of Man—"coming in the clouds with great power and glory"—to describe Christ.[54] Not to put too fine a point on it, it would seem that Baal becomes Christ.

This possible connection between Baal and Son of Man would, no doubt, be a cause consternation for some interpreters, because of the connection to Canaanite sources.[55] Though the Baal attested in the older Ugaritic sources (Baal Haddad) is likely not identical with the Baal often mentioned in the Hebrew Bible (possibly a Phoenician Baal),[56] the name "Baal" becomes a signifier for ancient Israelite idolatry, against which the Hebrew scriptures rail. Baal is one of the chief gods that the God of Israel says should be stamped out in the colonization of Canaan (producing an oppressive racialization in the Bible that has carried over into colonial and neocolonial periods, where the Other has been identified with the Canaanites). Over time, Baal has come to represent all that is ungodly. As an icon of idolatry,

Baal's association with the bull form has been affiliated with the antichrist beast, at least in some versions of apocalyptic Christianity.[57] So if the figure of antichrist has been connected with the idolatrous Baal of the Canaanites— the Bible's racialized others—it only takes a short interpretive hop for some interpreters to identify the racialized enemy of another faith (i.e., Muslims) as the inhuman antichrist.

Yet it is more than plausible that the Canaanite Baal (the Ugaritic version) in fact produces Christ, by way of the Son of Man. The Canaanite Baal, then, gives rise both to the inhuman beast and to the victorious Son of Man figure, who becomes the divine-human son of God. The Christ figure is therefore replete with an alterity that is more or less impossible for many adherents to the Christian tradition. The figure of the in/human beast is both included in the genealogy of Christ, the exemplary human, and excluded as the basest of beastly gods, as the antichrist. The antichrist is both essential to the functioning of the Christian symbolic, and excluded from it. The antichrist is the boundary of the set that is the Christ, but when we start to look we notice that it forms an internal pocket larger than the whole. Christ is invaginated by the antichrist.

How might this invagination function as a permanent parabasis? Briefly, I'd like to offer several possibilities. Most obviously, the recognition of the Christ/antichrist symbiosis must at the very least change the understanding of the threat of the Other. If, in some virulent, xenophobic, anti-Islam Internet sites, Baal has been associated with Allah and with the antichrist, what happens to this insult if Baal is also genealogically affiliated with the Christ? Allah, and Allah's followers can no longer be associated with the satanic. It is not that any of these figures become one and the same, but the threat and taint of evil is removed (reduced to the literary).

Second, when the Ugaritic Baal cycle is read in its entirety, the figure of Baal can be read as ironically commenting on the narrative establishing Christ's divinity. Though Christ is understood to be the heroic final con- queror of death, his Canaanite heritage reads differently. In the Baal cycle, the dying and rising god cannot conquer death without help from his sister Anat. It is actually Anat who slays the god of death, and frees Baal. So though Baal is referred to as conqueror, he needs a little help. If the invagination of cultural difference were not enough, here we have the invagination of gender difference as well. Can the saving work of the Baal-Christ still be claimed as masculine? Can it continue to justify the need for the patriarchal decision? It seems to me that the genealogy of the Christ figure stands as ironic comment on the need to claim Christ as the exemplar of the masculine decision maker. It queers the norms of gender.

Third, and perhaps most important, the reason that the antichrist is so threatening is that he (or perhaps she?) is deceptive. It is truly difficult to tell the antichrist from the Christ. There is no telling who might be the antichrist and whether there might be more than one (as per the many antichrists referenced in 1 John 2:18). The antichrist could be anyone, even the most ostensibly upright person. Through deception, the antichrist leads human desire astray and perverts it. The antichrist's deceptiveness means that human and inhuman cannot be told apart, nor, apparently, their sexualities.[58] This deceptiveness threatens and queers every identity. Moreover, the double and separate identification of the antichrist as political enemy and as gay suggests that the political enemy might not be outside the nation at all, might not even wield weapons, but might simply desire nonheteronormative sex. In short, the deceptive presence of the antichrist puts the heteronormative, masculinist, messianic decisions of the United States into question. Any decision might be false. The antichrist troubles any declaration of an exacting moral decision. The antichrist is a queer figure of undecidability—one that puts into question the calculations so prevalent in our contemporary political moment, especially those based on sexual morality and ideological superiority.

When the racialized, sexualized antichrist is read in the realm of the literary—as a narrative that is both permissible and necessary to the political and ethical calculations performed in the name of the messianic—the chains of signification to which this figure is attached become visible. Yet we can also read this figure, like grace, as a kind of permanent parabasis to these very calculations. Such a reading disrupts "belief as faith." Indeed, as Gilles Deleuze suggests, it shows belief to be inhabited by a "violent atheist . . . [or we might say, a radical secularism, that is] the Antichrist, eternally given 'once and for all' within grace."[59] In short, attention to the literary formations of the antichrist puts into question gendered and politicized icons of righteousness, salvation, and evil, as well as their presumed sexualities. Moreover, it represents an inability to *know*: to know gender or sexuality, to know evil, or to know salvation when we see it. To apply Davis's words, the antichrist is the site of an inability to know that "reconstitutes the will to know" that is so entwined with colonial processes and power relations.[60] As mentioned, Davis and Spivak call this "not-knowing" in the encounter with the Other a form of love. What I am suggesting then, queerly, and against all the odds, is that we consider antichristic forms of loving as a political principle.

❧ Comparative Theology
after "Religion"

JOHN J. THATAMANIL

The word "Aryan," which, for Max Müller and his generation, had a purely linguistic meaning, was now in the hands of less academic persons, poisoners, who were speaking of races of men, races of masters and races of servants and other races too, races whose fundamental impurity necessitated drastic measures, races who were not wanted on the voyage, who were surplus to requirements, races to be cut, blackballed and deposited in the bin of history.
SALMAN RUSHDIE, *The Ground beneath Her Feet*

CONTAINING DIFFERENCE BY DELIMITING OUR INTERLOCUTORS

Christian reflection has, from its inception, been situated in a world of difference. Indeed, it would be possible to craft a history of Christian thought and practice written as a series of interactions with and transmutations of movements and traditions that Christians have come to demarcate as non-Christian. Such a history would demonstrate not only that many of the central categories, practices, and symbols of Christian life are borrowed from Hellenistic philosophical schools, mystery religions, and, of course, most vitally from what we now call "Judaism," but that for long stretches of history, no clearly defined and rigid boundaries existed between "Christianity" and those traditions we now take to be Christianity's others. Important components of such a history are now being written, and Daniel Boyarin's *Border Lines* is just one recent example that comes readily to mind.[1] Alongside such a history, a companion work could be written that would take note of tremors within (especially Western) Christian self-awareness when such profound entanglements come to surface. I suspect that such a companion history would unearth moments of widespread anxiety among custodians of tradition at just those junctures when "the unbearable proximity"[2] of those whom Christians customarily regard as other is most keenly felt.

Arvind Mandair has written several important essays that together amount to a critical contribution to the latter sort of history.[3] Mandair's work is motivated by a basic question: "Why is it that despite the recent proliferation of postcolonial critiques of Indology, its modern successors such as the history of religions and area studies . . . continue to reconstitute past imperialisms, such as the hegemony of theory as specifically Western and/or the division of intellectual labor between universal and particular knowledge formations?"[4] Mandair is especially interested in interrogating the dichotomy between the normative/theoretical work of philosophy of religion (universal) and the history of religions (particular). As a result of this dichotomy, the religious traditions of Asia are understood as data to be studied by history of religions but are not permitted to furnish conceptual resources to and for the normative work of philosophy of religion. The persistence of this divide, as Mandair notes, is all the more peculiar since "cultural theory has helped not only to dismantle well-worn dualisms such as religion/politics, theism/atheism, sacred/secular, but, more importantly has helped to narrow the gap between academic practices and cultural practices such as religion that scholars seek to study."[5]

Mandair rightly observes that the work of cultural and critical theory has been especially productive for Christian theology. Pointing to "a reversal of critical theory's atheistic roots in 'the masters of suspicion,'" Mandair notes that Christian theologians have not only managed to "dispute the atheistic presuppositions of modern secular thinking in the social sciences" but also to legitimize "the use of phenomena from these particular traditions as resources for critical thinking about religion per se."[6] Mandair cites as evidence a variety of texts, including John Milbank's groundbreaking work, *Theology and Social Theory*.[7] In texts such as these, Christian theology is not merely the object of social theory but claims for itself the conceptual power and resources to engage in social analysis itself.

Despite such gains in the case of Western traditions, no comparable turn is evident in the case of Asian religions. There, the unmitigated divide between the universal and the particular, between theory and data persists. Why? Ironically, one answer that Mandair advances is that postcolonial critics have been so anxious to protect Indian culture from the "religious effects" of imperialism—the configuration of Indian traditions as "religions" on the West's own terms, terms extrinsic and alien to Indian traditions—that the only form of anti-imperialist critique permitted is a secular one.[8]

As we shall soon see, Mandair's own indebtedness to postcolonial critique is too profound to suggest that he wishes to dismiss such scholarship. He too is worried about the consequences for both West and East when the universal translatability of *religio* is assumed.[9] He contends that Gayatri Chakravorty Spivak and others have accurately identified key figures who were responsible for instantiating the very dichotomy between a dynamic, historically self-aware West and a frozen and timeless East. What Mandair wishes to interrogate is the peculiar way in which an exclusive commitment to secular critique repeats the long-standing depiction of the West as the scene of dynamic *history* over against South Asia, which remains bound to *religion* now characterized as static and even atavistic.[10] On such accounts, Indian religious traditions remain objects to be theorized and not subjects who are agential contributors to theorizing.

My own questions are akin to Mandair's: Why do Christian theologians, by and large, remain unwilling to enter into a substantive engagement with the normative claims and aims of other traditions? What conceptions of the theological task make it permissible for Christian theologians to pretend that the truth-seeking work of theology need not take account of the normative commitments of Hindus, Buddhists, and others? Why does comparative theology remain relatively marginal to regnant movements within contemporary theology? Most concisely put, is not all theology *necessarily* comparative? What grounds the persistent dichotomy between systematic theology proper and comparative theology? Why is comparative work relegated to history of religions and not itself a constitutive feature of Christian theology?

This final formulation best discloses the kinship between my theological questions and Mandair's work as a philosopher of religion. With Mandair, I seek to interrupt the duality between theory and data, between those traditions that are accorded the status of universality and others that remain merely particular. This challenge may well be greater within Christian theology than in philosophy of religion just to the extent that Christian thinkers rarely recognize the practices and claims of other traditions *even as data* for theological reflection. Even narrowly apologetic encounters with other religious traditions would amount to a recognition (albeit problematic) that such traditions are conversation partners who make normative claims. What prevails instead is a failure of engagement. Christian theologians largely proceed without feeling any compulsion to reckon with religious alternatives. They have largely contained the effects of religious diversity by arbitrarily delimiting their interlocutors. While Western philosophical traditions and secularity as such are worthy of interrogation and perhaps even refutation, traditions of the East are too often simply ignored.[11]

MANAGING PROXIMITY BY INVENTING RELIGIONS

Both philosophy of religion and Christian theology presume and presuppose a divide between the universal and the particular, between the West and the Rest. What are the roots of this dichotomy? Mandair believes that the roots of the divide between the universal and the particular can be traced back to a critical historical moment: the early Indological discovery of the antiquity of Sanskrit and the common origin of European and Indian languages in some form of Proto-Indo-European.[12] Mandair argues that these discoveries threatened the ideological foundations of the colonial project by undermining European notions of civilizational separateness and superiority. Just as accounts that seek to depict human communities as divided into discrete biological groups marked by asymmetrical intellectual endowments are interrupted by Darwin's theory of evolution, so it is with the Indological discovery of common linguistic and cultural origins. Monogenetic accounts of origin, whether biological or cultural, prove inconvenient for theorists of racial or cultural superiority who seek to posit essentialist disjuncture as a precondition for claims of superiority.[13] The proximity of South Asia was especially threatening, Mandair argues, because the work of noted Indophiles such as Schelling offered intellectually credible and appreciative engagements with Eastern pantheism, and in so doing, ventured alternative possibilities for the future of European Christianity.[14]

Mandair contends that the disruptive potential of the challenge posed by philology was managed most effectively by Hegel, especially in his *Lectures on the Philosophy of Religion*. Central to Mandair's reading of Hegel is the latter's claim that the origin of thought is coincident with the origins of religion. Therefore, if the historical evidence suggests that the origin of religion can be traced back to Indian antiquity, then a monogenetic account of history, religion, and thought would undercut the claims to radical difference necessary to support the superiority claims of one culture over against all others.[15] Mandair argues that positing a typology of religions—the plural is important—alleviated this threat to "Western man's" claim to be historically different from "the Rest" by serving both to reify and to map the religions and their respective civilizations over against each other. Mandair's argument—which draws on and advances Spivak's work on Hegel[16]—is too rich to treat here without distortion.[17] It must suffice to note that Hegel is a critical figure because he generates a typology of religions that allows non-Western traditions to be fixed to more primitive evolutionary strata and hence no longer relevant to the ongoing unfolding of history. Mandair contends that Hegel, in so doing, reduces these religions to the status of mere objects of the historian's gaze. Henceforth, these traditions can be studied by the history of religions, but they cannot figure into the normative work that constitutes philosophy of religion proper, which is necessarily grounded in and appeals only to more advanced Western religious materials.

Mandair's turn to Hegel goes a long way toward answering the question, "[W]hy can the turn toward critical and cultural theory not be done using Indian religious phenomena/materials/thinking?"[18] However, it is worth noting that Mandair does not so much answer the question as subvert it. He reminds readers that the very invention of the radical separation between East and West, between Indic and non-Indic is itself a historical creation that needs to be remembered rather than repeated. Mandair, by citing the work of Naoki Sakai, indicates that he does not thereby wish to undercut the possibility of thinking from "geo-politically specific locations," but calls us only to be "attentive to the trans-cultural dissemination of global traces with theoretical knowledge produced in geo-politically specific locations and which explores how theories are themselves transformed by their practical effects when they are performed in other sites."[19]

INTERROGATING "RELIGION" AND "RACE"

Mandair is just one of many scholars who are now demonstrating that the utterly ubiquitous categories "religion" and "religions" are neither innocent nor cross-cultural universals that are somehow ontologically given. These categories have a complex and determinate history—a history that remains largely underappreciated—and vast material consequences that we are only now beginning to understand. These include the following:

> The category "religion" has a provincial origin in the West but has come to be employed universally. Thus, the category has been applied to

peoples and traditions that did not themselves order their lives by appeal to these notions prior to the colonial project.

These Western habits of thought are problematic because these distinctions are hardly intelligible for "other cultural complexes."[20] Moreover, once these distinctions are securely in place and taken for granted, it is easy to characterize traditions that do not recognize and abide by our distinctions as "fundamentalist" in character.

By a complex set of colonial mechanisms—including but not limited to mission schools, the teaching of English and English literature, divide-and-conquer administrative policies rooted in appeals to communal religious law, and the census—colonized peoples were constrained to think of themselves as religious and as members of particular religions.

On the Indian scene and elsewhere, learning to think by way of the category "religion" has given rise to the very idea of singular religious identity.

The notion of singular religious identity, in circular fashion, is generated by and in turn generates the idea that religions are neatly separated by clearly demarcated and impermeable borders.

A relatively fixed set of traditions is accorded the status of "world religions." Arriving at that status requires candidate traditions to take on markers of identity that define Christianity as a prototypical world religion, including most especially a written sacred scripture.[21]

The consequences of these vast, indeed global, transformations generated by "religion" are difficult to grasp. My own sense is that they are best approached, at least initially, by way of another category that has likewise come to be globalized but also had a relatively provincial origin in the West, namely the idea of race. Indeed, it is entirely possible to argue that the idea of race has also played a decisive role in managing, curtailing, and containing the consequences of just the very same Indological discovery of Proto-Indo-European. Rather than turn to theory to make this case, I propose a turn to fiction, in particular Salman Rushdie's 1999 novel, *The Ground beneath Her Feet*, quoted in the epigraph.[22]

Early in the novel, Rushdie depicts two characters—one British, William Methwold (who, it should be noted, had to bear the weight of actual existence before assuming the added, albeit posthumous burden, of becoming a character in a Rushdie novel), and the other an (entirely fictional but nonetheless compelling) Anglophile Bombay Parsi named Darius Xerxes

Cama—doing their very best to avoid, ignore, and altogether escape the unmaking of the colonial world, a world of which they are exceedingly fond and to which they are quite accustomed. For them, Gandhi and the nationalist movement of the 1930s and 1940s are nothing more than disturbers of the Pax Britannica. They choose as their avenue of scholarly escapism the deliberately arcane and far removed world of philology. Their heroes are Max Müller and Georges Dumézil. They pass their days examining parallels between the *Iliad* and the *Ramayana*, between Helen of Troy and Sita, relishing the happy knowledge that Indological philology has demonstrated that British and Indian alike are all "barbarians," and that the East is not so far removed from the West. Their blissful sanctuary comes crashing down when news blows into their scholarly haven that the word "Aryan" and indeed the entire legacy of their escapist labors has been sullied by the use to which this discourse has been put by the Nazis. The temporal priority of Müller and Dumézil does not shield their heroes from the poison that "works its way backward through time and sideways into the reputation of innocent men" and brings their own life passion to naught.[23] Their labors turn out to be far from arcane; a world in which all alike are barbarians is replaced by another populated by races, races everywhere, most of whom are impure, tainted, inferior, and dangerous.

Mandair and Rushdie—each in his own fashion and idiom—demonstrate how the discourse of religion and the discourse of race have been deployed to reify and thereby to separate peoples and traditions whose complex and intertwined histories hardly permit of essentialist disjuncture. Both have demonstrated just how a moment in which knowledge of the radical proximity of the other was not just managed but eventually contained and ultimately negated.

At the close of the first decade of the twenty-first century, we find ourselves in an analogous moment. Ours is a time of persistent and multidirectional transnational flows of peoples, images, ideas, institutions, and practices; the world we inhabit admits of no neat cartographies that affix hard-and-fast boundaries between communities and traditions. And yet we see both in Christian theology and beyond ever more vehement arguments that insist on the fundamental incommensurability of civilizations and their respective religions. Indeed, some contend that "the religion line" is replacing W. E. B. Du Bois's "color line." My sense is that the category "religion" is being deployed—and, as we have seen, not for the first time—precisely to manage and contain proximity in ways that are strikingly akin to the uses to which the category "race" has been put. Hence, it seems reasonable to examine the work of critical race theorists and their critique of the category "race" if similar moves are to be made in a critique of "religion."

The careful work of scholars of racism has done much to displace long-standing conceptions of race as a biological or ontological given. Like Rushdie, we are more than ever aware that we can trace, if not date, the origins of notion of race and the idea of multiple, discrete races; understanding these contingent origins has helped us appreciate that these categories are fictions, albeit dangerous and recalcitrant ones. The work of Paul Gilroy and Robert Miles, in particular, has done much to cultivate a genealogical sensibility around the category of race. Miles's work has, I contend, special importance for theologians and religious studies scholars because of his stringent and rigorous critique of the "race relations" paradigm in racism studies.[24] Perhaps the fundamental conviction that drives Miles's work is the following:

If "races" are not naturally occurring populations, the reasons and conditions for the social process whereby the discourse of "race" is employed to label, constitute and exclude social collectivities requires explanation rather than be assumed to be a natural and universal process. In other words, the construction and reproduction of the idea of "race." is something that requires investigation. This task is circumvented by the transformation of the idea itself ("race") into an analytical concept. Thereby, what needs to be represented as a social process and explained is reconstructed as a social fact that can be used to explain other social facts.[25]

And that is precisely the problem with the race relations paradigm: race continues to be treated as ontologically real. Of course, Miles and his colleague Malcolm Brown are not claiming that race does not have real and brutal social consequences; they mean only to insist that there is no way to undo those social consequences apart from undoing and unmasking the very idea of race. Miles and Brown stipulate that "The analytical task is not to explain 'race relations'; rather, it is the generation of concepts with which one can grasp and portray the historical processes by which notions of 'race' become accepted and/or used in a plurality of discourses."[26]

INTERRELIGIOUS DIALOGUE AND COMPARATIVE THEOLOGY
AFTER "RELIGION"

What are the implications of deconstructing and historicizing the category of "race" for the work of religionists and theologians, especially for theologians whose work is dedicated to improving interreligious relations? How might religious studies and theology need to be reconfigured if, mutatis mutandis, the very claim advanced by Miles and Brown were to be applied to our disciplinary discourses about "religion"? I find the question both daunting and even mind-bending, despite the fact that there is now in religious studies a veritable cottage industry dedicated to demonstrating that "religion," far from being a universal and timeless feature of human experience as such, is not only of Western provenance but perhaps one of the West's most successful exports. It should be noted that although there is considerable agreement on the matter of geographical origins within this literature, no such consensus exists on the question of temporality. There is wild disagreement about whether religion is a product of Enlightenment modernity (Talal Asad)[27] or an invention of Christian antiquity (Daniel Dubuisson)[28] or perhaps both. Who should be awarded the patent—Herbert of Cherbury or Lactantius? A great deal hinges on these questions; answering them determines whether religion will be considered a product of the West as such or a product of modernity in particular.

These questions concerning the provenance of "religion" are important. They are also unlikely to be resolved in short order. What matters at this particular juncture is the more basic and fundamental task of transmuting the question posed by Miles into religious studies and theology. What might it mean for theology to think beyond and after "religion"? Is such thinking even possible? Does thinking after and against religion compel Christian theologians to counter and work against too ready an embrace of interfaith and interreligious dialogue? Are theologians of religious pluralism the theological doppelgängers of race relations theorists? Do we inadvertently reaffirm the very category that must be called into question? More disturbingly still, does the very project of dialogue require that our neighbors adopt "religious identities" that mirror conceptions of identity formulated and authorized in the West? Does the discourse of religion and interreligious dialogue already presume that the other is constructed in our image before he or she is permitted and perhaps obligated to respond? Does not interreligious dialogue, as presently constituted, take for granted the universal translatability of the category *religio*? Just what are the operative politics of translation at stake in presuming that such translatability is even possible?

As a Christian comparative theologian, I am committed to theological reflection that seeks to learn from multiple religious traditions and to rethink my own theological commitments and those of the Christian tradition in the light of these encounters. Comparative theology is constructive reflection that insists on learning from and with—and here we immediately run into difficulties that we now know are more than merely terminological—"other religions." Comparative theology, with a few notable recent exceptions, has operated and indeed continues to operate as a close sibling to another subspecialty within Christian theology, namely theology of religions or theology of religious pluralism (TRP). The focal questions that drive TRP are well known and include the following: Are other religions also means of salvation, and if so, how? Are they independently efficacious "soteriological vehicles" that lead to the same destination (John Hick), or are they efficacious precisely because, in some perhaps hidden and anonymous fashion, the Christ or the Spirit is operative within those traditions (Karl Rahner)? More recently, Mark Heim has argued that exclusivists, inclusivists, and even pluralists such as John Hick have not arrived at a genuine pluralism. Heim notes that exclusivists believe that there is only one worthwhile religious goal or aim, which only their tradition can access. Heim argues, rather strikingly, that the so-called pluralists fail to live up to their name because they agree with exclusivists that there can be at most one and only one worthwhile religious goal or aim; they just happen to believe that all religions can access that selfsame goal. The central operative metaphors that structure the pluralist imagination are well known: the religions are paths up the same mountain, rivers flowing to the selfsame sea, or planets in equidistant orbit around the same sun. Hardly pluralistic, as Heim observes. Against these options, Heim advances what he takes to be a genuine pluralism, one that posits the existence of genuinely different and compelling religious goods. In effect, Heim proposes that the religious terrain is mountainous; each religion is its own mountain and ascending any particular mountain leads to its own singular and distinctive religious good.[29]

Heim's alternative adds a new possibility to the extant options, but every one of these alternatives, including Heim's, traffics in homogeneities. All take for granted that the world is composed of discrete and clearly demarcated religious traditions that are other to each other. Excluding some exclusivists, all are committed to improving relations between the religions, but, as is the case with those committed to improving race relations, they continue to re-create and thereby reaffirm a world composed of religions. A provincial Western category continues to exert an irresistible gravitational pull that none can resist, a pull that warps the very fabric of experience.

As is the case with race, to fall under the spell of religion is to become vulnerable to a host of essentialisms. Within a given religion, sameness reigns, and without, there is only difference. Hence, the fact that most "religions" contain alternative and indeed sharply different salvations, to use Heim's plural term, hardly registers in conversations within TRP. As is the case with race, in religion too, singular identity is normative and multiple identities are aberrant, abnormal, or at the very least, atypical. The coercive power of the category, by constituting traditions as spaces of homogeneity, erases what should be obvious to any clear-eyed observer: religious traditions are internally marked by the widest and wildest kinds of difference, even on central questions of soteriology and eschatology. There is no consensus within Christian communities or within Hindu communities about such central questions as the possibility or nature of postmortem existence, whether persons can or should aspire to union with divinity or at best communion. But perhaps the most subtle and consequential work accomplished by the category "religion," particularly in its plural version, is the way in which the category generates, without anything so blatant as an assertion, the clear demarcation between the religions themselves, between internal and external, between self and other.

Paulo Gonçalves's marvelous essay "Religious 'Worlds' and Their Alien Invaders" offers the shrewdest account both of religion's power to generate homogeneity within a tradition and why such homogeneity serves the interests of those who aspire to gain authoritative control over a tradition.[30] Gonçalves aims his laser-like critique at Christian theologians within the radical orthodoxy and postliberal theology movements. Theologians in both camps, he notes, are explicitly committed to rejecting the kind of homogenizing reflection about religion that drives the work of pluralists like John Hick. In the name of affirming genuine pluralism, both camps appeal to notions of narrativity to assert that religions are tightly woven, seamless, and integrated metanarratives or cultural-linguistic worlds. Each religion is, on such accounts, a world unto itself with its own, albeit nonfoundational, narrative integrity. About such positions, Gonçalves makes a telling observation, one that must be quoted at length:

I am concerned that, precisely in their attempts to affirm the particularity, alterity and difference of various traditions, such approaches are not, as they claim, so much *describing*, but rather *generating, promoting and perpetuating* idealized or romanticized fantasms of quasi-autonomous and homogenous religious traditions—fantasms which are possibly far removed from their actual and historical forms, and which ignore the agonistic history of their constitution as "traditions" or "religions." In this manner, approaches which rightfully criticize the universalist notions of mysticism and essential religiosity which have dominated the discourse on religions are now seduced by what I will suggest is another chimera of strongly differentiated religious identities.[31]

Gonçalves's argument is powerful just to the extent that it demonstrates that the category "religion" and the further idea of "religious worlds" disfigure not only Asian traditions—as has been rightly pointed out by scholars such as Mandair and Richard King[32]—but also Christian traditions. He observes that *"the very same forms* of homogenization, and thus the very same problems, occur in the representation of Christian identity, theology and history, and that consequently these representations can and should be challenged by the same sort of critique."[33]

This contribution alone would be enough to establish the signal importance of Gonçalves's essay, but he proceeds to demonstrate that such homogenization serves the controlling interests of the postliberals and radical orthodoxy theologians. Their readings of tradition are rendered authoritative inasmuch as these theologians can insist that their proposal is not just one among many contested alternatives but instead represents *"the* biblical story."[34] Regarding the practice by radical orthodoxy thinkers of "the use of 'theology' without qualifiers, presenting it as a clear univocal practice, and the ascription to it of a *'fundamental nature'* and *'original form,'"* Gonçalves poses the following trenchant questions:

Does theology have a "fundamental nature" and "original form"? Who decides what this "fundamental nature" is, and what interests does this serve? Is there a uniform and homogenous pre-modern Christian theology? Can we speak "theology" in this abstract manner? Is it accurate to depict the Enlightenment as an alien invasion of theology . . . ?[35]

Gonçalves's argument demonstrates that the creation of homogenous accounts of Christian theology serves not only to mask and privilege the interests of postliberal and radical orthodoxy theologians but also makes it entirely unnecessary for theologians to take account of those they deem to be external to *the* tradition. The creation of stark boundaries generates a neat duality between those who are inside and those on the outside. Accounts of Christian theology that regard theology as an exercise in faithfulness to the deep grammar of Christian practice or keeping faith with the singular biblical metanarrative inoculate theology from having to engage all those who stand outside the tradition, all those who are othered. These others are to be repulsed as threats, and dissenters are but heretics.

Comparative theology is spurious when theology is so conceived. Because postliberals and the radical orthodoxy theologians take persons to be situated within homogenous matrixes and because there is no neutral arbiter—no generalized reason derived from Enlightenment sources—that might serve as mediator between these matrixes, reflective engagement across religious boundaries is ipso facto impossible and ruled out of court.[36] After all, religions in this view are impermeable worlds. The only traffic possible between these worlds is conversion or contest. One can understand a religious world only by taking up residence therein, which is to say by conversion. Persons can be driven to conversion only by way of contest that discloses aporia internal to the other's religious system. Driven by such discontent, one can jump ship and leave one religious world for another, but the reasons and claims of "other religions" cannot make a positive contribution to one's own tradition; there is no possibility of mutual transformation or of double inhabitation. Most peculiarly, theological movements that are utterly enamored of the metaphor of language are unable to imagine that persons might become bilingual or multilingual.[37] The way to multiple religious identities or even to a serious vision of collaborative comparative theology is foreclosed.

If comparative theology is prohibited by postliberal theology and by radical orthodoxy, can we discover resources for comparative theology by engaging postcolonial theory? The argument ventured thus far—that postcolonial theory can help disrupt the reifications and homogeneities that come with a colonial deployment of the category "religion"—suggests that comparative theology can find in postcolonial theory a powerful resource and partner. However, poststructuralist and postcolonial theorists are unlikely to offer their resources to comparative theology without contest and challenge. After all, there is reason to believe that the stern warning regarding the untranslatability of *religio* applies to "theology" as well. The work of engaging the resources of other traditions in the work of Christian theology might succumb to the danger that the very project—and naturally the object too—of theology is taken to be universal. The theologian is duly warned that neither religion nor theology can be taken as universals, and that warning interrupts any premature and unreflective movement to comparative theology or even interreligious dialogue.

We have already seen that extreme caution is warranted in the matter of interreligious dialogue: the very idea of interreligious dialogue or interfaith conversation, while advanced in the name of peaceful coexistence, might replicate the problems of race relations discourse. As already noted, to speak of improving race relations is to endorse, at least tacitly, the very idea that race is a biological or ontological reality and thus writ into the very fabric of things—rather than writ into the fabric of things by various acts and regimes of power. Likewise to talk about interreligious or interfaith dialogue is to take for granted that the world is naturally divided up into various impermeable world religions along with some other minor traditions that do not properly rise to the status of world religions. Postcolonial theorists—Spivak in particular—would caution theologians to take account of the very real material asymmetries of power between traditions. Who represents whom? For whose interests? In what language?[38] The cumulative force of these queries prevents any quick turn to comparative theology.

But is the way entirely barred? I think not. What is decisively foreclosed—and thankfully so—is any mode of religious reflection wedded, either in theory or in practice, to purity of identity. Any theology that knows beforehand—that is to say before conversation and encounter—what its proper agenda is and ought to be is bound to co-opt, assimilate, and domesticate other traditions. Resistance is futile. But is it possible to imagine that theology might proceed otherwise than by way of appeal to questions and criteria established before and apart from dialogue? Can one imagine the possibility of a theology that is aware from the outset that no tradition is itself pure, singular, homogenous, and thus "uncontaminated"?

Just this possibility is suggested by Gonçalves himself. Gonçalves proposes a turn to Derrida and poststructuralism in order to undermine the structuralist philosophical underpinnings of postliberal theology. Gonçalves rightly observes that postliberal theology's talk about "the internal logic or grammar of religions" is heavily indebted to the structuralism of Clifford Geertz and William Christian.[39] What theology needs to countermand structuralist fictions, he asserts, is "alternative modes of theorizing religious identity and its representation which are sensitive to blurred boundaries, variations of interpretation, marginalization by influential elites and the dynamics of innovation and transformation."[40] For Gonçalves, Derrida's work—especially his critique of the closure of metaphysics—offers invaluable resources. He cites Derrida: "The closure of metaphysics, above all, is not a circle surrounding a homogenous field, a field homogenous with itself on its inside, whose outside then would be homogenous also. The limit has the form of always different faults, of fissures whose mark or scar is borne by all the texts of philosophy."[41]

Gonçalves looks to the disruptive power of deconstruction in order to counteract "forces of 'thetic abstraction,'" which persistently "attempt to 'normalize' the agonistic history of the genesis, transformation and constitution of those things we call 'religions.'"[42] What does Gonçalves hope will result from this turn to deconstruction? He expects that the infusion of deconstructive energies will demonstrate that religious identities are always already hybrid and polyphonic. If such a vision of religious identity is taken to heart, Gonçalves expects that the end result will be a vision of "both 'religious studies' and 'theology' as carnivalesque, messy, agonistic, creative, critical, multiple, transformative and unpredictable areas of study."[43]

As a comparative theologian, I can do no other than to endorse the carnivalesque vision of theology that Gonçalves advances, for such a vision can help disrupt and deconstruct the idea that comparative theology is a special but marginal brand or subdiscipline within theology proper. When we realize that theology has always been "messy, agonistic, creative . . . multiple," the term "comparative theology" begins to sound more like a redundancy rather an oxymoron. How could theology be anything other than comparative? The call for a robust and interreligious comparative theology must be, on this account, understood as a call for reflection that lives into and thinks out of the inherent creative multiplicity of tradition(s), a multiplicity that already bears within it the mark of tradition's encounters with difference.

But for the comparative theologian, a turn to deconstruction alone is inadequate. Comparative theologians should insist that the theoretical resources for reconfiguring theology must be informed and enriched precisely by the traditions that they study. That is to say, comparative theology must demonstrate fidelity to its basic commitment to doing theology in conversation with a variety of religious traditions by refusing to reduce the insights and aims of other traditions solely to the status of data for reflection. *Resources from other traditions must shape comparative theological method itself.*

I agree with Gonçalves that we need richer accounts of identity, but I am persuaded that some of those richer accounts will ultimately come from non-Western traditions. Although I embrace Gonçalves's call for creative multiplicity, I am not entirely sanguine about turning to poststructuralist and postcolonial theory, not least because both streams of thought are, to my taste, much too enamored with the *tout autre*, with the wholly Other. I find the figure of the nondual more adequate to experience than recourse to talk about the wholly other. Elsewhere, I argue, inspired by the work of the philosopher of relationality, Harold Oliver, that Western theology has too often confused the Holy Other with the wholly Other.[44] The former bespeaks an encounter, a presence, a relation, and the latter suggests that which simply cannot enter into relation and therefore simply cannot be. The former points to that which exceeds my grasp; the latter is merely a postulate, a sheer fiction on the order of the hare's horn in Indian philosophy, something that can be uttered but has no being.

THINKING IDENTITY WITH A LITTLE HELP FROM NAGARJUNA

No thinker has done more to problematize the very idea of the Wholly Other than Nagarjuna, the founder of the Madhyamaka philosophical tradition. For Nagarjuna and the Madhyamikas more generally, such a refutation takes place by way of a rejection of *svabhava* (own-being or essence). Madhyamaka Buddhism is the antiessentialist tradition par excellence. Indeed, the two central terms of the Madhyamaka tradition—*pratitya-samutpada*, dependent co-arising, and *sunyata*, emptiness—are understood to be different but complementary ways of dislodging the innate human habit of reification—of taking the world to be composed of unrelated entities each with some essence entirely its own.

Dependent co-arising is an ancient notion rooted in the Buddha's own teaching; the idea, in the earliest stratum of Buddhist literature, refers to nexuses of factors that together perpetuate the cycle of transmigration. The idea of dependent co-arising can be understood as what Western philosophers might characterize as a doctrine of universal internal relations. Nothing at all arises apart from some set of antecedent causes and conditions. Nagarjuna's entire philosophical project can be read as a rigorous attempt to think through what is entailed by affirming just that proposition. What exactly does it mean to posit that nothing arises apart from causes and conditions? As it turns out, in Nagarjuna's hands, dependent co-arising can be rigorously understood only by appeal to emptiness.

But first a very small step back from metaphysics to soteriology: At the heart of Nagarjuna's religious vision is the conviction that human beings are driven by craving. That hardly counts as news for anyone acquainted with Buddhism, as it is but a restatement of the Second Noble Truth. Nagarjuna and the Madhyamaka tradition go further by insisting that the most subtle and so also the most recalcitrant manifestation of craving is evident in the cognitive habit of reification—of taking reality to be made up of things, of discrete entities. This point can be made by appeal to the double meaning of the English word "grasp" which signifies both taking a hold of something but also serves to signify the act of understanding. The cognitive activity of grasping can give rise to a mistaken and distorted vision of reality that takes experience to be composed of graspable particulars, by entities that have own-being or essence.

It should be noted that Madhyamika thinkers are speaking of innate cognitive patterns and not about formal philosophical position taking. Human beings habitually and prereflectively take reality to be composed of discrete entities each with own-being or self-existence. Under the force of such habituation, even the notion of dependent co-arising is misunderstood when it is formalized into a theory of causation. In any theory of causation, one inevitably asks about the relationship between cause and effect. When that question is posed, one quickly finds oneself in insoluble contradictions, because we revert to treating them as independent entities. When cause and effect are so imagined, no viable account of causation can be generated. Nagarjuna makes this point by way of a comprehensive critique of then extant theories of causation in the first chapter of his *Mulamadhyamakakarika*. His demonstration is too extensive to recount here; it suffices to note that if causes and effects have essences of their own, then it is impossible to get them back into relation. It will not do to attempt to argue either that effects, in some fashion, preexist in their causes or that an independently existing cause gives rise to an independently existent effect. If the effect exists independently of its cause, then it does not need to be caused. Demonstrating that absurdities follow from essentialization is the intention of the compressed first verse of Chapter 1:

Neither from itself nor from another,
Nor from both,
Nor without a cause,
Does anything whatever, anywhere arise.[45]

If dependent co-arising is to be rightly understood, it turns out that one needs to be cured of one's innate disposition toward substantialist habits of mind, and that is just precisely why one needs to understand rightly the meaning of *pratitya-samutpada* by way of *sunyata*, emptiness. Only when one understands that nothing whatsoever has essence or own-being—that everything is empty of self-existence—can one rightly understand the deep intention of the Buddha's teaching.

But suppose, Nagarjuna asks, we assume a given reality has own-being or *svabhava*. What would that mean? Well, first, if any being anywhere did enjoy own-being, then it would follow that such a reality would be changeless and eternal, terms much privileged in some classical accounts of divinity. Any such reality could never have come into being and could never cease to be. But of course, no world composed of such entities is conceivable, as it would be entirely changeless and hence static. What is changeless and static cannot enter in relation. Neither could we know it, nor could it make itself known. By means of extended reductio ad absurdum argumentation, Nagarjuna demonstrates that it is impossible to think the world in such fashion.

Nagarjuna then takes great care to see that emptiness itself is not reified and thereby treated as an absolute, on the order of Brahman. Emptiness, to quote the Heart Sutra, is not other than form, form not other than emptiness. Emptiness is not a substratum. It does not point to an absolute or ultimate reality that stands behind or beneath the world as experienced. To understand emptiness is to see the conventional, everyday world rightly, to see it on the far side of reification and essentialism, which amounts to saying that the world is the realm of dependent co-arising, a world of relation. The world without *svabhava* is wondrous, unthinkable, excessive, and mysterious but also utterly and profoundly ordinary. It is the world of quotidian experience seen rightly, seen outside the compulsive spell of reification. It is utterly refractory of the drive of thinking to grasp objects and essences, because there are no objects to be grasped anywhere.

This compressed and rather elementary sketch of Nagarjuna's thought, I suggest, is nonetheless a fecund and powerful resource for reflection that seeks to deconstruct notions of homogenous and unrelated identity operative in world religions discourse. Turning to Nagarjuna and the Madhyamaka tradition is a compelling move for the comparative theologian whose aim is not merely to think about, theorize, or otherwise to explain religious others and their "beliefs." In turning to Nagarjuna as a resource for theory as well as a religious resource for addressing enduring afflictions that plague the human predicament, the comparative theologian hopes to challenge those within religious studies and secularist area studies who remain perfectly content to theorize about the religious other, to let the other serve as native informant, but not as normative thinkers whose claims and arguments require us to rethink and reformulate our own. Indeed, the very idea of *sunyata* reminds us that all talk of self and other must be handled with extreme care. As a mode of ordinary language, as a way of negotiating day-to-day interactions, such language is both useful and, of course, unavoidable. But when such discourse leads us into essentializing patterns of reflection and behavior, we fall prey to ignorance, an ignorance that has profound ethical consequence because it overlooks the fundamental nonduality of self and other. To reify is to break communion and to violate compassion.

It goes without say that at least some Christian theologians are likely to be unsettled by a thoroughgoing encounter with the Madhyamaka affirmation of emptiness understood as the rejection of *svabhava*. Not only will Christian theologians encounter therein a mode of religious reflection that is not determined by divinity, but they will encounter a tradition that rejects the very idea that any reality whatsoever, whether mundane or transcendent, can be eternal and changeless—the instantiation par excellence of *svabhava*, of essence. To engage Madhyamaka seriously will require a substantive and difficult transformation of Christian theology.

Nonetheless, classical Christian theology has some resources for understanding Madhyamaka. From the first, classical Christian theology has been determined by two motifs that are through and through relational, the motif of incarnation and the motif of Trinity. The latter figure understands the divine life as perichoretic: each member of the Trinity is distinct but not separate. The former figure, incarnation, is the basis for the ancient but often forgotten theme that divinity is fundamentally communicable, a communicable wellness if you will. God became human so that the human might become divine. A deep encounter with emptiness might well allow theologians to reframe and revivify elements at the very heart of tradition that have remained muted or submerged for far too long.

Comparative theology has a complex and ambivalent relationship with "religion." On the one hand, the felt need for comparative theology is driven precisely by the desire not just to take account of religious difference but to learn from it. But on the other hand, the way to comparative theology can be barred precisely by the entrenched weight of the category "religion." The force of the category can undergird and authorize a conception of theology as determined wholly by past construals of revelatory sources and motifs. Consequently, it comes as no surprise that theology is customarily taken to be thinking from and for a particular religious tradition that engages "other religions" solely for apologetic contest.

The devastating price that theology pays when it buys into such conservative readings of its own work is hard to overstate. If as radical orthodoxy theologians have argued, Christian faith is driven by the quest for a peaceable kingdom, it will hardly do for theology to serve as the ideological handmaiden for the clash-of-civilizations discourse that now pervades and structures so much of our public life. Ironically and even tragically, theologians who aspire to give to faith countercultural power by forming Christian communities in sectarian fashion have proven to be accommodationists par excellence. Their vision of fundamentally different religions that ground and animate fundamentally different civilizations nicely serves the interests of those who wish to insist on the inevitability of conflict. A comparative theology that works against the reifying power of identity configurations, sanctified in the name of religion, is a powerful and desperately needed counterforce to those agonistic energies that are currently fracturing any hope for planetary loves.

❧ Toward a Cosmopolitan Theology: Constructing Public Theology from the Future

NAMSOON KANG

Let us take hold of the fact that there are two communities—the one, which is truly great and common, embracing gods and men, in which we look neither to this corner not to that, but measure the boundaries of our state by the sun; the other, the one to which we have been assigned by our birth.
SENECA

It makes no difference whether a person lives here or there, provided that, wherever he lives, he lives as a citizen of the world.
MARCUS AURELIUS

It is part of morality not to be at home in one's home.
THEODOR ADORNO

Ich bin du, wenn Ich Ich bin [I am you, when I am I].
PAUL CELAN

VISIONING FOR PLANETARY LOVE

The question of who one is, the question of one's identity, has been a contested and recurring issue in various discourses and movements. The "who-am-I" question was once for me only an existential question, meaning that I was not fully aware of my multiple locationality in the world. The exclusively existential nature of my "who-am-I" question began to take a new form after feminism touched my life. The awareness of my gender and race in a white dominant culture extended the "who-am-I" question from a mere existential question to a social, cultural, and geopolitical one. In contemporary identity politics, identity usually refers to the axis of race, ethnicity, gender, religion, and sexual orientation. One forms the collective dimension of this kind of identity based on the unique difference of one's particular group from the other groups. In order to claim a collective identity, one needs to create one's own categories that make one distinct from other categories. Once society labels a group of people as feminist, gay, African American, or Asian, ideas and categories about the people come to imply social, political, cultural, psychological, spiritual, and theological effects. These labels shape the ways people perceive themselves and their actions and advocacy. In this process of constructing collective identity, one begins to shape one's agency in the public sphere. One has no control over some criteria for establishing one's identity, such as gender, race/ethnicity, ability, or sexuality, but choice determines other criteria, such as feminist, Marxist, postcolonialist, philosopher, theologian, Muslim, Buddhist, or Christian.

Here identity politics faces a serious question: What is "the stronger mobilizing discourse,"[1] not merely for a particular group but for the globe? Gayatri Chakravorty Spivak offers an answer to this question: Love. This mind-changing love wins "the attention of the subaltern without coercion or crisis" and is "the possibility of an unascertainable ethical singularity."[2] The mind-changing love is more essential to move the world than "the collective efforts to change laws, relations of production, systems of education, and health care" because "without the mind-changing one-on-one responsible contact, nothing will stick."[3] Spivak goes on to say: "We all know that when we engage profoundly with *one* person, the responses—the answers—come from both sides. Let us call this responsibility, as well as 'answer'ability or accountability. . . . In this sense, ethical singularity can be called a secret encounter."[4]

How can "we," who dream of a planetary love but have ties to different identities, form a profoundly radical coalition and solidarity? Is "solidarity in multiplicity" possible? What kind of epistemology can guide such a radical coalition across the dividing line of identity, which a term such as planetary love expresses? One cannot appeal to some transparently universal ground of being but rather must negotiate the meaning of one's collective identity in relation to structures of language, gender, class, ethnicity, ability, sexual orientation, religion, and so forth. As Friedrich Nietzsche eloquently puts it:

[F]or the enrichment of knowledge it may be of more value not to reduce oneself to uniformity in this way, but to listen instead to the gentle voice of each of life's different situations; these will suggest the attitude of mind appropriate to them. Through thus ceasing to treat oneself as a single rigid and unchanging individuum one takes an intelligent interest in the life and being of many others.[5]

Historically marginalized groups based on gender, race, religion, class, or sexual orientation insist on their unique identity to avoid reducing themselves to universal uniformity. However, eventually one confronts the dilemma that one can no longer take whiteness, the middle class, Christianity, maleness, or heterosexuality, for example, as the ubiquitous, paradigmatic agent of oppression and marginalization. A simple classification of one's ontological and geopolitical location based on this axis of identities does not reflect the complex reality of the center and the margin or the need for the planetary love which listens "to the gentle voice of each of life's different situations" (Nietzsche) and which is possible through an act of "ethical singularity" (Spivak). This planetary love can be an expression of a *deterritorialization* through which one creates one's own identity out of the twisted skeins of one's backgrounds and locality, recognizes differences among/between people without seizing them as levers in a struggle for power, and moves toward a space of "radical planetary love" across all forms of boundaries.

I believe *cosmopolitanism* can be an effective discourse with which to advocate a politics of trans-identity of overlapping interests and heterogeneous or hybrid subjects in order to challenge conventional notions of exclusive belonging, identity, and citizenship, and to envision a planetary love through an ethical singularity aimed at a more peaceful and just world. I regard cosmopolitanism as a "stronger mobilizing discourse" that captures Spivak's call for a mind-changing love for the planet. This essay is an effort to illuminate cosmopolitanism as a discourse that calls simultaneously for a planetary love through ethical singularity, in accordance with Spivak's notion, and for a radical neighborly love, in accordance with the Christian notion. As such, it is also an effort to articulate a cosmopolitan theological discourse, which I believe can be a mobilizing discourse for a more just and egalitarian world regardless of who one is.

COSMOPOLITANISM: A MOBILIZING DISCOURSE
FOR PLANETARY NEIGHBORLY LOVE

Cosmopolitanism as Trans-Provincialism

"Cosmopolitanism" is not a new but a long-standing concept that a wide range of scholars has recently revisited. The term dates back to the Cynics, who first began to use the term "cosmopolitan," to denote "citizen of the cosmos." When asked where he came from, Diogenes the Cynic replied, "I am a citizen of the world/I am a *kosmopolites*,"[6] which meant he refused to be confined by his local origins and local group memberships. Diogenes meant to assert that local affiliations were of lesser importance than a primary affiliation with humanity. Some suggest that Socrates predates Diogenes as the first thinker to regard himself as a "world citizen."[7] When asked where he was from, he also replied, not "Athens," but "the world," thereby embracing the universe as his city.[8] Marcus Aurelius also made a cosmopolitan claim by saying, "It makes no difference whether a person lives here or there, provided that, wherever he [*sic*] lives, he lives as a citizen of the world."[9] Scholars have used this idea of "world-citizen" (*kosmopolites*), strongly related to contemporary human rights issues, as a ground of cosmopolitanism. An identity as *kosmopolites* obviously transcends a specific national boundary, and thereby moves beyond a community-bounded identity.

Communitarianism regards "community" as "a significant source of ethical value," whereas cosmopolitanism sees "individuals as the origin of moral worth."[10] In this sense, communitarianism reduces the application and demand of justice, rights, and hospitality to those bounded by specific community, but cosmopolitanism concerns the rights and justice of *individuals* across the specific communities bounded by gender, nation-state, race, ethnicity, sexual orientation, and so forth. This idea of world-citizen regards as accidental and secondary the individual markers based on nationality, gender, class, ethnicity, sexual orientation, and so forth. The recognition of the contingency of *where* and *how* one is born and the attitude of "world-citizen" give rise to the concept of a "moral community made up by the community of all human beings."[11] In this context, cosmopolitanism reflects a critically skeptical attitude toward a conventional concept and tradition of society, a refusal to confine one's sense of belonging to a particular polis and instead a claim to belonging to a wider human community, the universe or cosmos.

Historically, however, people have used the notion of cosmopolitanism in negative ways as well. Nazis, for instance, used it as a synonym for a death sentence, categorizing "all victims of the planned mass murder as cosmopolitans" and identified Jews as "cosmopolitans." The Stalinists also used the word "cosmopolitan" to mean "Jew."[12] People often criticize cosmopolitanism as elitist when it means a "lifestyle" that requires sufficient financial resources to afford world travels and an ability to embrace multiculturalism, when the majority of people simply do not have the option to participate in such a lifestyle. People often attribute cosmopolitanism to "North Atlantic merchant sailors, Caribbean au pairs in the United States, Egyptian guest workers in Iraq, or Japanese women who take *gaijin* lovers."[13] People have used and interpreted cosmopolitanism in many different ways, and, interestingly, a wide range of scholars has recently reactivated the concept of cosmopolitanism. Therefore, in a way, "cosmopolitanism is back."[14] Social and political theorists, especially, tend to use the term to argue that individuals and nations have obligations to ensure justice across national borderlines. Cosmopolitanism emerges by way of a proposed new politics, embodying an alternative perspective between "ethnocentric nationalism" and "particularistic multiculturalism."[15]

Ulrich Beck illustrates interconnected principles of the cosmopolitan outlook. These principles reveal awareness of the interdependence of the global community, which requires overcoming "the boundaries between internal and external, us and them, the national and the international." He contends, "Cosmopolitanism without provincialism is empty, provincialism without cosmopolitanism is blind."[16] Cosmopolitanism favors voluntary affiliations, embraces the intersecting character of many groups, and engages the complexity of one's multiple identities, moving beyond provincial enclosures.

Cosmopolitanism as Universal Rights and Radical Hospitality
Although one can take Diogenes as the originator of cosmopolitanism with his idea of *kosmopolites*, it is Stoicism that strengthened the notion of cosmopolitanism in the sense that endorses "cosmic community," which transcends one's national boundary, especially in terms of the scope of justice, peace, and equality. Diogenes' idea of *kosmopolites* triggered a significant notion that we should not confine one's belonging only to a national/geographical boundary but should extend it to a larger community, the cosmos. In this sense, Stoicism strengthened the theoretical ground and promoted the idea of cosmopolitanism. Zeno illustrates, "Our household

arrangements should not be based on cities or local populations, each one marked out by its own legal system, but we should regard all people as our fellow-citizens and local residents, and there should be one way of life and one order, like that of a herd grazing together and nurtured by a common law."[17]

Stoic cosmopolitanism, not as a "proposal for a world-state" but as the ideal of "world-citizen," is "strategically valuable in social life."[18] Thomas Aquinas rearticulates the Stoic cosmopolitan ideal in his notion of natural law that is accessible to all human beings as an expression of God's creation. For Aquinas, natural law is a creation of divine will and a form of moral law. In principle, even non-Christians could be included in the application of natural law.[19] The concept of cosmopolitanism in modern usage is based on the inherent human dignity and equality of all human beings, and therefore people often use "cosmopolitanism" in association with the concept of universal human rights. Kant's notion of "perpetual peace" argues for cosmopolitan values that defend the equal claim of every individual person to the recognition, protection, and universal obligations of justice that cross borders of nationality and provincial community.[20] In his often-cited essay, "Perpetual Peace: A Philosophical Sketch," which is the basis of his advocacy of cosmopolitanism, Kant rightly argues:

> The people of the earth have thus entered in varying degrees into a universal community, and it has developed to the point where a violation of rights in *one* part of the world is felt *everywhere*. The idea of a cosmopolitan right is therefore not fantastic and overstrained; it is a necessary complement to the unwritten code of political and international right, transforming it into a universal right of humanity. Only under this condition can we flatter ourselves that we are continually advancing towards a perpetual peace.[21]

Kant's emphasis on the interconnected nature of life of the "people of the earth" and thereby on the significance of implementing the idea of a "cosmopolitan right" are very important, especially in an era of globalization and neoimperialism. What Kant is concerned with is not "philanthropy" but "right," in which context "*hospitality* means the right of a stranger not to be treated with hostility when he [sic] arrives on someone else's territory."[22] The ontological ground of this universal hospitality is in the fact that "no-one originally has any greater right than anyone else to occupy any particular portion of the earth."²³ Kant clearly depicts the philosophical principles for achieving "perpetual peace" among nations, and at the same time, portrays cosmopolitanism as the fullest measure of human achievement. In his thesis on "civil constitution," he argues that the civil constitution of every state shall be republican, which "is founded upon three principles: "firstly, the principle of *freedom* for all members of a society (as men [*sic*]); secondly, the principle of the *dependence* of everyone upon a single common legislation (as subjects); and thirdly, the principle of legal *equality* for everyone (as citizens)."²⁴ For Kant, cosmopolitanism is about the *principles of universal hospitality* that would ensure "perpetual peace" in the world. Although there is a fundamental contradiction in Kant's own thinking between his Eurocentric hierarchical theory of race and his cosmopolitan ideal, which reveals a fundamental problem in the modern notion of "universality," his utopian ideal of cosmopolitanism has influenced scholars who envision an ideal world of justice and peace beyond national boundaries.

Hannah Arendt took up the Kantian idea of "universal rights and hospitality" in her dealing with the stateless people, the displaced, the dislocated —the *Heimatlosen*.²⁵ She argues that the declaration of human rights by international organizations still has its limits because it "operates in terms of reciprocal agreements and treaties *between sovereign states;* and, for the time being, a sphere that is above the nations does not exist."²⁶ Arendt invites us to reevaluate the term "human rights," because "human rights," by its very definition, should be the rights of people as individual human beings, not as citizens of a particular nation-state. Here one encounters the tensions between "the particularity of positive law," operated by the institutions of specific nation-states, and "the universality of ethical obligations" toward individual persons regardless of their national citizenship.²⁷ In fact, at least theoretically, the UN Declaration of Human Rights in 1948 made a shift from an "international" to a "cosmopolitan" ideal of justice and rights when the General Assembly of the UN declared in December of that year that

> All human beings are born free and equal in dignity and rights. . . .
> Everyone is entitled to all the rights and freedoms set forth in this
> Declaration, without distinction of any kind, such as race, colour, sex,
> language, religion, political or other opinion, national or social origin,
> property, birth or other status.²⁸

How can those *Heimatlosen* receive equal treatment as equal human beings? Jacques Derrida elaborates this idea by coining a new phrase, "free city," where "one could retreat in order to escape from the threat of injustice." The idea of "free city" is significant because "when dealing with the related questions of hospitality and refuge," the idea of "free city" could "elevate itself above nation-states or at least free itself from them."[29] A significant task for our time, where the interconnectedness of the globe is becoming a daily reality, is then a construction of discourse that reconciles the universality of human rights with the particularity of positive law.

It is worth noting that Derrida points out the ambivalence of the term "hospitality." Noting the fact that *hospis* (host) and *hostes* (enemy) have common roots, he coins the term, "hostipitality" (*hostipitalité*), to show the entanglement of hostility and hospitality.[30] Derrida brings our attention to the "phenomenological interrelationship between the moment of hospitality and that of hostility," when one has an initial encounter with the other.[31] The moment of initial encounter with the other is a liminal space between acceptance, hospitality, and rejection, hostility. When there is a disparity of rights and power between two subjects—the host and the guest, the other—hospitality means fundamental welcoming, unconditional receptivity by the host toward the other, because "radical hospitality consists, would have to consist, in *receiving without invitation*, beyond or before the invitation."[32] In a society, the position between these two subjects—the host and the guest—often hinges on citizenship, race, gender, nationality, class, ability, or ethnicity. However, this reversibility of the stance of hospitality and hostility in our everyday encounters is significant.

Emmanuel Levinas calls for a concept of humanity that transcends the economical and political realms. If there is no notion of humanity that transcends sociopolitical structures, what ground is there left for theology or philosophy to reconsider who/what we humans are? Levinas's approach to hospitality, to humanity, offers an important ethicotheological aspect to sociopolitical issues. Although those who work for justice focus on the power relations between different social groups, they often overlook the significance of individual responsibility in the legitimating of justice itself. The fundamental question of Being, the whole philosophical and theological tradition of the West, remains:

Each one, as an "I," is separate from all the others to whom the moral duty is due. . . . From then on, there is no moral awareness that is not an awareness of this exceptional position, an awareness of being chosen. Reciprocity is a structure founded on an original inequality. For equality to make its entry into the world, beings must be able to demand more of themselves than of the Other, feel responsibilities on which the fate of humanity hangs, and in this sense pose themselves problems outside humanity. . . . It is a particularism that conditions universality, and it is a moral category rather than an historical fact.[33]

Levinas calls on us never to lose sight of the other, our fellow humans, our "neighbors." Unless we acknowledge individual humans as our neighbors, and their rights as universal rights, we will likely reduce them to impersonal numbers. Regarding one's neighbors as oneself is the core of cosmopolitan rights and hospitality. Cosmopolitanism advances ethics as fundamental welcoming, unconditional receptivity for the other, and a notion of responsibility for the other, our neighbor.

Cosmopolitanism as Trans-Boundaryness

There is no discourse without problems, weaknesses, or dilemmas. One of the dilemmas that cosmopolitanism carries is "its perceived inability to acknowledge and properly account for the special ties and commitments that characterize the lives of ordinary men and women."[34] Nationality and patriotism, religious identity, racial/ethnic identity, gender identity, and sexual identity create those special ties and particular attachments for most people. Cosmopolitanism seems to rule out these particular attachments and advocacies of the marginalized group and therefore seems to be out of touch with what is of value to many people. But the universalistic implications of cosmopolitanism and the particularistic commitments that every identity politics entails do not have to conflict. They can be mutually enhancing and complementary.

Here I would like to make a double differentiation between cosmopolitanism as an ideal and as an institutional claim, on the one hand, and between cosmopolitanism as a claim about justice and as a claim about culture and identity, on the other. First, cosmopolitanism, as a moral ideal and a set of moral commitments, views "individuals" as entitled to equal consideration of justice regardless of their nationality or race/ethnicity,[35] whereas people commonly associate cosmopolitanism as an institutional claim with a world state, which is often the basis of objection to cosmopolitanism in general.[36] Second, there are also two kinds of cosmopolitanism: one is a claim about culture or identity and the other is a claim about justice. The former denies that membership in a particular cultural community is constitutive of a person's social identity, whereas the latter concerns the scope of justice and holds that social boundaries do not impose limits on justice.[37] The cosmopolitanism that I adopt from this political philosophical discourse is cosmopolitanism as a moral claim and as a claim about the scope of justice. One can use cosmopolitanism in both negative and positive ways. In a positive sense, cosmopolitanism is a "moral perspective" that is "impartial, universal, individualist, and egalitarian," and its fundamental idea is that "every human being has a right to have her or his vital interest met, regardless of nationality or citizenship."[38]

Despite the contradictory uses of and dilemmas of cosmopolitanism, I find it more enabling, empowering, and liberating than disempowering and confining, especially when the issue of global inequality has become a more and more serious issue in our time, which requires theological reflection and commitment. The discourse of cosmopolitanism enables one to break out of self-centered, balkanized, collective identity and national/patriotic narcissism and to expand the application of justice and solidarity across and beyond national, regional, group-based boundaries and confinements. Cosmopolitanism is a standpoint that vindicates impartial, planetary, and egalitarian justice and solidarities across all the different forms of boundaries that divide people. For Jacques Derrida, the concept of cosmopolitanism signifies an "undeconstructable concern for justice."[39] Cosmopolitanism for me maintains principles of justice and compassion that transcend nationality, citizenship, and other boundaries and that defend the application of justice to all individuals of the cosmos as a whole.

Paul reflects this "oneness of humanity" in his statement, "[T]here is no longer Jew or Greek, there is no longer slave or free, there is no longer male and female; for all of you are one in Christ Jesus."[40] Another text also conveys this idea of oneness of humanity of cosmopolitanism: "So then you are no longer strangers and aliens, but you are citizen with the saints and also members of the household of God."[41] Cosmopolitanism and its theological adoption is, in this context, a theological response to the issues of global inequality that we are facing. I view the *impartiality* of the scope of justice and concern in cosmopolitanism as the very essence of the Christian teaching of "neighborly love," and it does not necessarily rule out the *partiality* of one's local attachments and commitments. The spirit of cosmopolitanism also requires us to radically extend the category of "neighbor," to cross and transcend various borders, and to embrace every human person and, furthermore, nature itself, as our "neighbors."

Cosmopolitanism as Trans-Identity Politics

Questions of identity have increasingly become interlaced with issues of power and representation. The battle to grant rights and justice to new social groups dominates the current political, cultural, and ideological landscape. There seems to be a deep conflict between the diverse identities and the politics of representation. Articulating the relationship among identities along the axes of gender, race, class, ethnicity, sexual orientation, ability, and so forth is not easy. People have taken up genders, races, ethnicities, sexual orientations, cultural differences, and diverse political and religious views in the struggle to construct counternarratives and practices. Identity politics covers complex and diverse theoretical positions, and discourses have evolved around the questions of subjectivity, representation, culture, difference, struggle, and liberation. Identity politics has become one of the more powerful commonsense constructions developed by marginalized groups. Therefore, "the complex, even contradictory character of identity politics must be accounted for in efforts to develop a politically effective critical perspective" and "will remain a persistent feature of our political landscape in part because it produces limited but real empowerment for its participants."[42]

Identity politics since the 1960s has played a central role in politicizing marginalized groups, challenging the mainstream hegemonic power, and providing spaces for the marginalized groups to claim their voices and experiences as legitimate. However, it has often failed to move beyond an unproblematized notion of difference and has thereby clung to the polarized "we-they" binarism. In doing so, identity politics has appealed uncritically to a discourse of essentialized "authenticity." As a result, identity politics becomes a "politics of heterogeneity" in attempting to construct "*identity-in-differential*." Here we need to make a distinction between "heterogeneity as bohemianism, anarchism, and political indifference and heterogeneity as political destiny." Furthermore, it is significant to acknowledge the distinction between "a categorical heterogeneity, that is, a heterogeneity construed by the homogeneous logic of the 'category' and an a-categorical heterogeneity that finds its 'self-expression' through the break-down of the 'categorical.'"[43] What we often experience in identity politics is its fall into a "categorical heterogeneity" where "[d]ifference is transformed into that

which must be specified within a concept, without overstepping its bounds,"
and the "swarming of individualities."[44] For instance, Orientalist and neo-
Orientalist concerns have shaped much scholarship on Asian subjects by
presenting the Asian other as product of a timeless, unchanging culture.
Here people still confine "being Asian" to the static images of "authentic"
Asianness.[45] An essentializing notion of Asian-ness continues to dog Asian
theological discourse, and homogenization and singularization of this vast
ethnic group, "Asian," continue to lurk in the field of theology. People
continue to homogenize "Asians," culturally, ethnically, and ontologically.
Furthermore, Asian scholars themselves selectively participate in and pro-
duce/reproduce Orientalist discourses. Homogenization of Asians by Asians
themselves in claiming their own identity-in-differential from the West is an
example of a "politics of categorical heterogeneity," and the politics of Asian
identity thereby turns into to a politics of "swarming individualities."

Identity politics has enabled formerly voiceless groups to claim their own
power and to establish their own identities and experiences. Nevertheless,
one of the dilemmas that the current identity politics carries is its tendency
to invoke a politics of separatism. Identity politics also makes people overlook the differences and power disparities within their own "group," because
that group becomes a homogeneously categorized community of "swarming individualities." Ellen Willis writes:

> The appeal of "identity politics" is that it arises from a radical insight—
> that domination is systematically structured into the relations between
> social groups. The problem is that [identity politics] gives rise to a logic
> that chokes off radicalism and ends up by supporting domination. If
> the present obsession with group identity as the basis of politics is hard
> to imagine, much less build, a broad-based radical collectivity, it has
> even more tellingly stood in the way of a principled commitment to
> the freedom and happiness of individuals, without which no genuine
> radicalism is possible.[46]

The reality of oppression and marginalization is very complicated and often
paradoxical. A person can belong to a socially privileged category but at the
same time to an unprivileged category. For instance, a middle-class, Asian,
heterosexual, woman, Christian professor like myself may blind herself to
issues of sexual orientation, class, and religious othering, and her experience
of racial/ethnic discrimination and inequality may have made her assume

that her experience of oppression based on her gender and race automatically guarantees her understanding of other forms of oppression and privilege. Identity politics often contributes to establishing another form of "interest group," rather than offering a claim for fundamental transformation of human relationship and its institutional implementation. "Identity politics" is necessary and legitimate only when its claim is to dismantle the discriminatory view of human beings, to claim dignity for the otherwise degraded group, and to enlarge the possibility of human liberation. But I am skeptical about identity politics when it is only for attaining and possessing more power for the formerly marginalized group without changing the fundamental nature of human relationships. Identity politics "produces limited but real empowerment for its participants."[47] However, it contains significant problems: First, its essentialist tendency; second, its we-they binary position; third, its homogenization of diverse social oppression; fourth, its simplification of the complexity and paradox of being privileged and unprivileged; and fifth, its ruling out of the intersectional space of diverse forms of oppression in reality.

Adopting cosmopolitanism discourse, I would like to articulate a theology that attempts to overcome the problems and dilemmas of identity politics. Central to my proposed cosmopolitan theology is the need to provide one with the vision to deconstruct the mythic notion of one's "frozen" identity, to address complex relations of representation, and to create liberative principles that make possible solidarity and coalition across different identities and borders. This theology embraces the "radical neighborly love" that is the profound message of Jesus' teaching, and which, I would argue, has certain affinities with Spivak's concept of "planetary love." The cosmopolitanism that I adopt entails a theological and geopolitical claim about the scope and value of justice, coalition, and allegiances, and not about culture and identity. The cosmopolitan spirit embraces but, at the same time, transcends the collective identity position and group-based allegiances across the borderlines of gender, race, ethnicity, sexual orientation, and ability. It is not therefore about boundary-making but about boundary-embracing and transcending.

CONSTRUCTING COSMOPOLITAN THEOLOGY

Cosmopolitanism from Above and Cosmopolitanism from Below
It is crucial to ask "what ends" one is claiming cosmopolitanism for in order to avoid a false universalization and totalizing grand-narrativization. I would

like to make a differentiation between two types of cosmopolitanism: *cosmopolitanism from below* and *cosmopolitanism from above*. One of the examples for the cosmopolitanism from above is Kant's cosmopolitanism. One of the criticisms of Kant involves his view on race with his argument that the white race achieves the greatest perfection of humanity.[48] Kant even argues that within the white race, the German "has a fortunate combination of feeling, both in that of the sublime and in that of the beautiful," while the English and French only have half of that feeling.[49] Kant's "cosmopolitan law" does not apply to certain races, as is evident when he writes that "humanity is at its greatest perfection in the race of the white. The yellow Indians do have a meager talent. The Negroes are far below them and at the lowest point are a part of the American peoples."[50] He goes on to argue that the Negro, found in dry, hot locations, is "well suited to his climate and grew strong, fleshy . . . lazy, soft and dawdling," and "all Negroes stink."[51] He further argues that "[t]he race of the Negroes, one could say, is completely the opposite of the Americans; they are full of affect and passion, very lively, talkative and vain. They can be educated but only as servants (slaves), that is if they allow themselves to be trained."[52]

He therefore argues that nature shows the inferiority of Blacks, which justifies the slavery system that uses Black as slaves. It is obvious that for Kant normative humanity is biologically both white and male. This deductive approach is typical of a cosmopolitanism from above because it is based on a discriminatory and hierarchical perception of human beings. Kant's deductive cosmopolitanism is not "cosmopolitan" enough to challenge the hierarchical anthropology that stands in opposition to the very spirit of cosmopolitanism. One can fully agree with Kant on his ideas of planetary peace, universal rights, hospitality, and equality, especially in relation to the issue of global justice and inequality in the era of globalization. However, the task of critical cosmopolitanism is to clear up the encumbrances of the past and move beyond Kant's prejudices and biases against certain races and female gender. Therefore, we are *"thinking with Kant against Kant."*[53]

In contrast to cosmopolitanism from above, cosmopolitanism from below is grounded in a radically egalitarian view of human beings that regards everyone as valuable and equal regardless of citizenship, ethnicity, gender, race, class, ability, religion, or sexuality, and on a radical sensitivity about all forms of injustice, discrimination, and oppression. Cosmopolitanism from below embraces the formerly devalued, silenced, and marginalized voices.

Moving forward for a transformative cosmopolitan project that adopts *border-thinking*,[54] it recognizes and transforms the hegemonic view from the perspective of people from below.[55] Here border-thinking offers an opportunity to engage the multiple contexts, communities, and identities that constitute different experiences of marginalization, oppression, and exclusion of people.

Cosmopolitanism from below does not affirm a "hierarchy of oppression" or that one can "own" a specific form of oppression simply because one is part of the oppressed group that has historical evidence of being oppressed or victimized. As an inductive cosmopolitanism, which arises from the concrete reality of ordinary people, cosmopolitanism from below calls for a radical sensitivity to the complexity and intersectionality of all forms of oppression. It cultivates what I would call a "theological anthropology of *regardless*" that promotes the actualization of the *imago dei* in every individual person in both spiritual and material reality.

Characteristics of Cosmopolitan Theology

The cosmopolitan theology that I propose here is grounded on cosmopolitanism from below and has five characteristics. First, cosmopolitan theology is a *theology of trans-identity*. Every identity politics should be provisional, temporal, and partial and move toward a larger community of radical equality and boundary-less inclusion, without undervaluing the significant meaning of "particular" engagement and commitment for implementation of justice and equality for all living beings. Theology of trans-identity is grounded in an understanding of the complexity of all forms of domination by extending it from merely one form of oppression, such as classism, to gender, sexual orientation, racial, or ethnic injustices. Oppression is a multilayered, complex process that affects different groups and different individuals in different ways and at different times across the various borders that structure our reality. We need to recognize, extend, and transform the ways power and knowledge operate because people now produce knowledge under the conditions of a globalizing neoliberal capitalism and emerging global public sphere. A single-issue movement, based on a single group identity, is unable to address the intersectional complexity of different forms of oppression. Despite its strength and significant contribution, *identity politics* or *politics of difference* cannot afford to have its connection to wider material relations occulted by a focus on theoretical issues often divorced from the lived experiences of oppressed, marginalized, and de-privileged groups. Being marginal or oppressed is not about one's "essence" based on race, gender, ethnicity, or sexual orientation, but about one's "position" and "location" in a material world. The material conditions include "widespread homelessness, joblessness, illiteracy, crime, disease (including AIDS), hunger, poverty, drug addiction, alcoholism as well as the various habits of ill health, and the destruction of the environment," and these are "the myriad social effects of the late multinational capitalism."[56] The politics of trans-identity that I propose does not deny one's identity but claims that one's identity is not fixed or essentialized. The politics of trans-identity relates personal identity to the struggle for justice and against the institutionalization of asymmetrical relations of various forms of hegemonic power and privilege. A theology of trans-identity seeks to move from the *politics of single identity* to the *politics of multiple solidarities* across various identities without abandoning one's personal attachments and commitments to the group that one finds significant. Here we should take up the issue of "difference" in ways that do not replay monocultural essentialism, such as Euro-U.S.-centrism, Anglocentrism, phallocentrism, androcentrism, gynocentrism, Christiancentrism, Asiancentrism, Blackcentrism, Whitecentrism, and the like. What we need is not to reverse and replay the "centrisms" but to create a politics of solidarity and alliance building, of dreaming together toward the "Reign of God" on earth that moves beyond a ghettoized, naturalized, idealized, romanticized, and essentialized "identity" politics, which actually serves to keep forms of institutionalized racism, sexism, classism, ethnocentrism, and homophobism intact.

Second, cosmopolitan theology is a *theology of radical affirmation of the Other*, and, at the same time, a theology of *radical neighborly love*. Cosmopolitan theology invites us to fundamentally ask and redefine who "the other" is and who "the neighbor" is in our time. Once the "neighbor" was very ethnocentric in Israelite/Jewish tradition, and then became "religiocentric" in Christian tradition through its invention of the "religious other" in its construction of doctrine, theology, and institutionalized practice. Theologians need to transform Christian anthropology from a "reluctant affirmation" to a "radical affirmation" of the formerly constructed "other" and to a radical inclusion of that "other" into the community of "neighbor," theologically, institutionally, and systemically. Cosmopolitan theology is based on a Christology that envisions Jesus Christ as the one who is ever affirming the "other"—the racialized other, gendered other, sexualized other, religious other, ethnic other, and so forth. Jesus' radical affirmation of the other is, I believe, based not on doctrinal grounds or personal merit but on neighborly love and compassion for the entire being—both humans and nonhumans.

Third, cosmopolitan theology is *a theology of trans-religious solidarity*. Traditional Christian theology and its practices have contributed to the construction of its religious other. Christian theology of religion and ecumenism has evolved around the issue of interreligious "dialogue," primarily grounded on an ethics of tolerance. There is, however, what I would call an "ecumenical taboo" that one has to comply with whenever one comes to the table for interreligious dialogue. One should not raise, for instance, such questions as gender justice, sexual orientation issues, religious/theological constructions of the other, multiple forms of violence, or religious co-optation by neo/imperialism. Each religion has its own "history of sin" that has justified and perpetuated oppression and exclusion of certain groups of people through its own religious teaching, doctrine, and practice. In order for us to be "nice" and "tolerant" to each other, our interreligious dialogue has not challenged the very fundamental issues of injustice that each of our religions has practiced and perpetuated in various ways. Interreligious dialogue has been based on an ethic of tolerance and has played a significant role in easing the antagonism between religions, at least among the "leaders" of established religions. However, I argue that an authentic ecumenism and theology of religion should be grounded in an *ethic of transformation*, and the encounter with one another should be a process of revisiting, reexamining, rechallenging, and reconstructing the very foundations of each religious discourse and practice, from the perspective of justice, as it impinges on the lives of ordinary people. In so doing, interreligious encounters will serve to dismantle the very way a religion constructs its discourse and identity, which has contributed to the construction of the "other" in multiple ways—not just a religious *other* but also a racialized, ethnicized, gendered, sexualized, or culturally essentialized *other*.

A final goal of ecumenism and interreligious dialogue is to work for the justice and betterment of the "cosmos." Unless we pursue a fundamental transformation of our own theological discourses and practices, multireligious education and ecumenical dialogue will be nothing but "religious voyeurism" or "ecumenical tourism." Trans-religious solidarity does not mean that everyone thinks the same way. However, it begins when people of different religions have the confidence to disagree over issues because they believe in transformation for the betterment of the world, not merely in coming up with doctrinal common ground among different faiths and religious traditions. This trans-religious solidarity maximizes mutual interaction, challenge, and transformation, rather than pursuing a neutral balance between and among different religions.

Fourth, cosmopolitan theology is a theological discourse of counter-empire. Cosmopolitan theology is a theological discourse of resistance against any form of imperialism. Empire building is all about building power by creating a devalued other. The empire then dominates the othered subject. The construction of the other is perpetuated through the surveillance, appropriation, aestheticization, classification, negation, idealization, naturalization, or eroticization of the other.[57] In cosmopolitan theological discourse, theologians must fundamentally scrutinize the issue of hegemony through the construction of the other and the intersectionality of various form of hegemony. Today we are facing multiple forms of hegemony: hegemony of English as a form of linguistic and discursive imperialism; hegemony of Westcentrism as a form of cultural, political, economic, discursive imperialism; hegemony of Whiteness as a form of racial/ethnic imperialism; hegemony of androcentrism and homophobia as a form of sexual imperialism; hegemony of Christianity as a form of religious imperialism, and so forth. In this context, the real question would not be *"whether* Empire but *whose* Empire."[58] This question is not only to check the abuses of power by others, but also to check our own abuses of power, and therefore to bring us into critical awareness of and engagement with the interests of all our relations.

Fifth, cosmopolitan theology is a *theology of boundary-transcending solidarity.* The cosmopolitan theology that I am proposing is a theological discourse and practice that cultivates planetary solidarity for justice, peace, and equality of all living beings. It embraces and transcends the diverse "subject positions" in a world of extreme inequalities. We can see the extreme inequality today in the following example:

> A child born in Sweden today has a life expectancy at birth of 79.7 years. A child born in Sierra Leone has a life expectancy at birth of 38.9 years. In the US, GDP per capita is $34,142, in Sierra Leone, GDP per capita is $490. Adult literacy rates in the top twenty nations are around 99 percent. In Sierra Leone, the literacy rate is 36 percent.[59]

The "global inequalities in income increased in the twentieth century by orders of magnitude out of proportion to anything experienced before," and the disparity "between the incomes of the richest and poorest country was about 3 to 1 in 1820, 35 to 1 in 1950, 44 to 1 in 1973 and 72 to 1 in 1992."[60] We are living in a world of unprecedented inequality between and among nations, regions, and peoples. Cosmopolitan theology offers the opportunity for us to engage the multiple realities that constitute different cultural, political, economic codes, and invites us to cross the borders in order to practice an impartial neighborly love and to be in solidarity with those on the margins. Global political and economic inequality and injustice have become serious issues because "these inequalities are mostly greater today than 50 or 100 years ago, and there is reason to believe that the gap will continue to grow."[61]

Cosmopolitan theology seeks to build solidarity based on the "we-hermeneutics" of cosmopolitanism in the sense that "I am because we are; and we are because I am."[62] Here "we" is not based on hierarchical/vertical relationships, as is the case in *cosmopolitanism from above*, but on radical egalitarian/horizontal democratic relationship among and across gender, age, race, ethnicity, class, orientation, or religions and culture.

COSMOPOLITAN THEOLOGY AS PUBLIC THEOLOGY FROM THE FUTURE

A distinctive phenomenon within theology over the past few decades has been the emergence of the various theologies of liberation such as Latin American and Black liberation theologies, feminist/womanist theologies, and LGBT (lesbian, gay, bisexual, and transgendered) theologies. All theologies of liberation and transformation focus on the marginalized, the excluded, the silenced, or the oppressed. A contribution of theologies of liberation is the repositioning of the role and the task of theology in the world. As one can define public theology as a theology that gets involved in the public affairs of society, liberation theologies have paved a way for the emergence of public theology in our times. Cosmopolitan theology is a new form of public theology that concerns the oppressed in our society. Its goal is to resist all forms of "oppression against humanity" and to be in solidarity with the marginalized. It further wrestles with the intersecting issues of social oppression and discrimination in society today and the conflicts among various advocacy groups and particular bounded communities. I regard the prospect of cosmopolitan theology as public theology, which has to do with the public relevance of a theology that has a concern for the coming of the Reign of God in the world of human history through the cosmopolitan justice of planetary neighborly love.

Cosmopolitanism from below is a discourse of hope and compassion that has not yet had the opportunity to actualize its utopian potential.[63] In this regard, cosmopolitan theology is a theology from the future. However, cosmopolitan consciousness transforms the goal of doing theology and the task of theologians. Traditionally people have viewed theologians not as active participants in public affairs, but as mere observers, and the role of theologians was often that of transmitter or interpreter of "divine truth." But I believe theologians must become "cosmopolitans," who cross the borders of differences and are capable not just of interpreting but also of "reinventing" traditions that serve to liberate and enlarge human possibilities regardless of one's nationality, gender, race, ethnicity, ability, religion, sexual orientation, and so forth. Cosmopolitan theology represents the voice of an all-embracing view of life. However, it challenges the liberal, humanist notion of the unified, essentialized subject, and views the subject as contradictory and multilayered. It rejects the politics of single-group identity if it essentializes the subject, and invites us to rethink fundamentally how we are constituted as subjects within a rapidly changing set of political, social, economic, cultural, and religious conditions. Cosmopolitan theology further calls for solidarity across borders, a community of radical inclusion, and deep compassion for the other regardless of who one is. It points to solidarity, community, justice, and compassion as essential aspects of how we experience the world and ourselves in a meaningful way.

Cosmopolitanism calls for a "planetary neighborly love" and "deep and radical compassion" for living beings, which I believe should be the central message of Christianity. In his book *The Coming of the Cosmic Christ*,[64] Matthew Fox examines how compassion is dying in the face of all the contemporary crises throughout the world: Mother Earth is dying, hope is dying, the youth are dying, and native peoples, cultures, religions, and wisdom are dying. He calls us to enact the resurrection of the living Cosmic Christ in our beings and then our actions to transform society and bring healing to all its suffering, broken parts through love, imagination, peacemaking, and environmental, moral, and social justice. Fox argues, with conviction and enthusiasm, that in restoring the mystical mind of compassion, the Christian work of love can bring a global renaissance to the entire world, including every aspect of society, from religion to sexuality, from peacemaking and disarmament to mentoring the young. Remaking the world will require "planetary love"—the mind-changing love for the planet, that Spivak calls for.

Cosmopolitan theology envisions a new Cosmic Christ who urges us to begin a great work to live and build the Reign of God on earth, where "almost half of the world's population of 6 billion people live on less than $2 a day, and 1.2 billion (a fifth of the world's population) live in absolute poverty on less than $1 day," and "800 million do not get enough food; and 500 million are chronically malnourished."[65] We need to expand the sites of theology so that it resides not merely in theological schools and institutions but in the wider public sphere; in doing so we would be extending the possible terrains of struggle for justice as well. I hope that theology addresses major social issues, fully engages matters of power and inequality in all aspects of daily life, and fosters in every way possible the imperatives of justice across the boundaries. Doing theology today may be one of the few spheres left for us to provide the conditions for people to become critically engaged social agents, and to create the conditions for people to struggle anew to sustain the promise of the Reign of God on earth and continuously expand into a world of new possibilities and opportunities for keeping justice and hope alive.

In this context, the theologian is an active participant in public affairs, not an objective and neutral observer, not just an academic scholar who resides only within an "ivory tower." If "reading the signs of our time" is one of the tasks of theologians, what constitutes "reading" becomes an important question, and redefining the role of theologians becomes an urgent task. Theologians are not to be passive transmitters of "divine truth" but active participants within multiple communities and public sectors, engaging with and providing theological discourses that foster and promote solidarities with the marginalized within, against, and between dominant powers and institutions on local and global levels. They are, in this sense, the boundary-crossers, who cross the boundaries of gender, nationality, race, ethnicity, ability, sexual orientation, and religion, in order to bring the Divine Will to earth, where justice, peace, equality, and compassion will flow like a river. Here theologians are "artists" in the sense that they create and re-create religious traditions and their practices of transformation and liberation. The languages that theologians use, create, and construct should be the languages of boundary-crossing, radical inclusion, hope, trans-boundary solidarity, and justice. The theologians' public responsibility is to contest sociogeopolitical relations and institutions that keep privilege, exclusion, discrimination, and oppression of one group over against the other alive in daily life. Cosmopolitan theological discourse is then a public theology from the future of *passion for the impossible, longing for the impossible, dreaming of the impossible, hope for the impossible.*

What can theology offer in the public sphere and to political action? Asked in an interview how philosophy could or should react to the problems of globalization, such as "the dissolution of the state and the impotence of politics," Derrida replied: "All political innovation touches on philosophy. The 'true' political action always engages with a philosophy. All action, all political decision making, must invent its norm or rule. Such a gesture traverses or implies philosophy."[66] Can theology function as philosophy does in political action? My answer is yes. Theology can be an ardent "interlocutor" in public discourse, disseminate its ideals in the public sector, and promote political action for enhancing "hospitality" to humanity. Theology should be a discourse that helps the sociopolitical approach to justice to maintain its human face and not to become "impersonal."

Cosmopolitan Theologians as Public Theologians without a Passport
Who are theologians? What kind of self-identity could or should a theologian claim? Should a theologian be a defender or transmitter of Christian "tradition"? What if the "tradition" itself carries a dark side, implicitly or explicitly, bounded by religious or cultural superiorism, ethnocentrism, homophobia, exclusive nationalism, sexism, racism, and so forth? What kind of "identity" would then justify me as a "theologian"? This question has been lingering in my mind throughout the time I have been working on cosmopolitan theology. It may sound simple, but for me the identity issue has been fundamental. The following remarks by Derrida resonate with what I think of as a proper language for the "identity" of a public theologian: public theologians, like philosophers in Derrida's sense, are those *without a passport*:

> In principle, a philosopher should not have a passport, or any kind of identity documents, he [*sic*] should never be required to have a visa! He should not represent any nationality, not even a national language. The will to be a philosopher, in principle and in relation to the most firm of traditions, is the will to make a contribution to the universal community. Not just cosmopolitan, but universal; beyond citizenship, beyond state, even beyond the cosmopolitan.[67]

Once one comes to possess an "identity document," one is bound to the ground of that identity document, whether it be about national or religious affiliation, or a particular advocacy cause, and so on. One begins then to be "attached" to the very ground of such "identity." Here a *passport* symbolizes classification, categorization, homogenization, totalization, genderization, sexualization, racialization, ethnicization, and so forth. The *passport* fundamentally limits the endless dimension of one's "neighbors," one's "friends," to a certain "category," especially when there is, in our reality, a "strong" passport and a "weak" one. *Theologians-without-passports* intentionally dissociate themselves from the dominant power, practice, or discourse that totalizes, categorizes, classifies an individual person into a stereotypical box, numbers, and data. *Theologians-without-passports* commit themselves to "make a contribution to the universal community," to the Reign of God, where every individual human being is equal to everyone else, treated justly, accepted fully as who one is. The word, "beyondness" well captures the spirit of cosmopolitan theologians as public *theologians-without-passports*. Theologians are to look to the beyond-community—beyond nationality, skin color, gender, sexual orientation, citizenship, religious affiliation— because the God, the Divine, who is the primary frame of reference of theologians, is for, with, in, among those individual human beings. It is to reaffirm the sheer truth: No one is better or worse, superior or inferior than any other; and "Ich bin du, wenn Ich Ich bin [I am you, when I am I]."[68]

✤ *Pax Terra* and Other Utopias? Planetarity, Cosmopolitanism, and the Kingdom of God

DHAWN B. MARTIN

Let's assume then that globalization is a set of designs to manage the world while cosmopolitanism is a set of projects toward planetary conviviality.
WALTER D. MIGNOLO, "The Many Faces of Cosmo-polis: Border Thinking and Critical Cosmopolitanism"

The Earth is a paranational image that can . . . perhaps provide, today, a displaced site for the imagination of planetarity.
GAYATRI CHAKRAVORTY SPIVAK, *Death of a Discipline*

Thy kingdom come. Thy will be done, on earth as it is in heaven.
MATTHEW 6:10, RSV

Mapped, divided into spheres of influence, and navigated by a wireless "net" accessed through palm-cradled devices, our micromanaged globe appears sufficiently contained.[1] "The globe" thus compacted, notes Gayatri Chakravorty Spivak, "allows us to think that we can aim to control it."[2] Efforts to control, however, inevitably stumble on the unexpected or unconquered. Cartographers of old warned that at the limits of the known globe and in the mists of unchartered waters, "here be monsters." The warning stands inscribed. Difference, or that which eludes categorization, bears the scar of the monstrous or foreign, so marked by the forces of hegemony. Orbiting in a universe resistant to the multiply particular, the globe—thus mapped, inscribed, and scarred by centuries of "design"—swirls about an axis tilted toward the reigning sociopolitical imaginaries of the time. In this particular time, images and policies of globalization twist the compressed orb into a "system of exchange" funded by economies of the same.[3]

These economies, driven by the homogenizing effects of capital and consumption, push the globe's diverse peoples, languages, beliefs, soils, and waters to the verge of material and conceptual extinction. The biodiversity of local environments falters beneath the weight of the same. Around the globe, the "other" ceases to be imagined or encountered except as a derivative from the same. In an effort to disrupt the derivative, Spivak "propose[s] the planet to overwrite the globe." For the planet, unlike the globe, "is in the species of alterity"—an alterity "underived."[4] The species Spivak names planet, in its overwriting alterity and "planetarity," serves as "a catachresis for . . . collective responsibility as right."[5] As to whether this "right" alludes to a matter of law or an alternative to "wrong," the text remains ambivalent. Yet when considered as an element in Spivak's work, this right likely speaks not so much of the inviolable as of the irreducible. For the inviolable dwells potentially in the comfort of the codified, with the collective and its responsible acts neatly defined—without deviation.[6] The irreducible, alternatively, inhabits the uncanny (*unheimlich*) and undecided. It refrains from absolute pronouncements but rather prays to be not only haunted by but also "imagined . . . without guarantees, by and in another culture," another collective.[7] Collectives of the irreducible, therefore, roam the unfamiliar terrains of a planet barren of certainty yet bursting with diverse encounters.

Spivak's proposed planetarity envisions the (im)possibility of ethical relationship with "the wholly other" emergent not from clearly delineated positions or oppositions, but from alterity.[8] Cast in opposition, the globe too readily splits between "here be monsters" and "there be the civilized"—or translated in twenty-first-century terms, here be the developing and there be the developed. Imagined in alterity, the planet opens beyond binary divisions and the "paranational" Earth gives place to "a politics of friendship to come."[9] (Im)possible though it be, Spivak's earthy vision demands attentive effort to picture and enact an ever-arriving politics of conviviality—to add Walter Mignolo's cosmopolitan idea of planetary relations. Yet conviviality and friendship, however deferred, risk devolution into an "unexamined benevolence" that once again partitions the globe into polar here and there, "First" and "Third" world designations.[10] So that this earth-nurtured ethics of collective responsibility does not deflate into global exchanges of the same, Spivak locates planetarity within radical alterity—an alterity she recognizes in the name of God, among other names.[11]

The Earth, altered relations, God, and a "yet to come" political paradigm: the prayers of planetarity and petitions for the divine kingdom voice hauntingly similar visions. Shared vision, bereft of consideration of irreducible rights and collective responsibilities, however, too readily flounders in unexamined complacence. It is, therefore, through the strategies of critique, postcolonial, cosmopolitan, and theopolitical, this essay exposes those "displaced site[s]" where Spivak's planetarity and "kingdom of God" parables share common, if uncanny, ground. On this uncertain yet sacred ground seeds root, lost sheep are found, the first shall be last, and "[p]lanet-thought" dares to imagine and relate to the other not as the same but as wholly/holy other.[12]

THY KINGDOM COME: A POLITICS OF CONVIVIALITY, COME!

The displaced functions practically and poetically in the call to an ever-arriving politics of the convivial—so too in planet-thoughts of the kingdom of God. The imperative—"come!"—prays for a political theology open to the images and acts, the poetry and praxis of sites continually displaced—the trans*terra*torial. This essay, informed by Spivak's planetarity and Mignolo's "critical cosmopolitanism," constructs a theology of the trans*terra*torial that seeks not an originary paradise or a monolithic telos. Neither Eden nor the globe contains a theopolitics of friendship. The kingdom of God envisioned as planetary cosmopolis, however, offers parables and practices of the convivial in an ever-to-come, ever-displaced universe.

Convivial practices of the displaced and displacing emerge from critique—a love act integral to the deconstruction of those social policies and theological doctrines designed, as Mignolo asserts, "to manage" the known world. A planetary cosmopolis displaces the globe and its economies of the same not by decrees of transcendent power but through relationships of critical vulnerability. The thoughts and practices leading to this earthy polis of God, as elaborated in the opening sections of this essay, draw primarily on the liberation theology of Dorothee Soelle and the poststructural insights of Spivak and Jacques Derrida. The cosmopolitan aspects, for the most part, reflect the influence of Mignolo and Homi K. Bhabha with a Kantian twist.

Through various twists and turns, including some God-talk and an open-ended account of atonement theory and cosmology, this essay constructs a political theology from the uncanny (in this case, *ou topos*) ground of a *strategic utopianism*. Akin to Spivak's strategic essentialism, this strategy resists universal absolutes, yet recognizes the import (and inevitability) of universals employed as bearers of irreducible rights and collective responsibilities. The essay concludes with a parable of the divine planetary cosmopolis: *Pax Terra*.

Political Theology as Hermeneutic of Critique:
The "Which" and "What" of Theo/logos

Political theology holds that human practices imply (perhaps even implicate) the divine. As Dorothee Soelle observes, with echoes of Martin Luther's *Small Catechism* and Paul Tillich's ultimate concern, "The correct theological question is . . . not whether someone lives with or without a god, but rather which god is worshiped and adored in a particular society" or, we might add, political system.[13] In other words, show me your politics—how you organize your polis, who is locked up, locked out and locked in, where and where not the dollars flow, who the protected and exploited are, those convenient lies and inconvenient truths of power regimes—and I'll show you your God.[14] If politics revels in or reveals a particular conception of the divine, it is the task of political theology to engage in a critique both of that politics and of the theo/logos and theo/praxis expressing that divinity.[15] Thus, the "which God?" question commences inquiry into the ultimacy or alterity invoked by divine (de)nominations—be they of the state or the church, be they of an underived planetarity or kingdom come.

To resist the designs both of idolatry and globalization, the *theos* of theo/logos, whether considered a name or *the* name among others, must speak of a radical alterity that challenges economies of the same. The wholly other transcends efforts by any "same" to grasp, control, civilize, or globalize. This transcendence reveals not the extraterrestrial but rather the trans*terra*torial. The wholly/holy other transcends in the very midst of humus and human relations. Through this in-the-midst transcendence the other displaces, making space—however uncanny and *ou topos* (not-place)—for encounter. Soelle reconfigures transcendence, divine and human, as vulnerability. Security, she asserts, is not transcendence, but the ascendance of destructive isolationism. Pushing the limits of traditional doctrines of an impassible God, Soelle declares that "transcendence is dangerous [precisely] because it makes us vulnerable"; it fosters the risk of openness in divine and human relations.

The theme of vulnerability before others emerges also in Spivak's understanding of deconstruction: "I think of it myself as a radical acceptance of vulnerability."[16] This "radical acceptance" confesses both "what . . . [it] cannot do" and the inevitability of loose ends. "When an end is defined, other ends are rejected, and one might not know what those ends are."[17] The confession of unknowable and therefore loose ends speaks again to vulnerable openness—an openness that challenges closed or seemingly secure systems. Thus, planetarity functions for Spivak as a catachrestic figure for the critique of those ends too conveniently or benevolently tied up by derivative alterity. The transcendent other calls to vulnerable responsibility—"without," as Spivak declares, "guarantees."[18]

Thoughts of a planetary cosmopolis relate the question of "what kind of transcendence the wholly/holy other bears" to the query "which God?" If the radical alterity voiced in the name "God" transcends in and through mutual relations and if this transcendence disrupts the benevolent and secure, then the words, practices, and strategies formed to express this *theos* necessarily involve vulnerable ventures. Human word-works imply the divine and that "which" is worshipped displaces in and through these very word-works. In other words, the human and divine mutually and vulnerably implicate one another. This vulnerability opens to a dangerous relationality. It dares and bears both vulnerable (and therefore open) critique and critical (and therefore questioning) vulnerability. In the absence of vulnerability or critique, a planetary cosmopolis and its *theos* revert to the merely global.

Neither catachrestic nor catechistic, god-talk arises in Mignolo's article, "The Many Faces of Cosmo-polis: Border Thinking and Critical Cosmopolitanism," only through discussion of Christianity as a primary example of global management. The "which" and "what" questions of a transcendent other do not concern Mignolo's text. Rather, the other embodies the "*exteriority* . . . the outside that is needed by the inside" of social and global structures based on here be/there be power differentials—specifically the colonial other.[19] Situating his "critical cosmopolitanism" as a disruptive challenge to "modern/colonial" imaginaries emergent from the sixteenth century and continuing into this century, Mignolo seeks "options beyond both benevolent recognition . . . and humanitarian pleas for inclusion."[20] Planetary conviviality represents one of these options.

Conviviality hinges on, though Mignolo refrains from employing the word, vulnerability as openness toward multiple others. It entails a "yielding generously . . . toward diversity as a *universal* and cosmopolitan project in which everyone participates."[21] The critical and vulnerable—or yielding—couple once again. And the same shudders, hopefully, before alterity. For

Mignolo, alterity (or exteriority) speaks both to diversity as a particularly open universal and to rights as informed not by global designs but by "border thinking."[22] In the strategic utopianism offered here, the wholly/ holy other—in all its displacing diversity—inspires border thoughts and deeds of a planetary cosmopolis of God: a collective of profound relationality, divine, human, and earthy, emergent from critical and vulnerable engagement with the powers and truth regimes that be.

The expansive religiosociopolitical vocabularies and structures punctuating U.S. domestic and international politics tend to confess a profoundly bellicose god—the god of absolute and necessarily enforced borders, scarce resources, and unilateral military action. This God promises yet withholds gifts—of citizenship, social welfare, and foreign aid—as weapons of mass control. *God almighty, hear our fear.* This God punishes—anticipating and aborting "sins" before their birth, perhaps even before their conception. A political double predestination emerges: the damned are damned before the damnable act, bombed and blown to (and out of the) kingdom come. Preventive military strikes from on high secure the globe below for peace and prosperity. *God almighty, hear our fear.* Billion-dollar "Great Walls" and self-anointed militia protect the borders of this God's kingdom from heretics (or immigrants) intent on crossing those First and Third, here be/there be differentials, while trespasses of any kind require atoning sacrifices before the altar of security.[23] *God almighty, hear our fear.*

Liturgies of unilateral, omnipotent power and litanies of crimes against divinity or against human kingdoms cloaked in the divine seemingly reinforce one another. The "which God?" worshipped implicates the "how" and "why" of human social and political constructs. These constructs likewise implicate God. As evident in certain U.S. policies and professions of faith, divine-human relations born of a fear-filled spirit imprison God within too-secured structures of impassible transcendence. With the "what" of divine transcendence locked up in heaven and locked out of vulnerable relation with all of creation, the globe and its reigning hegemonies take on the mantle of godly omnipotence. Thy kingdom come, thy will be done around the globe as it is in heaven?

Informed by transdisciplinary analyses of the phenomenon of civil religion and by the tragic history of the frequent alliance of church and empire/ state, a strategic utopianism offers no metanarrative solution to recalcitrant myths of U.S. manifest (double pre-) destiny or the divine right of political leaders to execute the will of gods worshipped and adored. Rather, it offers a (re)vision of divine transcendence and the politics it inspires. The planetary cosmopolis of God imagines and enacts just relations in the very soil and elements of interdependent earth-dwelling. For the wholly/holy other transcends in-the-midst and soils of terra relations. Trans*terra*torial practices of the cosmopolis, then, dare to: displace unexamined certainties; transgress those divides that both relegate the divine to heavenly residence and facilitate here be/there be global designs; reside in compromised borders; and embrace sustained conversations over contested terrains of thought, experience, and land.

ATONING ECONOMIES OR RECONCILING ACCOUNTS

For Spivak, an embrace—what she calls the "deconstructive embrace"—represents neither a glib gesture nor a globe-grabbing design. Rather, the embrace of deconstruction is the effort-filled " 'setting to work' " toward the convivial, toward life "lived as the call of the wholly other, which must necessarily be answered."[24] This call and response speak to the aporetic character of encounter with the other experienced as the impossible—indeed, as justice and ethics. Encounters with the just and ethical demand neither purity nor piety, but rather invite the risk of critical and vulnerable response before radical alterity. Responsive and "responsible action" in the wake of this impossible experience involves the work of "calculus"—manifest but not limited to laws and politics.[25] This calculus, more than mere mathematics, includes the task of decision making by means of a critical (and therefore vulnerable) reading, for "reading," as Spivak articulates, "is translation."[26] And if, as she further contends, "[B]ecoming-human is an incessant economy of translation," then informed decision making and expansive readings of the contexts of the human condition necessitate "transnational literacy."[27]

As "an interruptive praxis,"[28] Spivak's transnational literacy entails "learning to ask" questions "of the names of nation-states that assemble and disassemble a *universal* meta-message that is the incessantly written but never readable synonym for the 'globe' standing in for the 'universe.' "[29] We meet once more, as in Mignolo's discussion of diversity, those persistent universals of cosmo-political import. The "universal" multiply assembled by nation-states and targeted by transnational literacy serves as primary currency within the global economy criticized by Spivak. The exchange rate in the meta-message economy rises and falls upon a substitution with cosmic consequences: "[T]he 'globe' stand[s] in for the 'universe.'" Globalization— that "synonym" for exchanges of the same—replaces with a singular universal the universe and all its planetary alterity. The system of substitution described by Spivak functions, literally and figuratively, in an economy driven by an inflated currency of the universal. In the language of globalization, the inevitable flow of capital, consumerism, and—even—democracy, bears the name this universal currently dons. If the vast economies of the globe are to reconcile with the universal assembled by ruling nation-states and their policies, they are forced to sacrifice their diverse currencies, pecuniary and cultural, to the one. This sacrifice represents a secular practice of at-one-ment with the universal. The globe overwrites the planet.

Former President George W. Bush's declaration of a *"global* war on terror" delivered a planet-overwriting call for the forces of "democracy," dressed in military garb, "to fight the enemy *wherever* it makes its stand." The invasion and consequent "liberation" of Iraq, as a first stand, fostered "democracy in the heart of the Middle East"—according to the meta-message of Bush's foreign policy. These benevolent acts not only spread "the hope of liberty" in the region, but also will "help free societies to take root—and when they do, freedom will yield the peace that *we* all desire."[30] The "we" of a multiply assembled, U.S.-led coalition performed a "heart" transplant or substitution of a different, global kind. Peace on earth, good will to all who reconcile with the same, and—as Bush frequently signed off, "God bless America!" Whether or not the "which God?" blesses, we dare not rest at ease until all is well and at-one with the globe.

Translated into a religious vernacular, both the "standing in" substitution questioned by Spivak and the war-secured peace pursued by Bush eerily echo certain doctrinal articulations of atonement theory. An omnipotent power, proclaimed by a frequently redacted good news, relays a global(izing) vision. The good news—or meta-message—of this vision articulates a particular universal to those with ears to hear. This universal divides the globe into believers and nonbelievers, into priests, prophets, citizens, and benevolent rulers, on the right hand, and skeptics, heretics, aliens, and archnemeses, on the other. And yet all fall short of the glory of the universal, of the one. The sanctity and security of this global vision thus demands a sacrifice to reconcile fallen and debt-laden particularities with the universal. The demanding vision, once appeased by its chosen sacrifice, substitutes a universe of possible human-divine relations with a single way, a sole path both to reconciliation with the omnipotent and to residence in the kingdom of God.

The preceding paragraph highlights elements of the substitution theory of atonement that potentially rehearse what Mignolo refers to as "designs to manage" rather than nurture the diverse possibilities of planetary conviviality. Mignolo identifies the sixteenth century, with its Christian missions and "Atlantic commercial circuit," as governed by the social imaginary of "orbis universalis christianus."[31] This single orb cast as the universe and universal, similar to Spivak's figure of the globe, marks for Mignolo the nascence of a recalcitrant colonial/modern imaginary that continues to affect contemporary social constructions and movements of globalization.[32] The orb overwrites and stands in for the planet; the modern eclipses yet depends on the colonial other; globalization substitutes an abstract universality for a convivial diversity. Critical cosmopolitanism steps out of and examines from the exterior the interior that orbis christianus and other meta-message generators seek to establish as the dominant picture of reality.[33]

Neither Mignolo nor Spivak articulate anything resembling atonement, thus a reading of substitution into their texts represents a liberal translation. And yet references to orbs and globes that attempt to stand in place of or interiorize all exteriority suggest economies of an atoning substitution at the core of globalizing projects. A theological critique of globalization so construed grapples at once with the "which God?" question, the "what" of transcendence—be it a relation of unilateral power or vulnerable mutuality—and the "how" and "why" of social constructions that implicate that "which" is worshipped. As illustrated by the brief allusions to Bush's foreign policy, political imaginaries driven by a manifest double predestiny attempt not only to divinely sanctify division of the globe into good and evil, heretic and saint, but also to save the globe from the enemies of democracy and for a peace desired by the benevolent "we." The boundary between the religious and the political blurs in imaginaries replete with resonant vocabularies: the debts or "sins" of others, defined—perhaps forgiven—by another set of others, are reconciled by a single vision, whether labeled Christianizing, civilizing, or globalizing. Accounts are settled (except for the damned, of course) through a global vision of salvation incarnate in one particular geo-spot of the globe. The globe giveth and the globe taketh away. The kingdom comes, but only for those whose debts have been reconciled.

And so political theology informed by planetarity and cosmopolitanism must inquire into the nature of this globe and of the omnipotent powers that create it. Under and in what omnipotent names are Two-Thirds World debts generated, defined, (un)forgiven? What promise or problems lie dormant when theological and political economies of reconciliation and "forgiveness" employ similar images and vernaculars? How are the ways, means, and methods of various earth-kingdoms projected on the kingdom of God? These queries reflect the type of "learning to ask" hermeneutic this essay draws from Spivak's transnational literacy and Mignolo's critical cosmopolitanism. As vulnerable critique displaces, so too the trans*terr*atorial pushes beyond the homogenizing economies of globes and orbs toward the abundant and diverse provisions of the universe.

WHEN BEGINNING: ZERO BALANCES AND JOINT VENTURES

A planetary life lived together marks an inescapable aspect of the human condition. Spivak states, "To be human is to be intended toward the other."[34] Efforts to envision this other-intended life as provision-bearing rather than economy-bound necessitate shifts in perspective. Imaginaries of the economic tend to focus on beginning and ending balances and on meticulous calculations to reconcile accounts. Zero-sum tabulations not only designate winners and losers in the competition for global market shares, but also whose debts will and will not be forgiven (on earth as in heaven?). The zero or nil appears as origin, goal, and mediator of a global accounting unaffected by encounter with radical alterity, by experience of justice and ethics. This impassible calculus stands in direct contrast to the "calculus" Spivak names as bearing the trace of the impossible. The "which God?" of an unaffected economy deals not in vulnerable relations but in indifferent calculation. In other words, a globe and its universal, created out of the nil by an omnipotent and sovereign power, substitutes and stands in for the multiplicity of the universe. A twisted *creatio ex et a nihilo* frequently underpins economic imaginaries and cosmologies. The nil, the zero, when conceived as origin and telos, constructs a universal that serves as the one, the static truth about which a no-thing-generated globe orbits. The nil begets but the one; it supports but a system of binary constructions blind to multiple expressions of life, love, and community. The one that is the nil dominates; no diversity and no vision of mutual relationship populate this cosmic system.

Thoughts and images of the provision-bearing, to the contrary, arise from what theologian Catherine Keller calls *"creatio ex profundis."* The *profundis*, the depths and provisions of a vast cosmos, reveal not an origin of the nil, a creator of solitary and sovereign power, or a telos of universal singularity.[35] Rather, when "beginning: a plurisingularity of universe, earth echoing chaos, dark deep vibrating with spirit, creates."[36] Creation spills forth not as a once-in-a-universal event but in and through relations with a universe of others. The "which God?", the plurisingularity, of the provision-bearing names a radical alterity relationally engaged in *"creatio cooperationis,"* a creative, joint venture of "open interactivity."[37] Plurisingularity, earth, chaos, deep, spirit, together breathe forth and give witness to the pleroma of cosmic dwelling. This pleroma abounds in the provisional—in provisions offering the potential of sustenance, and not absolute surety. The universe, in all its multiplicity and diversity, provides not certainty, not perfectly balanced accounts, but an unfathomable complexity in which chance, risk, wonder, love, sorrow, and the impossible bid at every loose end, every questioned absolute, every traversed border.

The trans*terra*torial, therefore, challenges economies of the nil and the same, calling to open-ends and collective (ad)ventures in the creation of planetary conviviality. Attempts to establish definitive origins and teloi delimit expressions of creative relation within globe-managing models of economic calculation and transcendent autonomy. For it is amid the swirling depths, the *profundis* of vulnerable relation and impossible encounters that thoughts of the planetary cosmopolis of God emerge—born of "earth echoing chaos," grounded in the displaced and displacing *ou topos* of a strategic utopianism.

Chaotic depths and an underived, poststructuralist planetarity represent, admittedly, unlikely images to inspire utopian visions. Nevertheless, Spivak describes planetarity as a "utopian idea . . . for thinking ground," for envisioning our habitation of earth and cosmos as *"unheimlich* or uncanny."[38] And while Keller disavows "final utopias or transcendent escapes," she describes chaos as "a matrix of possibilities," of beginnings and co-creative endeavors.[39] Immersed in the uncanny and a fecund matrix, a strategic utopianism progresses not to a beatific ideal, but dives into the indeterminate, into the lived chaos of existence—not in resignation, but in thoughtful resistance. It recognizes the peril and promise of the (im)possible and of mutual interdependence. It performs what Derrida refers to as *"[t]eleiopoesis,"* a poetic practice "qualif[ying] . . . that which *renders* absolute, perfect, completed . . . which *brings* to an end." The teleiopoetic, for Derrida, "speaks to distance and the far-removed."[40] An imaginary not simply of the now, but also of the (im)possible not yet; the teleiopoesis of a planetary cosmopolis "begins at the end, it is initiated with the signature of the other."[41] It prepares for and anticipates, however imperfectly, an encounter with the wholly/holy other, an experience of the impossible that is just relations. Open, loose, and planetary ends inspire alternative imaginaries to closed, benevolent, and globe-compressing certainties.

The cosmopolis of God, then, proclaims no lost paradise to regain, but rather proposes a cosmos to reinhabit—strategically. Reinhabitation consists of diligent awareness of a fall not from grace but into planetary conviviality, into mutual interdependence immersed in structures both of oppression and liberation. The strategy entails both the trans*terra*torial and teleiopoetic: it dwells in the *ou topos* of fecund matrices of possibility; it prepares in the now and not-yet of earthy relations for the call of the wholly/holy other to collective responsibility; and it challenges beliefs and policies that attempt to constrain the magnificently poignant diversity of the universe within a particular sphere of influence or in static calculations.

Universal Particulars: A Dangerous and Endangered Political Ecotheology
The universe and all its particularities pervade, as evident in this essay, discussion of the planetary and cosmopolitan. The call to a "universe-all" entanglement with the particular and the diverse proves integral to a postcolonial reading of the increasingly endangered habitat of any bounded certainty, be it the kingdom of God, the nation-state, or theories of cosmopolitanism. The following sections, therefore, focus on the dangerous and endangered elements of this entanglement.

"THE DANGEROUS"
The danger intrinsic to universals is that they tend to claim the intrinsic, innate, absolute, and fundamental. Spivak's planetarity and Mignolo's critical cosmopolitanism speak of the universe and universals not as bounded, unquestioned absolutes but as expressions of the strategic and teleiopoetic. Spivak, drawing on the work of Luce Irigaray, declares that "[a]n ethical position must entail universalization of the singular," the particular. Necessary though it be, this universalization manifests the provisional, "keep[ing] the 'real universal' on the other side of différance."[42] The work of universalization, therefore, calls to the (im)possible, to a radical alterity underived from but enlivening particulars. In a political theology of a planetary cosmopolis, this work discovers provisions amid the provisional; it dares critical and vulnerable relation with God and humans in the chaos and ground of

the Earth and all its particular elements. Thus, it is the particular or, from Mignolo's perspective, the diverse elements of the cosmos that inform the strategies and teleiopoesis of the universal.

Mignolo's critical cosmopolitanism recasts the enterprise of universality as "diversality"; that is, "diversity as a universal and cosmopolitan project in which everyone participates."[43] Diversality blurs—in a transterratorial fashion—the boundaries between the universal and particular, yet emphasizes each element. Mignolo's exploration of those particular elements integral to planetary conviviality refers to a cosmopolitan tradition both rich and rife with concepts of the universal.

Stoic conceptions of the *kosmou polites*, citizen of the world/universe, reveal ancient struggles with the relation of the particular or local to the universal. Several themes emerge in their writings: reason (or *logos*) as an internal, defining, and therefore universal aspect of human being; the equality of all humans—based on the faculty of reason; and the contingent and random character of both local/state loyalties and external attachments.[44] Stoic philosophy challenges the sovereignty of any citizenship or rights bequeathing entity to define absolutely who is "in" and "out" of the polis. Thus, the *cosmo*politan opts for the universals of the cosmos as uncanny grounds for irreducible rights and collective responsibility. Yet the *kosmou polites* refrains from abandoning the questioned and qualified local. Rather, the cosmopolitan situates the local within "a series of concentric circles"— the all encompassing circle, human being.[45] Humans, in their particular and glorious capacity to reason inspire the universal. It is for love of the human universe, complicated but not dominated by the particular, that Stoics profess cosmopolitanism.[46]

Kant's essay "To Perpetual Peace: A Philosophic Sketch," with its call for "a *nation of peoples* (*civitas gentium*) that . . . will finally include all the people of the earth," stands as the next major Western marker in the journey of the *kosmou polites* here considered.[47] Martha Nussbaum notes the influence of Stoic thought—particularly as adapted from Cicero's *De Officiis*—on Kant's cosmopolitanism. In Stoic and Kantian logic the universal faculty of reason binds humans to each other and, as an expression of the pattern of nature, to "natural" laws. Laws and rights, evident to the enlightened mind that dares to know, thereby join all humanity to a "virtual polity, a cosmopolis that has an implicit structure of claims and obligations"—including the right to "universal *hospitality*."[48] Securing "the highest attainable development of mankind's capacities" represents for Kant the primary obligation and originating impulse of a "*universal* civil society."[49]

A thinker within the Kantian tradition, contemporary political theorist David Held envisions not a universal civil society, but transnational social democracies. In order for the "social," or the collective, of social democracies to thrive amid spheres of competition for local, national, and transnational loyalties, Held maintains that principles of cosmopolitanism provide needed ethical bounds. These principles, resonant with aspects of Stoic thought, include the equality of all humanity; "personal responsibility and accountability"; and active discourse and cooperation across a multitude of bounded territories—be they social imaginaries, communities, nation-states, or NGOs.[50] The multiple "territories" mapping the twenty-first century's encounter with globalization, as configured by Held, dispense with the neat concentric circles of Stoicism. Rather, the cartography of this century is one of "overlapping communities of fate" and of "collective fortunes."[51] The local, collective, and communal, therefore, compromise the distinction between particular and universal. While Kantian notions of universal human rights ground Held's cosmopolitanism, particulars—be they local or international collectives—create social democracy through deliberative discourse and participation.

The transterratorial, following Held's lead, conjugates the communal—the random fate-generated, the rational concept-developed, and the affective life-shaping allegiances—as bearer of the question and of the critique of political theology. In and through these various commitments and loves develops the potential to deconstruct omnipotent powers and absolute universals that demand both unquestioned loyalty and the sacrifice of the particular and diverse. Although the transterratorial embraces Kantian conceptions of the universal light of human reason and rights, it does so in a deconstructive mode that recognizes the dangerous shadings of universals posited solely from the Western perspective.[52] Bhabha's "vernacular cosmopolitanism," similar to Mignolo's critical cosmopolitanism, explores those imaginaries and lives exterior to Stoic and Enlightenment configurations of universals.

Bhabha proposes an ethical praxis of the "right to difference in equality."[53] This particular right neither establishes "an original [or essentialist] cultural or group identity" nor invokes a universality that places the plurality or particularity of human existence under erasure.[54] Instead, it articulates a "minoritarian perspective" which challenges political imaginaries of uniform, unitary citizenship and belonging. No universal civil society, no metropolitan city upon a hill, draws humanity into a glorious, rational, or ordered kingdom to come. And yet vernacular cosmopolitanism expresses "a political process that works *towards* the shared goals of democratic rule, rather than simply acknowledging already constituted 'marginal' political entities or identities."[55] And so, a "minoritarian perspective," those particular experiences of individuals and their communities, informs and transforms "the shared goals" of democracy. The Derridean concept of a "democracy to come" might function for Bhabha as a strategic universal never fully realized on this side but ever-beckoning on the other side of *différance*.[56] For Bhabha, too, locates the transformation of dominant imaginaries within the "act of *poesis*." This poetic space emerges as both the "right to narrate" and the "spirit of resistance."[57] Versed in democratic notions of equality before and beyond economies of the same, the vernacular voices the realities of globalization—realities questioned and potentially transcribed by the trans*terra*torial.

Each theory of cosmopolitanism presented here constructs a political paradigm and imaginary defined by universal and/or particular claims to human rights. It is the human as human, wildly and diversely human, but human nonetheless who emerges as locus of a plurality of spheres of influence and overlapping collectives. In a post-Holocaust era, cosmopolitan projects rightly seek to navigate the universality of human being and experience as expressed in particularity—with neither dominating the other. For as Hannah Arendt declares in her correspondence with Karl Jaspers, through the crimes of World War II "an organized attempt was made to eradicate the concept of the human being."[58] The concept and bodies of the human and of human relations in a universe of diversity remain susceptible to eradication. Kant's desired universal cosmopolis of hospitality frequently is greeted not by open arms but armed borders. The human, then, appears to occupy a habitat as endangered as any.

"THE ENDANGERED"

Endangered habitat, employed as strategic metaphor—literally a carrying-over and across—endeavors to transgress the "unilinear and indivisible" borders sociopolitical and religiopolitical discourses readily erect between human and other than human creation.[59] This metaphor includes Derrida's notion of "limitrophy," which "complicates" the "abyssal rupture" delimiting the human and other than human. Derrida's *"trophe"* posits not an "opposing side," or a here be/there be boundary, but rather introduces thoughts of "an irreducible living multiplicity."[60] Envisioned in plurality and not opposition, limitrophy deconstructs philosophical traditions and theological discourses centered on notions of human "superiority over and subjugation of the animal."[61] An endangering metaphor similarly displaces, throws into crisis, "the human" as agent of domination and seeks to attend to an emerging solidarity among all creatures. By dis/locating the "human" as endangered habitat, the trans*terra*torial views the "human" and all terra bodies as living convivially and equally—without guarantees. Stated differently, to place autonomous agency within a zone of potential extinction fractures hierarchic models by recognition of the contingent nature of our mutual dwelling in compromised environments. Of course, humans, or more accurately human policies and activities of rampant industrialization, have endangered the habitat called earth. The deconstructive method of this essay impurely exploits this literal destruction in an effort to uncover the (im)possibility of a collective, ecological dwelling.

This exploitation calls for transposing Spivak's "becoming-human" as "incessant economy of translation," in a different slipperier key—one that might unlock liberating strains within the kingdom talk of Christian theology.[62] In this key becoming exceeds both the human sphere and the rules/ *nomos* of economic exchange. It attempts to abide in a space of ecology and ecopraxy liberated from a debt/salvation model and for revisioned relationship. A grateful supplement, both the trans*terra*torial and strategic utopianism arise from a *becoming-creaturely* that embodies ecstatic commitment to a theo-ecology of sociopolitical interdependence. As will be explored in the following sections, a planetary and cosmopolitan translation of the kingdom entails a critique of the practices of domination that endanger the *cosmos*, its vulnerable habitats, and its interdependent and ever-becoming creatures.

Political theology, thus, strives not to categorize, "not to represent," the other but, as Spivak encourages, "to learn to represent" itself to the other.[63] Representations necessarily call upon generalizations—or universal commonalities—that endanger the integrity of the particular. Yet, as Spivak famously writes, "[S]ince it is not possible not to be an essentialist, one can self-consciously use this irreducible moment of essentialism as part of one's strategy."[64] The irreducible moment, the particular in the midst of a universe of possibilities compromised—filled with both promise and peril—that is the space and place of *Pax Terra*.

On the way to and in the midst of *Pax Terra* we stumble across various (mis)interpretations of the kingdom of God. Thus the poetics and pragmatics of the planetary cosmopolis of God attempt to reimagine Christian community shorn, however imperfectly, of imperial vestments. A "really 'loving' political practice," this attempt necessarily "fall[s] . . . prey to its own critique."[65] It is a theopolitical practice absent absolutes and guarantees, but which listens to and learns from the wholly/holy other—for the love of God, planet, and "universe-all" entanglements. This love-praxis commences, then, not with beatific pontifications on the kingdom but with a trudge through some of the theopolitical thickets surrounding it.

"THY KINGDOM COME"?

Monarchial monadism, divine right of kings, kyriarchy, and manifest destiny—these phrases speak to oppressive theological themes and sociopolitical structures embedded in and derived from biblical testimony to the kingdom/ *basileia* of God. Alternatives to the hierarchy and empire-laden images of the kingdom abound. The feminist biblical scholar Elisabeth Schüssler Fiorenza finds within the political and scriptural term *ekklesia* a vast reservoir for thinking and enacting "radical equality, justice, and well-being for all wo/ men in the *cosmopolis*."[66] The theologian John B. Cobb Jr. offers "commonwealth" as a translation of *basileia* ("empire," in the Greek) that "besides not emphasizing the controlling power of a ruler, suggests that the realm may be organized for the common good."[67] And yet, images of a ruling kingdom continue to dominate contemporary theological, social, and political imaginaries. John Milbank, a theologian within the radical orthodoxy movement, calls for a "mixed government" model with a monarchy and aristocracy "balanced" democracy to administer "the universal human cosmopolis." The "monarchic" and "aristocratic" admit hierarchic elements into governance structures that, by appeal to the reign of justice and the rule of charity, check potential tyrannies or whims of the few or the many by truths reasoned and revealed. This political hybrid draws validity from the divine monarchy revealed in Christ the king and the new "charity" paradigm incarnated in God's gift of Godself.[68] In gestures less charitable, whether conceived as the globe-wrenching, heaven-sent conflict of the *Left Behind* series or alluded to in former President George W. Bush's division of the globe into axes of evil and good, the prayer "thy kingdom come" sounds a rallying cry to defend whatever hegemonic impulse happens to be invoking the image.[69]

Review of either the accidental allegiance or tragic complicity of Christianity with empire exceeds the bounds of this essay. As Spivak attests, "the history" of "the so-called great religions . . . is too deeply imbricated in the narrative of the ebb and flow of power."[70] Quests for a heavenly kingdom on earth governed by the divine rights of lordship—a sovereignty robed in the residue of Aristotle's unmoved mover and Aquinas's image of God as pure actuality—too readily devolve into the imperial or tyrannical. Thus, dangerous visions of a heavenly omnipotence indifferent to earthly loves lurk in certain theological discourses of the kingdom. If the omnipotent king, in absolute freedom, opts not to give, then no liberating or preferential option exists for anyone. The divine king gives at the king's pleasure, dispassionately dispensing good(s) and receiving tribute/worship; while all-too-human subjects fearfully negotiate theological, social, and political values—keenly aware of the possibility of a charity, a (debt-forgiving) grace withheld. The risk of this theopolitics resides not in mutual relation but in an omnipotence unaffected by relation. The globe of divine rights overwrites a planetary conviviality that seeks to enact Bhabha's call to "the right to difference in equality." Yet when released from a too-charitable transcendence or from defensive calculations, kingdom images might just rupture the link between God and almighty authority on earth and in heaven.

This essay commenced with the prayers both of Spivak's planetarity and the *basileia* of Christian discourse. Petitions for a kingdom and "politics of friendship" to come voice both a call and response to the wholly/holy other. A strategic utopianism discovers within the underived alterity of planetarity and the "learning to ask" of transnational literacy displaced and displacing sites for inquiring into the "which God?" worshipped, the "what" of transcendence, and the "how" and "why" of political structures. Amid a fecund matrix and the elemental soils of an uncanny yet provisional ground this particular strategy seeks to create, *ex profundis*, visions of resistance to economies and exchanges of the same. The questions and visions of this political theology critically engage not only U.S. manifest destinies or the management designs of globalization but also the texts and doctrines of the Christian tradition. Thus, in the images and content of the Nazarene's basileic pronouncements, the trans*terra*torial affirms, with John B. Cobb Jr., a "contra-imperial" message—however rarely it sounds in the halls of the imperium.[71] Yet affirmation of contra-imperial gestures in the word-works of Jesus—as relayed in the biblical text—are not the end, but the beginning of the story. Thanks be to the defiant One who announces love of God and neighbor as the infinite end of eternal life (Mt 19:16–19; 22:37–40; Mk 12:28–34). For a context to be living it must be loving. And as indicated earlier, a truly loving (and therefore living) theopolitical hermeneutic necessarily "fall[s] prey to its own critique." It exposes itself, its texts, traditions, and claims to critical and vulnerable interpretations.

The contra-imperial, parabolic tales of the Nazarene defy those monad-ruled kingdoms mobilized for Christian imperial mission and for religion-infused political rhetoric, be they of the sixteenth century or the twenty-first.[72] For no single narrative defines the kingdom. The "smallest of all seeds" when planted in the generative soil of (a paranational) Earth grows into "the greatest of shrubs . . . a tree" so enormous its branches provide safe haven for "birds of the air" (Mt 13:31–32). Day laborers, whether working one or eight hours in the vineyard, receive equal wages—the last hired merits as much as the first (Mt 20:1–16). A missing sheep and coin compel extensive search and recovery efforts, concluding with the celebrated return of the one lost (Lk 15:3–10). Bucolic excess, divine generosity, tenacious quests for the particular among the many, and unfettered rejoicing appear to reign in the kingdom.

But what themes emerge from other images of the *basileia*—especially the "separating out" or postexpulsion scenes of weeping, wailing, and gnashing of teeth? Might these jarring portrayals illustrate the potentially fractured and faction-creating citizenship and belonging requirements of the kingdom?[73] Might they inspire inquiry into the rights afforded or not in discourses of the kingdom? The seemingly indissoluble link between the basileia and the imperium and the mixed message of its parables demonstrate the "profound ambivalence" of the kingdom with regard to what rights, irreducible or other, anyone enjoys in this political vision.[74] Is the kingdom an (im)possible site of collective responsibility and interdependent relation or an exclusive realm of the chosen few? An uncertain fate awaits dwellers in the kingdom as depicted in the marriage banquet: a guest plucked from the street is just as suddenly tossed back out (Mt 22:1–14). You're out; you're in; you're out; you're. . . . The day laborers, too, experience a sense of tenuous and ruptured rights as the vineyard owner declares, "So the last will be first, and the first last" (Mt 20:16).

No one parable expresses the magnanimity of transformed social status (the last shall be first) or the anonymity of exile to outer isolation. The kingdom is not absolutely single—nor singularly utopian—it reveals, perhaps, the no-place (*ou topos*) of every place of displaced belonging. It opens those innumerable sites from which particular voices must join to express what place, however *ou topos*, the irreducible right to difference, diversity, and particularity in equality occupies within social imaginaries and political structures. The profoundly contradictory character of this kingdom, with its chosen and denied, its globe-shattering calls to justice and collective-dissolving claims to segregation splits open a space for a transterratorial articulation of the rights and responsibilities practiced in the planetary cosmopolis of God.

Cosmopolitanism, in its Kantian, critical, or vernacular form, envisions a plane of universal human existence attuned to particular rights. Articulated through Mignolo's "border thinking" or Bhabha's "difference in equality," these rights seek the convivial and imagine different configurations of political community. For Kant, not only the cosmopolitan civil society but also a Christianity *"worthy of love"* fosters an ethics—rational and theological—in which "freedom in choosing ultimate ends" is tempered by "the free integration of the will of another into one's maxims."[75] Translated in the language of the transterratorial, love freely invites the wholly/holy other to displace individual ends and collective rights. Without guarantees, then, the divine cosmopolis calls to and for irreducible rights: of love—critical and vulnerable; of teleiopoesis—to be imagined by the other in and for the other *and* to imagine poetic practices of life lived convivially; of the displaced and displacing—to transgress those boundaries that would constrain the planet within mapped, here be/there be hierarchies.

These rights, nurtured in the soils of the uncanny, offer a planetary twist to the strategic utopianism drawn from critical and vernacular cosmopolitanisms. They emerge from a critically vulnerable love for the particular and universal. The relation neither hierarchic nor relativistic, particulars and universals join together in refrains—both chaotic and harmonic—to create a cosmos, a universe of verse . . . of turns and the upturned, literally "ploughed" earth (form the Latin, *vertere/versus*).[76] And so, perhaps, in the poetry of verse and in the fecund matrix of irreducible rights we discern the never seamless, ever unseemly ground of theopolitical practices of love. The universe is composed of its particulars, and particulars upturn and transform universals. The human and nonhuman, the local and global, the national and transnational necessarily inform one another. The earth gives of its elements to nourish all creatures, and all creatures return to enrich the elements. It is in the soil of this cosmos, an ecology of encounter—not an economy of accounts—in which the seeds of the kingdom dwell. Where particulars and universals twist, turn, question, and nurture one another.

And so we return to a kingdom complicated, where the last shall indeed be first unless, of course, you're thrown out of line or booted from the table altogether. Expulsion or exile threatens in the seedier side of this kingdom and its political parties. And that is precisely the trans*terra*torial point. No manifest (double pre-) destiny of the damned or saved, the indebted or debt-free, determines citizenship or rights in the kingdom. Strategic utopianism discovers in the last-shall-be-first displacements a gloriously com/promised proposition: this image of the *basileia* depicts not a social reversal but a radical rehearsal of equality affirmed and practiced. The last shall be first. The "here" shall be "there." The First and Third worlds shall be debt-free or indebted together—their communities of fate inextricably intertwined and interdependent with all of creation. These are the claims of a planetary cosmopolis to come, now and not quite yet.

Undaunted and yet haunted by contradictions in the *basileia* with its universal vision upturned by the particulars of lives lived—human and non-human, the trans*terra*torial dives into ambiguity and ambivalence. It questions and uproots assumptions: What if the mixed messages of parables of the *basileia* so dislocate the kingdom from an absolute telos as to render absurd any idolatrous imaginaries of absolute sovereignty (divine or other) unconcerned with the *demos* and *humus* of the cosmos? Might the "tensive symbol" of the kingdom rend notions of sovereignty and citizenry based on economic models, and thus translate *basileia* or even the *polis* of cosmopolitanism as *oikos*/dwelling—in which all of creation both dwells in God and is indwelt by God (Eph 2:19–22)?[77] "The kingdom of God is in the midst of you" (Lk 17:21). But it is not you, not me, not democracy, not any named omnipotent that demands loyalty and banishes love—a love that questions and in questioning loves more resolutely. The basileia, in all its ambivalence, portrays a dwelling, mutual, mutable, and multiple. It is an ecopraxy of collective responsibility, not an economos of debt-generating and forgiving meta-messages.

The kingdom of God, therefore, is like a cosmopolis, where the universe and all its universals provide the space, the soil and ground for the various turns and particular expressions of existence lived and loved together, voiced in a cacophony of vernaculars. The kingdom of God is like a *Pax Terra*, a world of theopolitical practices that seek not an idealized piece of an increasingly compressed globe, but peace on Earth—however tenuous, however perpetually compromised.[78] It is lived—convivially, but not exhausted or exhaustible. It is a hope translated by reality—the reality of upturned universals and of particulars rooted in provisional universals (transitory yet abounding both in sustaining provisions and [re]visioned possibilities).

Pax Terra roots in the very soil and elements of our political, social, ecological, and theological interdependence. It receives seed (mustard and other), water (baptismal and oceanic), fire (of spirit and the nucleic), earth (embodied as human and humus), and air—those irrepressible gusts of liberation. It gathers and is gathered by particular elements of the "universe-all" entanglements creation shares in and with God. And last, but certainly not least, *Pax Terra* loves. It professes love for both the particular grounds in which one finds nurture and for "universe-all" rights to sustainable and just community. These are rights of way, rights to question, rights of abundant dwelling, rights to root and uproot, to become as welcoming as an arbor in which birds of the air might nest, as sturdy as an oak that stands against tempests of injustice, and as fecund with possibility and surprise as a seed . . . so that when the winds of liberation blow even sovereign mountains, those globe-busting omnipotents, might be moved.

✦ Crip/tography:
Of Karma and Cosmopolis

SHARON V. BETCHER

Suppose we raise the possibility of a God who belongs not to the fixed order of presence, but to the (dis)order of the deconstruction of presence . . . [and] in favor of a paradigm where . . . sovereign power slips out of favor? Suppose . . . that the event that is sheltered in the name of God does not belong to the order of power and presence, but rather withdraws from the world in order to station him or herself [Godself] with everything that the world despises? Suppose we think of God as someone who prowls the streets and disturbs the peace of . . . Christendom? Suppose we imagine God as a street person with a definite body odor, like Lord Shiva living as a beggar?
JOHN CAPUTO, *The Weakness of God*

The human being is human in answer to an "outside call."
GAYATRI CHAKRAVORTY SPIVAK, *"Righting Wrongs"*

Rockefeller Center, Christmas 1999

We, knowing we would soon be moving to the other edge of the continent, wanted her to have the enchanted memory of skating at night under the Christmas tree at Rockefeller Center. After waiting in line for two and a half hours, my daughter Sarah, along with her friend and my partner, Jeff, take to the skating rink. I make my way to a glass concourse at rink level that should allow me to build my own memory—that of watching my daughter set against the jeweled night lights of the city, dusted with the twinkle of snowflake, enfolded in this celebration of humanity turned, by the touch of frost and holiday celebration, toward the warmth of one another.

But this is Giuliani's New York after the first bombing of the World Trade Towers and at the time of the cleanup of unwanted bodies that can clutter the aesthetic appeal of the streets and therefore undermine the economic profitability of a global city; and my body easily slides off the mark of civility. There being no benches, I sit on the floor of the rink-level concourse as tight against the window as I can squeeze and there slip into the bittersweet mesmerization of trying, as a bench-warmer in this situation, to absorb the pleasure of those on the ice. A security guard breaks into my reverie: "Move or you will be charged with loitering," is the message I receive through the exchange of versions of my still Midwestern as distinct from his recent immigrant English. One recent immigrant, with his own ill fit into the straitjacket of civility (and trying to access the economic circuit through that newly created and often ironically immigrant-based "security" industry), forced to confront the fact that my body won't stay upright and mobile. "I just want to watch my twelve-year-old daughter skate," I protest. "Look at me," I say, insisting that he take in the disability, the crutches. "I can't join her on the ice. Please let me watch." "Crutches? As likely pipe bombs. How would I know? Please move. I don't want to lose my job; I can't risk it," he counters. Between the irony of his surveillance of my lack of compliance with civility and our mutual empathy, we are caught, finally working out a deal that I can stay ten minutes (only!); he will look the other way, but if I hear him whistle, it's a warning that I need to move immediately, because his supervisor will have spotted this infraction. We strike a deal, try to come to solidarity below the radar of civility, which each of us in our own way threatens.

I.

"Picture the world in motion," theologian Ray Bakke invites us: "the southern hemisphere is coming north, east is coming west, and on all six continents migrations are to the city."[1] Indeed, "globalization as urbanization seems," the postcolonial theorist Gayatri Chakravorty Spivak nonchalantly adds, "one of the least speculative strands in the thinking of globalization."[2] Given "the general drive for order, cleanliness and beauty, which Freud put at the center of the civilizing project, . . . it is only a small exaggeration [here at the dawn of the twenty-first century] to say that cities are us, and we are cities," suggests the philosopher and culture critic Mark Kingwell.[3] Spivak adds her facile agreement: Everywhere across the planet, "we can *see* cities exploding their spatial outlines and virtualizing into nexuses of telecommunication." "That is," Spivak dryly notes, "the canonical account of globalization."[4] But, warns Spivak, catching us romanticizing the glass and twinkles, the thick of the crowds, such visibility can lull us into not perceiving "the invisible power lines that make and unmake the visible." To get at the latter, she advises, "requires archaeology, genealogy."[5] In this essay, I assume her challenge toward archaeology of the invisible powerlines of "globalicities." Aspirations for planetary well-being must today be asserted by swerving such trajectories. After opening out the gestural articulations of civility, Spivak's renovation of Western anthropology will be assumed as key to theological geographies hoping to counter urban grids of fear.

Such massive, planetary urban in-migration as is now agitated in the name of globalization implies that formerly colonial territories, held apart by the buffers of ocean, are today humanly enfolded—like origami—into any of the planet's "global" or "world cities."[6] "In contemporary cities people connected by imperial histories," the postcolonial theorist Jane M. Jacobs observes, "are thrust together in assemblages barely predicted, and often guarded against, during the inaugural phases of colonialism. Often enough this is a meeting not simply augmented by imperialism but still regulated by its constructs of difference and privilege."[7] If urbanization provides humanity with its ultimate test case—namely, "to create living patterns harmonized with nature's rhythms,"[8] to create cities of refuge and solidarity amid difference (including those of religions and their degrees of resort to absolutes), to work out our hopes for "planetarity" (Spivak) and "conviviality" (Gilroy)—colonialism lingers on in the choreography of bodies within our urban geography, where "that racism which is not so much ethnic as biological" sorts bodies along the razor edge of the performance of "civility."[9] As the doubly loaded scene at Rockefeller Center suggests, the work of "civilizing"—of sorting bodies into publicly acceptable appearance coupled with the assumption of their regularity, rationality, productivity, symmetry, and independence—has not dropped off the agenda in this age of globalization. Fear—engorged with the nightmare of terror—conduces to this renovated straitjacket of urban civility. As global cities increasingly re-create themselves as "experience museums" of culture and the cultured, civility not only dispenses with bodies burdened with such difference but continues, within the space of cities, to colonize and collapse space within which such bodies might take place.[10]

And yet if both disabled persons (by reference to the index of the fit, economically productive body of earlier industrial capitalism and of the aesthetically, acceptable body of consumer capitalism) and the postcolonial find themselves surveilled "for fear of . . . ," cities also hold out the possibility, as Jacobs notes, of unraveling imperial trajectories[11]—hence, the hope of cosmopolis, of mongrel cities, of cities where diversity, plurality, and heterogeneity can prevail without fear.[12] Thus, as David Harvey's integration of "body talk" with "globalization talk" suggests, postcolonial practice must address the construction and choreography of bodies in order "to redefine in a more subtle way the terms and spaces of political struggle open to us in these extraordinary times."[13] "[B]oiled down to its simplest determinations, globalization is," Harvey explains, "about the socio-spatial relations between billions of individuals."[14] Jacobs concurs: "The geographical articulations of imperialism are not simply laid out across the landscape" but "exist in the 'opaque' intersections between representational practices, the built form and a range of other axes of power which . . . includes the uneven geography of capital investment, legal and judicial regulatory regimes as well as the various territorialisations and deterritorialisations of space which occur through protest, violence, ironic artistry, or simple dwelling in place."[15] In other words, we might begin to redress the imperial aspects of globalization by swerving one of its lines of force—namely here, civility—informing bodies, their choreography, their right to take place. For civility not only displaces bodies loaded with difference but configures urban space accordingly.

Crip/tography thus attempts to think a postcolonial theology in and for life in the global city, a theology that hopes to work under the rubric of Susan Stanford Friedman's "locational approach to feminism."[16] Theology, like many of the humanist disciplines, has yet to begin thinking "from site rather than text."[17] True to most axial religions, Christian theology has assumed the categories of time—hence, eschatology and kairos—as the realm of freedom. But, warns Jacobs: "[H]istory that speaks only of time on the deactivated 'stage' of space (space as an 'empty interval, a natural given') is imperial history." Christian theologies turning toward postcolonial conscientization will want to cultivate Jacobs's insight that "to activate space, to produce a spatial history, is fundamental to [the] project of taking history beyond imperialism."[18]

So crip/tography attempts to think crip, like "queer," not as "a positivity but as a positionality, a location or strategically marginal position from which to resist the norm."[19] Crip/tography assumes (as per Foucault) that "progressive politics does not require a vision, but an awareness of the intolerable and an historical analysis that informs political strategies."[20] It pays disciplined attention to the geography and choreography of our urban-ized bodies in hopes of producing the social and psychic ruptures that engender detachment from normativity—here, civility. Crip/tography seeks religious passion disciplined into practices that might—like the mad monks of Myanmar[21]—break through the restraints of civility. In this vein, I want to rethink the now failed or failing relationship of liberal theology with culture by assuming with Yvonne Sherwood that "the Bible is in some respects radically other to the modern project of the care and growth of the self."[22] Sherwood's conclusion evolves from her reading of the *Akedah*, the story of the binding of Isaac (Genesis 22), as but "simply the most famous of a series of tableaux."[23] Reading this as a series of tableaux, beginning with the night wrestler, left "crip" hero, Jacob, and the "limping nation" bearing his name,[24] allows also for the possibility that the cripped iconography at the heart of Christianity might interpolate us into a different location on the streets of today's mongrel cities.

Donna Haraway sounds a postcolonial echo, urging us to "set aside the Enlightenment figures of coherent and masterful subjectivity, the bearers of rights, holders of property in the self," encouraging us to think beyond humanism by thinking with "brokenness"—specifically, by recalling Jesus as a historical grotesque.[25] Interpolated through Isaiah's figuration of the suffering servant-slave, Jesus emerges as related to colonialism's "in/appro-priate/d others."[26] If Christianity might recall itself to the cripped iconography at its heart as the possibility for a spreading rhizome of bodies among whom "*eros* and *thanatos* no longer agree to be compliantly contra-dictory,"[27] how might this lead toward a practice of navigating civility otherwise? Such a resetting of Jesus into the tableaux stretching from the cripped Jacob to today's "inappropriate/d others" already displaces the mod-ernist portraiture of Jesus as "vital, pure and busy" healer set over against the "miserable wash of humanity" at the heart of colonial mission.[28] In so doing, it may also allow for the passional renegotiation of fear among those otherwise straitjacketed into globalizing culture's body politics.

After delving into "the rubric of civility" so as to consider how this psychology of liberal humanism already assumes a strategy for managing the burden of difference,[29] I turn to two projects from very different sources that might be heard as sharing my concern for renegotiating this colonially limned line of force named civility. Neither theologian abides the Freudian "Berlin Wall" segregating pain from pleasure—and hence they do not with-hold either pain or pleasure from religious passion; both askew the modern calculus of loss/gain—and thus move with passion into agentially unsafe scenes. In these ways, both challenge a civil and controlled Christianity that considers itself "the comforter, resolver, or even eliminator of suffering."[30] Graham Ward situates his theological proposal, *Cities of God*, as an express attempt to counter cultural individualism (a posture civility does assume) with an ontology of participation, an ontology that Ward insists will be good news for "the brokenness of bodies in postmodernity":[31] "'This is my body' announces, for the Christian, the scandal of both crucifixion and resurrection, both a dying-to-self-positing and an incorporation into the city of God. Here is announced a theology for the disabled, the sick, the racked, the torn, the diseased, the pained."[32] I will next take as theological midrash the contemporary novel *Broken for You* by Stephanie Kallos, which assumes as an epigraph "the fracture" (the narrative of blessing at the heart of Christian Eucharistic ritual, i.e., "He took bread, . . . brake it, and gave it to his disciples, saying, Take, eat, this is my Body, which is given for you").[33] Kallos's novelistic reimagination of the negotiation of a life economy sets out from her intuition that the breaking open of the body, even if by pain and disease, enables the passional capaciousness invoked by Sherwood.

Amid these analyses, I turn to think with and through biblical exegesis and theological analysis of how Eucharist, this *sacramentum* or "oath of loyalty" taken among cripped bodies, might have been released as anticolonial commentary or strategy about the ancient city, thus inviting our own reimagination.[34] Sacrifice, as a rite, founded the ancient city; it was understood to secure the well-being of the city.[35] How might we read ourselves into Christianity's iconic embrace of the body pivoted upon "the fracture," this mimetic retort to the ancient, imperial economy of well-being in the city? "God's new order"—ever and again imaged as contagious (like mustard seeds) and contaminating (like yeast)—"is about the reclamation of human space as the arena for economic and social justice," about challenging the valorization "of people, places and activities," challenging "the value placed upon them by the cultic leaders, their urban masters, or their Roman overlords," theologian Andrew Davey insists.[36] If "the ancient city was founded on sacrifice," then might Christian sacrament have been suggesting a mimetically resistive wisdom—given its own location and "oath taking" among imperially displaced, dislocated, and iconically cripped bodies?

II.

The age of decolonization—namely, the 1960s–'70s, when the decolonized began rushing like flood water toward their colonial metropoles—was, observes the sociologist Sharon Zukin, "a watershed in the institutionaliza-tion of urban fear."[37] Zukin connects the onset of the "institutionalization of urban fear," so much at the heart of urban politics today, to the urban in-migration of formerly colonized persons—those who, like the disabled, can loose a psychic storm surge of dread on mere visual encounter. Where the myth of development took, there followed in its wake a certain primal anxiety around "lack," hence the colonial missions to redress "degeneracy." But colonial mission had its metropolitan history—specifically, the rehabili-tating of disability. Disability—like presumed "degeneracy"—marks those who have not managed to become or to stay self-sovereign, who have failed the privatized work of managing the mutable body as bounded territory, of preserving order. "Empire" has recently been able to incorporate by capital-izing on the "ethnic" computation of difference of earlier stages of colonialism.[38] But colonialism's "'computation of normalities' and 'degrees of deviancy' from the white norm"—this standard for measuring bodies fit for civilization, based on being categorically proper—remains in effect.[39] The bodies of the urban homeless are, in this regard, comparable to those marked disabled (and indeed these categories significantly overlap each other). Social research suggests that "disorder—like crime—is caused by conditions like poverty and a lack of trust between neighbors" and that civility legislation—like that prohibiting homeless persons from parks, even prohibiting them from benches (as I discovered)—does not reduce but sim-ply displaces their numbers. However, citizens—under the auspices of securing the city—prefer enacting civic ordinances that restrict which bodies will be allowed in public space, especially in its decorous zones (the city center of fashion, the sites of tourism, and the neighborhoods of the rich).[40]

Economies of global cities—like the young nation of America following the Civil War, when prosthetics were cosmetically deployed to project a national image of virility and vitality—depend on sequestering bodies pre-sumably burdened with this "biologized" difference.[41] Given that "profit maximization, rather than the fulfillment of social needs, is the leading motive of the private land economy that produces most of the built environ-ment of capitalist cities," disabled persons find ourselves hemmed in, landlocked.[42] The analysis of disabled bodies as unproductive has been built into spatial, geographical impediments, thus "perpetuating the dominance of 'able-bodied' persons."[43] But this equally extends to aesthetics: The emer-gence of a consumer economy has been tied, explains Harlan Hahn, an urban studies and disabilities theorist, to "a vision of satisfaction that could become available to those prepared to reshape themselves." As urbanization developed, image became the medium for negotiating the interface with strangers (hence, the role of advertising as persons attempted to fit themselves into a community of strangers). "In cities that were supposed to be havens of heterogeneity," Hahn concludes, with a bite of irony, "influences promoting conformity may have imposed an even more severe burden on visibly disabled men and women than in the rural environs that had flourished prior to the so-called industrial revolution."[44] Although Don Mitchell's analysis of the "annihilating economy" has been worked from an outrage over antihomeless laws, disability experience resonates with his assessment that "what is at work . . . at the urban scale . . . is the implementation . . . of a regulatory regime—and its ideological justification—appropriate to the globalizing neoliberal political economy."[45] What emerges as the supposedly public space of the globalized city resembles an idealized landscape, "a privatized view suitable only from the passive gaze of the privileged," substituted "for the (often uncomfortable and troublesome) heterogeneous interactions of urban life."[46] As global cities come to depend on the culture industry (replacing former industrial cores), the "aestheticization of fear" becomes a major civic strategy for determining who belongs on the streets of global cities.[47]

Decolonization and the Rubric of Civility

So global cities' aesthetic image and their promise of personal security (hence, their own economic profitability) borrow upon this primal anxiety registered as lack or degeneracy, this psychological wiring of fear, in order to generate notions of civil space. As global cities, like New York City and Vancouver (one of the smaller but still *"global"* cities, owing to the fact that Vancouver has one of the highest immigration rates on the planet), now aspire to serve as "experience museums" of culture and the cultured, the legislation of civility has become the epitome of civic-mindedness.[48] The aesthetics of civic space remains limned then with dread of the biologized other. The choreography of civility, along with its mapping of civic space,[49] may be, I am suggesting, one of the lines of force where humanism continues to work a colonial agenda.[50] If civility might constitute what Spivak calls an "enabling violence," comparably also here then her strategy: "the enablement"—namely, civility—"must be used even as the violation is renegotiated."[51]

That cities exist "as human settlements in which strangers are likely to meet," as Richard Sennett explained in his 1976 text *The Fall of Public Man* (released then amid what Zukin has identified as the first wave of the institutionalization of fear), calls in turn "for a rather special and sophisticated type of skill"—namely, "the rubric of civility."[52] Civility, according to Sennett, might be defined as that "activity which protects people from each other and yet allows them to enjoy each other's company." In this way, civility "shield[s] others from being burdened with oneself." "Wearing a mask" becomes the epitome of civility, since "[m]asks permit pure sociability, detached from the circumstances of power, malaise and private feelings of those who wear them."[53] Equally, however, civility—a psychosocial line of force—protects the transcendent plain of value, that growth capitalist scale of valuing unlimited potential, opportunities innumerable, and unencumbered ability.

If we immediately recognize the choreography to which Sennett refers us, we can also, recalling the scene at Rockefeller Center, contemplate how this line of force we call "civility," this expectation that we shield each other from the burden of ourselves, might negatively affect what Spivak calls "the lost imperative to responsibility."[54] I am somewhat intrigued, given Spivak's provocation, to think back to the story of Cain and Abel (Genesis 4), a tight theological hub from which spins out the biblical narrative addressing the first or original sin (that is, fratricide, at least in some accounts), the founding of the city and the haunting question, "Am I my brother/sister's keeper?" Not only does "a city represent a masked structure of dependence on various 'elsewheres,'" for example, agricultural lands as well as nonadjacent industrial zones and maquiladoras,[55] the city equally allows us—by encouraging the mask of civility—to avoid carrying the burden of the other. The temptation to secure our own well-being by capitalist accumulation, to become invulnerable to interdependence by building the infrastructure of city, also allows us to avoid being our brother and sister's "keeper." Daily, then, we face the temptation to murder—in the Levinasian sense—of refusing recognition to the face of the other. In this vein, civility protects the practice of the rights and freedoms of the sovereign self, but avoids negotiating our interdependence, avoids carrying the burden of the other, of his/her difference.

Called across the Apartheid of the Cultured and the Class/ified
If civility spatially protects the practice of individual rights, it may also generatively aggravate today's planetary fault-line—the divide between the resource rich and the resource poor. This apartheid, Spivak's analysis suggests, might better be defined as dividing the cultured from the class/ified,

dividing those scaled to the human rights agenda from the biologized—that "class" created by "the aestheticization of fear" (Zukin) and "the unequal distribution of agency."[56] (Need it be noted that the disabled, the homeless, and, to a certain extent, postcolonial subjects of Western metropoles can easily find themselves subjected to this latter classification, i.e. the biologized?) Spivak, concerned with the rural poor or those "removed from lines of social mobility," suspects that "the idea of human rights . . . may carry within itself the agenda of a kind of social Darwinism."[57] Spivak's analysis doesn't deny that the subject constructed by the human rights agenda practices a certain kind of responsibility. But human rights, caught into the myth of development, makes responsibility accidental or supplemental to subjectivity; and further, such a subjective posture carries the presumption of "development," of serving as helper-rescuer of the needy other. Thus, the humanist has an alibi for furthering his/her own narcissistic view of the world and, on an international basis, for justifying control.[58] The globalized world, she counters, "must be filled with the more robust imperative to responsibility that capitalist social productivity was obliged to destroy."[59] Consequently, Spivak charges us with something of a religious responsibility—that of, "suturing the lost cultural imperative to responsibility" into the human rights agenda.[60] This ethical imperative, she insists, must be established at the heart of our understanding of the subject and prior to humanism.[61] For a religious person, Spivak's anthropological starting point—"the human being is human in answer to an outside call"—carries an intriguingly strong theological impulse—the concept of *vocare*, to be called.[62]

Like Spivak, the sociologist Zygmunt Bauman in "Modernity and Its Outcasts" notices something of an apartheid.[63] As modernization goes global, we face "an acute crisis of the human waste disposal industry," Bauman observes. "The production of 'human waste,' or more correctly wasted humans (the 'excessive' and 'redundant' . . .) is," Bauman contends, "an inevitable outcome of modernization, . . . an inescapable side-effect of order-building (each order casts some parts of the extant population as 'out of place,' 'unfit' or 'undesirable') and of economic progress (that cannot proceed without degrading and devaluing the previously effective modes of 'making a living' . . .)."[64] But this globally produced problem forces localities—like global cities—to seek solutions.[65] With freedom definitively indexed to capitalism's unwillingness to tolerate any impediment to its mobility, a certain "mechanics of movement has invaded . . . modern experience"—actualized in the choreography of bodies on the street as much as in NAFTA and GATT.[66] In this vein, Bauman suspects that "civility" (Bauman here reading with Sennett) protects the "people who move and act faster, who come nearest to the momentariness of movement," from the burdened bodies, those whose differences mark them as "mobility impaired." "Domination," he concludes, "consists [today] in one's own capacity to escape, to disengage, to be elsewhere, and the right to decide the speed with which all this is done." Public civility ensures one's ability to move through consumer corridors unimpeded, assures power of the speed necessary to elude accountability. "In liquid modernity, it is the most elusive, those free to move without notice, who rule," Bauman concludes, insinuating that these function as something of an absentee landlord class.[67] The practice of civility—increasingly fused with this class's power to rule through the "synopticon" (the power of being watched, observed, imitated)[68]—assumes that we will meet up with difference in the city, but has already internalized a means to avoid the burden of difference (that difference marked today as "human waste"), has developed the means of stripping the encounter of its challenges, has already substituted techniques of escape and elision for engagement and mutual commitment. In Bauman's terms, the choreography of civility, already assuming techniques of escape and elision in place of engagement and mutuality, results in "the pathology of public space."[69] Free to talk (or not), we are also free to avoid commitment, the call of the other.[70]

From Lotusland with Love (or, Even Christians Here Speak of Karma)
Admittedly, for those of us trained within the mythos of humanism, the recognition that "the psychological foundations of liberalism" have been based on a repression by abjection of the burden of difference and thus aggravate this apartheid of bodies, that our humanist posture has been and thus remains limned with colonialism as we walk the streets of the city, can be a difficult admission. Theologically more troublesome would be the insight that this class apartheid might well have to do with the order of the body generated within Protestantism: "Capitalism could not make sense, it could not be the social organization for accomplishing certain types of material labor, if the disciplining of the body in Protestant terms did not already make sense," writes Janet Jakobsen, recalling the insights of Max Weber.[71] Self-sovereignty has crept willy-nilly into our notions of religious

subjectivity. If we crip that posture, if we bend it to the call of the other, then the religious subject might affirm with Spivak that "to be human is to be called by the other." "We are obligated to respond to our environment and other people in ways that open up rather than close off the possibility of response," suggests Kelly Oliver, echoing Spivak.[72] Assuming such a theological anthropology might begin to break with the lines of force hemming us into civility.

Let me demonstrate with a scene from "Lotusland" (Vancouver), where even Christians speak of karma: Vancouverites emerge like moles to the few hours of sunlight breaking open life in the rainforest. On one such morning I make my way to Capers Organic Grocery and Deli, where I'm something of a regular. (Cripped bodies often require the interdependence of face-to-face relations.) On the corner of 4th and Vine, the other regulars (street people, whom Capers does not restrict) greet me—without my professional garb and therefore passable mask as "the professor"—with a touch of admiration and a bit of ironic laughter. (To be disabled is to share an affinity with street persons, and I am, after all, an uncivil body inside the civility of academia.) Capers Deli presents one with an interesting cross-section of life in the global city—émigrés of former British colonies enter North America through our port, Vancouver having the fourth highest immigration rate among cities on this planet. Behind the deli counter, I am consequently likely to meet up with someone whose professional status outranks my own, but who cannot get relicensed in this country, a Sikh forced into the food industry, a street person from the Downtown Eastside in recovery and job retraining or, owing to our informal status as an international gay refuge, an M to F trannie. Shanti from Singapore often teaches me about non-Western traditions, like roasting goat and making oil lamps for Diwali.

But today there's a new presence in deli-prep—Indo-Canadian, I think. And when she spots me twelve deep in the line-up for the comfort of tea and a muffin on this still damp and dripping morning, she gasps and nearly drops her pans. Sure that I have yet again been fixed in the stare, the horrific clench of fear that keeps my disabled body tenuously on the edge of civil acceptance, I grow stone cold, psychically suck myself in. (I, you see, have the body that can bring the world to a standstill. Almost, but not quite the picture of civility: "You have one leg," the most common utterance after the gasp. Duh, I know; but the onlooker seems to be just now getting used to the idea.) But no: her energies surge toward me not as fear, but as—could it be?—a surge force of reverence. I am apparently an honored guest. And then without any command of English but under karmic command, she moves the twelve others aside, shaming them with her finger.[73] I'm embarrassed, shocked, amazed: Is this the energy of spiritual passion?

Could Christians not just learn to speak of karma but practice crip/tography—this capaciousness of being bent toward, because called by, the other? The other twelve were not intending to be mean, just aiming to give me the cloak of civil decency, that is, tolerant inclusion, by making no fuss about my difference in their line-up. But she has just shown me an energy that might breach the retaining walls of all of these different zones set up by the command force of civility in the global city. Whereas liberalism has typically gotten stuck enforcing "decency theologies" (Marcella Althaus-Reid),[74] here the naturalized ethos of the city was burst by something like responsibility to karma, a locus or region of value not civilly scripted. Or if not karma, here at least was something that re-related humans to the mystery of the ineffable in a way that provoked another human geography, the promise of another economy of value.

Where civility offloads responsibility, and where liberal theological anthropology has been conflated with it, civility cedes its interests to imperialism, avoids the encounter with strangeness, refuses to engage and therefore to live with difference by putting difference—as in Giuliani's "Project Civil City"—in geographic set aside. " '[P]roduction-consumption values inevitably place a central priority upon utility, upon reward for people who can perform useful tasks," explains biblical scholar Walter Brueggemann. And, I would add, at this point in the globalization of consumer capitalism, it places priority upon appearance. "Such values," Brueggemann continues, "tend to discard people without utility. And Jesus, the center of land-history, announced and embodied the conviction that in the new land (the kingdom) the issue of utility as a means of entry was not pertinent (cf. Luke 14:12–14, 21–24)."[75] So crip/tography—this christological excursus—takes up its location amid the social pressures of civility within the regions of the citizen-consumer, imagining "Christianity as Path and Practice" setting out from a locus other than that of the transparency that each of our bodies agrees to practice within empire.

Like the industrious Jack and Jill, who went up the hill to fetch water, my body too was born under the regime of self-sovereignty demanded by capitalist economy and within which we treat ability like a piece of property for enclosure. But I broke my crown and had a falling out with that notion of self-sovereignty. I have consequently suggested that civility—protecting us from the burden of the other but with and through the "aestheticization of fear" (Zukin) of the degenerat/ing body—holds this sense of self-sovereignty in play. Whether we name our horizon of hope "planetarity" (Spivak) or "conviviality" (as does the postcolonial scholar Paul Gilroy, from amid the mongrel city of London), this sovereign self must be fissured, fractured, by something like religious passion. That's the conviction of those like Haraway, but also Salman Rushdie in *Midnight's Children*, and Inosh Arani in *The Cripple and His Talisman*, who hold before us the iconography of the broken body as figural map of the postcolonial. Because the en/crip/tion of pain exposes self-sovereignty as illusion, the crip may figurally open out the way for going "post/al" in cosmopolis. Given the ways in which civility plays upon the "aestheticization of fear," can Christianity—"the practices of others made odd"[76]—be lived cryptographically—as a geography of resistance? Geographies of resistance don't necessarily seek to "mirror geographies of domination," but rather to uncouple from domination by creating and insinuating alternative spatialities.[77] "To suture . . . the torn and weak responsibility-based system into a conception of human dignity as the enjoyment of rights one enters ritual practice transgressively . . . , as a hacker enters software," advises Spivak.[78] The ritual site—not unrecognized by the likes of Graham Ward or Stephanie Kallos—where bodies targeted for waste figurally enter ritual practice—has been that of the Eucharistic fracture.

III.

Generosity—a "desire to redistribute," in other words—does not necessarily (Spivak reminds us) flow or even trickle down from the well-laden table; it "is not the unproblematic consequence of a well-fed society."[79] The heart of those ensconced as self-sovereign turns rather, Richard Sennett advises, toward narcissism: "[N]arcissism is now mobilized in social relations by a culture deprived of belief in the public and ruled by intimate feeling as a measure of the meaning of reality."[80] Indeed, "Narcissism is the Protestant Ethic of Modern Times," Sennett charges, obviously averting to, by escalating, Max Weber's intuition that Protestantism supplied capitalism with an amenable anthropology.[81] If "worldly asceticism" erased sociability and turned subjective impulse inward, today's cult of narcissism borrowed on that initial structure of ascetic distance from society, but now makes subjective feeling an obsessive—even if doomed to fail (since narcissistic desire can never be sated)—index of well-being.[82] Publicly eulogized as "enlightened self-interest" and made normative, this sense of cultured subjectivity, a privatized and inflated subjective individualism, closed in on its own feelings and ravenous for experience, discriminates itself from class/ified or biologized difference. The self—gone missing from public sociality, but immersed in culture consumption—practices a sovereignty over the body in similar manner as it assumes to property rights, to the right to capitalize upon property, to geographically map the city.[83] With the advance of capitalist globalization, those bodies which do not similarly hold property "privately"—private property being asserted as neoliberal realism and common law regarding the global city—literally cannot take place: "When capital is believed to have no need for any particular place [as has been true within the myth of capital in network society], then cities do what they can to make themselves attractive to capital. . . . 'Quality of life' laws [like that to which I was subjected in Giuliani's New York City]—making urban areas attractive to footloose capital and to mid-to-upper classes—annihilate the space of those who do not own property, who have no legal right to place."[84] Recognizing then that even those of liberal vision are "obliged to admit that there is no continuous line from rights to responsibilities,"[85] Christians might agree with Spivak that "the only way to make these sweeping changes" into a postproductive economy is "to take seriously the necessary but impossible task to construct a collectivity among the dispensers of bounty as well as the victims of oppression,"[86] to angle subjectivity toward the call of the other.[87]

Can Crips "Participate"?

Theologian Graham Ward, concerned about the challenges meeting the planet in the form of the emergence of global cities and wanting to induce a generosity of being, recalls Christians to Eucharist as a heuristic ritual for an "ontology of participation."[88] Where "cities become variants on the theme-park, reorganized as sites for consumption, sites for the satisfaction of endless desire,"[89] "where the "social [becomes] the cultural,"[90] we require another kind of theological response, Ward writes in his *Cities of God*.[91] In that assertion, he criticizes an earlier Christian social liberalism that could, by petition or plea, whisper its ideological suggestions and assume their respectful hearing in the channels of the political state, a Christianity that was, however, also imbricated in the politics of rescue.[92] But Ward's comment is equally meant to push theologians to think in new terms—

specifically, to think analytically with and through the lines of force loosed in a culture, rather than only redressing, by criticism, national policy. The line of force which Ward addresses particularly is desire, since the body is the principal site for the operation of contemporary power.[93] According to Ward, an adequate Christian response to the atomism of Western culture (which appears as his primary culture complaint) has to include "a strong doctrine of participation" so as "to undermine the social atomism which contemporary cyberspace, global cities, and new forms of mobile, short term 'employment' . . . develop."[94] "The Christian theology outlined in [*Cities of God*]," Ward writes, "starts from what it is to be called by God as an embodied soul to participate in Christ's body."[95] In this way, he assumes Christian subjectivity must "start . . . with the collective," not the individual,[96] stressing participation and interdependence—hence, the Eucharist as map. All in all, Ward's analytic intuitions would seem to be on the same page as Spivak's.

With Eucharist as ontological map in mind and having marked "the racked and viral-ridden bodies of the sick" and disenfranchised, including earth, as well as "the engineered bodies of the beautiful, the power-hungry,"[97] as his primary concern in chapters 3 ("Corporeality: The Ontological Scandal") and 4 ("The Displaced Body of Jesus Christ") of *Cities of God* as well as in his essays, "Bodies: The Displaced Body of Jesus"[98] and "Suffering and Incarnation,"[99] Ward then circles around this question: "[W]hat kind of bodies is Christianity concerned with . . . , if . . . this Eucharistic and Christic body informs all other understandings of 'body' . . . ?"[100] Ward, on the one hand, asserts that "the manner in which [the iconic status of the body of Jesus] draws us is configured through an identification with the suffering of the body," eventuating in an economy of desire no longer libidinal, but experienced as mourning.[101] Yet Ward, on the other hand, presumes to facilitate these analytic suggestions and his question of the spatial relations among bodies by introducing the analogical worldview, by "announcing to the postmodern city [Christianity's] own vision of universal justice, peace, and beauty,"[102] or, variously, by—in an act of "ontological madness"— renaming the world as "bread" or "body."[103] Ward's economy of desire tinged with mourning, with eternal longing,[104] here seems to have returned with transcendent vigor or vengeance.

"The analogical worldview," Ward explains, "issues, methodologically, from re-inscribing the urban symbolic production and exchange . . . within a Christian theology of signification . . . : we live . . . in a world mediated to us, interpreted to us; governed by the Word of God the signs become sacramental—dense with mystery."[105] In one sense, then, Ward picks up the work of theology as cosmology, of teaching us a different way to live in the world, by resort to a logos-saturated world to counter "this soulless materialism—materialism without mystery."[106] Where worldviews have yielded to realist materialism, Ward's theological cosmology may recall liberal Christians away from the myth of development to a different, operative economy of value. In the quest for a sustainable world, such a religious reorientation, which "forges emotional connection with the natural world"—and especially where that natural world is "second nature," the city—may not be insignificant.[107]

But I worry that Ward, while intending to challenge us toward Eucharistic sharing of the common elements of life, has not yet paid sufficient attention to fissuring open the sovereign self of the human rights agenda, which (as Spivak has made clear) is not without a helper mentality. The modern subject has always been something of a "wounded identity," Wendy Brown warns, mourning something of an ideal, a lost transcendent, which has made it conducive to capitalism.[108] Further, I suspect that Ward's analogical worldview—itself a reappropriation of an undeconstructed Neoplatonic theology—presumes to cultural resistance by mere oppositionalism. In Roman imperial iconography, the emperor—just as do today's globalizing forces—carried a vision of worldwide peace, sufficiency, and reconciliation; the agenda does not itself yet distinguish one regime from another. Christ, explains John S. Dunne, in The City of the Gods, stands in a long line of savior-kings, ruling over an eternal city.[109] And Ward well knows that "sacrifice founded the ancient city."[110] Intuitively then, we might ask how the Eucharist, itself an ancient rite affiliated with sacrifice, might have mimetically generated an alternative choreography among subjugated bodies as distinct from imperial theology. Where ancient emperor cults appreciated the self-composed, sober, civil self, what might have been loosed by putting the body of a torture victim—a crip, a grotesque—iconographically on the throne of that savior-king, the emperor? Ward's invocation of Eucharistic ritual appears oddly already culturally transparent.

This methodology for "dwelling . . . in complex communities which constitute the cities of God" by negotiating "an analogical relation" with "Christian theological cosmology"[111] avoids (it seems to me) being challenged by the subaltern. Invoking idealization at this juncture avoids "open[ing] the mind to be 'othered' by the subaltern," avoids subjecting the self to "a fractured relation to subjectivity"; instead it assumes, as did modernity, to "yoke the emotions to belief, which then is led to/by reason."[112] At this juncture, I can only concur with Althaus-Reid's assessment that "Radical orthodoxy . . . fails to take into account the epistemological plateau of the excluded."[113] Although fashioned as an anti-metaphysics (and Ward, as a good poststructuralist, recognizes changing cultural epistemes), this method appears to reassemble some version of absolute transcendence—if more tenuously called "analogical." Although Ward recognizes "how the body . . . disseminates itself through a myriad of other bodies" and how "ghettoisations and the segregations" of structural violence "injure me,"[114] the analogical worldview, it appears to me, takes into account neither the call of the other nor, when it comes to the practice of responsibility, the willingness to let the subaltern teach us. "In opening myself to be 'othered' by the subaltern," Spivak explains, "it is this broader more mysterious arena of the subject that the self hopes to enter." Without a working engagement with subalterns, "without this effortful task of 'doing' in the mode of 'to come' [because "the subaltern is my teacher"], . . . 'thinking' [remains] in the mode of 'my way is the best.'"[115] One might hear rather Peter Brown's narration of early Christianity's move to identify with the poor, to posit its inheritance among the poor, as something in the order of being called by the other.[116]

To be sure, Ward does not hand us yet again the modern Jesus—the Healer and Savior of the degenerate, figural map for the politics of rescue. If we read cripped bodies from within Ward's proposal, Ward would insist, I think, on a soulful, supplemental value not encoded by culture—something like Richard Kearney's *prosopon*, a relational sense of the irreducible alterity of the other, which does prevent the wholesale devaluation of bodies.[117] And yet, Eucharistic participation—as evidenced perhaps by the ways in which even liturgical ritual can foreclose upon disabled bodies—may not reach across today's worldwide apartheid.[118] Disability, I am assuming, might be indicative of today's worldwide apartheid dividing the subaltern—"those removed from lines of social mobility"[119]—from the cultured. Disability may then be indicative of "out-lier groups," since this difference—as distinct from race and gender—can never aspire to the subjective idealization at the heart of liberal humanism nor to the "translocationality" of the body in today's globalizing capitalism.[120]

Whatever these differences marked by "disability" and its cognate resonance with the biologized "waste" of globalization, they "defy assimilation," such that these bodies end up as but passive recipients.[121] Justice construed as "a matter of distributing benefits produced by mutual cooperation among those capable of contributing" will never arrive among those seen as in-crip-ted on today's city streets. Crips, Anita Silvers, a disabilities ethicist, insists, rather require something "like a project for engendering trust,"[122] where trust implies "accepting one's vulnerability to another . . . in the confidence that such exposure of vulnerability will not be used to harm the other."[123] Trust might here then be said to be an extension of responsibility inasmuch as it holds open the call of the other.[124] But then again it may not simply be "out-liers" who today require the renegotiation of trust: while the disembedding technologies of modernity have required trust in hard and soft infrastructure technologies, these dry up human social trust.[125] Fear—including its aesthetic modes—may need to be redressed not so much by participation as by a trust culture.

Christology and the Akedah of In/Appropriate/d Others

"Christianity," Ward contends, quoting Michel de Certeau directly, "was founded upon the loss of a body—the loss of the body of Jesus Christ, compounded with the loss of the 'body' of Israel, of a 'nation' and its genealogy."[126] "It is the loss," Ward then concludes, "which prepares the way for the mystical." Correcting himself, Ward explains: "Rather than loss, I wish to speak of 'displacement'—. . . , the displacement of the one, arche-typal body, which engenders a transcorporeality in which the body of Christ is mapped onto and shot like a watermark through physical bodies, social bodies, institutional bodies, ecclesial bodies, sacramental bodies."[127] But what shall we make of this Christic wound that allows for its own disappear-ance, a wounded body made more spiritually capacious because it is displaced? As one with some experience of bearing what for this culture appears as stigmata, I wonder how this torture victim, this victim of imperial power, this uncivil grotesque (Isaiah 53), comes to be so easily disappeared and what that disappearance affects. For the colonized, the body—visually fixed as hemorrhaging, bleeding, stigmatic (as Frantz Fanon first sug-gested)—can never disappear, can never pretend to transparency. Rather our bodies circulate outside in/vested desire, civility patrolling any allow-ance of/for their desire (for instance, the disabled are typically assumed to be as asexual as Althaus-Reid's lemon vendors).[128] As Bauman, among others, persistently points out, for the bodies of those "absentee landlords" and the cult/ure of public appearance, disappearance or transparency is the norm of power. So might Ward's dispersion of the wounded body, its "translocationality,"[129] rather unwittingly serve the absentee landlord class who live an absence of presence to relational accountability?

What might religiously emerge, I wonder, if we figurally remembered here the stigmatic, because colonized, body that resisted cultural power's disappearing act. Might our responsibility to the call of the other here begin to cross through cultural apartheid? Rather than analogical idealization (because vision we have, but no practiced paths opening out therefrom), might we consider how the iconography of the inappropriate/d other could be worked (again?) to promote a geography of resistance? Might this geography have been opened off from feeling with and for the wound of the other, of assuming pain, and our empathic engagement, as of the nature of human life? The model of self-sovereignty avoids, and something in Ward's proposal skirts, precisely such an empathic interdependence. Wounds, streets, disappear when thinking analogically—as if we could find the muscle named "responsibility" by shutting our eyes.[130] By referring us outside of social context, Ward's analogical method avoids encountering the geographical thicket of discerning among immanental intelligibilities, of risking commitment to the possible good—not some idealized good.[131] And, I might suggest, invoking Spirit—that intriguing biblical concept accompanying bodies colonized and cripped, that theological concept scaled to negotiate the political and not so much the universal[132]—might itself avoid the dualism of transcendence/immanence into which Ward's methodology might otherwise return us.

To reread Christian iconography as rather decisively "cripped"—as engaging "wounds" that refuse displacement—may open out a different suggestive possibility: If pain is always culturally symbolically interpreted, then what might "de-crip-tion" of culture's abject and in/appropriate/d others suggest? Isaiah 53 constitutes the greatest hypertext for our synoptic passion narratives. Traditionally, Isaiah's suffering servant, when conflated with Jesus as victim of Roman torture tactics, has lent itself to atonement theories. Feminist theologians have accused such theologies of perpetuating—by embracing justification through the actions of a vicarious sufferer—abusive relationships. Yet the servant songs of deutero-Isaiah, composed within and/or consequent to the exile of Judah in Babylon, could be read to expose, not legitimate, imperial conditions—to expose the powers which occasion the enslaving or colonizing of subjugated peoples, manifest in/as physical torture, hobbling, humiliation, and shame. On rereading, then, Isaiah 53 might suggest not vicarious suffering, but a ritual of insight therapy:[133] "Surely he has borne our griefs and carried our sorrows; yet we accounted him stricken." Rather than justifying vicarious suffering, does it not expose the mechanism of social scapegoating? Used for insight therapy, Isaiah 53 invites persons to discerningly confront the relations occasioning exclusion and rejects the shame that others are attempting to impose on the humiliated other. Like disability or biologizing of class, ringed by aestheticization of fear, projecting suffering onto another obscures our participation in the distorted relations of empire. But if Isaiah 53 were turned into such a ritual of insight therapy, might the de-crip-tion of the in/valid (only so as understood within the myth of development, of course) occasion a confession of the ways in which we presume upon "the philanthropy of the poor"?[134]

"Following Jesus, the torture victim, means daily negotiation of Roman power," observes biblical scholar Warren Carter.[135] The salvific potential of proclaiming the cross, as Neil Elliott explains, was the exposure of unjust and terrorizing political relations that then could be identified and collectively resisted.[136] Similarly, the Pauline instructions on the need to discern the body of the crucified Christ at the Eucharist: If persons joined themselves to the body of Christ and still live unrighteously with others, they were participating in the same systems of judgment and condemnation that crucified Jesus (1 Corinthians 11:23–26).[137] Perhaps such discernment might be lived in relation to the subalterns of our culture—as crip/tographic iconography, as a locus for a geography of resistance.

"Of Splintered Glazes, Hairline Fractures, Cracks and Other Prerequisites of Intimacy"

If literature occupies that other theological venue in the West, extending the imagination of our humanity, Stephanie Kallos's novel *Broken for You* might offer us not so much a vision of new humanity as a suggestion for living the fractures of human life as a possible spiritual path.[138] Margaret Hughes, the protagonist of the novel, has been encrypted within her 15,000-square-foot Seattle mausoleum of a mansion since the death of her eight-year-old son and her consequent divorce from her husband. For decades then, the seventy-five-year-old has tended the porcelain and art glass collections gathered in by her father—these, the ill-gotten wealth of a man who dealt with the Nazis to procure stolen Jewish goods during World War II. As if the sins of the father were visited upon the child, Margaret develops an astrocytoma—a star-shaped, incurable malignant tumor of the brain. But now leveraging illness as a chance to break with old habits, that choreography of a life tending but "the objects of my affection," she invites in one melancholic boarder after another to disorder the isolating decorum of her wealth—first, Wanda, the orphaned dramaturge, chasing an impossible love; then stolid and asexual Susan, a nursing assistant; next Bruce, the caterer become community cook, seeking gay refuge, and so on—the handyman, a gardener, a lover. Born from her "fracture" and theirs—in a way that echoes the medieval christological concept of "wound become womb," but without disappearing the historied hurt—is an adoptive family—including, with thanks to a turkey baster, a second generation, Bruce and Susan's little Augie. As individual lives fracture, the members of this adoptive family hold and redeem one another. Gathering energy from their shared accountability, they finally even invent a ritual of atonement to loose the palpable guilt exuding from the porcelain collections, none of the pieces ever returnable. Inverting the horror of Kristallnacht "when bodies had been shattered but things had not,"[139] each soup tureen will break its silence and tell its family history, even if invented—each goblet, each figurine, each egg coddler, and saucer. Visitors to the mansion as well as family members, each having held himself or herself accountable to history's horror in the telling of such an invented story, smash each plate, each vase, each teacup in turn, redeeming the fragments as mosaic tiles for Wanda's art.

This adoptive community, taking shape here in the popular imagination, resonates with Foucault's queer geography of resistance by adoption[140] and with Spivak's sensibilities for turning the bearer of rights toward collectivity. Spirit adoption, one of the earliest strategic practices of Christianity within the conditions of empire (which tends to strew bodies hither and yon and make genealogies impossible), was a redemption strategy for mortal bodies (Romans 8).[141] Far from promising grace to overly moralistic and guilt-ridden consciences, the apostle Paul connected Spirit to the liberation of history's humiliated—from political oppression into economic mutuality, from the relational alienation induced by urban in-migration and slavery into sociocommunal, ecclesial belonging. Disrupting the power plays of empire, its land grab, and its legalized terror of the poor, Spirit revealed itself as in solidarity with and as threading transcendence, if also "history," among those empire humiliated.

But Kallos's text appears intriguingly to address itself to "the bearers of right" (to those in that crypt of sovereign-selfhood, even if at the top of the proverbial ladder) and seeks to redress not just atomization (as did Ward),

but the dehumanization of wealth,[142] the social ills accruing amid the afflu-
ent. "The rise in aggregate wealth has not," qualitative studies have insisted,
"raised reported subjective well-being."[143] Rather, wealth—presenting us
with the ways and means to ensure ourselves against the vicissitudes, fluc-
tuations, and volatilities of interdependence—has "coincided with an
epidemic expansion of mental-health disorders."[144] Avner Offer, presenting
study after study, asks us to consider the correlation between material abundance and a wide range of social and personal disorders—family breakdown,
child and youth anxiety, addiction, crime, declining social trust, and, often
among youth, "attachment disorders."[145] Seen from the psychic inside out,
affluence—as a way of embargoing ourselves against interdependence—not
only undermines social commitment, but psychic well-being: "Strong mate-
rialistic values were associated with a pervasive undermining of well-being,
from low life satisfaction and happiness, to depression and anxiety, physical
problems such as headaches, personality disorders, narcissism and antisocial
behavior."[146] That modernity chose to relate us but through the cash nexus
makes this a social, not one-to-one, correlation. Kallos seems intuitively to
catch us in that condition.

Consider Kallos's work, then, a training manual in breaking with "the
objects of [our] affection" so as to move away from "sentiment," which she
describes as "ascribing a value to something above and beyond what its
value is to God,"[147] toward relational embeddedness and the love of a mortal
and transient life. Kallos, moving momentarily into the voice of the spiritual
director, instructs: "Look . . . at the faces and bodies of people you love.
The explicit beauty that comes not from smoothness of skin or neutrality
of expression, but from the web of experience that has left its mark. Each
face, each body is its own living fossilized record. A record of cats, combat-
ants, difficult births; of accidents, cruelties, blessings. . . . [T]hese records
are what render your beloved beautiful."[148] You see, Kallos writes at one
point, "We're worth more broken."[149]

Wounds, breaking through the solid encryptions of social civility, here
become capacious because of their invitation for deterritorialization of the
body. Illness breaks open the tacit infrastructure of the real, of what is
presumed to make life meaningful, of what is of value, even of how we
articulate health. (From an alternative position, "health" might well be
indexed to humane practice—not the perfection of the boundaries of the
body.) In Frida Kahlo's famous painting, "Roots 1943," Kahlo's broken body
lays like a mirror-image of the parched and fissured land of Mexico; her

broken and bleeding spinal column nevertheless sprouts rhizomes, green vines inching their way out of the frame. In Stephanie Kallos's imaginative pedagogy for pain, such rhizomes might even map a way out of economism. Echoing Spivak's sensibilities that the only way "to persuade global finance and world trade to jettison the culture of economic growth" would be "to take seriously the necessary but impossible task to construct a collectivity among the dispensers of bounty as well as the victims of oppression,"[150] Kallos tracks the passing of capitalist inheritance into the collective of cripped bodies adopted into a household.

Living like the "Zen Tea Box Broken in a Hundred Places"
As Kallos details Margaret's use of illness to breach old habit, I too have found in physical and in disability's sociopsychic suffering something like the possibilities of a spiritual practice. With the psychic and physical sheering of my health crisis has also come something of a shift in the register of a life, of consciousness. Perhaps this shouldn't be surprising if "spiritual waking arrives ever as the dis/abling of the ableist dream."[151] As Ward's account of religious subjectivity also recognized, there is not "a spectrum with pain at one extreme and pleasure at the other." Rather, religious accounts have historically "appealed to experiences which are simultaneously both painful and consummately beatific." If "the mystic's cry of ecstasy, the mathematician's speechless awe at the dark spaces between the stars, the exquisite intellectual confession of what is beautiful sheers towards the edge of the tremendum," if "each testif[ies] to experiences that exceed the neat categorization, the spectrum extremities, of pain and pleasure,"[152] might becoming disabled or falling ill not also serve as something like the slap of a Zen master?

By suggesting that we live our fissures and fractures "like the Zen tea box broken in a hundred places"[153]—in other words, as a spiritual discipline toward deterritorialization from our existing ideological regime, I mean to point toward (1) the discipline of attentively spending one's energies and learning to open spaces of time for retreat; (2) the discipline of not following the veins of envy, jealousy, hatred, anger; (3) the discipline of releasing the romantic harmonies of life, those presumed harmonies not after all unrelated to the power and punishment of judgment; (4) the practice of sympathy for the other who startles and flees in fear from my in-crip-tion (their fear cannot be but of their own humble contours of flesh); (5) the practice of reentering the geography of a life trusting that if I should slip, fall, become "landlocked" by failure of crutch or wheelchair, that someone will actually be humane. I am learning to trust myself again to human interdependence, a risk from which wealth is an insulator. The recognition of the meagerness and volatility of ego; the blessing of the crack through which one begins to recognize the ideological arteries of a culture; the reminder of life transpiring before the ineffable; an awareness of a resplendent plenitude out of which I can at times manage to live mindfully: in regard to all of these, I here claim nothing more than situated knowledge. Anyone can cultivate subjective fractures, which tumble us from the transcendental cult of public appearance, as insight therapy.

Could Karma Retrain Us to Be Each Others' Keeper?

David Harvey reads globalization as the lines of force moving through bodies. Deconstructing such lines of force, he hopes might also conversely swerve globalization.[154] I have, by deconstructing the lines of force yoking civility and the politics of public appearance, assumed Harvey's conviction in my own work. But in regards to Harvey's resolve, I now find myself in a bit of quandary: Given the ubiquity of "body" amid consumer discourse, might we Christians need—so as to underscore the practice of responsibility (Spivak), the practice of being each other's keeper—to speak of karma or its like? If Christianity is dead or in "near-terminal decline," we are left with the values and valorizations of rationalism.[155] Even Spivak intimates, when reading Kant, that she could understand that something like a God-supplement would help us imagine "responsibility" toward subalterns: "[T]his name ["God"] may be seen as a name of the radical alterity that the self as 'the narrative center of gravity' is programmed to imagine in an ethics of responsibility."[156] At least here in Lotusland, something meaningful about an alternative economy of value gets asserted by speaking of karma, whether by assuming a reference to alterity or by yoking ourselves to another trajectory of wisdom.

For now I hold this place in Christian theology with the concept "Spirit": "A notion of 'postcolonial spirit' can engender postcolonial theology," Mark Lewis Taylor submits, and I concur.[157] "Spirit," Mircea Eliade first found, digging into the texts of Hebrew prophets and priests (Genesis, Ezekiel, Isaiah), was developed as a sacred metaphor during times of catastrophic dislocation, when religious persons were disarticulated from their sacred lands. If with exile "space threatened to become permanently emptied of meaning," Hebrew prophets suggestively constructed "Spirit" as the place-holder spelling "the potential sacrality of all spaces," even "the decentralized spaces of [peoples'] exile."[158] To be sure, Spirit would come in colonial time to reign over a regime of accruing land, Spirit then linked into the voracious dialectic delivering the primitive into the civilized. But such colonial choreography of imperial sovereignty need not be construed as inherent to Spirit. So let Spirit name this other karmic-like economy of passion—namely, the choice to live "out of a desire beyond one's immediate control for a good one cannot fully know for others who are quite different."[159] Spirit— something of a prosthesis, as much a desire as a conviction that the world be hospitable—does not yet have a vision but has a generosity of presence.[160] And—as in the Buddhist practice of *tonglen*—Spirit assumes, as civility does not, to carry "the burden" of the other. Tonglen—the meditative practice of breathing in the pain and suffering of others, while breathing out the offering of compassion, wishing the other happiness—reverses the usual logic of avoiding suffering and seeking pleasure.[161] Crip/tography assumes this calculus of Spirit, assumes that Christic iconography can invite us to such spacious and fearless empathy. Given that "fear is as great a threat to the future stability of cities and regions as the much more talked about economic forces,"[162] crip/tography of this calculus might occasion a new choreography among bodies moving along the corridors of cosmopolis.

IV.

Here, in Vancouver, named the most livable of the planet's global cities, social Christianity—that "enabling violence" (Spivak) of the modern era of progress and its impetus for nationhood, not itself devoid of commitments to structural justices—has come to an end. Postcolonial studies have challenged the ways in which social mission, both nationally and within Christian community, has inherently carried colonial imbrication, even as the social justice practices inherent in these liberal traditions has also bequeathed a national infrastructure committed to multiculturalism, social welfare, civil rights, labor rights, and health care. If not directly owed to postcolonial theory, a subconscious decolonizing movement has also occasioned, if not forced, this edge of the western continent, the Pacific Northwest, to dream of a Christianity "post-Christendom"—if "Christianity" at all.

Liberal Protestantism, which has at least on its edges politically garnered inclusion of bodies differing, has nonetheless "been the form of Christianity hardest hit [by the postmodern challenges to authority] because it accommodated most fully to modernism with its emphasis on individualism and notions of progress and mastery."[163] Not surprisingly then, liberal theologies are having difficulty getting traction in post-Christendom. And yet in this situation—strewn with evangelicalisms, fundamentalisms (new age and environmental as well as textual), and cosmopolitans (tempted to collapse all sense of value into the discourse of materialism), attention to the complex valences of desires (to which postcolonial theory aspires), has, within lived religious practice, significant political work to do. I hope here to have begun to parse liberal theology in such a way that we can recognize and then deterritorialize its imbrication with "project civility"—a sentiment Edward Said recognized in his reading of the parlor spirituality of Jane Austen's *Mansfield Park*.[164] By developing crip/tography, an intentional way of "becoming minor" (à la Deleuze) as a practice, I am encouraging progressive theologies to redress their own infatuation with the myth of development.

Theology, Ward insists, "produces a space for belief within particular cultures."[165] I might agree, if I can assume here H. Richard Niebuhr's sense of faith as "fiduciary responsibility" to one another,[166] thus generating with Luce Irigaray "felicity in history."[167] Entrustment to life has been hemmed in by an aesthetics of fear, which itself has been coupled with the class decorum of civility. Disabled and other bodies assigned to the waste heaps of modernity carry the stigmatic refusal of today's sovereign self, that power of capital that tries to outrun the vulnerability and vicissitudes of interdependence. "Capital" insures the self against the frustrations of mutuality. Liberal social contract has consistently wedged apart interdependent subjectivities, interdependence being something of the "nature" of being disabled. Disabled persons—and to the extent that we share some of the disposition of the subalterns and/or postcolonials—"cannot bargain [but] still can trust."[168] Then again, if crip/tography begins by relating to stigmatic bodies iconographically, hoping to follow their rhizomes outside the frame-ups of civil decorum, cosmopolitan culture itself suffers from illnesses accruing because of the undercutting of interdependent relations, of mutuality, the inability to trust. "When we habitually employ a shutdown strategy"—to close off the overwhelming psychic pain/distress of contemporary culture, and among which strategies is depression, which dampens energy, enthusiasm, desire, concentration, memory—"the very strategy used to shut down pain can create more pain."[169]

Crip/tography attempts to move toward thinking theology "on location," given the challenges of the new urbanism and postcolonial conscientization. It hopes to open a passage beyond ideological envisionment. By cultivating the ever epistemically interpolated figure of the crip—a biblical tableau recuperated in these postcolonial times so as to move us beyond the whole-some self with which theology has gotten imbricated, it opens—by practice—on a path of compassionate, interdependent trust. Disrupting the urban grid of fear, crip/tography invites a different choreography from that which joined liberal Christians to the web of civility. Crip/tography reminds us yet again that to become human it is not necessary to become whole but to attend to the call of the other—and thus to become just, to practice love, pardon, tenderness, mercy, welcome, respect, compassion, solidarity, and communion among all our relations.

NOTES

A TENTATIVE TOPOGRAPHY OF POSTCOLONIAL THEOLOGY | MAYRA RIVERA AND STEPHEN D. MOORE

1. For an outline of the development of postcolonial biblical criticism, see Stephen D. Moore, *Empire and Apocalypse: Postcolonialism and the New Testament,* The Bible in the Modern World, no. 12 (Sheffield, UK: Sheffield Phoenix Press, 2006), 3–23. For a multiauthored attempt to situate postcolonial biblical criticism in relation to other important theoretical and political currents both inside and outside the field of biblical studies, see Stephen D. Moore and Fernando F. Segovia, eds., *Postcolonial Biblical Criticism: Interdisciplinary Intersections,* The Bible and Postcolonialism, no. 6 (New York: T. & T. Clark International, 2005). And for the most ambitious product of postcolonial biblical criticism to date, see Fernando F. Segovia and R. S. Sugirtharajah, eds., *A Postcolonial Commentary on the New Testament Writings,* The Bible and Postcolonialism, no. 7 (New York: T. & T. Clark International, 2007).

2. Early influential examples of postcolonial biblical hermeneutics include Laura E. Donaldson, ed., *Postcolonialism and Scriptural Reading,* Semeia, no. 75 (Atlanta: Scholars Press, 1996); R. S. Sugirtharajah, ed., *The Postcolonial Bible,* The Bible and Postcolonialism, no. 1 (Sheffield: Sheffield Academic Press, 1998); idem, *Asian Biblical Hermeneutics and Postcolonialism: Contesting the Interpretations* (Maryknoll, N.Y.: Orbis Books, 1998); Tat-siong Benny Liew, *Politics of Parousia: Reading Mark Inter(con)textually,* Biblical Interpretation, no. 42 (Leiden: E. J. Brill, 1999); Musa W. Dube, *Postcolonial Feminist Interpretation of the Bible* (St. Louis: Chalice Press, 2000); and Fernando F. Segovia, *Decolonizing Biblical Studies: A View from the Margins* (Maryknoll, N.Y.: Orbis Books, 2000).

3. Kwok Pui-lan, *Discovering the Bible in the Non-Biblical World* (Maryknoll, N.Y.: Orbis Books, 1995); idem, "Discovering the Bible in the Non-Biblical World,"

Semeia 47 (1989): 25–42. See also Kwok Pui-lan, "Response to the *Semeia* Volume on Postcolonial Criticism," *Semeia* 75 (1996): 211–18, and her "Jesus/the Native: Biblical Studies from a Postcolonial Perspective," in *Teaching the Bible: The Discourses and Politics of Biblical Pedagogy,* ed. Fernando F. Segovia and Mary Ann Tolbert (Eugene, Ore.: Wipf and Stock, 1998), 69–85.

4. Laura E. Donaldson and Kwok Pui-lan, eds., *Postcolonialism, Feminism, and Religious Discourse* (London and New York: Routledge, 2002). Historians of religion influenced by critical theory or postcolonial studies have also analyzed the self-fashioning of Christianity in the context of modern colonialism, focusing particularly on the symbiotic relationship between modern Christian identity and its construction of "other religions"; see, for example, Richard King, *Orientalism and Religion: Postcolonial Theory, India, and "The Mystic East"* (London and New York: Routledge, 1999); Talal Asad, *Genealogies of Religion: Discipline and Reasons of Power in Christianity and Islam* (Baltimore and London: Johns Hopkins University Press, 1993). Although these analyses have profound implications for the study of Christian self-definition, they have not had a significant impact on theology. Kwok Pui-lan's "Beyond Pluralism: Toward a Postcolonial Theology of Religious Difference" in her *Postcolonial Imagination and Feminist Theology* (Louisville, Ky.: Westminster John Knox, 2005) is a notable exception. John Thatamanil's essay in the present volume also contributes to this area.

5. Catherine Keller, Michael Nausner, and Mayra Rivera, eds., *Postcolonial Theologies: Divinity and Empire* (St. Louis: Chalice, 2004). The colloquium in question was the second Drew Transdisciplinary Theological Colloquium, entitled "Com/promised Lands: The Colonial, the Postcolonial, and the Theological." The colloquium of the following year (2003) had as its theme "An American Empire? Globalization, War, and Religion." The 2007 colloquium, from which the present volume derives, was titled "Planetary Loves: Postcoloniality, Gender, and Theology," while the 2008 colloquium also had a postcolonial theme: "Decolonizing Epistemology: New Knowing in Latina/o Philosophy and Theology."

6. See, for example, Mayra Rivera Rivera, "En-Gendered Territory: U.S. Missionaries Discourse in Puerto Rico (1898–1920)," in *New Horizons in Hispanic/Latino(a) Theology,* ed. Benjamin Valentin (Cleveland, Ohio: Pilgrim Press, 2003), 79–100; Joerg Rieger, "Theology and Mission between Neocolonialism and Postcolonialism," *Mission Studies* 21 (2004): 201–27; Letty M. Russell, "God, Gold, Glory and Gender: A Postcolonial View of Mission," *International Review of Mission* 93 (2004): 39–49; idem, "Cultural Hermeneutics: A Postcolonial Look at Mission," *Journal of Feminist Studies in Religion* 20 (2004): 23–40; Marion Grau,

"'We Must Give Ourselves to Voyaging': Regifting the Theological Present," in *Interpreting the Postmodern: Responses to "Radical Orthodoxy,"* ed. Rosemary Radford Ruether and Marion Grau (New York and London: T. & T. Clark, 2006), 141–60. Also relevant is Catherine Keller's analysis of Cristobal Colón's apocalyptic imagery in the chapter "Place: De/Colon/izing Spaces," in her *Apocalypse Now and Then: A Feminist Guide to the End of the World* (Boston: Beacon Press, 1996), 140–80.

7. See, for example, Gayatri Chakravorty Spivak, *A Critique of Postcolonial Reason: Toward a History of the Vanishing Present* (Cambridge, Mass.: Harvard University Press, 1999), 211–13. "Worlding" is Spivak's term for the process whereby a colonizing agent assimilates a subject people through acts of epistemic violence, such as renaming or remapping.

8. Kwok Pui-lan, Don H. Compier, and Joerg Rieger, eds., *Empire and the Christian Tradition: New Readings of Classical Theologians* (Minneapolis: Fortress, 2007).

9. Joerg Rieger, *Christ and Empire: From Paul to Postcolonial Times* (Minneapolis: Fortress Press, 2007).

10. Catherine Keller, *God and Power: Counter-Apocalyptic Journeys* (Minneapolis: Fortress Press, 2005). See also Mark Lewis Taylor, "Empire and Transcendence: Hardt and Negri's Challenge to Theology and Ethics," in *Evangelicals and Empire: Alternatives to the Political Status Quo,* ed. Bruce Ellis Benson and Peter Goodwin Heltzel (Grand Rapids, Mich.: Brazos Press, 2008), 201–17. For a postcolonial theological reading of the economy of empires, both ancient and modern, see Marion Grau, *Of Divine Economy: Refinancing Redemption* (New York and London: T. & T. Clark International, 2004).

11. For this aspect of Spivak's work, see Moore, "Situating Spivak," in the present volume.

12. R. S. Sugirtharajah, *The Bible and the Third World: Precolonial, Colonial and Postcolonial Encounters* (Cambridge: Cambridge University Press, 2001), 244. Pages 203–75 of this book deal with the relationship of liberationist and postcolonial hermeneutics. An abridged and lightly rewritten version of the same material appears in R. S. Sugirtharajah, *Postcolonial Criticism and Biblical Interpretation* (Oxford: Oxford University Press, 2002), 103–23.

13. A theme that Kwok explores in her essay in the present volume.

14. Cf. Walter D. Mignolo, *Local Histories/Global Designs: Coloniality, Subaltern Knowledges, and Border Thinking* (Princeton, N.J.: Princeton University Press, 2000), 91–126.

15. See, for example, Jung Mo Sung, *Desire, Market and Religion* (London: MSC Press, 2007); Ivan Petrella, *Liberation Theology: The Next Generation* (Maryknoll, N.Y.: Orbis Books, 2005); Ivone Gebara, *Longing for Running Water: Ecofeminism and Liberation* (Minneapolis: Fortress Press, 1999).

16. Considerations of sexuality have been less formative, although the influence of Marcella Althaus-Reid's work in this area is notable.

17. Namsoon Kang, "Who/What Is Asian?" in Keller, Nausner, and Rivera, *Postcolonial Theologies*, 100–117.

18. See, for example, Ada María Isasi-Díaz, "A New *Mestizaje/Mulatez*: Reconceptualizing Difference," in *A Dream Unfinished: Theological Reflections on America from the Margins*, ed. Eleazar S. Fernandez and Fernando F. Segovia (Maryknoll, N.Y.: Orbis Books, 2001), 203–219; Michelle Gonzalez, "Who Is Americana/o? Theological Anthropology, Postcoloniality, and the Spanish-Speaking Americas," in *Postcolonial Theologies*, ed. Keller, Nausner, and Rivera, 58–78; Manuel A. Vásquez, "Rethinking Mestizaje," in *Rethinking Latino(a) Religion and Identity*, ed. Miguel A. De la Torre and Gastón Espinosa (Cleveland, Ohio: Pilgrim Press, 2006), 129–57.

19. Susan Abraham, *Identity, Ethics, and Nonviolence in Postcolonial Theory: A Rahnerian Theological Assessment* (New York: Palgrave Macmillan, 2007).

20. Jeannine Hill Fletcher, *Monopoly on Salvation? A Feminist Approach to Religious Pluralism* (New York and London: Continuum, 2005).

21. John Thatamanil observes that such absence is evident in the extent to which the work of scholars such as Richard King and, more recently, Timothy Fitzgerald, Arvind Mandair, and Tomoko Masuzawa has gone unnoticed (personal communication).

22. Gayatri Chakravorty Spivak, "Three Women's Texts and a Critique of Imperialism," in *The Post-Colonial Studies Reader,* ed. Bill Ashcroft, Gareth Griffiths, and Helen Tiffin (London and New York: Routledge, 1995), 269–72.

23. See, for example, Serene Jones, *Feminist Theory and Christian Theology: Cartographies of Grace* (Minneapolis: Fortress Press, 2000), 42–48; Kwok Pui-lan, "Feminist Theology as Intercultural Discourse," in *The Cambridge Companion to Feminist Theology,* ed. Susan Park Parsons (Cambridge: Cambridge University Press, 2002), 23–39; Margaret D. Kamitsuka, *Feminist Theology and the Challenge of Difference* (Oxford: Oxford University Press, 2007), 90–97; Susan Abraham, *Identity, Ethics, and Nonviolence in Postcolonial Theory*, 105–15.

24. Gayatri Chakravorty Spivak, *In Other Worlds: Essays in Cultural Politics* (London and New York: Methuen, 1987), 205. Spivak seems unsure about the origins of the term "strategic essentialism," the first use of which she states has been attributed to both Jacques Derrida and Stephen Heath (Swapan Chakravorty, Suzana Milevska, and Tani E. Barlow, *Conversations with Gayatri Chakravorty Spivak* [London, New York, and Calcutta: Seagull, 2006], 63).

25. Gayatri Chakravorty Spivak, *Outside in the Teaching Machine* (New York and London: Routledge, 1993), 4.

26. Chakravorty, Milevska, and Barlow, *Conversations with Gayatri Chakravorty Spivak*, 64.

27. Marcella Althaus-Reid, *Indecent Theology: Theological Perversions in Sex, Gender and Politics* (London and New York: Routledge, 2000), 27–33.

28. Gayatri Chakravorty Spivak, "Can the Subaltern Speak?" in *Marxism and the Interpretation of Culture*, ed. Cary Nelson and Larry Grossberg (Urbana: University of Illinois Press, 1988), 271–313. For an introduction to the essay, see Moore, "Situating Spivak," in the present volume.

29. Mark Lewis Taylor, "Subalternity and Advocacy as *Kairos* for Theology," in *Opting for the Margins: Postmodernity and Liberation in Christian Theology*, ed. Joerg Rieger (Oxford: Oxford University Press, 2003), 23–45; Vítor Westhelle, "Margins Exposed: Representation, Hybridity and Transfiguration," in *Still at the Margins: Biblical Scholarship Fifteen Years after the Voices from the Margin*, ed. R. S. Sugirtharajah (New York: T. & T. Clark International, 2008), 69–87. See also Abraham, *Identity, Ethics, and Nonviolence in Postcolonial Theory*, 109–20.

30. Wonhee Anne Joh, *Heart of the Cross: A Postcolonial Christology* (Louisville, Ky.: Westminster John Knox, 2006); Sharon V. Betcher, *Spirit and the Politics of Disablement* (Minneapolis: Fortress Press, 2007); Mayra Rivera, *The Touch of Transcendence: A Postcolonial Theology of God* (Louisville, Ky.: Westminster John Knox, 2007).

31. Gayatri Chakravorty Spivak, "Imagination, Not Culture: A Singular Example," William James Lecture on Religious Experience, Harvard Divinity School, April 10, 2008.

SITUATING SPIVAK | STEPHEN D. MOORE

1. For an account of that arrival, see "A Tentative Topography of Postcolonial Theology," Rivera and Moore in the present volume.

2. Not that such a task can be adequately accomplished in a short introduction. See further Stephen Morton, *Gayatri Chakravorty Spivak*, Routledge Critical Thinkers (London and New York: Routledge, 2003); idem, *Gayatri Spivak: Ethics, Subalternity and the Critique of Postcolonial Reason* (Cambridge, UK: Polity Press, 2007); Mark Sanders, *Gayatri Chakravorty Spivak: Live Theory* (New York: Continuum, 2006); and Sangeeta Ray, *Gayatri Chakravorty Spivak: In Other Words* (Oxford: Wiley-Blackwell, 2009). Still essential reading, although now in need of updating, is Bart Moore-Gilbert, *Postcolonial Theory: Contexts, Practices, Politics* (London and New York: Verso, 1997), 74–113 (a chapter titled "Gayatri Spivak: The Deconstructive Twist"). Worth reading too is the chapter "Spivak Reading Derrida," in Michael Syrotinski, *Deconstruction and the Postcolonial: At*

the Limits of Theory (Liverpool, UK: Liverpool University Press, 2007), 40–61. Useful for other reasons, although also in need of updating, is *The Spivak Reader: Selected Works of Gayatri Chakravorty Spivak*, ed. Donna Landry and Gerald MacLean (London and New York: Routledge, 1995). Also worth consulting is "Gayatri Spivak's Influences: Past, Present, Future," *PMLA* 123, no. 1 (2008): 235–49, a special section of six short articles with a response from Spivak.

3. Jacques Derrida, *Of Grammatology*, trans. Gayatri Chakravorty Spivak (Baltimore: Johns Hopkins University Press, 1974), ix–lxxxix. Spivak's treatment of Derrida was considerably more comprehensive, for example, than that of Vincent Descombes in his *Le même et l'autre: Quarante-cinq ans de philosophie française (1933–1978)* (Paris: Editions de Minuit, 1979), where Derrida shares a chapter with Deleuze.

4. Jonathan Culler, *On Deconstruction: Theory and Criticism after Structuralism* (Ithaca, N.Y.: Cornell University Press, 1982); Christopher Norris, *Deconstruction: Theory and Practice* (London and New York: Methuen, 1982); Vincent B. Leitch, *Deconstructive Criticism: An Advanced Introduction* (New York: Columbia University Press, 1983).

5. Gayatri Chakravorty Spivak, *A Critique of Postcolonial Reason: Toward a History of the Vanishing Present* (Cambridge, Mass.: Harvard University Press, 1999), 423.

6. For a recent example, see Gayatri Chakravorty Spivak, "Learning from de Man: Looking Back," *boundary 2* 32, no. 3 (2005): 21–35. "The de Man affair" is the standard expression for the posthumous discovery of 170 literary articles written by de Man between 1940 and 1942 for a collaborationist newspaper in Nazi-occupied Belgium. One of the articles, on most readings, is explicitly anti-Semitic.

7. Gayatri Chakravorty Spivak, with Serene Jones, Catherine Keller, Kwok Pui-lan, and Stephen D. Moore, "Love: A Conversation," 64, in this volume.

8. Ibid. See Jacques Derrida, *Le toucher: Jean-Luc Nancy* (Paris: Galilée, 1999). In an earlier recounting of the anecdote, we learn what Derrida said in reply: "When I called myself a 'forme tachée' in the field of deconstruction he said, gently, '"tache" has another meaning. You are the task in the field of deconstruction.'" Gayatri Chakravorty Spivak, "Touched by Deconstruction," *Grey Room* 20 (Summer 2005): 95.

9. Gayatri Chakravorty Spivak, *In Other Worlds: Essays in Cultural Politics* (London and New York: Methuen, 1987; repr. London and New York: Routledge, 1988).

10. Sangeeta Ray, "An Ethics on the Run," *PMLA* 123, no. 1 (2008): 238, quoting Spivak, "Not Really a Properly Intellectual Response: An Interview with Gayatri Spivak," conducted by Tani E. Barlow, *Positions* 12, no. 1 (2004): 153.

11. Paul de Man, *Blindness and Insight: Essays in the Rhetoric of Contemporary Criticism* (Minneapolis: University of Minnesota Press, 1971), 136, referring specifically to Rousseau's text; but it is also a general claim he would never tire of making, albeit with variations, for the literature he most admired. Parallel claims could be cited from the work of Miller, Johnson, Shoshana Felman, and, after a certain point, Derrida himself.

12. Frank Lentricchia's *After the New Criticism* (Chicago: University of Chicago Press, 1980), in particular, contained a scathing critique of de Manian deconstruction as formalism (282-317). New Criticism had been the dominant mode of Anglo-American literary criticism from the late 1930s through the 1950s and was associated with a conception of the literary work as an autonomous, organic whole and a consequent rejection of "extrinsic" approaches to it, not least historical approaches.

13. Edward W. Said, *Orientalism* (New York: Vintage Books, 1978).

14. Ibid., 3; cf. 94. For Foucault, discourse is that which covertly conspires to produce that which it purports to describe. In place of an "enigmatic treasure of 'things' anterior to discourse," he posited "the regular formation of objects that emerge only in discourse" (Michel Foucault, *The Archaeology of Knowledge*, trans. Alan Sheridan [New York: Pantheon Books, 1972], 47).

15. See especially Frantz Fanon, *Black Skin, White Masks*, trans. Charles Lam Markmann (New York: Grove Press, 1967), 161 n. 25.

16. Not that Foucault has not also been an important interlocutor for Spivak at times; see most recently her *Other Asias* (Oxford: Blackwell, 2008), 132-60. Already in 1992, however, she had indicated that her appreciation of Foucault's work was increasing; see her "The Politics of Translation," in *Destabilizing Theory: Contemporary Feminist Debates*, ed. Michèle Barrett and Anne Phillips (Stanford, Calif.: Stanford University Press, 1992), 191-92. Meanwhile, Said's appreciation of Foucault's work had decreased; in *Culture and Imperialism* (New York: Knopf, 1993), for instance, Said takes Foucault to task for his "theoretical oversight" of "the imperial experience" (41; cf. 26-27).

17. Spivak, *A Critique of Postcolonial Reason*, xi.

18. See Rashmi Bhatnagar, "Seminars on Reading Marx," *PMLA* 123, no. 1 (2008): 236, commenting on Spivak.

19. Spivak et al., "Love," 63.

20. Even while thus engaged, Spivak has frequently insisted that her academic training was as a "Europeanist."

21. Bhatnagar, "Seminars on Reading Marx," 235. Spivak's signal statements on Marx have included: "Marx after Derrida," in *Philosophical Approaches to Literature: New Essays on Nineteenth- and Twentieth-Century Texts*, ed. William E.

Cain (Lewisburg, Penn.: Bucknell University Press, 1983), 227–46; "Scattered Speculations on the Question of Value," *Diacritics* 15, no. 4 (1985): 73–93; "Speculations on Reading Marx: After Reading Derrida," in *Post-Structuralism and the Question of History*, ed. Derek Attridge, Geoff Bennington, and Robert Young (Cambridge: Cambridge University Press, 1987), 30–62; "Limits and Openings of Marx in Derrida," in her *Outside in the Teaching Machine* (London and New York: Routledge, 1993), 97–120; "Ghostwriting," *Diacritics* 25, no. 2 (1995): 65–84; "Supplementing Marxism," in *Whither Marxism?* ed. Steven Cullenberg and Bernd Magnus (London and New York: Routledge, 1995), 109–19; and *A Critique of Postcolonial Reason*, 67–111.

22. Gayatri Chakravorty Spivak, "Feminism and Critical Theory," in *The Spivak Reader*, 57.

23. Gayatri Chakravorty Spivak, "The Rani of Sirmur: An Essay in Reading the Archives," *History and Theory* 24, no. 3 (1985): 247–72; "Subaltern Studies: Deconstructing Historiography," in *Subaltern Studies IV: Writings on South Asian History and Society*, ed. Ranajit Guha (New Delhi: Oxford University Press, 1985), 330–63; "Three Women's Texts and a Critique of Imperialism," *Critical Inquiry* 12, no. 1 (1985): 243–61; "Can the Subaltern Speak? Speculations on Widow Sacrifice," *Wedge* 7/8 (Winter/Spring 1985): 120–30. For "Scattered Speculations" see n. 21 above.

24. It reappeared in a much-expanded form, without its original subtitle, in *Marxism and the Interpretation of Culture*, ed. Cary Nelson and Larry Grossberg (Urbana: University of Illinois Press, 1988), 271–313. All citations below are from this version. A symposium to mark the twentieth anniversary of the essay, featuring a distinguished slate of speakers ranging from Toni Morrison to Homi Bhabha, was held at Columbia University in February 2004. The proceedings have been published as follows: Rosalind Morris, ed., *Can the Subaltern Speak? Reflections on the History of an Idea* (New York: Columbia University Press, 2010).

25. Spivak, "Can the Subaltern Speak?," 308. In the final version of the essay that is woven into her *Critique of Postcolonial Reason*, Spivak appears to withdraw her claim: "[I]n the first version of this text, I wrote, in the accents of passionate lament: the subaltern cannot speak! It was an inadvisable remark" (308 [somewhat eerily, the same page number as in the essay]).

26. See, for example, Ranajit Guha and Gayatri Chakravorty Spivak, eds., *Selected Subaltern Studies* (Oxford: Oxford University Press, 1988), which leads off with a reprint of Spivak's "Subaltern Studies: Deconstructing Historiography" (3–34).

27. Spivak uses the term "subaltern" in apposition with the terms "detritus" and "flotsam" in "A Literary Representation of the Subaltern," in her *In Other Worlds*, 245–46.

28. Spivak, *A Critique of Postcolonial Reason*, 309.

29. Spivak, *Other Asias*, 36. The historical moment in question is one "that has taken capital and empire as telos" (ibid.).

30. Spivak, *A Critique of Postcolonial Reason*, 310.

31. Gayatri Chakravorty Spivak, "The New Historicism: Political Commitment and the Postmodern Critic," in *The Post-Colonial Critic: Interviews, Strategies, Dialogues*, ed. Sarah Harasym (London and New York: Routledge, 1990), 158. Cf. Spivak, *Other Asias*, 27: "I hope it is clear that I have no interest in keeping the subaltern poor."

32. See further Spivak et al., "Love," 65, along with her "Extempore Response," also in the present volume.

33. Spivak, "Can the Subaltern Speak?" 287.

34. Ibid., 307–8. Those details resist easy summarization.

35. Srinivas Aravamudan, "The (Teleo)Poiesis of Singularity," *PMLA* 123, no. 1 (2008): 245, quoting Spivak, *Outside in the Teaching Machine*, 281.

36. Spivak's engagement with Devi was only beginning; see further, for example, Mahasweta Devi, *Imaginary Maps: Three Stories*, trans. and introduced by Gayatri Chakravorty Spivak (London and New York: Routledge, 1995); idem, *Breast Stories*, trans. and introduced by Gayatri Chakravorty Spivak (Calcutta: Seagull Books, 1997); and idem, *Chotti Munda and His Arrow*, trans. and introduced by Gayatri Chakravorty Spivak (Oxford: Blackwell, 2003).

37. Spivak, "French Feminism in an International Frame," 153.

38. If "Can the Subaltern Speak?" became Spivak's signature essay, "Three Women's Texts and a Critique of Imperialism" has been her most frequently reprinted essay (to date it has appeared in at least ten anthologies in English alone), and also, one suspects, her most frequently photocopied essay. It received an initial boost into prominence from the fact that the thematic issue of *Critical Inquiry* in which it first appeared (an issue published in monograph form the following year as *"Race," Writing, and Difference*, ed. Henry Louis Gates, Jr. [Chicago: University of Chicago Press, 1986]) quickly became emblematic of the politicization of poststructuralism then under way in U.S. literary studies.

39. Gayatri Chakravorty Spivak, "Imperialism and Sexual Difference," *Oxford Literary Review* 7, nos. 1/2 (1986): 225–40.

40. Gayatri Chakravorty Spivak, "Versions of the Margin: J. M. Coetzee's *Foe* Reading Defoe's *Crusoe/Roxana*," in *Consequences of Theory: Selected Papers of the English Institute, 1987–88*, ed. Jonathan Arac and Barbara Johnson (Baltimore: Johns Hopkins University Press, 1990), 154–80. Much of "Three Women's Texts" centers on Jean Rhys's *Wide Sargasso Sea* as a rereading of Charlotte Brontë's *Jane Eyre*.

41. Spivak, *In Other Worlds*, xxi.
42. Sangeeta Ray, "Shifting Subjects Shifting Ground: The Names and Spaces of the Postcolonial," *Hypatia* 7, no. 2 (1992): 191.
43. See Bill Ashcroft, Gareth Griffiths and Helen Tiffin, eds., *The Post-Colonial Studies Reader* (London and New York: Routledge, 1995); idem, *Key Concepts in Post-Colonial Studies* (London and New York: Routledge, 1998; reprinted in 2001 as *Post-Colonial Studies: The Key Concepts*); Ania Loomba, *Colonialism/Postcolonialism* (London and New York: Routledge, 1998); Ato Quayson, *Postcolonialism: Theory, Practice or Process?* (Cambridge: Polity Press, 2000); Robert J. C. Young, *Postcolonialism: An Historical Introduction* (Oxford: Blackwell, 2001); Bart Moore-Gilbert et al., eds., *Postcolonial Criticism* (London: Longman, 1997); Leela Gandhi, *Postcolonial Theory: A Critical Introduction* (New York: Columbia University Press, 1998); Moore-Gilbert, *Postcolonial Theory;* Patrick Williams and Laura Chrisman, eds., *Colonial Discourse and Postcolonial Theory* (New York: Columbia University Press, 1994); Peter Childs and Patrick Williams, *An Introduction to Post-Colonial Theory* (London and New York: Prentice Hall/Harvester Wheatsheaf, 1997); Mongia Padmini, ed., *Contemporary Postcolonial Theory: A Reader* (London: Arnold, 1996); John McLeod, *Beginning Postcolonialism* (Manchester: Manchester University Press, 2000); Robert J. C. Young, *Postcolonialism: A Very Short Introduction* (Oxford: Oxford University Press, 2003); Henry Schwarz and Sangeeta Ray, eds., *A Companion to Postcolonial Studies* (Oxford: Blackwell, 2000); John C. Hawley, ed., *Encyclopedia of Postcolonial Studies* (Westport, Conn.: Greenwood Press, 2001); Ian Adam and Helen Tiffin, eds., *Past the Last Post: Theorizing Post-Colonialism and Post-Modernism* (London and New York: Harvester Wheatsheaf, 1991); Fernando de Toro, Alfonso de Toro, and Kathleen Quinn, eds., *Borders and Margins: Post-Colonialism and Post-Modernism* (Frankfurt: Vervuert, 1995); Crystal Bartolovich and Neil Lazarus, eds., *Marxism, Modernity, and Postcolonial Studies* (Cambridge: Cambridge University Press, 2002); Reina Lewis and Sara Mills, eds., *Feminist Postcolonial Theory: A Reader* (Edinburgh: Edinburgh University Press, 2003); John C. Hawley, ed., *Postcolonial Queer: Theoretical Intersections* (Albany: State University of New York Press, 2001); Jan Campbell, *Arguing with the Phallus: Feminist, Queer and Postcolonial Theory* (New York: St. Martin's Press, 2000); Jeffrey Jerome Cohen, ed., *The Postcolonial Middle Ages* (New York: St. Martin's Press, 2000); R. S. Sugirtharajah, ed., *The Postcolonial Bible* (Sheffield: Sheffield Academic Press, 1998); Patricia M. Pelley, *Postcolonial Vietnam: New Histories of the National Past* (Durham, N.C.: Duke University Press, 2002); Clare Carroll and Patricia King, eds., *Ireland and Postcolonial Theory* (Notre Dame, Ind.: Notre Dame University

Press, 2003); C. Richard King, ed., *Postcolonial America* (Urbana and Chicago: University of Illinois Press, 2000); Jacques Haers, Norbert Hintersteiner, and Georges De Schrijver, *Postcolonial Europe in the Crucible of Cultures: Reckoning with God in a World of Conflicts* (Amsterdam and New York: Rodopi, 2007); Epifanio San Juan, Jr., *Beyond Postcolonial Theory* (New York: St. Martin's Press, 1998); Ania Loomba et al., eds., *Postcolonial Studies and Beyond* (Durham, N.C.: Duke University Press, 2005).

44. Robert J. C. Young, *Colonial Desire: Hybridity in Theory, Culture, and Race* (London and New York: Routledge, 1995), 163: "[I]t would be true to say that Said, Bhabha and Spivak constitute the Holy Trinity of colonial discourse analysis, and have to be acknowledged as central to the field."

45. Robert J. C. Young, *White Mythologies: Writing History and the West* (London and New York: Routledge, 1990), chaps. 7–9. Bart Moore-Gilbert followed Young's lead in his field-consolidating study *Postcolonial Theory* (see n. 2 above), centering the book even more determinedly on the Holy Trinity, as did Peter Childs and Patrick Williams in their *An Introduction to Post-Colonial Theory* (see note 43 above).

46. Gayatri Chakravorty Spivak, *Myself Must I Remake: The Life and Poetry of W. B. Yeats* (New York: Crowell, 1974).

47. The title Spivak originally had in mind for the book, however, was more querulous still: *Don't Call Me Postcolonial: From Kant to Kawakubo*. According to Michèle Barrett, Spivak "had to be restrained" from conferring that title on her work (Barrett, "Can the Subaltern Speak?" *History Workshop Journal* 58, no. 1 [2004]: 359).

48. Spivak, *A Critique of Postcolonial Reason*, 1.

49. Ibid, 360; see also 358.

50. Spivak, "The New Historicism," 164.

51. Spivak, *A Critique of Postcolonial Reason*, ix–x.

52. Ibid., x; cf. 359: "[O]ne woman teetering on the *socle mouvant* of the history of the vanishing present, running after 'culture' on the run, failure guaranteed." Further on this *socle mouvant* ("moving base/substrate"), a term she seems to have borrowed from Foucault, see Spivak, *Outside in the Teaching Machine*, 31.

53. Ibid., 3; see also 172.

54. Such is the case even when the era is other than contemporary. The East India Company, for instance, is styled "the first great transnational company before the fact" (220), and analyzed as such. In *Other Asias*, Spivak remarks of the East India Company's gradual standardization of Indian monetary currencies: "[W]e are on the way, however remotely, to globalization" (203).

55. Spivak, *A Critique of Postcolonial Reason*, xii.

56. Cf. Jacques Derrida, *Writing and Difference*, trans. Alan Bass (Chicago: University of Chicago Press, 1978), 280–81: "[W]e can pronounce not a single deconstructive proposition which has not already had to slip into the form, the logic, and the implicit postulations of precisely what it seeks to contest."

57. Spivak, *A Critique of Postcolonial Reason*, 357.

58. Ibid., xi, 200. All that being said, much of her direct engagement with globalization in the *Critique* occurs in footnotes, a point to which I shall return.

59. For the genesis of the term "postcolonial," see Ashcroft, Griffiths and Tiffin, eds., *Post-Colonial Studies*, 186. It appears to have been first employed in such expressions as "the post-colonial nation-state."

60. See Loomba et al., eds, *Postcolonial Studies and Beyond*.

61. Graham Huggan, "Postcolonialism, Globalization, and the Rise of (Trans)cultural Studies," in *Towards a Transcultural Future: Literature and Society in a "Post"-Colonial World*, ed. Geoffrey V. Davis, Peter H. Marsden, Bénédicte Ledent, and Marc Delrez (Amsterdam and New York: Rodopi, 2004), 32–33. The first issue of *Postcolonial Studies* carried an article by Simon During, an early advocate of the view that globalization has superseded postcolonialism as an analytic category. See During, "Postcolonialism and Globalisation: A Dialectical Relation after All?" *Postcolonial Studies* 1, no. 1 (1998): 31–47; and see further his "Postcolonialism and Globalisation: Towards a Historicization of Their Inter-Relation," *Cultural Studies* 14, nos. 3/4 (2000): 385–404.

62. Revathi Krishnaswamy and John C. Hawley, eds., *The Postcolonial and the Global* (Minneapolis: University of Minnesota Press, 2008).

63. Ibid., 106. All in all, Spivak plays a more effaced role in a related work released the following year—Sankaran Krishna, *Globalization and Postcolonialism: Hegemony and Resistance in the Twenty-First Century* (Lanham, Md.: Rowman & Littlefield, 2009). Krishna does discuss Spivak's work (see especially 98–105), but it is not clear that he sees it as being significantly engaged with globalization.

64. Gayatri Chakravorty Spivak, *Imperatives to Re-Imagine the Planet/Imperative zur Neuerfindung des Planeten*, ed. Willi Goetschel, trans. Bernhard Schweizer (Vienna: Passagen, 1999); idem, *Death of a Discipline*, The Wellek Library Lectures in Critical Theory (New York: Columbia University Press, 2003), 81. *Imperatives* is a dual-language transcription and translation of the Mary Levin Goldschmidt Bollag Memorial Lecture that Spivak delivered in Switzerland in 1997; and *Death* originated in the Wellek Library Lectures in Critical Theory that she delivered at the University of California, Irvine, in 2000. Spivak takes us behind the Swiss lecture in "Love," 61–63.

65. Spivak, *Death of a Discipline*, 72.

66. Quotation from Spivak et al., "Love," 61. What *is* more about "that"—i.e., ecological justice—is the absorbing two pages on ecology and religion in the *Critique of Postcolonial Reason* (382–83; cf. "Love," 55, 60–63). It is "nature," not "the planet," that is the theoretically torqued term in that brief discourse, begging the question of the precise relationship between the two in Spivak's thought. Setting her remarks on nature, ecology, and religion, on the one hand, into dialogue with her remarks on the planet and planetarity, on the other (which might well entail reading Spivak against Spivak), is unfortunately beyond the scope of this essay.

67. Gayatri Chakravorty Spivak, "Reply," *PMLA* 123, no. 1 (2008): 247.

68. Spivak, *Death of a Discipline*, 73; cf. idem, *Imperatives to Re-Imagine the Planet*, 46.

69. Cf. Revathi Krishnaswamy, "Postcolonial and Globalization Studies: Connections, Conflicts, Complicities," in *The Postcolonial and the Global*, ed. Krishnaswamy and Hawley, 2.

70. Spivak, *Death of a Discipline*, 37.

71. Jacques Derrida, *Glas*, trans. John P. Leavey Jr. and Richard Rand (Lincoln: University of Nebraska Press, 1986 [French original 1974]), 151a. Cf. Gayatri Chakravorty Spivak, "*Glas*-Piece: A Compte-Rendu," *Diacritics* 7, no. 3 (1977): 22–43.

72. Spivak, *Death of a Discipline*, 97; cf. ibid, 72: "When I invoke the planet, I think of the effort required to figure the (im)possibility of this underived intuition."

73. Ibid., 101–2; cf. Spivak, *A Critique of Postcolonial Reason*, 382–83.

74. Spivak, *A Critique of Postcolonial Reason*, x. Self-pigeonholing, however, is something that Spivak has never gone in for. Ambivalence thus reasserts itself by the end of the volume: "[T]ransnationality, a new buzzword for cultural studies" (412).

75. Spivak, *Death of a Discipline*, 81.

76. Ibid., 95.

77. Ibid., 85. Cf. Spivak, *Other Asias*, 25, and "Love," 65–66, for related statements.

78. Spivak, *A Critique of Postcolonial Reason*, x.

79. The first essay, "The Letter as Cutting Edge," which stems from 1977, is representative of the first four essays of the collection. French high theorist (Lacan) meets canonical English author (Coleridge) in Spivak's brilliant, beguiling musings. The essay has profound affinities with those of Barbara Johnson and Shoshana Felman from the same period. What sets it apart from Spivak's slightly later work is a lack of any triangulation of the French high theory–European literary canon coupling with a text from the Two-Thirds World. "In 1979–80, concerns of race and class were beginning to invade my mind," she tells us in "Feminism and Critical Theory" (84), the fifth essay in the volume.

80. This is less surprising in light of the fact that the seven essays from which *Other Asias* is constructed stem from 1992 to 2002, which means that most of them predate the lectures that were the source for *Imperatives to Re-Imagine the Planet* and *Death of a Discipline*.

81. Spivak, *A Critique of Postcolonial Reason*, x; cf. 359.

82. Globalization is also the central topic of Spivak's published dialogue with Judith Butler; see Judith Butler and Gayatri Chakravorty Spivak, *Who Sings the Nation-State? Language, Politics, Belonging* (Calcutta: Seagull Books, 2007).

83. The term "global cultural studies" seems to occur only twice in the book, however, and is used in passing in both instances (*Other Asias*, 106, 162).

84. Chapter 2 of *Other Asias*, for example, is titled "Responsibility—1992: Testing Theory in the Plains," and "offer[s] two readings, of Derrida's *Of Spirit*, and of a conference on the World Bank's Flood Action Plan in Bangladesh" (61), whereas chapter 5 is titled "Megacity—1997: Testing Theory in Cities." Chapter 3 asks "Will Postcolonialism Travel?"—to Armenia, and chapter 4 takes Foucault to Afghanistan.

85. Spivak, *Death of a Discipline*, 85.

86. Jacques Lacan, *Le Séminaire de Jacques Lacan; Livre XX: Encore (1972–1973)*, ed. Jacques-Alain Miller (Paris: Seuil, 1975), 114, translated and quoted in Spivak, "The Letter as Cutting Edge," in *In Other Worlds*, 14.

WHAT HAS LOVE TO DO WITH IT? PLANETARITY, FEMINISM, AND THEOLOGY | KWOK PUI-LAN

1. Kwok Pui-lan, *Discovering the Bible in the Non-Biblical World* (Maryknoll, N.Y.: Orbis Books, 1995), 71–83.

2. Kwok Pui-lan, "Jesus/the Native: Biblical Studies from a Postcolonial Perspective," in *Teaching the Bible: The Discourses and Politics of Biblical Pedagogy*, ed. Fernando F. Segovia and Mary Ann Tolbert (Maryknoll, N.Y.: Orbis Books, 1998), 69–85.

3. Kwok Pui-lan, "Unbinding Our Feet: Saving Brown Women and Feminist Religious Discourse," in *Postcolonialism, Feminism, and Religious Discourse*, ed. Laura E. Donaldson and Kwok Pui-lan (New York: Routledge, 2002), 62–81.

4. Gayatri Chakravorty Spivak, *A Critique of Postcolonial Reason: Toward a History of the Vanishing Present* (Cambridge, Mass.: Harvard University Press, 1999), ix–x.

5. Kwok Pui-lan, "Fishing the Asia Pacific: Transnationalism and Feminist Theology," in *Off the Menu: Asian and Asian North American Women's Religion and Theology*, ed. Rita Nakashima Brock et al. (Louisville, Ky.: Westminster John Knox Press, 2007), 3–22.

6. Colin MacCabe, Foreword to *In Other Worlds: Essays in Cultural Politics,* by Gayatri Chakravorty Spivak (New York: Routledge, 1987), ix.

7. Toni Morrison, *The Dancing Mind* (New York: Alfred A. Knopf, 1996).

8. Spivak, *Critique of Postcolonial Reason,* 382–83.

9. Ibid., 383.

10. Gayatri Chakravorty Spivak, *Death of a Discipline,* Wellek Library Lectures in Critical Theory (New York: Columbia University Press, 2003), 72.

11. Ibid.

12. Ibid., 84.

13. Ibid., 73.

14. Laura E. Donaldson, "Gospel Hauntings: The Postcolonial Demons of New Testament Criticism," in *Postcolonial Biblical Criticism: Interdisciplinary Intersections,* ed. Stephen D. Moore and Fernando F. Segovia (London: T. & T. Clark International, 2005), 100–101; Catherine Keller, "The Love Supplement: Christianity and Empire," in *God and Power: Counter-Apocalyptic Journeys,* by Catherine Keller (Minneapolis: Fortress Press, 2005), 126–32; Mayra Rivera, *The Touch of Transcendence: A Postcolonial Theology of God* (Louisville, Ky.: Westminster John Knox Press, 2007), 122–24.

15. Gordon D. Kaufman, *An Essay on Theological Method,* rev. ed. (Missoula, Mont.: Scholars Press, 1979), 13.

16. Spivak, *Death of a Discipline,* 92.

17. Tissa Balasuriya, *Planetary Theology* (Maryknoll, N.Y.: Orbis Books, 1984).

18. Spivak, *Critique of Postcolonial Reason,* 382 n. 96.

19. Ofelia Schutte, *Cultural Identity and Social Liberation in Latin American Thought* (Albany: State University of New York Press, 1993), 175–205.

20. Balasuriya was excommunicated in 1997 based on his book *Mary and Human Liberation,* but the excommunication order was lifted in 1998.

21. Gayatri Chakravorty Spivak, *Imaginary Maps: Three Stories by Mahasweta Devi* (New York: Routledge, 1995).

22. Gayatri Chakravorty Spivak, Afterword to *Imaginary Maps,* 199.

23. Ibid.

24. Aruna Gnanadason, *Listen to the Women! Listen to the Earth!* (Geneva: World Council of Churches, 2005), 1–9.

25. Ibid., 95–96.

26. Ibid., 100.

27. Karen Baker-Fletcher, "Dust and Spirit," in *Strike Terror No More: Theology, Ethics, and the New War,* ed. Jon L. Berquist (St. Louis: Chalice Press, 2002), 281.

28. Ibid., 284.

29. Karen Baker-Fletcher, *Dancing with God: The Trinity from a Womanist Perspective* (St. Louis: Chalice Press, 2006).

30. Spivak, *Death of a Discipline*, 72.

31. Gayatri Chakravorty Spivak, "A Moral Dilemma," in *What Happens to History? The Renewal of Ethics in Contemporary Thought*, ed. Howard Marchitello (New York: Routledge, 2001), 215, as quoted in Rivera, *The Touch of Transcendence*, 122, 129.

32. Balasuriya, *Planetary Theology*, 187–88.

33. Thich Nhat Hanh, *Interbeing: Fourteen Guidelines for Engaged Buddhism*, 3rd ed. (Berkeley, Calif.: Parallax, 1998).

34. Homi K. Bhabha, *The Location of Culture* (London: Routledge, 1994), 1–2, 37; Jonathan Rutherford, "The Third Space: Interview with Homi Bhabha," in *Identity, Community, Culture, Difference*, ed. Jonathan Rutherford (London: Lawrence & Wishart, 1990), 207–21.

35. Chang Tung-sun, "A Chinese Philosopher's Theory of Knowledge," trans. Li An-che, *Yenching Journal of Social Studies* 1 (1939): 169, 172.

36. See W. Anne Joh's essay in the present volume.

37. See Tang Kejing, *Shouwen jiezi jinshi* (Modern Commentary on *Shouwen jiezi*), (Changsha, China: Yuelu shushe, 1997), 2:1438–39. It is interesting to note that W. Anne Joh uses Julia Kristeva's maternal semiotic to illuminate the meaning of *jeong*, though she does not allude to the Chinese understanding of *jeong* as yin energy. See her *Heart of the Cross: A Postcolonial Christology* (Louisville, Ky.: Westminster John Knox Press, 2006), 109.

38. Li Qing-Zhao, "Tune: Slow, Slow Tune," in *100 Tang and Song Ci Poems*, ed. and trans. Xu Yuan-zhong (Hong Kong: Commercial Press., 1986), 149–51. I modified the translation of the final two lines. Spivak discusses Julia Kristeva's comments on this poem in "French Feminism in an International Frame," in *In Other Worlds: Essays in Cultural Politics* (New York: Routledge, 1988), 139.

39. Donna Landry and Gerald Maclean, Introduction to "Bonding in Difference: Interview with Alfred Arteaga," in *The Spivak Reader: Selected Works of Gayatri Chakravorty Spivak*, ed. Donna Landry and Gerald Maclean (New York: Routledge, 1996), 15–16.

40. Gayatri Chakravorty Spivak, "French Feminism Revisited," in *Outside in the Teaching Machine* (New York: Routledge, 1993), 144.

41. Gayatri Chakravorty Spivak, "Bonding in Difference: Interview with Alfred Arteaga," in *The Spivak Reader*, 28.

42. Spivak, "French Feminism in an International Frame," in *In Other Worlds*, 134–53.

43. Julia Kristeva, *About Chinese Women*, trans. Anita Barrows (New York: Urizen Books, 1977).

44. Spivak, "French Feminism in an International Frame," 150.

45. Spivak, *Death of a Discipline*, 73.

46. Gayatri Chakravorty Spivak, "Not Virgin Enough to Say That [S]he Occupies the Place of the Other," in *Outside in the Teaching Machine*, 175.

47. Spivak, "French Feminism Revisited," 141–69.

48. Ibid., 161.

49. It was first published as Gayatri Chakravorty Spivak, "Can the Subaltern Speak? Speculations on Widow-Sacrifice," *Wedge* 7, no. 8 (1985): 120–30. The longer version was reprinted in *Colonial Discourse and Post-Colonial Theory: A Reader*, ed. Patrick Williams and Laura Chrisman (Hemel Hempstead: Harvester Wheatsheaf, 1993), 66–111.

50. Gayatri Chakravorty Spivak, "The New Historicism: Political Commitment and the Postmodern Critic," in *The Post-Colonial Critic: Interviews, Strategies, Dialogues*, ed. Sarah Harasym (New York: Routledge, 1990), 158.

51. Miroslav Volf, *The End of Memory: Remembering Rightly in a Violent World* (Grand Rapids, Mich.: Eerdmans, 2006), 45.

52. Gayatri Chakravorty Spivak, "Subaltern Talk: Interview with the Editors," in *The Spivak Reader*, 290.

53. Spivak, *Critique of Postcolonial Reason*, 308.

54. Emilie M. Townes, *Breaking the Fine Rain of Death: African American Health Issues and a Womanist Ethics of Care* (New York: Continuum, 1998).

55. Spivak, "Can the Subaltern Speak?" 73.

56. See the criticism of Spivak on this point in Bart Moore-Gilbert, *Postcolonial Theory: Contexts, Practices, Politics* (London: Verso, 1997), 106–7.

57. Laurel C. Schneider, *Beyond Monotheism: A Theology of Multiplicity* (New York: Routledge, 2007), 173.

THE LOVE WE CANNOT NOT WANT: A RESPONSE TO KWOK PUI-LAN | LAUREL C. SCHNEIDER

1. Gayatri Chakravorty Spivak, *A Critique of Postcolonial Reason: Toward a History of the Vanishing Present* (Cambridge, Mass.: Harvard University Press, 1999), 383.

2. Gayatri Chakravorty Spivak, "Bonding in Difference: Interview with Alfred Arteaga," in *The Spivak Reader: Selected Works of Gayatri Chakravorty Spivak*, ed. Donna Landry and Gerald Maclean (New York: Routledge, 1996), 15–16.

3. James Baldwin, *The Fire Within* (New York: Dell, 1962), 128, quoted in Laurel C. Schneider, *Beyond Monotheism: A Theology of Multiplicity* (New York: Routledge, 2007), 238.

4. See Mayra Rivera, *The Touch of Transcendence: A Postcolonial Theology of God* (Louisville, Ky.: Westminster John Knox Press, 2007).

LOVE: A CONVERSATION | GAYATRI CHAKRAVORTY
SPIVAK, WITH SERENE JONES, CATHERINE KELLER, KWOK
PUI-LAN, AND STEPHEN D. MOORE

"Love" was Gayatri Chakravorty Spivak's own choice of title for the transcript
of this conversation.

1. Gayatri Chakravorty Spivak, *A Critique of Postcolonial Reason: Toward a History of the Vanishing Present* (Cambridge, Mass.: Harvard University Press, 1999), 383.

2. Ibid.

3. See Ellen T. Armour, "Planetary Sightings?" in this volume.

4. Spivak, *A Critique of Postcolonial Reason*, 382–83.

5. Alluding to Gayatri Chakravorty Spivak, *Outside in the Teaching Machine* (London and New York: Routledge, 1993), 34, which suggests that "power/knowledge," the inevitable translation of Foucault's *pouvoir/savoir*, "monumentalizes Foucault unnecessarily." Spivak finds it a "pity that there is no word in English corresponding to *pouvoir* as there is 'knowing' for *savoir*. *Pouvoir* is of course 'power.' But there is also a sense of 'can-do'-ness in *pouvoir*, if only because, in various conjugations, it is the commonest way of saying 'can' in the French language" (ibid.).

6. Rey Chow, *The Protestant Ethnic and the Spirit of Capitalism* (New York: Columbia University Press, 2002).

7. Laurel C. Schneider, *Beyond Monotheism: A Theology of Multiplicity* (London and New York: Routledge, 2007).

8. Catherine Keller, *The Face of the Deep: A Theology of Becoming* (London and New York: Routledge, 2003).

9. Gayatri Chakravorty Spivak, "Not Virgin Enough to Say That [S]he Occupies the Place of the Other," in her *Outside in the Teaching Machine*, 173.

10. The space in question was Craig Chapel at Drew Theological School, from which the main cross, which normally hangs suspended from the ceiling, had been removed to make the space more hospitable for the Transdisciplinary Theological Colloquium.

11. A lesser cross, overlooked in the light secularization of the space for the colloquium.

12. Gayatri Chakravorty Spivak, *Imperatives to Re-Imagine the Planet/Imperative zur Neuerfindung des Planeten*, ed. Willi Goetschel, trans. Bernhard Schweizer (Vienna: Passagen, 1999).

13. Jacques Derrida, *Le toucher: Jean-Luc Nancy* (Paris: Galilée, 2000); *On Touching—Jean-Luc Nancy*, trans. Christine Irizarry (Stanford, Calif.: Stanford University Press, 2005).

14. Gayatri Chakravorty Spivak, "French Feminism in an International Frame," *Yale French Studies* 62 (1981): 154–84.

15. Gayatri Chakravorty Spivak, "'Draupadi' by Mahasweta Devi," *Critical Inquiry* 7, no. 2 (1981): 381–402.

16. Mahasweta Devi, *Chotti Munda and His Arrow*, trans. and introduced by Gayatri Chakravorty Spivak (Oxford: Blackwell, 2003).

17. Gayatri Chakravorty Spivak, "Can the Subaltern Speak?" in *Marxism and the Interpretation of Culture*, ed. Cary Nelson and Larry Grossberg (Urbana: University of Illinois Press, 1988), 271–313.

18. Jacques Derrida, "Faith and Knowledge: The Two Sources of 'Religion' at the Limits of Reason Alone," in *Religion*, ed. Jacques Derrida and Gianni Vattimo, trans. David Webb et al. (Stanford, Calif.: Stanford University Press, 1998), 4.

19. Alain Badiou, *Saint Paul: The Foundation of Universalism*, trans. Ray Brassier (Stanford, Calif.: Stanford University Press, 2003).

20. Gayatri Chakravorty Spivak, "Three Women's Texts and a Critique of Imperialism," *Critical Inquiry* 12, no. 1 (1985): 243–61.

21. Homi K. Bhabha, *The Location of Culture* (London and New York: Routledge, 1994), 166 and passim.

22. Gayatri Chakravorty Spivak, "In a Word: Interview" (with Ellen Rooney), in her *Outside in the Teaching Machine*, 11.

23. Spivak, *A Critique of Postcolonial Reason*, 213.

24. Ibid., 211.

25. Ibid., 213.

26. Ibid., 216.

27. Gregory Bateson, *Steps to an Evolution of Mind: Collected Essays in Anthropology, Psychiatry, Evolution, and Epistemology* (Chicago: University of Chicago Press, 2000).

28. W. E. B. Du Bois, *The Souls of Black Folk* (1903; New York: Signet, 1995); Gayatri Chakravorty Spivak, *Death of a Discipline* (New York: Columbia University Press, 2003), 97–100.

29. Gayatri Chakravorty Spivak, "Righting Wrongs," *South Atlantic Quarterly* 103, no. 23 (2004): 523–81.

THE PTERODACTYL IN THE MARGINS: DETRANSCENDENTALIZING POSTCOLONIAL THEOLOGY | SUSAN ABRAHAM

1. Gayatri Chakravorty Spivak, "Moving Devi—1997: The Non-Resident and the Expatriate," in *Other Asias* (Malden, Mass., and Oxford: Blackwell, 2008),

175–208. She writes: "'Moving Devi,' read inattentively, may seem too 'religious.' . . . [I]t is an example of the effort to detranscendentalize the sacred, to move it towards imagination, away from belief, in which the secular humanities must forever engage" (10). In my view, Spivak's plea to "detranscendentalize" attempts to counter the specifically theological, that is, based in a system of beliefs without giving thought to the cultural, material, and interreligious frame in which beliefs (or nonbeliefs) are constructed. For Christian theologians, her word might signal a rather thin understanding of ontotheological commitments. Spivak is not a theologian, but her argument to move theology into a cultural and material plane has definite merits in the postcolonial context.

2. Spivak, *Other Asias*, 259.

3. Gayatri Chakravorty Spivak, *Death of a Discipline* (New York: Columbia University Press, 2003), 47. "Logofratrocentric" is Spivak's denunciative term for the sort of "democracy" based on legalism and masculinist privilege she is determined to deconstruct.

4. Pope Benedict XVI is following the late Pope John Paul II here: "In addition to the irrational destruction of the natural environment, we must also mention the more serious destruction of the *human environment,* something which is by no means receiving the attention it deserves. Although people are rightly worried—though much less than they should be—about preserving the natural habitats of the various animal species threatened with extinction, because they realize that each of these species makes its particular contribution to the balance of nature in general, too little effort is made to *safeguard the moral conditions for an authentic 'human ecology.'"* And again: "The first and fundamental structure for 'human ecology' is the family, in which man receives his first formative ideas about truth and goodness, and learns what it means to love and to be loved, and thus what it actually means to be a person. Here we mean the *family founded on marriage,* in which the mutual gift of self by husband and wife creates an environment in which children can be born and develop their potentialities, become aware of their dignity and prepare to face their unique and individual destiny. . . . It is necessary to go back to seeing the family as the *sanctuary of life.* The family is indeed sacred: it is the place in which life—the gift of God—can be properly welcomed and protected against the many attacks to which it is exposed, and can develop in accordance with what constitutes authentic human growth. In the face of the so-called culture of death, the family is the heart of the culture of life" (*Centesimus Annus,* 1991, 38, 39, original emphases).

5. Spivak, *Death of a Discipline,* 73.

6. Gayatri Chakravorty Spivak, Afterword to *Imaginary Maps: Three Stories* (New York and London: Routledge, 1995), 198.

7. In an interview by Robert Young, Spivak asserts that what goes by the name of "postcolonialism" in the liberal Western academy is "just totally bogus." "Neocolonialism and the Secret Agent of Knowledge," *Oxford Literary Review* 13, no. 1–2 (1991): 224.

8. Spivak, *Death of a Discipline*, 27.

9. Ibid., 81.

10. Ibid., 88.

11. Spivak, *Imaginary Maps*, 200.

12. Gayatri Chakravorty Spivak, *Outside in the Teaching Machine* (New York and London: Routledge, 1993), 61.

13. See Susan Abraham, "What Does Mumbai Have to Do with Rome? Postcolonial Perspectives on Globalization and Theology," *Theological Studies* 69 (June 2008): 386.

14. Spivak, *Outside in the Teaching Machine*, 63.

15. Ibid.

16. Elisabeth Schüssler Fiorenza, *The Power of the Word: Scripture and the Rhetoric of Empire* (Minneapolis: Fortress Press, 2007), 195. It might seem to some cultural and material feminists that simply speaking about transcendence and immanence sanctions and sustains the power of imperializing theological frameworks. For feminists working in the fields of comparative religion or theology, the words "immanence" and "transcendence" bear the significant weight of missionary Christianity. My argument is that detranscendentalizing theology, that is, advancing its discussion into the cultural, material and specifically interreligious frame, requires an active, deconstructive engagement with theological words and ideas in view of decolonizing theology.

17. Nancy Frankenberry, "Classical Theism, Panentheism, and Pantheism: On the Relation between God Construction and Gender Construction," *Zygon* 28, no. 1 (1993): 29–46.

18. Ibid., 30.

19. Ibid., 32.

20. Ibid., 29.

21. Sarah Coakley, "God and Evolution: A New Solution," *Harvard Divinity Bulletin* (Summer 2007): 8–13.

22. See Spivak's analysis of Kant's *Critique of Pure Reason* in *A Critique of Postcolonial Reason: Toward a History of the Vanishing Present* (Cambridge, Mass.: Harvard University Press), 38. She writes: "I always use the shocking 'he' when that is true to the spirit of the author. Kant's system cannot be made socio-sexually

just by pronominal piety, without violating the argument. This also reminds some of us, as we speculate about the ethics of sexual difference, that traditional European ethical philosophy simply disavows or benevolently naturalizes its sexual differentiation."

23. Elizabeth Johnson, *She Who Is: The Mystery of God in Feminist Theological Discourse* (New York: Crossroad, 1993), 104–20.

24. Ibid., 104.

25. Ibid., 229.

26. Ibid., 112.

27. Spivak, *Imaginary Maps*, 199.

28. Johnson, *She Who Is*, 114.

29. Ibid., 119–20.

30. Frankenberry, "Classical Theism, Panentheism, and Pantheism," 35.

31. Grace Jantzen, *Becoming Divine: Toward a Feminist Philosophy of Religion* (Bloomington and Indianapolis: Indiana University Press, 1999), 257.

32. Ibid., 260.

33. Ibid., 263.

34. Ibid., 269.

35. Spivak, *Other Asias*, 11.

36. Ibid.

37. Spivak, *Death of a Discipline*, 80.

38. Mahasweta Devi, "Pterodactyl, Puran Sahay and Pirtha," in *Imaginary Maps*, 155–56.

39. Spivak, Afterword to *Imaginary Maps*, 197.

40. Devi, "Pterodactyl, Puran Sahay and Pirtha," 196.

41. Ibid., 178, emphasis added.

42. Ibid., 97.

43. Ibid., 124.

44. Ibid., 146.

45. Ibid., 178.

46. Ibid.

47. Spivak, "Moving Devi," 179.

48. Spivak, *Death of a Discipline*, 73.

49. Spivak, "Moving Devi," 196.

50. Ibid., 208.

51. Jantzen, *Becoming Divine*, 271.

52. Johnson, *She Who Is*, 230.

53. Ibid., 231.

54. Devi, "Pterodactyl, Puran Sahay and Pirtha," 196.

LOST IN TRANSLATION? TRACING LINGUISTIC AND ECONOMIC TRANSACTIONS IN THREE TEXTS | TAT-SIONG BENNY LIEW

1. Gayatri Chakravorty Spivak, *Death of a Discipline* (New York: Columbia University Press, 2003), 72.

2. Gayatri Chakravorty Spivak, *A Critique of Postcolonial Reason: Toward a History of the Vanishing Present* (Cambridge, Mass.: Harvard University Press, 1999), 428. See also Spivak, *Death of a Discipline*, 71–102; and Swapan Chakravorty, Suzana Milevska, and Tani E. Barlow, *Conversations with Gayatri Chakravorty Spivak* (New York: Seagull, 2006), 30.

3. Spivak, *Critique of Postcolonial Reason*, 50.

4. Chakravorty, Milevska, and Barlow, *Conversations with Gayatri Chakravorty Spivak*, 30.

5. Karl Marx, *Capital: A Critique of Political Economy*, vol. 1: *The Process of Capitalist Production*, trans. Samuel Moore and Edward Aveling, ed. Frederick Engels (New York: International, 1967), 74.

6. Ferdinand de Saussure, *Course in General Linguistics*, trans. Wade Baskin, ed. Charles Bally and Albert Sechehaye (New York: Philosophical Library, 1959), 79.

7. David Damrosch, *What Is World Literature?* (Princeton, N.J.: Princeton University Press, 2003), 113.

8. Gayatri Chakravorty Spivak, "Three Women's Texts and a Critique of Imperialism," *Critical Inquiry* 12, no. 1 (1985): 243–61.

9. Mahasweta Devi, *Imaginary Maps: Three Stories*, trans. Gayatri Chakravorty Spivak (New York: Routledge, 1995); and Mahasweta Devi, *Breast Stories*, trans. Gayatri Chakravorty Spivak (Calcutta: Seagull, 1997).

10. Rodney Koeneke, *Empires of the Mind: I. A. Richards and Basic English in China, 1929–1979* (Stanford, Calif.: Stanford University Press, 2004), 2.

11. See, for example, Sarah J. Dille, *Mixing Metaphors: God as Mother and Father in Deutero-Isaiah* (New York: T. & T. Clark, 2004), 5; and Antje Labahn, "Fire from Above: Metaphors and Images of God's Actions in Lamentations 2.1–9," *Journal for the Study of the Old Testament* 31, no. 2 (2006): 241 n. 7.

12. I. A. Richards, *Science and Poetry* (London: Kegan Paul, Trench, Trubner, 1926), 82.

13. Ibid., 33; Richards, *Complementarities: Uncollected Essays*, ed. John Paul Russo (Cambridge, Mass.: Harvard University Press, 1976), 259; and Koeneke, *Empires of the Mind*, 2, 40–41.

14. Koeneke, *Empires of the Mind*, 1–2, 4.

15. Richards, *Complementarities*, 257.

16. Cited in Q. S. Tong, "The Bathos of a Universalism: I. A. Richards and His Basic English," in *Tokens of Exchange: The Problem of Translation in Global Circulations*, ed. Lydia H. Liu (Durham, N.C.: Duke University Press, 1999), 337.

17. C. K. Ogden and I. A. Richards, *The Meaning of Meaning: A Study of the Influence of Language upon Thought and of the Science of Symbolism* (New York: Harcourt, Brace Jovanovich, 1989), 17, 29.

18. I. A. Richards, *Nations and Peace* (New York: Simon and Schuster, 1947).

19. I. A. Richards, Introduction to *The Republic of Plato: A Version in Simplified English* (New York: W. W. Norton, 1942), 11.

20. Koeneke, *Empires of the Mind*, 24.

21. Edward Said, *Orientalism* (New York: Vintage, 1979), 254.

22. Koeneke, *Empires of the Mind*, 14.

23. I. A. Richards, "Basic English," *Fortune* 23 (June 1941): 90.

24. C. K. Ogden, *Basic English: International Second Language* (New York: Harcourt, Brace and World, 1968), 12.

25. Winston Churchill, *His Complete Speeches, 1897–1963*, 8 vols., ed. Robert Rhodes James (New York: Chelsea House, 1974), 7:6825.

26. Winston Churchill, *Onwards to Victory: War Speeches*, ed. Charles Eade (Boston: Little, Brown, 1944), 342; emphasis mine.

27. Bernard Faure, *Double Exposure: Cutting Across Buddhist and Western Discourses*, trans. Janet Lloyd (Stanford, Calif.: Stanford University Press, 2004), 96.

28. Gayatri Chakravorty Spivak, *Other Asias* (Malden, Mass.: Blackwell, 2008), 5; emphasis mine. See also 15–18.

29. Ibid., 23.

30. See, for instance, Gayatri Chakravorty Spivak, *Imperatives to Re-Imagine the Planet/Imperative zur Neuerfindung des Planeten*, ed. Willi Goetschel (Vienna: Passagen, 1999), 72; and Spivak, *Other Asias*, 25–33.

31. See Yunte Huang, *Transpacific Displacement: Intertextual Travel in Twentieth-Century American Literature* (Berkeley: University of California Press, 2002), 128–31.

32. Susan Stanford Friedman, "Unthinking Manifest Destiny: Muslim Modernities on Three Continents," in *Shades of the Planet: American Literature as World Literature*, ed. Wai Chee Dimock and Laurence Buell (Princeton, N.J.: Princeton University Press, 2007), 62–100. See also Spivak, *Death of a Discipline*, 82.

33. Stuart Hall, "Race, Articulation, and Societies Structured in Dominance," in *Black British Cultural Studies: A Reader*, ed. Houston A. Baker, Manthia Diawara, and Ruth H. Lindeborg (Chicago: University of Chicago Press, 1996), 16–60.

34. David Szanton, "Introduction: The Origin, Nature, and Challenges of Area Studies in the United States," in *The Politics of Knowledge: Area Studies and the*

Disciplines, ed. David Szanton (Berkeley: University of California Press, 2004), 24–25.

35. See, for example, Stuart Hall, "The Local and the Global: Globalization and Ethnicity," in *Culture, Globalization, and the World System*, ed. Anthony D. King (Minneapolis: University of Minnesota Press, 1997), 1–29; Arjun Appadurai, "Grassroots Globalization and the Research Imagination," in *Globalization*, ed. Arjun Appadurai (Durham, N.C.: Duke University Press, 2001), 1–21; Ranjana Khanna, *Dark Continents: Psychoanalysis and Colonialism* (Durham, N.C.: Duke University Press, 2003), 223, 228–29; and Homi K. Bhabha, "Global Minoritarian Culture," in *Shades of the Planet: American Literature as World Literature*, ed. Wai Chee Dimock and Lawrence Buell (Princeton, N.J.: Princeton University Press, 2007), 184–95.

36. Nicholas B. Dirks, "South Asian Studies: Futures Past," in *The Politics of Knowledge: Area Studies and the Disciplines*, ed. David Szanton (Berkeley: University of California Press, 2004), 378.

37. Spivak, *Other Asias*, 1.

38. Spivak, *Imperatives to Re-Imagine the Planet*, 50.

39. Emily S. Apter, *The Translation Zone: A New Comparative Literature* (Princeton, N.J.: Princeton University Press, 2006), 3.

40. Richards, *Basic in Teaching: East and West* (London: Kegan Paul, Trench, Trubner, 1935), 22–23.

41. Marc Shell, *Money, Language, and Thought: Literary and Philosophical Economies from the Medieval to the Modern Era* (Berkeley: University of California Press, 1982), 107.

42. Amitava Kumar, *World Bank Literature* (Minneapolis: University of Minnesota Press, 2002).

43. Spivak, *Critique of Postcolonial Reason*, xii.

44. Chakravorty, Milevska, and Barlow, *Conversations with Gayatri Chakravorty Spivak*, 62, 72–73.

45. For example, Addison G. Wright, "The Widow's Mites: Praise or Lament?—A Matter of Context," *Catholic Biblical Quarterly* 44, no. 2 (1982): 256–65; and Elizabeth Struthers Malbon, *In the Company of Jesus: Characters in Mark's Gospel* (Louisville, Ky.: Westminster John Knox, 2006), 166–88.

46. Robert G. Bratcher, *A Translator's Guide to the Gospel of Mark* (New York: United Bible Societies, 1981).

47. Gayatri Chakravorty Spivak, "The Politics of Translation," in *Destabilizing Theory: Contemporary Feminist Debates*, ed. Michèle Barrett and Anne Phillips (New York: Polity, 1992), 179.

48. Gayatri Chakravorty Spivak, "Can the Subaltern Speak?" in *Marxism and the Interpretation of Culture*, ed. Cary Nelson and Larry Grossberg (Urbana: University of Illinois Press, 1988), 296. See also Tat-siong Benny Liew, "Postcolonial

Criticism: Echoes of a Subaltern's Contribution and Exclusion," in *Mark and Method: New Approaches in Biblical Studies*, ed. Janice Capel Anderson and Stephen D. Moore, 2nd ed. (Minneapolis: Fortress, 2008), 224–30.

49. Spivak, *Death of a Discipline*, 77–78.

50. Walter Benjamin, *Illuminations*, trans. Harry Zohn, ed. Hannah Arendt (New York: Schocken, 1969), 74–80.

51. Spivak, *Critique of Postcolonial Reason*, 190.

52. King-kok Cheung, *Articulate Silences: Hisaye Yamamoto, Maxine Hong Kingston, Joy Kogawa* (Ithaca, N.Y.: Cornell University Press, 1993).

53. Wai Chee Dimock, "African, Caribbean, American: Black English as Creole Tongue," in *Shades of the Planet*, ed. Wai Chee Dimock and Lawrence Buell (Princeton, N.J.: Princeton University Press, 2007), 291.

54. Dawn Rae Davis, "(Love Is) The Ability of Not Knowing: Feminist Experience of the Impossible in Ethical Singularity," *Hypatia* 17, no. 2 (2002): 154.

55. Stephen J. Greenblatt, *Marvelous Possession: The Wonder of the New World* (Chicago: University of Chicago Press, 1991), 99.

56. Mary Louise Pratt, "The Traffic in Meaning: Translation, Contagion, Infiltration," *Profession* (2002): 34–35.

57. Ludwig Wittgenstein, *Lectures and Conversations on Aesthetics, Psychology, and Religious Belief*, ed. Cyril Barrett (Berkeley: University of California Press, 1967), 11.

58. Franz Boas, "The Aims of Ethnology," in *Race, Language, and Culture* (New York: Free Press, 1940), 631. See also Dimock, "African, Caribbean, American."

59. Michael North, "Ken Saro-wiwa's *Sozaboy*: The Politics of 'Rotten English,'" *Public Culture* 13, no. 1 (2001): 97–112.

60. Evelyn Nien-Ming Ch'ien, *Weird English* (Cambridge, Mass.: Harvard University Press, 2004).

61. Apter, *Translation Zone*, 147.

62. Khanna, *Dark Continents*, 164.

63. Gilles Deleuze and Felix Guattari, *On the Line*, trans. John Johnston (New York: Semiotext[e], 1983), 1–68.

64. Fatima Mernissi, *Dreams of Trespass: Tales of a Harem Girlhood* (New York: Perseus, 1994), 15.

65. Ch'ien, *Weird English*, 137. See also Brent Hayes Edwards, *The Practice of Diaspora: Literature, Translation, and the Rise of Black Internationalism* (Cambridge, Mass.: Harvard University Press, 2003), 21–22.

66. Spivak, *Critique of Postcolonial Reason*, 384.

67. Derrida, *Of Spirit: Heidegger and the Question*, trans. Geoffrey Bennington and Rachel Bowlby (Chicago: University of Chicago Press, 1989), 109.

68. Apter, *Translation Zone*, 9.

69. Peter Hallward, *Absolutely Postcolonial: Writing between the Singular and the Specific* (Manchester: Manchester University Press, 2001). See also Friedrich Schleiermacher, *On Religion: Speeches to Its Cultured Despisers*, trans. Richard Crouter (Cambridge: Cambridge University Press, 1996), 18–54.

70. Spivak, *Other Asias*, 10, 21, 178.

71. Spivak, *Death of a Discipline*, 73; emphasis mine. See also Spivak, *Imperatives to Re-Imagine the Planet*, 46.

72. Spivak, Afterword to *Imaginary Maps*, by Devi, 199.

73. Mayra Rivera, *The Touch of Transcendence: A Postcolonial Theology of God* (Louisville: Westminster John Knox, 2007).

74. Spivak, *Imperatives to Re-Imagine the Planet*, 44, 56; and Spivak, *Death of a Discipline*, 71–102.

75. Spivak, *Imperatives to Re-Imagine the Planet*, 44; and Spivak, *Other Asias*, 57.

76. Tzvetan Todorov, *The Poetics of Prose*, trans. Richard Howard (Ithaca, N.Y.: Cornell University Press, 1977), 189.

77. Spivak, *Death of a Discipline*, 72.

78. Spivak, *Critique of Postcolonial Reason*, 383. See also Spivak, *Other Asias*, 2.

79. Spivak, *Critique of Postcolonial Reason*, 116. See also Catherine Keller, *God and Power: Counter-Apocalyptic Journeys* (Minneapolis: Fortress, 2005), 113–34.

80. Gayatri Chakravorty Spivak, "Setting to Work (Transnational Cultural Studies)," in *A Critical Sense: Interviews with Intellectuals*, ed. Peter Osborne (New York: Routledge, 1996), 166.

81. Spivak, *Critique of Postcolonial Reason*, 153.

82. See also Davis, "(Love Is) The Ability of Not Knowing."

83. Apter, *Translation Zone*, 8.

84. Spivak, *Critique of Postcolonial Reason*, 427–28; Spivak, *Imperatives to Re-Imagine the Planet*, 84.

85. Davis, "(Love Is) The Ability of Not Knowing," 156–57.

86. Julia Kristeva, *Powers of Horror: An Essay on Abjection*, trans. Leon S. Roudiez (New York: Columbia University Press, 1982).

87. Gayatri Chakravorty Spivak, *The Post-Colonial Critic: Interviews, Strategies, Dialogues*, ed. Sarah Harasym (New York: Routledge, 1990), 50–58.

88. Jonathan Arac, "Global and Babel: Language and Planet in American Literature," in *Shades of the Planet*, ed. Wai Chee Dimock and Lawrence Buell (Princeton, N.J.: Princeton University Press, 2007), 30.

89. Jacques Derrida, *Monolingualism of the Other, or, The Prosthesis of Origin*, trans. Patrick Mensah (Stanford, Calif.: Stanford University Press, 1998), 65.

90. Rey Chow, "In the Name of Comparative Literature," in *Comparative Literature in the Age of Multiculturalism*, ed. Charles Bernheimer (Baltimore: Johns Hopkins University Press, 1995), 107–16.

91. Lawrence Venuti, *The Translator's Invisibility: A History of Translation* (New York: Routledge, 1995), 1.
92. Spivak, *Death of a Discipline*, 82.
93. Ibid., 97.
94. Robert Gooding-Williams, *Look, A Negro! Philosophical Essays on Race, Culture, and Politics* (New York: Routledge, 2006), 107–8.
95. Spivak, *Death of a Discipline*, 74; emphasis mine.
96. David Kyuman Kim, *Melancholic Freedom: Agency and the Spirit of Politics* (New York: Oxford University Press, 2007), 77.
97. Jacques Derrida, *Demeure: Fiction and Testimony*, trans. Elizabeth Rottenberg (Stanford, Calif.: Stanford University Press, 2000), 31.
98. Spivak, *Critique of Postcolonial Reason*, 5.
99. Spivak, Afterword to *Imaginary Maps*, by Devi, 201.
100. Spivak, *Imperatives to Re-Imagine the Planet*, 86.

GHOSTLY ENCOUNTERS: SPIRITS, MEMORY, AND THE HOLY GHOST | MAYRA RIVERA

The epigraph poem is "The Comforter," by Donald Davie, from *Collected Poems* (Chicago: University of Chicago Press, 1991), 412–13. My thanks to Joe Driskill for sharing this poem with me.

1. Sandra Cisneros commented in a lecture in 1986, "If I were asked what it is I write about I would have to say I write about those ghosts inside that haunt me, that will not let me sleep, of that which even memory does not like to mention." Sandra Cisneros, "Ghosts and Voices: Writing from Obsession," *Americas Review* 15, no. 1 (1987): 73.
2. Allende claims to have had no empirical knowledge of the mass grave at a mine in Chile that she describes in *Of Love and Shadows* until long after the novel was published, when the priest who had discovered the site asked her how she had found out about it. She explains: "The dead told me, I replied, but he did not believe me." Isabel Allende, *Paula: A Memoir*, trans. Margaret Sayers Peden (New York: HarperCollins Publishers, 1996), 284–85.
3. Translation is a central part of the story of this character, to be sure, but what would traditioning entail if not the accumulation of marks of such translations and displacements?
4. For instance, in a recent and invaluable eco-pneumatology, Mark Wallace laments the "mistaken" translation of the Hebrew and Greek terms (*ruach* and *pneuma*) as "Holy Ghost" rather than "Holy Spirit." "The Spirit is to be understood as God's visible and benevolent power in the cosmos, not a spook or a ghost," he argues. "The Spirit is not a heavenly phantom," he protests

(Mark I. Wallace, *Finding God in the Singing River: Christianity, Spirit, Nature* [Minneapolis: Fortress Press, 2005], 7). Stephen D. Moore adds a key element to this discussion: "for Anglophone mainline Protestants the term 'Holy Ghost' tends to conjure up Pentecostals and other biblical literalists clutching their King James Bibles in which the archaic translation 'Holy Ghost' is forever enshrined. There's a class element in play here, in other words" (personal communication).

5. David L. Miller, *Hells and Holy Ghosts: A Theopoetics of Christian Belief* (New Orleans: Spring Journal Books, 2004), 111.

6. For Augustine, for instance, the Spirit is love itself, the bond of intertrinitarian relationships (*De Trinitate*).

7. For a comprehensive survey of images of the Holy Spirit in both testaments see Michael Welker, *God the Spirit: A Theology of the Holy Spirit*, trans. John F. Hoffmeyer (Minneapolis: Augsburg Fortress, 2004).

8. I borrow this phrase from Richard Rodriguez, *Hunger of Memory: The Education of Richard Rodriguez* (Boston: David R. Godine, 1982).

9. Friedrich Nietzsche, *Thus Spoke Zarathustra*, in *The Portable Nietzsche* (New York: Viking Penguin, 1977), 251–52.

10. Andreas Huyssen, *Present Pasts: Urban Palimpsest and the Politics of Memory* (Stanford, Calif.: Stanford University Press, 2003), 6.

11. Gayatri Chakravorty Spivak, "Extempore Response," in the present volume.

12. W. G. Sebald, *Austerlitz* (Munich: Hanser, 2001), 24, quoted in Huyssen, *Present Pasts*, xiii.

13. Gayatri Chakravorty Spivak, *A Critique of Postcolonial Reason: Toward a History of the Vanishing Present* (Cambridge, Mass., and London: Harvard University Press, 1999), 203.

14. Ibid.

15. Ibid.

16. Ibid.

17. Thus, Spivak resists descriptions of the historical tasks that rely on metaphors like the psychoanalytic transference, attractive as they may seem, because they place the critic/scholar in the position of the analyst, given the "sanctioned authority" to effect the "cure" (ibid., 207).

18. Gayatri Chakravorty Spivak, "Ghostwriting," *Diacritics* 25, no. 2 (1995): 70. Spivak further explains: "Cultural memory is a privatization of history and it happens with an insistent collective rememoration 'this really happened, this really happened'; one can be deeply suspicious of cultural memory" (Gayatri Chakravorty Spivak, "More Thoughts on Cultural Translation," *Translate.epicp .net*, 2008).

19. Spivak, "Ghostwriting," 70.

20. Spivak, *Critique of Postcolonial Reason*, 207.

21. Spivak, "Ghostwriting," 66.

22. Kathleen Brogan, *Cultural Haunting: Ghosts and Ethnicity in Recent American Literature* (Charlottesville and London: University Press of Virginia, 1998), 9.

23. Ibid.

24. For an affirmative theological reading of spirit possession as a way in which ancestors participate in the present, see Monica A. Coleman, *Making a Way Out of No Way: A Womanist Theology* (Minneapolis: Augsburg Fortress, 2008), 101–23.

25. Assia Djebar, "The Dead Speak," in *Women of Algiers in Their Apartment* (Charlottesville and London: University of Virginia Press, 1992), 79.

26. Huyssen, *Present Pasts*, 9.

27. Spivak, "Ghostwriting," 79.

28. Gayatri Chakravorty Spivak, *Death of a Discipline* (New York: Columbia University Press, 2003), 39–46, 91–100; Spivak, "Ghostwriting."

29. Spivak, "Ghostwriting," 71.

30. Ibid., 79, 71. Spivak further insists that the structure of haunting does not even depend on whether the ancestors are real or imagined.

31. Jacques Derrida, *Specters of Marx: The State of Debt, the Work of Mourning, and the New International*, trans. Peggy Kamuf (New York and London: Routledge, 1994).

32. Peter Stuhlmacher, "Spiritual Remembering: John 14:26," in *The Holy Spirit in Christian Origins: Essays in Honor of James D. G. Dunn*, ed. Graham N. Stanton, Bruce W. Longenecker, and Stephen C. Barton (Grand Rapids, Mich., and Cambridge, UK: William B. Eerdmans, 2004). "Certainly, all Gospels were written from the perspective of hindsight, but John is the only evangelist expressly to thematize this viewpoint" (Udo Schnelle, quoted in Stuhlmacher, "Spiritual Remembering," 61).

33. Tat-siong Benny Liew, "The Word of Bare Life: Workings of Death and Dream in the Fourth Gospel," in *Anatomies of Narrative Criticism: The Past, Present, and Futures of the Fourth Gospel as Literature*, ed. Tom Thatcher and Stephen D. Moore (Atlanta: Society of Biblical Literature, 2008), 167–94.

34. Kiran Desai, *The Inheritance of Loss* (New York: Atlantic Monthly Press, 2006).

35. The only other use of the word *parakletos* in the New Testament is in 1 John 2:1: "[W]e have a Paraclete with the Father, Jesus Christ the righteous."

36. The term "postresurrection," commonly used to describe these sections of the Jesus story, seems to occlude the spectrality that I seek to foreground in this reading, placing Jesus decisively beyond, rather than in-between, life and death.

I retain the term here (in quotation marks) only to reflect the scholarly convention.

37. Gail R. O'Day, "'I Have Overcome the World' (John 16:33): Narrative Time in John 13–17," *Semeia* 53 (1991): 153, 157.

38. It is also, from the beginning, an announcement of impending death as soon as it names Jesus the "lamb of God," as Tat-siong Benny Liew observes. Indeed, Liew argues that John's Gospel is intensely concerned with, if not obsessed by, death—a mark of the colonial context in which it was produced, but also of the text's "desire to get out of the 'death zone'" (Liew, "Word of Bare Life," 179–80).

39. These details suggest parallels in form between John's story of these ghostly encounters and the tale of the grateful dead. See Miller, *Hells and Holy Ghosts*, 140.

40. Derrida, *Specters of Marx*, 9.

41. Ibid.

42. Nietzsche, *Thus Spoke Zarathustra*, 251–52.

43. Raymond E. Brown, *The Gospel According to John I–XII* (New York: Doubleday, 1966), 1002.

44. Fredric Jameson, "Marx's Purloined Letter," in *Ghostly Demarcations: A Symposium on Jacques Derrida's Specters of Marx*, ed. Michael Sprinker (London and New York: Verso, 2008), 43.

45. Jean-Luc Nancy, *Noli me tangere: On the Raising of the Body*, trans. Sarah Clift, Pascale-Anne Brault, and Michael Naas; Perspectives in Continental Philosophy (New York: Fordham University Press, 2008), 27–30.

46. Derrida, *Specters of Marx*, 6.

47. Karmen MacKendrick, *Word Made Skin: Figuring Language at the Surface of Flesh* (New York: Fordham University Press, 2004), 29.

48. Ibid., 44, 47.

49. Spivak, "Ghostwriting," 78.

50. Derrida, *Specters of Marx*, 6.

51. Avery F. Gordon, *Ghostly Matters: Haunting and the Sociological Imagination* (Minneapolis and London: University of Minnesota Press, 1997), 8.

52. Liew, "Word of Bare Life," 191.

53. Johann Baptist Metz, *Faith in History and Society: Toward a Practical Fundamental Theology*, trans. J. Mathew Ashley (New York: Herder & Herder, 2007), 105.

54. Ibid. On the importance of dangerous memories for liberation theologies, see Sharon D. Welch, *Communities of Resistance and Solidarity: A Feminist Theology of Liberation* (Maryknoll, N.Y.: Orbis Books, 1985), 32–54.

55. Metz, *Faith in History and Society*, 105.

56. Ibid., 101.

57. Ibid., 105; my italics.

58. However, like some of the Marxist utopianisms with which they danced, the founding fathers of Latin American liberation theology often dreamt of, "announced and called for a presence to come"—fully, without specters (Derrida, *Specters of Marx*, 101). The controversy around utopianism in liberation theology is well known, and still controversial. Ivan Petrella's recent manifesto faults Metz for lacking a specific program, reacting against Metz's insistence that *memoria passionis* rejects any attempt by any subject, nation, or race to "define itself as this subject [of divine will]" (Ivan Petrella, *The Future of Liberation Theology: An Argument and Manifesto* [Aldershot-Hampshire: Ashgate, 2004], 127–28).

59. Metz's conceptualizations of time and memory are deeply influenced by Walter Benjamin's work. Cf. Steven T. Ostovich, "Epilogue: Dangerous Memories," in *The Work of Memory: New Directions in the Study of German Society and Culture,* ed. Alon Confino and Peter Fritzsche (Urbana: University of Illinois Press, 2002), 239–56.

60. Metz, *Faith in History*, 109.

61. Gayatri Chakravorty Spivak, "Touched by Deconstruction," *Grey Room* 20 (Summer 2005): 99.

62. For a recent depiction of theological narrative (of Exodus and Christ's passion) as "regulative memories," see Miroslav Volf, *The End of Memory: Remembering Rightly in a Violent World* (Grand Rapids, Mich.: William B. Eerdmans, 2006).

63. Metz, *Faith in History*, 109f.; my italics.

64. Spivak, "Ghostwriting," 79.

65. See Susan Abraham, *Identity, Ethics, and Nonviolence in Postcolonial Theory: A Rahnerian Theological Assessment* (New York: Palgrave Macmillan, 2007), 30–38.

66. Liew, "Word of Bare Life."

67. Kwok Pui-lan, *Postcolonial Imagination and Feminist Theology* (Louisville, Ky.: Westminster John Knox, 2005), 37. As Elisabeth Schüssler Fiorenza puts it: "History is best figured not as an accurate record or transcript of the past but as a perspectival discourse that seeks to articulate a living memory for the present and the future" (*In Memory of Her: A Feminist Theological Reconstruction of Christian Origins* [New York: Crossroad, 1994], xxii).

68. Spivak, "Ghostwriting," 82.

69. Metz, *Faith in History*, 109.

70. Gayatri Chakravorty Spivak, "'The Slightness of My Endeavor': An Interview with Gayatri Chakravorty Spivak," *Comparative Literature* 57, no. 3 (2005): 259.

71. Spivak, "Ghostwriting," 70. The call to be haunted by forgotten possibilities is beautifully illustrated by Spivak's reading of Virginia Woolf (and of José Martí) in Spivak, *Death of a Discipline*.

72. Spivak, "The Slightness of My Endeavor," 259.

73. Marcella Althaus-Reid, "Feetishism: The Scent of a Latin American Body Theology," in *Toward a Theology of Eros: Transfiguring Passion at the Limits of Discipline*, ed. Virginia Burrus and Catherine Keller (New York: Fordham University Press, 2006), 144.

74. John D. Caputo has proposed a hauntological hermeneutics based on the secret, the "solemn silence," that characterizes both the dead and God. The secret, he argues, "takes up residence" in this excess. But for Caputo the spectral qualities that I have been tracing here belong to "another ghost" who disturbs the Holy Ghost. Thus he follows the Derridean model, seeking to identify a messianic structure that troubles concrete messianisms, leading him to assert that "the messianic specter disturbs the concrete messianisms with the spectral thought that they are a historical garment" (John D. Caputo, "Hauntological Hermeneutics and the Interpretation of Christian Faith: On Being Dead Equal before God," in *Hermeneutics at the Crossroads*, ed. Kevin J. Vanhoozer, James K. A. Smith, and Bruce Ellis Benson [Bloomington and Indianapolis: Indiana University Press, 2006], 103). I'd like to avoid establishing a separation between the messianic and its "historical garment" that could lead to imagining an ahistorical Spirit. It is evidently not Caputo's intention to establish that division, as he clarifies in the text, but his insistence that we are all "dead equal before God or death" (99) seems to reinscribe the classical distinction between the plurality of history and the uniformity of the divine. I am grateful to Marion Grau for alerting me to this text.

75. Liew, "Word of Bare Life," 192.

76. Spivak, "Extempore Response," in the present volume.

77. Reading process theology though the African religious sensibilities of womanist theologies, Monica Coleman develops a metaphysical framework for the possibility of ancestral immortality and memory. In process metaphysics, each entity becomes, at each moment, in relation to past becomings, embracing or rejecting elements of the past. The past leaves its traces on the new—even if the past is negatively incorporated. Process theology further asserts that as entities pass away, their objective existence is immortalized in God. "When a human being dies," Coleman suggests, "she becomes an ancestor. Inside the being of God, this ancestor has actuality. . . . [T]he ancestor can be said to 'commune' with other ancestors" (*Making a Way Out of No Way*, 117). As past

experiences become part of Godself, they also become part of the present through God's relation to it, to the extent that the present opens itself to it. In this view, the ancestors' activity becomes part of divine agency to which the present can relate. Through ritual practices persons may "position themselves 'to hear the voices'" of particular ancestors. In this reading of ancestral agency, the divine is an agent of memory where nothing is lost (119).

78. Spivak, "Ghostwriting," 67.

EXTEMPORE RESPONSE TO SUSAN ABRAHAM, TAT-SIONG BENNY LIEW, AND MAYRA RIVERA | GAYATRI CHAKRAVORTY SPIVAK

1. Ngugi wa Thiong'o, *Decolonizing the Mind: The Politics of Language in African Literature* (London: J. Currey, 1986).

2. Jacques Derrida, *The Politics of Friendship*, trans. George Collins (London: Verso, 2005).

3. Gayatri Chakravorty Spivak, Afterword to *Imaginary Maps*, by Mahasweta Devi, trans. Gayatri Chakravorty Spivak (London and New York: Routledge, 1995).

4. William Shakespeare, *Henry IV*, Part I, 3.1.2:
Glendower: I can call spirits from the vasty deep.
Hotspur: Why, so can I, or so can any man;
But will they come when you do call for them?

5. Located in Brooklyn, the college is named after Medgar Wiley Evers, the slain African American civil rights leader. Professor Spivak was honored by the college on November 5, 2007.

6. Jacques Derrida, *Spectres de Marx: l'état de la dette, le travail du deuil et la nouvelle Internationale* (Paris: Editions Galilée, 1993); *Specters of Marx: The State of the Debt, the Work of Mourning, and the New International*, trans. Peggy Kamuf (London and New York: Routledge, 1994).

7. William Shakespeare, *Hamlet*, 1.1.42.

8. Derrida, *Spectres de Marx*, 225.

9. Gayatri Chakravorty Spivak, "The New Historicism: Political Commitment and the Postmodern Critic," in *The Post-Colonial Critic: Interviews, Strategies, Dialogues*, ed. Sarah Harasym (London and New York: Routledge, 1990), 158.

PLANETARY SUBJECTS AFTER THE DEATH OF GEOGRAPHY | JENNA TIITSMAN

1. Rama Lakshmi, "India Call Centers Suffer Storm of 4-Letter Words, Executives Blame American Anger Over Outsourcing," *Washington Post*, February 27, 2005, A22.

2. President James Buchanan to Queen Victoria, 16 August 1858, in Henry Martyn Field, *History of the Atlantic Telegraph* (London: Sampson Low, Son & Marston, 1866).

3. For discussion of the representation of South Asian religions in European narratives of religious origins, see Richard King, *Orientalism and Religion: Postcolonial Theory, India and "the Mystic East"* (New York: Routledge, 1999), and Tomoko Masuzawa, *The Invention of World Religions* (Chicago: University of Chicago Press, 2005).

4. For more on this definition of postmodernism, see Fredric Jameson, *Postmodernism, or, The Cultural Logic of Late Capitalism* (Durham, N.C.: Duke University Press, 1991).

5. Gayatri Chakravorty Spivak, *Death of a Discipline* (New York: Columbia University Press, 2005), 72.

6. Gayatri Chakravorty Spivak, *Imperatives to Re-Imagine the Planet/Imperative zur Neuerfindung des Planeten*, ed. Willi Goetschel (Vienna: Passagen, 1999), 46.

7. Ibid.

8. Thomas Tweed, *Crossing and Dwelling: A Theory of Religion* (Cambridge, Mass.: Harvard University Press: 2006), 133.

9. Spivak, *Imperatives to Re-Imagine the Planet*, 46.

10. Ibid., 36.

11. Randall Styers, *Making Magic: Religion, Magic, and Science in the Modern World* (New York: Oxford University Press, 2004), 17.

12. See Bruno Latour, *We Have Never Been Modern*, trans. Catherine Porter (Cambridge, Mass.: Harvard University Press, 1993).

13. Jonathan Z. Smith, "Religion, Religions, Religious," in *Critical Terms for Religious Studies*, ed. Mark C. Taylor (Chicago: University of Chicago Press, 1998), 269.

14. Ibid., 271.

15. Styers, *Making Magic*, 5.

16. Herbert of Cherbury, *De Veritate*, trans. Meyrick H. Carré (1625; Bristol: University of Bristol, 1937).

17. Ibid., 291.

18. David Hume, *Dialogues and Natural History of Religion*, ed. J. C. A. Gaskin (1757; New York: Oxford University Press, 1993), 141–42. For further discussion of Hume's role in the development of the category of religion, see Smith, "Religion, Religions, Religious," 273–74.

19. Marcel Mauss, *The Gift: The Form and Reason for Exchange in Archaic Societies*, trans. W. D. Halls (1923–24; New York: Routledge, 2002), and Edward Tylor, *Primitive Culture* (1871; New York: J. P. Putnam's Sons, 1920).

20. Robert R. Marett, *The Threshold of Religion* (1900; New York: Kessinger, 2004).

21. Styers, *Making Magic*, 98–104.

22. Bryan Wilson, *Religion in Sociological Perspective* (Oxford: Oxford University Press, 1982), 171–74, cited in Styers, *Making Magic*, 101–2.

23. Styers, *Making Magic*, 102.

24. Jeffrey Sachs, *The End of Poverty: Economic Possibility for Our Time* (New York: Penguin Books, 2005), 5–25.

25. Ibid., 41.

26. Ibid., 50.

27. Thomas L. Friedman, *The World Is Flat: A Brief History of the Twenty-First Century* (New York: Farrar, Straus and Giroux, 2005), 10.

28. Spivak, *Death of a Discipline*, 72.

29. Ibid.

30. Ibid.

31. Spivak, *Imperatives to Re-Imagine the Planet*, 46.

32. Gayatri Chakravorty Spivak, "World Systems and the Creole," *Narrative* 14, no. 1 (2006): 107.

33. Ibid., 108.

34. Spivak, *Death of a Discipline*, 72.

35. Ibid.

36. Mary Louise Pratt, *Imperial Eyes: Travel Writing and Transculturation* (New York: Routledge, 1992), 18.

37. For an in-depth discussion of this and its influential part in shaping the category of religion, see David Chidester, *Savage Systems: Colonialism and Comparative Religion in Southern Africa* (Charlottesville: University of Virginia Press, 1996).

38. Lisa Parks, *Cultures in Orbit: Satellites and the Televisual* (Durham, N.C.: Duke University Press, 2005), 1–2.

39. President Buchanan to Queen Victoria, in Field, *History of the Atlantic Telegraph*.

40. James Carey, *Communication as Culture: Essays in Media and Society* (New York: Routledge, 1988), 204.

41. Telkom SA Ltd, *SAT-3/WASC/SAFE*, 8 November 2004, 30 April 2003, http://www.safe-sat3.co.za/HomePage/SAT3_WASC_SAFE_Home.asp (accessed May 16, 2008).

42. For a more detailed discussion of postcolonial economic reforms and the development of India's success in information technologies, see Sachs, *The End of Poverty*, 170–87.

43. Ibid., 182.

44. Parks, *Cultures in Orbit*, 2.

45. See José Rabasa, "Allegories of *Atlas*," in *The Post-Colonial Studies Reader*, ed. Bill Ashcroft, Gareth Griffiths, and Helen Tiffin (New York: Routledge, 2002),

360: "Since the totality of the world can never be apprehended as such in a cartographical objectification, maps have significance only within a subjective reconstitution of the fragments. . . . Memory and systematic forgetfulness suspend the elucidation of a stable structure and constitute the need for an active translation."

46. Parks, *Cultures in Orbit*, 4.

47. Raymond Williams, *Television Technology and Cultural Form* (1974; New York: Routledge, 2003), 19.

48. Ibid., 21.

49. Scott DeGarmo, "High-Tech Havens," *Broadband House* 2 (2001): 6, cited in Lynn Spigel, "Designing the Smart House: Posthuman Domesticity and Conspicuous Production," *European Journal of Cultural Studies* 8, no. 4 (2005): 403.

50. Spigel, "Designing the Smart House," 421–22.

51. Ibid., 422.

52. Parks, *Cultures in Orbit*, 47–75.

53. Ibid., 54–56.

54. Ibid., 54.

55. Ibid., 49.

56. Ibid., 47.

57. Ibid., 48.

58. Ibid., 49.

59. Ibid., 70.

60. Spigel, "Designing the Smart House," 422.

LOVE'S MULTIPLICITY: *JEONG* AND SPIVAK'S NOTES TOWARD PLANETARY LOVE | W. ANNE JOH

1. Hannah Arendt's own struggle with love as "antipolitical" and one that "destroys the in-between which relates us to and separates us from one another" is apparent in her work, *The Human Condition* (Chicago: University of Chicago Press, 1998). However, the other side of her dialectical struggle with love is intensely felt in *Love and Saint Augustine*, ed. Joanna Vecchiarelli Scott and Judith Chelius Stark (Chicago: University of Chicago Press, 1996). She argues that love serves as the basis for our in-betweenness. The question that continues to haunt many theologians and philosophers is "Can love and human agency combine to bring about freedom rather than enslavement?"

2. Gayatri Chakravorty Spivak, "Terror: A Speech after 9-11," *boundary 2* 31, no. 2 (2004): 98.

3. Gayatri Chakravorty Spivak, *Death of a Discipline* (New York: Columbia University Press, 2003), 73.

4. Wonhee Anne Joh, *Heart of the Cross: A Postcolonial Christology* (Louisville, Ky.: Westminster John Knox Press, 2006).

5. Cf. Gayatri Chakravorty Spivak, "World Systems and the Creole," *Narrative* 14 (January 2006): 102–12.

6. See James R. Martel, *Love Is A Sweet Chain: Desire, Autonomy and Friendship in Liberal Political Theory* (New York: Routledge, 2001). In this book, Martel offers an excellent critique of how love has been sentimentalized. In thinking the politics of love, he argues that one must examine the historical concept of love in order to enable us to examine ourselves and our society by visiting the intimate and the often violent realm that is presupposed by the political.

7. There are theologians both past and present who have done fine work of reconfiguring love in all its complexity and imperfections. For an excellent example of such scholarship, see Gary Chartier, *The Analogy of Love: Divine and Human Love at the Center of Christian Theology* (Devon, UK: Imprint Academic, 2007). Among other arguments, Chartier outlines what a theology that is centered on love would look like. He asserts that such a theology must: emerge from community, be relational, be praxis sensitive, integrated with spirituality, and be *fun*.

8. Jean-Luc Nancy, *Being Singular Plural* (Stanford, Calif.: Stanford University Press, 2000), xiii.

9. Gayatri Chakravorty Spivak, "The Politics of Translation," in *Destabilizing Theory: Contemporary Feminist Debates,* ed. Michele Barrett and Anne Phillips (Stanford, Calif.: Stanford University Press, 1992), 177–200.

10. Trinh T. Minh-ha, *Cinema Interval* (New York: Routledge, 1999), 61–62.

11. Spivak, *Death of a Discipline,* 75.

12. For distinctions between globalization and planetarity and Spivak's own preference for planetarity, see her *A Critique of Postcolonial Reason: In Search of the Vanishing Present* (Cambridge, Mass.: Harvard University Press, 2000) and *Death of a Discipline.* For an excellent review of the latter, see Stephen Slemon, "Lament for a Notion," *ESC* 29, no. 1 (2003): 207–18.

13. I would like to develop the various ways that this learning of and practicing of *jeong* might take place in non-Korean contexts (while acknowledging, too, that the Korean context itself is heterogeneous). For example, how might Edouard Glissant's "creolity" influence the way we translate *jeong*? What about Homi Bhabha's "hybridity"? How do creolization, hybridization, and pluralization structure the form and practices of *jeong*?

14. Eric Hayot, "The Slightness of My Endeavor: An Interview of Gayatri Spivak" (transcript of unpublished interview conducted at the University of California, Irvine, on May 26, 2005), 257–58.

15. Spivak, *Death of a Discipline*, 92.

16. Julia Kristeva, *Powers of Horror: An Essay on Abjection* (New York: Columbia University Press, 1982), 9. The Oedipus complex attempts to account for the emergence of the speaking subject. This psychic process has been traditionally understood as divided into two stages: presubjectivity, and the period follow-ing, which allows entrance to the Symbolic at the cost of abjecting and/or repressing the Semiotic. See Martha Reineke, *Sacrificed Lives: Kristeva on Women and Violence* (Bloomington: Indiana University Press, 1997), 22.

17. For an excellent critique of the "neutrality" of psychoanalysis, see Jacques Derrida, "Geopsychoanalysis: '. . . and the rest of the world,'" in *The Psycho-analysis of Race*, ed. Christopher Lane (New York: Columbia University Press, 1998), 65–90.

18. Spivak cautions against easy uses of identity in the way we navigate ourselves when she observes that the term "subaltern" has "lost its power to indicate people from the very bottom layer of society, excluded even from the logic of the class structure." In our haste to claim otherness from the metropolitan majority, we forget the other. See Gayatri Chakravorty Spivak, "Moving Devi," *Cultural Critique* 47 (2001): 121. Also see her caution against the "seductive winning of the assent of the colonized, so that the result is a kind of ventrilo-quism that then stands in for free will. Our own complicity in our production is another kind of translation of cultures, access to a 'museumized' identity, roots in aspic." Gayatri Chakravorty Spivak, "Acting Bits/Identity Talk," *Criti-cal Inquiry* 18, no. 4 (1992): 798.

19. Stephen Morton, *Gayatri Spivak: Ethics, Subalternity and the Critique of Postcolo-nial Reason* (Cambridge: Polity Press, 2007), 143.

20. Spivak, *A Critique of Postcolonial Reason*, 5.

21. Cf. Butler's use of foreclosure in Judith Butler, *Excitable Speech* (New York: Routledge, 1997), and *The Psychic Life of Power* (Stanford, Calif.: Stanford Univer-sity Press, 1997).

22. Morton, *Gayatri Spivak*, 149.

23. Due to the limits of this essay, I cannot here go into the critique of psychoanal-ysis as a "colonial discipline that reveals to us an ethnography of the West" and that is born out of the epistemic violence of colonial discipline. See Ranjana Khanna, *Dark Continents: Psychoanalysis and Colonialism* (Durham, N.C.: Duke University Press, 2003). This particular critique can be leveled at the emergence of psychoanalysis as a field during the time of colonization of many "conti-nents" in addition to the regulation of sexuality and gender. Excellent analysis of this can be located in Anne McClintock's *Imperial Leather: Race, Gender, and Sexuality in the Colonial Contest* (New York: Routledge, 1995).

24. What is most often not acknowledged in psychoanalysis is the privileged position of the dominant identity. Kelly Oliver argues that often these unexamined and privileged positions influence the many ways in which identity is shaped and even deformed. As she notes, theories that do not start from the subjectivities of those other-ed but rather from the dominant subjectivity presuppose a need to exclude some other to fortify and shore itself up in order to reassure that all subjects are alike: "[W]e level differences, we develop a normative notion of the subject formation based on one particular group, gender or class of people." See Kelly Oliver, *The Colonization of Psychic Space: A Psychoanalytic Social Theory of Oppression* (Minneapolis: University of Minnesota Press, 2004). Also see Karen Shimakawa, *National Abjection: The Asian American Body Onstage* (Durham, N.C.: Duke University Press, 2002).

25. Gayatri Chakravorty Spivak, "The Trajectory of the Subaltern in My Work," unpublished lecture delivered at the University of California, Santa Cruz, September 13, 2004.

26. Julia Kristeva, *Strangers to Ourselves* (New York: Columbia University Press, 1991), 2. See Cecilia Sjoholm, *Kristeva and the Political* (New York: Routledge, 2005), especially 59–86.

27. Spivak, "World Systems and the Creole," 108.

28. Dawn Rae David, "(Love Is) The Ability of Not Knowing: Feminist Experience of the Impossible in Ethical Singularity," *Hypatia* 17, no. 1 (2002): 146.

29. Ibid., 147.

30. Spivak, "World Systems and the Creole," 110.

31. Elizabeth Povinelli, *The Empire of Love: Toward a Theory of Intimacy, Genealogy, and Carnality* (Durham, N.C.: Duke University Press, 2006), 6.

32. Ibid.

33. Ibid., 175.

34. Ibid., 10.

35. Ibid., 178.

36. Ibid.

37. Ibid., 241. More questions to ponder at a later time: Can we really maintain the dialectic of "Occidental freedom and Oriental bondage"? Must we choose between intimacy with strangers as only promiscuity and intimacy with kin or only one as the only valid love? What, then, about intimate promiscuity?

38. Nancy, *Being Singular Plural*, xiii.

39. For an excellent examination of the complexity of *hesed,* see Katherine Doob Sakenfeld, *The Meaning of Hesed in the Hebrew Bible* (Atlanta: Scholars Press, 1978), 23.

40. Gayatri Chakravorty Spivak, "Use and Abuse of Human Rights," *boundary 2* 32, no. 1 (2005): 148.

41. For a feminist postcolonial theology of incarnality and love, see Catherine Keller, *God and Power: Counter-Apocalyptic Journeys* (Minneapolis: Fortress, 2005), 113–34. This chapter is really, as far as I am aware, the first postcolonial feminist theology that is in conversation with Gayatri Spivak's work on "love."

42. Spivak, "Terror," 94.

43. Spivak, *Death of a Discipline*, 52.

44. Gayatri Chakravorty Spivak, "Harlem," *Social Text* 81, no. 22 (2004): 116.

45. Spivak, *Death of a Discipline*, 100.

46. Julia Kristeva, *Intimate Revolt: The Powers and Limits of Psychoanalysis* (New York: Columbia University Press, 2002), 20.

47. Michel de Certeau, *The Practice of Everyday Life* (Berkeley: University of California Press, 1984), xix.

48. Spivak, *A Critique of Postcolonial Reason*, 116–17.

49. Ibid., 332–34.

50. Spivak, "Terror," 83.

51. Ibid., 98.

52. Kelly Oliver, *Witnessing: Beyond Recognition* (Minneapolis: University of Minnesota Press, 2001), 68.

53. I am well aware that this notion of the "we" can be rightly critiqued, especially from a feminist perspective, as inclusive dynamics of coercion. However, many, who so well know the violence of abjection, have relied and depended on the collective, the sense of "we," to mobilize collective resistance against violence. Judith Butler also examines the necessity of the "we" as she observes that "we are something other than 'autonomous' in such a condition, but that does not mean that we are merged or without boundaries. It does mean . . . that when we think about who we 'are' and seek to represent ourselves, we cannot represent ourselves as merely bounded beings, for the primary others who are past for me not only live on in the fiber of the boundary that contains me, but they also haunt the way I am, as it were, periodically undone and open to becoming unbounded." Judith Butler, *Precarious Life: The Powers of Mourning and Violence* (New York: Verso, 2004), 27–28. See also Judith Butler and Gayatri Spivak, *Who Sings the Nation-State? Language, Politics, Belonging* (London: Seagull Books, 2007).

54. Gayatri Chakravorty Spivak, "Righting Wrongs," *South Atlantic Quarterly* 103, no. 2 (2004): 523–81 (now also in her *Other Asias* [Malden, Mass.: Blackwell, 2008], 14–57).

55. Spivak, "Use and Abuse of Human Rights," 139.

56. Spivak, *Death of a Discipline*, 35.

57. Spivak, "Use and Abuse of Human Rights," 139.

58. Ibid., 148.

59. Ibid., 165.

60. Simon Critchley, *Infinitely Demanding: Ethics of Commitment, Politics of Resistance* (New York: Verso, 2007), 61.

61. Spivak, *A Critique of Postcolonial Reason*, 3n, 69n, 89, 101, 220, 419, and especially 363–64.

62. Spivak, "Terror," 83.

63. Edouard Glissant, *Poetics of Relation* (Ann Arbor: University of Michigan Press, 1997), 194.

64. Spivak, "Use and Abuse of Human Rights," 139.

65. Gayatri Chakravorty Spivak, "The Trajectory of the Subaltern in My Work," http://www.youtube.com/watch?v=2ZHH4ALRFHw (accessed October 14, 2008).

66. Spivak, "World Systems and the Creole," 107.

67. Spivak, "Use and Abuse of Human Rights," 189, referring to Orlando Patterson's phrase.

NOT QUITE NOT AGENTS OF OPPRESSION: LIBERATIVE PRAXIS FOR NORTH AMERICAN WHITE WOMEN | LYDIA YORK

1. Melanie Morrison, Eleanor S. Morrison and Ann Flescher, *Doing Our Own Work Training Handbook*, sec. II, p. 2 (Lyons, Mich.: Allies for Change, 2003), from "Definitions of Key Terms," which is indebted to *cultural bridges*, a racial justice consortium in Questa, New Mexico; The Women's Theological Center in Boston, Mass.; and The National Council for Community and Justice in New York City. Recently, the Doing Our Own Work trainers have begun to use the phrase "non–target group members" instead of "agents of oppression" to avoid reobjectifying people of color as those without agency. Even so, they continue to find significance in the power of the original diction.

2. Trinh T. Minh-ha and Marina Grzinic, "Inappropriate/d Artificiality," Interview with Marina Grzinic, *The Digital Film Event* (1998): http://arch .ced.berkeley.edu/people/faculty/bourdier/trinh.

3. North American women publishing are "not-quite-not-native informants, even for feminist scholars." Gayatri Chakravorty Spivak, *A Critique of Postcolonial Reason: Toward a History of the Vanishing Present* (Cambridge, Mass.: Harvard University Press, 1999), 113.

4. Ibid., 116.

5. See Gloria T. Smith Hull and Patricia Bell-Scott, *All the Women Are White, All the Blacks Are Men, but Some of Us Are Brave: Black Women's Studies* (Old Westbury, N.Y.: Feminist Press, 1982).

6. See Laurel C. Schneider, "What Race Is Your Sex?" in *Disrupting White Supremacy from Within: White People on What We Need to Do*, ed. Jennifer Harvey, Karin Case, and Robin Hawley Gorsline (Cleveland: Pilgrim Press, 2004), 142–62; and Anne McClintock, *Imperial Leather: Race, Gender, and Sexuality in the Colonial Contest* (New York: Routledge, 1995).

7. Schneider, "What Race Is Your Sex?" 142.

8. Ibid., 145.

9. Ibid., 154.

10. See bell hooks, "Representations of Whiteness," in *Black Looks: Race and Representation* (Boston, Mass.: South End Press, 1992), 165–78; and David Theo Goldberg, *Racial Subjects: Writing on Race in America* (New York: Routledge, 1997).

11. Alfred J. López, *Posts and Pasts: A Theory of Postcolonialism* (Albany: State University of New York Press, 2001), 94–96.

12. Alfred J. López, *Postcolonial Whiteness: A Critical Reader on Race and Empire* (Albany: State University of New York Press, 2005), 13.

13. Richard Dyer, *White* (New York: Routledge, 1997), 80.

14. Ibid., 4.

15. Ibid., 46–47.

16. Booker T. Washington (1900) on the one-drop or one-percent rule: "It is a fact that, if a person is known to have one percent of African blood in his veins, he ceases to be a white man," as quoted in John G. Mencke, *Mulattoes and Race Mixture: American Attitudes and Images, 1865–1918* (Ann Arbor, Mich.: UMI Research Press, 1979), 37.

17. Mayra Rivera, *The Touch of Transcendence: A Postcolonial Theology of God* (Louisville, Ky.: Westminster John Knox Press, 2007), 108.

18. Birgit Brander Rasmussen, Eric Klinenberg, Irene J. Nexica, and Matt Wray, eds., Introduction to *The Making and Unmaking of Whiteness* (Durham, N.C.: Duke University Press, 2001), 1–24.

19. López, *Posts and Pasts*, 119.

20. David R. Roediger, *The Wages of Whiteness: Race and the Making of the American Working Class* (London: Verso, 1991); and Thandeka, *Learning to Be White: Money, Race, and God in America* (New York: Continuum, 1999).

21. Mab Segrest, "The Souls of White Folks," in *The Making and Unmaking of Whiteness*, ed. Rasmussen et al., 45.

22. Segrest, "The Souls of White Folks," 54, quoting Mary Chesnut, *A Diary from Dixie*, ed. Ben Ames Williams (Cambridge, Mass.: Harvard University Press, 1980), 25–26.

23. Segrest, "The Souls of White Folks," 68.

24. bell hooks, *Black Looks*, 13–14.

25. Spivak is here giving final form to a reading of *Wide Sargasso Sea* that began in her highly influential 1985 article, "Three Women's Texts and a Critique of Imperialism," *Critical Inquiry* 12, no. 1 (1985): 243–61.

26. Jean Rhys, *Wide Sargasso Sea*, ed. Judith L. Raiskin (1966; New York: W. W. Norton, 1999), 61.

27. Spivak, *A Critique of Postcolonial Reason*, 125–26.

28. Ibid., 126.

29. Ibid., 126–27.

30. Ibid., 126.

31. Gayatri Chakravorty Spivak, "Echo," in *The Spivak Reader: Selected Works of Gayatri Chakravorty Spivak*, ed. Donna Landry and Gerald MacLean (New York: Routledge, 1996), 182, quoting *Metamorphoses* 3.463–71.

32. Ibid.

33. Ibid., 183.

34. Spivak, *A Critique of Postcolonial Reason*, 130.

35. Homi K. Bhabha, *The Location of Culture* (London: Routledge, 1994), 89.

36. Wonhee Anne Joh, *Heart of the Cross: A Postcolonial Christology* (Louisville, Ky.: Westminster John Knox Press, 2006), 69.

37. Lorraine O'Grady, quoted in Evelynn Hammonds, "Black (W)holes and the Geometry of Black Female Sexuality," as quoted in turn in Schneider, "What Race Is Your Sex?" 146.

38. Susan Friedman, *Mappings: Feminism and the Cultural Geographies of Resistance*, (Princeton, N.J.: Princeton University Press, 1998), 41–43.

39. Morrison, Morrison, and Flescher, *Doing Our Own Work Training Handbook*, sec. 1, p. 1. For more information on the *Doing Our Own Work* Seminar, contact *Allies for Change*, P.O. Box 138, Lyons, Mich. 48851, www.alliesforchange.org.

40. Ibid., sec. 1, p. 3.

41. Ibid.

42. Ibid.

43. Ibid, sec. 2, p. 6.

44. Donna K. Bivens and Nancy D. Richardson, "Naming and Claiming Our Histories," *The Brown Papers* 1, no. 2 (1994), as quoted in Melanie S. Morrison, "Why Offer an Anti-Racism Seminar for White People?" www.alliesfor change.org/documents.

45. Becky Thompson, *A Promise and a Way of Life: White Antiracist Activism* (Minneapolis: University of Minnesota Press, 2001), 165. Interviewing Ruth Frankenburg, Thompson writes, "Ruth learned that antiracist work for white people requires 'doing the work from a place of self-love.'"

46. Thandeka, *Learning to Be White*; Frantz Fanon, *The Wretched of the Earth*, trans. Richard Philcox (1961; New York: Grove Press, 2004); Anne Anlin Cheng, *The Melancholy of Race* (Oxford: Oxford University Press, 2001).

47. Paul Rasor, "Reclaiming Our Prophetic Voice: Liberal Theology and the Challenge of Racism," in *Soul Work: Anti-Racist Theologies in Dialogue*, ed. Marjorie Bowens-Wheatley and Nancy Palmer Jones (Boston: Skinner House Books, 2002), 123.

48. Gayatri Chakravorty Spivak, "Moving Devi," *Cultural Critique* 47 (Winter 2001): 124, quoting Jacques Derrida, "The Law of Genre," *Glyph* 7 (Spring 1980): 206.

49. Cheng, *The Melancholy of Race*, 7–9.

50. Thandeka, "The Self between Feminist Theory and Theology," in *Horizons in Feminist Theology: Identity, Tradition, and Norms*, ed. Rebecca S. Chopp and Sheila Greeve Davaney (Minneapolis: Fortress Press, 1997), 96.

PLANETARY SIGHTINGS? NEGOTIATING SEXUAL DIFFERENCES IN GLOBALIZATION'S SHADOW | ELLEN T. ARMOUR

1. Spivak's planet resembles other uncanny sites that also give place: the womb (according to Luce Irigaray) and *khora* (according to Jacques Derrida).

2. Other events contributed to this firestorm as well, including, for example, the creation of rites for same-sex unions by the New Westminster diocese of the Canadian branch of the Anglican church. Terry Mattingly views the current dispute as the latest round of an ongoing conflict within the communion that dates back decades. See his July 15, 2009, post "How about some ecclesiastical math?" at http://www.getreligion.org/?m=200907&paged=4 (accessed September 17, 2009).

3. Events continue to unfold. December 2008 saw the founding of the Anglican Church in North America as an alternative province to the American and Canadian churches. It held its first church-wide assembly in Texas in June 2009. See their website at http://www.anglicanchurch-na.org. In July 2009, the bishops of the Episcopal Church voted by an overwhelming majority to open all ministries of the Church to openly gay and lesbian persons. In the eyes of many, this move essentially ended the so-called moratorium called for by Rowan Williams, Archbishop of Canterbury. See Laurie Goodstein, "Episcopal Vote Reopens a Door to Gay Bishops," *New York Times*, July 14, 2009, at http://www.nytimes.com/2009/07/15/us/15episcopal.html (accessed July 14, 2009).

4. http://www.anglicancommunion.org.

5. William Saletan, "Sexual Reorientation: The Gay Culture War Is About to Turn Chemical," *Slate*. Posted June 18, 2008. http://www.slate.com/id/2193841/.

6. See Augustine, *City of God*, trans. Henry Bettenson (New York: Penguin Classics, 1972; rev. ed., 2003), Book XIV, chaps. 16–28. In *The Ethics of Sex* (Malden, Mass.: Blackwell, 2002), Mark D. Jordan demonstrates that, while the dominant strand of post-Augustinian Christian theology (up through Aquinas and the Reformers) certainly doesn't condone same-sex sex, it does not unabashedly endorse opposite-sex sex. Procreative sex is itself dangerous—even within marriage. Marriage is a prophylactic against desire, to borrow a phrase from Dale Martin's study of Paul, *The Corinthian Body* (New Haven, Conn.: Yale University Press, 1999). Husbands and wives owe each other access to their bodies to keep sex/desire in check.

7. Robert Marus and Greg Warner, "Mohler: Homosexuality Likely Genetic: Christians Should Support Prenatal Cure," http://www.abpnews.com/1855.article; originally published March 7, 2007.

8. Saletan, "Sexual Reorientation."

9. Of particular importance for this essay is Foucault's work, especially *The History of Sexuality: An Introduction* (New York: Random House, 1990). The subsequent volumes of this series focus on Greece and Rome, respectively. The fourth volume of Foucault's history of sexuality was to have been on Christianity. It has never been (and, by order of the estate, will likely never be) published. But Foucault sketched out portions of this argument in various lectures. Notes from these lectures have been collected in Part III of *Religion and Culture: Michel Foucault*, ed. Jeremy R. Carrette (New York: Routledge, 1999).

10. See, for instance, the "Statement on Homosexuality by the Anglican Province of Rwanda," issued January 31,1998, in which the signatories (all diocesan bishops) write, "We know that some Westerners have introduced homosexual practices in the Great Lakes Region of Africa, but we, as Africans, repudiate the practice and do not wish it to be seen in our Province." Available at http://andromeda.rutgers.edu/~lcrew/rwanda.html (accessed July 10, 2008).

11. Mark Jordan, *The Invention of Sodomy in Christian Theology* (Chicago: University of Chicago Press, 1997).

12. Ibid., 43.

13. Foucault, *History of Sexuality*, 43. On the emergence of heterosexuality as the sexual identity we take it to be today, see Jonathan Ned Katz, *The Invention of Heterosexuality* (Chicago: University of Chicago Press, 1997).

14. Indeed, the scientific research on homosexuality presupposes this very scheme insofar as it seeks out evidence of the feminization of what should be masculine and vice versa.

15. Scholarly works in religion on these topics include Dale Martin, *The Corinthian Body* (New Haven, Conn.: Yale University Press, 1995); certain essays in his *Sex*

and the Single Savior: Gender and Sexuality in Biblical Interpretation (Louisville, Ky.: Westminster John Knox Press, 2006); and Bernadette Brooten, *Love Between Women: Early Christian Responses to Homoeroticism* (Chicago: University of Chicago Press, 1996). Ken Stone's essay, "The Garden of Eden and the Heterosexual Contract," in *Bodily Citations: Religion and Judith Butler,* ed. Ellen T. Armour and Susan St. Ville (New York: Columbia University Press, 2006), 48–70, includes a helpful list of references to a larger body of scholarship on sexuality in the ancient world (see 67 n. 9).

16. Simone de Beauvoir, *The Second Sex,* trans. E. M. Parshley (New York: Vintage Books, 1973), 301.

17. On this, see especially Anne Fausto-Sterling, *Sexing the Body: Gender, Politics and the Construction of Sexuality* (New York: Basic Books, 2000).

18. Recent headlines bear this out. The effects of the collapse of the subprime mortgage market in the United States were felt locally and personally (on streets where homeowners defaulted on their mortgages thus affecting property values in the immediate vicinity) and internationally. According to a recent story on NPR's *Morning Edition* many of the so-called whales—unbelievably high rollers at Las Vegas casinos—are wealthy businessmen from China and Russia.

19. Stephen O. Murray and Will Roscoe, eds., *Boy-Wives and Female Husbands: Studies in African Homosexualities* (New York: Palgrave Macmillan, 2001), Martin Duberman, Martha Vicinus, and George Chauncey Jr., *Hidden from History* (New York: Meridian, 1990). Kevin Ward, "Same-Sex Relations in Africa and the Debate on Homosexuality in East African Anglicanism," *Anglican Theological Review* (Winter 2002): 1. http://newark.rutgers.edu/~lcrew/homosexualityAfrica.html.

20. Ward, "Same-Sex Relations in Africa."

21. David Greenberg, *The Construction of Homosexuality* (Chicago: University of Chicago Press, 1988), chap. 2. Cited by Ward, "Same-Sex Relations in Africa." For some historical records of same-sex practices, see Murray and Roscoe, *Boy-Wives and Female Husbands.* For contemporary Anglican voices on the subject from across the global South, see Terry Brown, ed., *Other Voices, Other Worlds: The Global Church Speaks Out on Homosexuality* (New York: Church Publishing, 2006).

22. Doug Ireland, "Nigeria: World's Worst Anti-Gay Law May Pass Soon," http://www.zmag.org/content/showarticle.cfm?ItemID = 12180.

23. Ward, "Same-Sex Relations in Africa."

24. Kevin Ward, "Marching or Stumbling towards a Christian Ethic?" in *Other Voices, Other Worlds,* ed. Brown, 133–34.

25. Kelly Brown Douglas, *Sexuality and the Black Church: A Womanist Perspective* (Maryknoll, N.Y.: Orbis Books, 1999); Marcella Althaus-Reid, *Indecent Theology: Theological Perversions in Sex, Gender, and Politics* (New York: Routledge, 2000), and *The Queer God* (New York: Routledge, 2003).

26. Willis Jenkins claims 15 million ("Episcopalians, Homosexuality, and World Mission," *Anglican Theological Review* 86, no. 2 [2004]: 295). The *New York Times* claims 17 million (Laurie Goodstein, "Gay and Dissident Bishops Excluded from '08 Meeting," http://www.nytimes.com/2007/05/23/us/23anglican.html [accessed October 1, 2007]). Philip Jenkins claims 20 million (*The Next Christendom: The Coming of Global Christianity* [New York: Oxford University Press, 2002], 59).

27. Cited by W. Jenkins in "Episcopalians, Homosexuality, and World Mission," 306–7. In a collect written in response to the consecration of Bishop Robinson, the Archbishop of Uganda writes, "We grieve because we remember the pain that has come from similar *imperial* actions in the past" (297).

28. Noting that the Episcopal church's financial contribution to the Anglican communion is the largest, Archbishop Drexel Gomez of the Province of the West Indies (part of the global South) said, "[A]s much as we need the money, the gospel must come first. We are prepared to suffer" (James Solheim, "International Reaction to Gene Robinson's Consecration in New Hampshire Mixed," *Anglican Communion News Service*, November 6, 2003, http://tiny.cc/ACNS). In April 2004, the Council of Anglican Provinces of Africa voted to reject funding from the ECUSA (Miranda Hassett, *Anglican Communion in Crisis: How Episcopal Dissidents and Their African Allies Are Reshaping Anglicanism* [Princeton, N.J.: Princeton University Press, 2007], 239).

29. Gledhill interview cited in "Akinola Unfiltered," at http//www.getreligion .org/?p + 2529.

30. This organization was involved in the recent founding of the Anglican Church of North America mentioned above. The Nigerian church was the first (and as of September 2009, the only) Anglican province to recognize ACNA. See http://www.anglicanchurch-na.org/stream/2009/03/anglican-church-north-america-recognized.html (accessed September 17, 2009).

31. For statistics, see P. Jenkins, *Next Christendom*, 2–3.

32. In addition to *The Next Christendom*, see also Philip Jenkins, *The New Faces of Christianity: Believing the Bible in the Global South* (New York: Oxford University Press, 2006).

33. Hassett's *Anglican Communion in Crisis* offers a fascinating and fulsome account of the background to Lambeth 1998 as well as an astute analysis of the larger controversy.

34. Thus, Sanneh calls this "world Christianity." He distinguishes it from "global Christianity," which still bears the strong imprint of its Western origins. See Lamin Sanneh, *Whose Religion Is Christianity? The Gospel Beyond the West* (Grand Rapids, Mich.: Eerdmans, 2003).

35. Brown, *Other Voices, Other Worlds.*

36. See Solheim, "International Reaction."

37. Hassett, *Anglican Communion in Crisis*, 91–92. This action was quickly and roundly denounced as an invasion by the North despite vocal protests to the contrary by local organizers. Hassett also notes that positions articulated in certain outlets in the Ugandan press document a wider range of opinion on same-sex sex among the populace at large than the Church's official reaction would suggest.

38. I note, for example, that a Metropolitan Community Church in Nigeria closed its physical doors in the face of threats and persecution, though it continues to find alternative routes to serve its constituency. See http://houseof rainbowmcc.blogspot.com/ (accessed September 18, 2009).

39. See Ireland, "Nigeria: World's Worst Anti-Gay Law." See also the International Gay and Lesbian Human Rights Commission's (IGLHRC) report, "Voices from Nigeria: Gays, Lesbians, Bisexuals and Transgendereds Speak Out Against the Same Sex Bill," at http://www.iglhrc.org/files/iglhrc/reports/Voices_ Nigeria.pdf. The bill went before the Nigerian National Assembly in January 2009 (see http://www.amnesty.org/en/news-and-updates/news/nigerias-proposed-ban-same-sex-partnerships-assault-human-rights-20090128). I have not been able to find any information about its current status.

40. Riazat Butt, "An Unheavenly Silence on Homophobia," guardian.co.uk, posted June 23, 2008, at http://www.guardian.co.uk/commentisfree/2008/jun/23/ anglicanism.gayrights (accessed July 1, 2008).

41. Our cause is not helped when Northern progressives speak of their Southern opposition in terms redolent of colonialist racism. Bishop John Shelby Spong raised the ire of many in the South when, just before Lambeth 1998, he described African Anglicans as "superstitious, fundamentalist Christians" who have "moved out of animism into a very superstitious kind of Christianity— [and have] yet to face the intellectual revolution of Copernicus and Einstein" (cited by Hassett, *Anglican Communion in Crisis*, 72).

42. W. Jenkins, "Episcopalians, Homosexuality, and World Mission," 310. As a result, Jenkins argues persuasively, Northern progressives are not as attuned as they need to be to the specific circumstances—including the pressures of globalization—that shape the African provincial churches' perspectives on homosexuality. He takes up this issue specifically in his "Ethnohomophobia?" *Anglican Theological Review* 82, no. 3 (2000): 551–63.

43. Gayatri Chakravorty Spivak, "Can the Subaltern Speak?" in *Marxism and the Interpretation of Culture*, ed. Lawrence Grossberg and Cary Nelson (Urbana and Chicago: University of Illinois Press), 296.

44. A salient contemporary example would be the use of the figure of the Muslim woman clad in a burqa to marshal support for the war in Afghanistan—an effort in which the Feminist Majority became involved. See Saba Mahmood, "Agency, Performativity, and the Feminist Subject," in Armour and St. Ville, *Bodily Citations*, 177–221; 207–8.

45. See, e.g., Ifi Amadiume, *Male Daughters, Female Husbands: Gender and Sex in African Society* (London: Zed Books, 1987).

46. This does not mean Northerners must wait for that careful work to be done before they can advocate on behalf of Southern sexual minorities. Globalization works in progressives' favor here. Archbishop Akinola's network now includes dissident Episcopalian parishes, effectively linking the global North with this Southern legislation. Those parishes seem legitimate sites for progressive attempts to ameliorate or at least protest some of the worst aspects of the legislation.

"EFFECTS OF GRACE": DETRANSCENDENTALIZING | ERIN RUNIONS

I thank Susan Abraham, Virginia Burrus, Catherine Keller, Hyo-Dong Lee, Stephen Moore, Mayra Rivera, and Mary-Jane Rubenstein for their helpful questions and engagements with the ideas in this essay.

1. Gayatri Chakravorty Spivak, "Terror: A Speech after 9.11," *boundary 2* 31, no. 2 (2004): 81–111.

2. Ibid., 100–101.

3. Ibid., 105.

4. Ibid., 111.

5. Russell T. McCutcheon, *Manufacturing Religion: The Discourse on Sui Generis Religion and the Politics of Nostalgia* (Oxford: Oxford University Press, 1997); Richard King, *Orientalism and Religion: Post-Colonial Theory, India and "The Mystic East"* (New York: Routledge, 1999).

6. Spivak, "Terror," 102.

7. Ibid.

8. Ibid., 103.

9. Ibid., 110 n. 43.

10. Kant distinguished between the transcendental—that is, the a priori conditions for knowledge—and the transcendent—that is, the realm beyond human knowledge.

11. Spivak, "Terror," 91.

12. Ibid., 107.

13. Ibid., 102, see also 108; Immanuel Kant, *Religion within the Boundaries of Mere Reason and Other Writings*, trans. and ed. Allen Wood and George Di Giovanni (1973; Cambridge: Cambridge University Press, 1998), 72–73, for his other remarks on these *parerga*, see 98–102, 140–47, 182–91.

14. Jacques Derrida, "Faith and Knowledge: The Two Sources of 'Religion' at the Limits of Reason Alone," in *Acts of Religion*, ed. Gil Anidjar (1996; New York: Routledge, 2002), 48–53.

15. Jacques Derrida, "The Parergon," trans. Craig Owens, *October* 9 (Summer 1979 [1978]): 22.

16. Spivak, "Terror," 108.

17. Ibid., 109.

18. Ibid.

19. Ibid.

20. Ibid., 106.

21. Gayatri Chakravorty Spivak, "Moving Devi," *Cultural Critique* 47 (Winter 2001): 124–27.

22. Jacques Derrida, "The Law of Genre," *Glyph: Textual Studies* 7 (Spring 1980): 206, quoted in Spivak, "Moving Devi," 124.

23. Spivak, "Moving Devi," 126–27.

24. Ibid., 124.

25. Ibid.

26. Ibid., 123.

27. Gayatri Chakravorty Spivak, *A Critique of Postcolonial Reason: Toward a History of the Vanishing Present.* (Cambridge, Mass.: Harvard University Press, 1999), 173, 427.

28. Gayatri Chakravorty Spivak, translator's preface to *Imaginary Maps*, by Mahasweta Devi (New York: Routledge, 1995), xxv.

29. Ibid., 200.

30. Spivak, *Imaginary Maps*, 201; *Critique*, 383.

31. Spivak, *Imaginary Maps*, xxv; *Critique*, 384.

32. Dawn Rae Davis, "(Love Is) The Ability of Not Knowing: Feminist Experience of the Impossible in Ethical Singularity," *Hypatia* 17, no. 2 (2002): 146.

33. Ibid., 149.

34. Spivak, *Critique of Postcolonial Reason*, 384.

35. Gayatri Chakravorty Spivak, foreword to *A Companion to Postcolonial Studies*, ed. Henry Schwarz and Sangeeta Ray (Oxford: Blackwell, 2000), xx.

36. Erin Runions, "Theologico-Political Resonance: Carl Schmitt between the Neocons and Theonomists," *Differences: A Journal of Feminist Cultural Studies* 18, no. 3 (2007): 43–80.

37. *God's Law and Society* (Alliance for Revival and Reformation, 1999), video series.

38. Kant, *Religion within the Boundaries of Mere Reason,* 72.

39. Spivak, *Terror,* 89.

40. Catherine Keller, *God and Power: Counter Apocalyptic Journeys* (Minneapolis: Augsburg Fortress, 2005). For the way the antichrist has figured in past U.S. political thought, see Robert C. Fuller, *Naming the Antichrist: The History of an American Obsession* (Oxford: Oxford University Press, 1995), 71–73, 136–60; Paul Boyer, *When Time Shall Be No More: Prophecy Belief in Modern American Culture* (Cambridge, Mass.: Harvard University Press, 1992), 282–84, 328–30.

41. Christopher Corbett, "The U.S. and Other U.N. Serfdoms," in *Foreshocks of the Antichrist,* ed. William T. James (Eugene, Ore.: Harvest House,1997), 203–30; Berit Kjos, "Classroom Earth: Educating for One World Order," in *Foreshocks of the Antichrist,* 45–80; Arno Froese, "United Europe's Power Play," in *Foreshocks of the Antichrist,* 275–300.

42. J. R. Church, "Riders of Revelation 6, Mount Up!," in *Foreshocks of the Antichrist,* 320.

43. E.g., Jerry Falwell, "Satan's Superman: Sermon for Nov. 4, 2001," Thomas Road Baptist Church, November 4, 2001, http://sermons.trbc.org/20011104 .html (accessed June 26, 2008).

44. George W. Bush, "President Discusses War on Terror at National Endowment for Democracy," October 6, 2005, www.whitehouse.gov/news/releases/2005/ 10/20051006-3.html (accessed June 26, 2008).

45. National Security Council, "National Strategy for Combating Terrorism: Overview," The Whitehouse 2006, http://www.whitehouse.gov/nsc/nsct/2006/ sectionI.html (accessed June 26, 2008).

46. See, respectively, George Bush, "President Bush and President Berger of Guatemala Participate in Joint Press Availability," March 12, 2007, www .whitehouse.gov/news/releases/2007/03/20070312-4.html (accessed June 26, 2008); Whitehouse, Homeland Security, "The National Strategy for Maritime Security," September 20, 2005, www.whitehouse.gov/homeland/maritime-security.html (accessed June 26, 2008); Whitehouse, Office of the Press Secretary, "2007 U.S.-EU Summit Promoting Peace, Human Rights and Democracy Worldwide," April 30, 2007, www.whitehouse.gov/news/releases/2007/04/ 20070430-13.html (accessed June 26, 2008).

47. Erin Runions, "Queering the Beast: The Antichrists' Gay Wedding," in *Queering the Non-Human,* ed. Noreen Giffney and Myra Hird (Aldershot, UK: Ashgate, 2008), 79–110.

48. David R. Reagan, "The Rise and Fall of the Antichrist," Lamb and Lion Ministries, http://www.lamblion.com/articles/articles_issues17.php (accessed

June 23, 2008); for other references to the gay antichrist see David Benoit, "Man Targeted for Extinction," in *Foreshocks of the Antichrist*, 313; Rob Boston, "Is the Antichrist Gay?: Stretching Scripture at the 'Values Voter Summit,'" Americans United for Separation of Church and State, November 2006, http://www.au.org/site/News2?page = NewsArticle&id = 8676&abbr = cs_ (accessed June 26, 2008).

49. C. L. Seow, *Daniel* (Louisville, Ky.: Westminster John Knox Press, 2003), 183; John Goldingay, *Daniel*, Word Biblical Commentary, 30 (Dallas: Word Books, 1989), 304. For similar readings, see also André Lacocque. *Le livre de Daniel* (Paris: Delachaux et Niestlé, 1976), 171; Norman W. Porteous, *Daniel: A Commentary*, The Old Testament Library (Philadelphia: Westminster, 1965), 169; W. Sibley Towner, *Daniel*, Interpretation (Atlanta: John Knox, 1984), 162.

50. Joseph Chambers, "Same Sex Marriage: Defiling the 'Marriage of the Lamb,'" Paw Creek Ministries, http://www.pawcreek.org/articles/endtimes/SameSexMarriage.htm (accessed May 23, 2008).

51. Watchmen Bible Study Group, "Emergence of the First Beast," http://biblestudysite.com/beast.htm (accessed May 23, 2008).

52. John J. Collins, "Stirring up the Great Sea: The Religio-Historical Background of Daniel 7," in *Seers, Sybils and Sages in Hellenistic-Roman Judaism*, Supplements to the Journal for the Study of Judaism (Leiden: Brill, 1997), 139–55; André Lacocque, "Allusions to Creation in Daniel 7," in *The Book of Daniel: Composition and Reception*, vol. 1, ed. John J. Collins and Peter W. Flint, with Cameron VanEpps (Leiden: Brill, 2001), 114–31; Paul Mosca, "Ugarit and Daniel 7: A Missing Link," *Biblica* 67, no. 1 (1986): 496–517; William H. Shea, "The Neo-Babylonian Historical Setting for Daniel 7," *Andrews University Seminar Studies* 24, no. 1 (1986): 31–36; John H. Walton, "The *Anzu* Myth as Relevant Background for Daniel 7?," in *The Book of Daniel: Composition and Reception*, 69–89; Robert R. Wilson, "Creation and New Creation: The Role of Creation Imagery in the Book of Daniel," in *God Who Creates: Essays in Honor of W. Sibley Towner*, ed. William P. Brown and S. Dean McBride Jr. (Grand Rapids, Mich.: Eerdmans, 2000), 190–203.

53. Collins, "Stirring up the Great Sea," 143–46.

54. Ibid., 142.

55. For instance, Collins notes Mosca's concern over a dependence on Canaanite sources; ibid., 151 n. 48. Mosca writes, "[W]hat I seriously doubt is that the impeccably orthodox Jewish author of Daniel 7 would turn to such a source for inspiration when presenting the heavenly scene which forms the very climax of his dream-vision" (Mosca, "Ugarit and Daniel 7," 499).

56. R. A. Oden, Jr., "Baal Samem and El," *Catholic Biblical Quarterly* 39, no. 4 (1977): 457–73; Mark S. Smith, *The Early History of God: Yahweh and the Other Deities in Ancient Israel*, 2nd ed. (Grand Rapids, Mich.: Eerdmans, 2002), 65–75.

57. For a discussion of the connection between bull iconography and Baal worship, see Smith, *Early History of God*, 83–85; he notes that there is some uncertainty as to the gods represented by bull figurines, and points out that the bull iconography may also have been a symbol for Yahweh.

58. Runions, "Queering the Beast," 102–4.

59. Gilles Deleuze, *Difference and Repetition*, trans. Paul Patton (1968; New York: Columbia University Press, 1994), 96.

60. Davis, "(Love Is) The Ability of Not Knowing," 155.

COMPARATIVE THEOLOGY AFTER "RELIGION"
| JOHN J. THATAMANIL

I am deeply indebted to the saintly patience of and editorial suggestions offered by Mayra Rivera and Stephen Moore and to Mary-Jane Rubenstein's response to this essay when delivered as a paper.

1. Daniel Boyarin, *Border Lines: The Partition of Judaeo-Christianity* (Philadelphia: University of Pennsylvania Press, 2006).

2. I borrow this phrase from Arvind Mandair. See his "The Repetition of Past Imperialisms: Hegel, Historical Difference, and the Theorization of Indic Religions," *History of Religions* 44, no. 4 (2005): 288.

3. Among these I am especially indebted to the essay just cited, Mandair's "The Repetition of Past Imperialisms," and the following: Arvind-Pal S. Mandair, "What if *Religio* Remained Untranslatable?" in *Difference in Philosophy of Religion*, ed. Philip Goodchild (Burlington, Vt.: Ashgate, 2003), 87–100; "The Global Fiduciary: Mediating the Violence of 'Religion,'" in *Religion and Violence in South Asia: Theory and Practice*, ed. John R. Hinells and Richard King (New York: Routledge, 2007), 211–25; "(Im)possible Intersections: Religion, (Post-)Colonial Subjectivity and the Ideology of Multiculturalism," in *A Postcolonial People: South Asians in Britain*, ed. N. Ali, V. S. Kalra, and S. Sayyid (New York: Columbia University Press, 2008). Taken together, these essays establish Mandair as among our foremost thinkers on the category "religion."

4. Mandair, "The Repetition of Past Imperialisms," 277.

5. Ibid., 277–78.

6. Ibid., 278.

7. John Milbank, *Theology and Social Theory: Beyond Secular Reason* (Malden, Mass.: Blackwell, 1990).

8. It is hard to determine precisely which postcolonial thinkers fall prey to this commitment to secular critique alone and the degree of guilt to be imputed to these various thinkers. Mandair lists a variety of figures, including Edward Said, Ronald Inden, and Gayatri Chakravorty Spivak. See "The Repetition of Past Imperialisms," 280.

9. Mandair's work on the question of the translatability of *"religio"* is, of course, profoundly indebted to Derrida's discussion of *globalatinization* in "Faith and Knowledge: Two Sources of 'Religion' at the Limits of Reason Alone," in Jacques Derrida, *Acts of Religion*, ed. Gil Anidjar (New York: Routledge, 2002), 40–101.

10. Mandair, "The Repetition of Past Imperialisms," 281.

11. For noteworthy exceptions to this rule, see the work of Robert C. Neville and Francis X. Clooney, S.J. For the most sophisticated articulation of a theological program that makes comparison integral to theology as such, see Neville's *On the Scope and Truth of Theology: Theology as Symbolic Engagement* (New York: T. & T. Clark International, 2006). For an appreciative though not uncritical assessment of the same, see my review of Neville's book in *Journal of Chinese Philosophy* 35, no. 3 (2008): 528–32. See also Clooney's *Hindu God, Christian God: How Reason Helps to Break Down the Boundaries between Religions* (New York: Oxford University Press, 2001).

12. Mandair, "The Repetition of Past Imperialisms," 281.

13. This is not to suggest that monogenetic accounts were immune to co-optation by colonial agendas. Mandair does well to demonstrate that early Indologists managed to allow for common origins between European and Indian cultures while simultaneously marking surviving Indian traditions as inferior because they have fallen away from an original and pure monotheism. The colonial project needed only the hypothesis that this original golden age of Aryan language and peoples was not preserved in India. Narratives of loss and decline were sufficient to support the need for a paternalistic colonialism that would restore to Indians their once noble cultural heritage. That said, Mandair argues that in subsequent periods of increased nationalism, the European strategy that eventually prevailed was a turn to polygenetic accounts of races and religions. See his "The Repetition of Past Imperialisms," 288–89. It is just here that Hegel emerges as a decisive figure.

14. Mandair writes that Hegel explicitly sought "to counter the influence of Indophiles such as Schelling in whose philosophy the prevailing definition of God/religion brought the origins of Oriental and Occidental civilizations unbearably close, such that the dominant vantage point of Euro-Christian identity based on its exclusionary claims to history, reason, and metaphysics, not to mention the colonial enterprise itself, would be threatened." Ibid., 289.

15. Ibid., 290.

16. Mandair is entirely in agreement with Spivak's claim that what Hegel offers in *Philosophy of History* is an "epistemography" and not an epistemology, but Mandair claims that it is in Hegel's *Lectures on the Philosophy of Religion* that one

finds Hegel's fully articulated solution to the threat posed by the philological discovery of common origins of European and Indian civilizations. Mandair's work also traces the processes by which Indians came to accept the translatability of *"religio"*—a Latinate term with no equivalent in Indian languages—and more importantly maps the monumental consequences of that acceptance. In this regard, Mandair's work is a critical contribution toward understanding what Spivak aptly calls the "epistemic seduction of the culture of imperialism." See Gayatri Chakravorty Spivak, *A Critique of Postcolonial Reason: Toward a History of the Vanishing Present* (Cambridge, Mass.: Harvard University Press, 1999), 41–49.

17. This complexity has much to do with Mandair's argument that for Hegel the decisive test for a religion's maturity was its capacity to approach the ontological proof for God's existence. See his "The Repetition of Past Imperialisms," 292–93. Traditions that have not realized the identity of being and thinking as exemplified in that argument remain deficient and trapped in earlier stages of cultural development. By appeal to this criterion, Hegel is able to distance Indian religion from Christianity by showing that "The Indian idea of divinity was as yet 'confused,' 'monstrous,' 'terrifying,' 'idolatrous,' 'absurd,' 'erroneous'—clear evidence for Hegel that Hindu thinking was limited to thinking nothingness." See "The Repetition of Past Imperialisms," 292.

18. The quote is from Mandair, "The Repetition of Past Imperialisms," 282.

19. Ibid., 299. See also Naoki Sakai, *Translation and Subjectivity: Japan and Cultural Nationalism* (Minneapolis: University of Minnesota Press, 1997), 91, cited in Mandair's "The Repetition of Past Imperialism," 299.

20. Of course, the very idea that the world can be divided into discrete cultural complexes or civilizations is an artifact of contingent historical processes. We are, on all sides, constrained by the very language and modes of thought that we seek to resist and escape.

21. It is striking that the work of generating scripture-like texts apparently took place even in the study of nonliterate indigenous religions. David Chidester reports that the philologist and student of South Africa Wilhelm Bleek even "arranged oral testimony into chapters and verses as if it represented a Zulu Bible." David Chidester, "'Classify and Conquer': Friedrich Max Müller, Indigenous Religious Traditions, and Imperial Comparative Religion," in *Beyond Primitivism: Indigenous Religious Traditions and Modernity*, ed. Jacob K. Olupona (New York: Routledge, 2004), 79.

22. Salman Rushdie, *The Ground beneath Her Feet* (New York: Henry Holt, 1999), 44. I should note here that I am not endorsing the historical accuracy of Rushdie's novelistic treatment of Müller. My intention in this chapter is to

demonstrate that there has long been an intimate and problematic connection between our thinking about "religions" and our thinking about "races."

23. Ibid. It should be noted that Rushdie's charitable treatment of the philological greats stands in need of qualification. For a nuanced and historically sensitive reading of Müller that demonstrates that his comparative religion was deeply tied up in justifying British imperial ambition, see the just cited essay by David Chidester. Chidester focuses on Müller's reading of the South African context in which colonized "savages" were understood to be "the original 'primitives' of the human race" and thus a critical tool in mapping the religious evolution of humanity. Chidester contends that, "Like imperial exhibitions, imperial comparative religion collected, condensed, and displayed the Empire as a sign and signal of its global scope and domination." See "Classify and Conquer," 84–85.

24. Robert Miles, *Racism After "Race Relations"* (New York: Routledge, 1993).

25. Robert Miles and Malcolm Brown, *Racism*, 2nd ed. (New York: Routledge, 2003), 91.

26. Ibid., 91–92.

27. See especially Talal Asad's "The Construction of Religion as an Anthropological Category," in *Genealogies of Religion: Discipline and Reasons of Power in Christianity and Islam* (Baltimore: Johns Hopkins University Press, 1993), 27–54.

28. Daniel Dubuisson, *The Western Construction of Religion* (Baltimore: Johns Hopkins University Press, 2003).

29. On these questions, see Mark Heim's *Salvations: Truth and Difference in Religion* (Maryknoll, N.Y.: Orbis Books, 1995) and *The Depth of the Riches: A Trinitarian Theology of Religious Ends* (Grand Rapids, Mich.: Eerdmans, 2000).

30. Paulo Gonçalves, "Religious 'Worlds' and Their Alien Invaders," in *Difference in Philosophy of Religion*, ed. Philip Goodchild (Burlington, Vt.: Ashgate, 2003), 115–34.

31. Ibid., 116.

32. Richard King, *Orientalism and Religion: Post-Colonial Theory, India and "The Mystic East"* (New York: Routledge, 1999).

33. Gonçalves, "Religious 'Worlds' and Their Alien Invaders," 116.

34. Ibid., 117.

35. Ibid.

36. Part of the problem here is that radical orthodoxy theologians work with limited alternatives. Either reason itself is deeply traditioned and therefore unlikely to be persuasive to those standing outside of a given tradition, or we have to make do with an Enlightenment account of rationality. Of course, the latter no longer appears to be a credible option now that Enlightenment reason

has been shown to be anything but neutral. But are these the only two broad options available to us? I think not. The most compelling account of reason and argumentation that avoids these two false options looks to Indian traditions of philosophical debate across traditions. See John Clayton's posthumously published book, *Religions, Reasons and Gods: Essays in Cross-Cultural Philosophy of Religion*, prepared for publication by Anne M. Blackburn and Thomas D. Carroll (New York: Cambridge University Press, 2006). Summarizing the difference between the Enlightenment conception of reason and Indian traditions of debate, Clayton offers the following observations: "1. In the Enlightenment model, tradition-specific reasons have no place in public rationality. In the *vada* model, tradition-specific reasons can have a place in public rationality. Admission to the public space is gained through contestability, not neutrality. 2. In the Enlightenment model, universal reason is a 'given' and is simply applied to particular cases. In the *vada* model, reason constructs itself in and through its operations in public debate. 3. In the Enlightenment model, the Other is not necessary for public rationality. In the *vada* model, the Other is necessary in that it is through engagement that both the Self and the Other construct themselves" (57). Clayton's account of rationality is particularly compelling because it accurately depicts tradition formation in general, whether inside or outside India, as accomplished by encounter and relation.

37. Of course, this is not to say that becoming religiously bilingual is easily accomplished. Spivak offers an extraordinarily rigorous account of the degree of bilingual competency required by those who aspire to take on the work of translating third world texts. See her essay "The Politics of Translation," in *Outside in the Teaching Machine* (New York: Routledge, 1993), 179–200. We are compelled to ask, What might it mean to be religiously bilingual in a sense that keeps fidelity with Spivak's criteria for translation?

38. See Spivak, "The Politics of Translation."

39. Gonçalves, "Religious 'Worlds' and Their Alien Invaders," 124.

40. Ibid., 125.

41. Jacques Derrida, *Positions*, trans. A. Bass (Chicago: University of Chicago Press, 1981), 57, quoted in Gonçalves, "Religious 'Worlds' and Their Alien Invaders," 126.

42. Gonçalves, "Religious 'Worlds' and Their Alien Invaders," 128.

43. Ibid., 132.

44. See my *The Immanent Divine: God, Creation, and the Human Predicament* (Minneapolis: Fortress Press, 2006), 205; See also Harold H. Oliver's *Relatedness: Essays in Metaphysics and Theology* (Macon, Ga.: Mercer University Press, 1984), 163–64.

45. Nagarjuna, *The Fundamental Wisdom of the Middle Way: Nagarjuna's* Mulamadhyamakakarika, trans. and commentary by Jay Garfield (New York: Oxford University Press, 1995).

TOWARD A COSMOPOLITAN THEOLOGY: CONSTRUCTING PUBLIC THEOLOGY FROM THE FUTURE | NAMSOON KANG

1. Gayatri Chakravorty Spivak, *A Critique of Postcolonial Reason: Toward a History of the Vanishing Present* (Cambridge, Mass.: Harvard University Press, 1999), 383.

2. Ibid.

3. Ibid.

4. Ibid., 384.

5. Friedrich Nietzsche, *Human, All too Human: A Book for Free Spirits* (Cambridge: Cambridge University Press, 1996), 196.

6. Diogenes the Cynic, in Diogenes Laertius, *Lives of the Philosophers,* Loeb Classical Library (Cambridge, Mass.: Harvard University Press, 1925), 6.63. One may distinguish between *cosmopolitans*, who are "basically indifferent to where they live," and *cosmopolites*, who are "habitants of a vast universe," placing a more positive value on the latter. See Yi-Fu Tuan, *Cosmos and Hearth: A Cosmopolite's Viewpoint* (Minneapolis: University of Minnesota Press, 1996), 159–60.

7. Here, however, the meaning of "citizen of the world" must be different from how we now tend to perceive it because Athenian "citizenship" at that time explicitly excluded women, slaves, and foreigners. See Jeremy Waldon, "Minority Cultures and the Cosmopolitan Alternative," *University of Michigan Journal of Law Reform* 25, no. 3 (1992): 751–93.

8. Patrick Hayden, *Cosmopolitan Global Politics* (Burlington, Vt.: Ashgate, 2005), 12.

9. Marcus Aurelius, *The Meditations* (Indianapolis: Hackett, 1983), 10.15.

10. Charles Jones, *Global Justice: Defending Cosmopolitanism* (Oxford: Oxford University Press, 1999), 16.

11. Martha Nussbaum, "Kant and Cosmopolitanism," in *Perpetual Peace: Essays on Kant's Cosmopolitan Ideal,* ed. James Bohman and Matthias Lutz-Backmann (Cambridge, Mass.: MIT Press, 1997), 31.

12. Ulrich Beck, *Cosmopolitan Vision,* trans. Ciaran Cronin (Cambridge, UK: Polity Press, 2006), 3.

13. Bruce Robbins, "Actually Existing Cosmopolitanism," in *Cosmopolitics: Thinking and Feeling beyond the Nation,* ed. Pheng Cheah et al. (Minneapolis: University of Minnesota Press, 1998), 1.

14. David Harvey, "Cosmopolitanism and the Banality of Geographical Evils," *Public Culture* 12, no. 2 (2000): 529.

15. For this argument, see Sharon Anderson-Gold, *Cosmopolitanism and Human Rights* (Cardiff: University of Wales Press, 2001); Darrel Moellendorf, *Cosmopolitan Justice* (Boulder, Colo.: Westview Press, 2002); Jones, *Global Justice*; Hayden, *Cosmopolitan Global Politics*; Luis Cabrera, *Political Theory of Global Justice: A*

Cosmopolitan Case for the World State (London and New York: Routledge, 2004); Steven Vertovec and Robin Cohen, *Conceiving Cosmopolitanism: Theory, Context, and Practice* (Oxford: Oxford University Press, 2002); Beck, *Cosmopolitan Vision*.

16. Beck, *Cosmopolitan Vision*, 7.

17. Zeno, cited in A. A. Long, "The Concept of the Cosmopolitan in Greek and Roman Thought," *Daedalus* (Summer 2008): 55.

18. Nussbaum, "Kant and Cosmopolitanism," 31.

19. Anderson-Gold, *Cosmopolitanism and Human Rights*, 11.

20. Cf. Bohman and Lutz-Bachmann, eds., *Perpetual Peace*.

21. Immanuel Kant, "Perpetual Peace: A Philosophical Sketch," in *Kant's Political Writings*, ed. Hans Reiss, trans. H. B. Nisbet (Cambridge: Cambridge University Press, 1971), 107–8.

22. Ibid., 105.

23. Ibid., 106.

24. Ibid., 99.

25. Seyla Benhabib argues that although Kant's cosmopolitan thought and his moral theory have influenced Arendt, she, as a "political existentialist," "remains committed to a civic republican vision of political self-determination." Seyla Benhabib, *Another Cosmopolitanism* (Oxford: Oxford University Press, 2006), 15.

26. Hannah Arendt, *The Origins of Totalitarianism* (London: George Allen and Unwin, 1967), 285; my emphasis.

27. Benhabib, *Another Cosmopolitanism*, 2.

28. United Nations, "Universal Declaration of Human Rights," 1948, articles 1 and 2.

29. Jacques Derrida, *On Cosmopolitanism and Forgiveness*, trans. Mark Dooley and Michael Hughes (London and New York: Routledge, 2001), 9.

30. Jacques Derrida, "Hostipitality," in *Acts of Religion*, ed. Gil Anidjar (London and New York: Routledge, 2002), 358–420.

31. Seyla Benhabib, *Another Cosmopolitanism* (Oxford: Oxford University Press, 2006), 157.

32. Derrida, "Hostipitality," 360.

33. Emmanuel Levinas, *Difficult Freedom: Essays on Judaism* (Baltimore: Johns Hopkins University Press, 1990), 22.

34. Kok-Chor Tan, *Justice without Borders: Cosmopolitanism, Nationalism and Patriotism* (Cambridge: Cambridge University Press, 2004), 1.

35. For this position, see Charles Beitz, *Political Theory and International Relations* (Princeton, N.J.: Princeton University Press, 1979); idem, "Cosmopolitan Ideals and National Sentiment," *Journal of Philosophy* 80, no. 10 (1983): 591–600; Nussbaum, "Kant and Cosmopolitanism"; Tan, *Justice without Borders*.

36. For the distinction of two types of cosmopolitanism, see Charles Beitz, "International Liberalism and Distributive Justice: A Survey of Recent Thought," *World Politics* 51, no. 2 (1999): 269–96.

37. Samuel Scheffler, *Boundaries and Allegiances* (Oxford: Oxford University Press, 2001), 112.

38. Jones, *Global Justice*, 15–17.

39. Derrida, *On Cosmopolitanism and Forgiveness*, viii.

40. Galatians 3:28, NRSV.

41. Ephesians 2:19, NRSV.

42. Stuart Alan Clarke, "Fear of a Black Planet," *Socialist Review* 21, no. 3–4 (1991): 46.

43. R. Radhakrishnan, *Diasporic Mediations: Between Home and Location* (Minneapolis: University of Minnesota Press, 1996), 75.

44. Michel Foucault, "Theatrum Philosophicum," in his *Language, Counter-Memory, Practice: Selected Essays and Interviews* (Ithaca, N.Y.: Cornell University Press, 1980), 182.

45. For a detailed discussion of this issue, see Namsoon Kang, "Who/What is Asian: A Postcolonial Theological Reading of Orientalism and Neo-Orientalism," in *Postcolonial Theologies: Divinity and Empire*, ed. Catherine Keller, Michael Nausner and Mayra Rivera (St. Louis: Chalice Press, 2004), 100–117.

46. Ellen Willis, "Multiple Identities," *Tikkun* 6, no. 6 (1991): 58.

47. Clarke, "Fear of a Black Planet," 46.

48. David Harvey, "Cosmopolitanism and the Banality of Geographical Evils," *Public Culture* 12, no. 2 (2000): 529–64.

49. Immanuel Kant, "Observations on the Feeling of the Beautiful and Sublime" (1764), cited in Emmanuel Chukwudi Eze, ed., *Race and the Enlightenment: A Reader* (Oxford: Blackwell, 1967), 48–49. It is questionable whether Kant is merely reflecting the general view of his time or inventing his own idea.

50. Immanuel Kant, *Physical Geography*, in *Gesammelte Schriften*, vols. 2 and 8 (Berlin: Reimer, 1900–66), cited in Eze, *Race and the Enlightenment*, 63.

51. Immanuel Kant, "On the Different Races of Man" (1775), cited in Eze, *Race and the Enlightenment*, 49, 46.

52. Immanuel Kant, *Kants philosophische Anthropologie*, ed. Friedrich Christian Starke (Leipzig, 1831), 353, cited in Emmanuel Chukwudi Eze, *Achieving our Humanity: The Idea of the Postracial Culture* (London and New York: Routledge, 2001), 99.

53. Robert Fine and Robin Cohen, "Four Cosmopolitan Moments," in *Conceiving Cosmopolitanism: Theory, Context, and Practice*, ed. Steven Vertovec and Robin Cohen (Oxford: Oxford University Press, 2002), 140.

54. I am indebted to Henry Giroux for the term, *border-thinking*. See Henry Giroux, "Border Pedagogy in the Age of Postmodernism," in *The Giroux Reader*, edited and introduced by Christopher Robbins (Boulder, Colo., and London: Paradigm Publishers, 2006), 47–66.

55. Although I do not buy into an exclusive polarity of *people from above* and *people from below*, my strategic use of the term *people from below* here is to denote the significance of one's positionality/locationality and solidarity with the marginalized people based on whatever grounds are available to one.

56. Michele Wallace, "Multiculturalism and Oppositionality," *Afterimage* (October 1991): 6.

57. Cf. David Spurr, *The Rhetoric of Empire: Colonial Discourse in Journalism, Travel Writing, and Imperial Administration* (Durham, N.C.: Duke University Press, 1993).

58. Sharon Welch, *After Empire: The Art and Ethos of Enduring Peace* (Minneapolis: Fortress Press, 2004), xvi.

59. *Human Development Report 2002*, United Nations Development Programme, 141–44, cited in Martha Nussbaum, "Beyond the Social Contract: Capabilities and Global Justice," in *The Political Philosophy of Cosmopolitanism*, ed. Gillian Brock and Harry Brighouse (Cambridge: Cambridge University Press, 2005), 196.

60. *Human Development Report 2000*, United Nations Development Programme, cited in Nussbaum, "Beyond the Social Contract," 196.

61. Charles Beitz, "Does Global Inequality Matter?" in *Global Justice*, ed. Thomas W. Pogge (Oxford: Blackwell, 2001), 106.

62. Karen Baker-Fletcher and Garth Kasimu Baker-Fletcher, *My Sister, My Brother: Womanist and Xodus God-Talk* (Maryknoll, N.Y.: Orbis Books, 1997), 203–4.

63. Here it is important to note that there are, according to Karl Mannheim, two types of utopia: the absolutely unrealizable utopia and the relatively unrealizable utopia. See Karl Mannheim, *Ideology and Utopia: An Introduction to the Sociology of Knowledge*, trans. Louis Wirth and Edward Shils (1927; New York: Harvest/HBJ, 1985), 196–99. A utopian idea is "unrealizable only from the point of view of a given social order which is already in existence" (ibid., 196), which means it can be realizable in a different social order.

64. Matthew Fox, *The Coming of the Cosmic Christ: The Healing of Mother Earth and the Birth of a Global Renaissance* (New York: HarperSanFrancisco, 1988).

65. Tan, *Justice without Borders*, 20.

66. For the interview with Derrida, see "Intellectual Courage: An Interview," *Culture Machine* 2 (2002). http://culturemachine.tees.ac.uk/frm_f1.htm (accessed May 25, 2008).

67. Jacques Derrida, *Le Figaro Magazine*, October 16, 1999, cited in Obrad Savic, "Introduction—Duty of Unconditional Hospitality," *Parallax* 11, no. 1 (2005): 4.

68. Paul Celan, cited in Emmanuel Levinas, *Otherwise Than Being, or Beyond Essence*, trans. Alphonso Lingis (Pittsburgh: Duquesne University Press, 1998), 99.

PAX TERRA AND OTHER UTOPIAS? PLANETARITY, COSMOPOLITANISM, AND THE KINGDOM OF GOD | DHAWN B. MARTIN

1. Walter D. Mignolo names sixteenth-century maps and their trade route connections as "the first step of the imaginary of the modern/colonial world that we today call globalization." Walter D. Mignolo, "The Many Faces of Cosmopolis: Border Thinking and Critical Cosmopolitanism," *Public Culture* 12, no. 3 (2000): 726.

2. Gayatri Chakravorty Spivak, *Death of a Discipline* (New York: Columbia University Press, 2003), 72.

3. "Globalization," Spivak observes, "is the imposition of the same system of exchange everywhere" (ibid).

4. Ibid.

5. Ibid., 101–2.

6. Spivak, following Derrida, distinguishes between the human as "repository of a 'unique and essential quality' that can only clamor for rights" and the human as "called by the other—to responsibility." Gayatri Chakravorty Spivak, *A Critique of Postcolonial Reason: Toward a History of the Vanishing Present* (Cambridge, Mass.: Harvard University Press, 1999), 388–89 n. 101.

7. Spivak, *Death of a Discipline*, 52. For detailed discussion of *unheimlich*, see 73–78.

8. For explication of Spivak's conception of the other or "wholly other," see "French Feminism Revisited," in Gayatri Chakravorty Spivak, *Outside in the Teaching Machine* (London: Routledge, 1993), 141–71. In discussing the "second phase" of Derrida's work with deconstruction, Spivak locates "justice and ethics" in "'experiences of the impossible': experiences of radical alterity." Spivak, *A Critique of Postcolonial Reason*, 426.

9. Spivak, *Death of a Discipline*, 13. Spivak draws and expands on Derrida's theme of an ever-arriving politics. See Jacques Derrida, *The Politics of Friendship*, trans. George Collins (1997; London: Verso, 2005).

10. Benevolence as a theme recurs throughout Spivak's writing and is intimately related to the "civilizing mission" and various social activists' "unexamined" participation in the "financialization of the globe." See Gayatri Chakravorty Spivak, "Practical Politics of the Open End," in *The Post-Colonial Critic: Interviews, Strategies, Dialogues*, ed. Sarah Harasym (New York and London:

Routledge, 1990), 95–112, and the last chapter of *A Critique of Postcolonial Reason* for two examples.

11. "[W]e have seen how Kant may be read as suggesting that the human being is programmed to supplement rational morality by the name of God. . . . [T]his name may be seen as *a* name of the radical alterity that the self . . . is programmed to imagine in an ethics of responsibility. The agency of the call of responsibility that is the program of being is then placed in a wholly other that makes (no = all the) difference." Spivak, *A Critique of Postcolonial Reason*, 354–55 n. 59. It is crucial to note, however, Spivak's insistence that for her, "radical alterity cannot be named 'God,' in any language." Gayatri Chakravorty Spivak, "Righting Wrongs," *South Atlantic Quarterly* 103, no. 2/3 (2004): 564.

12. Spivak, *Death of a Discipline*, 73.

13. Dorothee Soelle, *The Window of Vulnerability: A Political Spirituality* (Minneapolis: Fortress Press, 1990), 7. In an earlier work, Soelle declares that "politics is understood as the comprehensive and decisive sphere in which Christian truth should become praxis." Dorothee Soelle, *Political Theology* (Philadelphia: Fortress Press, 1974), 89, cited in Sharon Welch, *Communities of Resistance and Solidarity: A Feminist Theology of Liberation* (Maryknoll, N.Y.: Orbis Books, 1985), 47.

14. "Tell me how you think and act politically, and I will tell you who your God is." Soelle, *Window of Vulnerability*, 106.

15. John Cobb, in his review of the political theologies of Metz, Moltmann, and Soelle, identifies a "hermeneutic" of the "self-critical" as constitutive to the discourse of political theology. John B. Cobb Jr., *Process Theology as Political Theology* (Manchester: Manchester University Press/Philadelphia: Westminster Press, 1982), 10, 15ff. In a different vein, Mark Lilla casts political theology as a dangerous vestige of premodern thought before the "Great Separation" and the experiment of Western secularism. Mark Lilla, *The Stillborn God: Religion, Politics, and the Modern West* (New York: Knopf, 2007).

16. Gayatri Chakravorty Spivak, "The Post-modern Condition: The End of Politics?" in *The Post-Colonial Critic*, 18.

17. Ibid., 18–19.

18. Spivak, *Death of a Discipline*, 52. See note 9 also.

19. Mignolo, "The Many Faces of Cosmo-polis," 724.

20. Ibid.

21. Ibid., 744; my emphasis.

22. Ibid., 742–43.

23. Debate—national and transnational—continues with regard to the "Great Wall" under construction between the United States and Mexico.

24. Spivak, *A Critique of Postcolonial Reason*, 427.

25. Ibid., 427–28.

26. Gayatri Chakravorty Spivak, "Questioned on Translation: Adrift," in *Public Culture* 13, no. 1 (2001): 14.

27. Ibid., 14–15.

28. Gayatri Chakravorty Spivak, "Teaching for the Times," *Journal of the Midwest Modern Language Association* 25, no. 1 (1992): 16. The article is part of a thematic issue titled "Oppositional Discourse."

29. Spivak, "Questioned on Translation," 15; my emphasis.

30. Quotes are from a speech delivered by former President George W. Bush at the Pentagon in March 2008 on the fifth anniversary of the invasion of Iraq. "President Bush Discusses Global War on Terror," http://www.whitehouse .gov/news/releases/2008/03/20080319-2.html (accessed July 6, 2008); my emphasis.

31. Mignolo, "The Many Faces of Cosmo-polis," 726.

32. It is important to note that Mignolo challenges historical and contemporary cosmopolitan projects that participate in the colonial/modern paradigm he identifies in a multitude of convergent imaginaries, times, and designs. According to Mignolo, the imaginary of the *orbis* morphed into one of the *cosmos* in eighteenth-century projects of the Enlightenment. Ibid.

33. Ibid., 727.

34. Spivak, *Death of a Discipline*, 73.

35. Catherine Keller, *Face of the Deep: A Theology of Becoming* (London and New York: Routledge, 2003), 40.

36. Ibid., 238.

37. Ibid., 117–18.

38. Spivak, *Death of a Discipline*, 81, 74. Spivak's work with the concept of utopia reveals a certain ambivalence. See "Righting Wrongs," 575 n. 53, and *A Critique of Postcolonial Reason*, 318: "Most utopias forget that utopia is nowhere. . . . In certain conjunctures, they can be productive."

39. Keller, *Face of the Deep*, 230, 171.

40. Jacques Derrida, *The Politics of Friendship*, 32.

41. Ibid.

42. Spivak, "French Feminism Revisited," 165.

43. Mignolo, "The Many Faces of Cosmo-polis," 744. Mignolo names the "subaltern perspective" as definitive of the universal project that is his conception of critical cosmopolitanism. Ibid., 743, 745.

44. For a review of and for other sources on Cynic and Stoic thought see Martha Nussbaum, "Kant and Cosmopolitanism," in *Perpetual Peace: Essays on Kant's*

Cosmopolitan Ideal, ed. James Bohman and Matthias Lutz-Bachmann (Cambridge, Mass.: MIT Press), 27–37. My sketch of Stoicism here is drawn primarily from Nussbaum's treatment.

45. Ibid., 32.

46. As Nussbaum summarizes, for Stoics "love of humanity as such should be our basic affective attitude" (ibid., 46).

47. Immanuel Kant, "To Perpetual Peace: A Philosophical Sketch," in *Immanuel Kant: Perpetual Peace and Other Essays,* trans. Ted Humphrey (Indianapolis: Hackett, 1983), 117.

48. Nussbaum, "Kant and Cosmopolitanism," 37. For more on the link between reason and natural law see 28–30. According to Kant, the equal rights of all humans and their "common ownership of the earth's surface" demand a "universal *hospitality*" ("Perpetual Peace," 118).

49. Immanuel Kant, "Idea for a Universal History with a Cosmopolitan Intent," in *Immanuel Kant: Perpetual Peace and Other Essays,* 33.

50. David Held, *Global Covenant: The Social Democratic Alternative to the Washington Consensus* (Cambridge, Mass.: Polity Press, 2004), 171. Held views cosmopolitanism as an effective and already pervasive tool for adapting post–World War II nation-state structures and policies to the increasing demands of transnational capital and communication flows. The political theorist William E. Connolly further dislocates concentricity as an element in cosmopolitanism, proposing "eccentric flows that cross and disrupt these circles, the concentric images" that, in Connolly's analysis, "point . . . either to the bellicose particularism of the nation/civilization . . . or to the impatient universalism of concentric cosmopolitanism (Nussbaum)." William E. Connolly, *Neuropolitics: Thinking, Culture, Speed* (Minneapolis: University of Minnesota Press, 2002), 192.

51. David Held, "Culture and Political Community: National, Global, and Cosmopolitan," in *Conceiving Cosmopolitanism: Theory, Context, and Practice,* ed. Stephen Vertovec and Robin Cohen (Oxford: Oxford University Press, 2002), 57–58.

52. Mignolo presents extensive discussion of Kant's "Eurocentric bias" and "geopolitical" bigotry. Mignolo, "The Many Faces of Cosmo-polis," 732–35. For other discussion of biases prevalent in Kant's work in geography see David Harvey, "Cosmopolitanism and the Banality of Geographical Evils," *Public Culture* 12, no. 2 (2000): 529–64.

53. Bhabha draws heavily on Etienne Balibar's "right to difference in equality" to explicate an ethos of vernacular cosmopolitanism. Homi K. Bhabha, "Looking Back, Moving Forward: Notes on Vernacular Cosmopolitanism," preface to the 2006 edition of *The Location of Culture* (London and New York: Routledge, 2006), xvii.

54. Ibid.

55. Ibid., xvi, xviii.

56. For Derrida, "[A] democracy to come . . . *would therefore be a matter of thinking an alterity without hierarchical difference at the root of democracy"* (*The Politics of Friendship*, 232).

57. Bhabha, *The Location of Culture*, xx.

58. Hannah Arendt and Karl Jaspers, *Correspondence: 1926–1969* (New York: Harcourt Brace, 1992), 69, as quoted in Robert Fine and Robin Cohen, "Four Cosmopolitan Moments," in *Conceiving Cosmopolitanism*, ed. Vertovec and Cohen, 150.

59. Jacques Derrida, "The Animal That Therefore I Am," trans. David Wills, *Critical Inquiry* 28, no. 2 (2002): 399.

60. Ibid., 397, 409.

61. Ibid., 413. Derrida's essay engages in a prolonged critique of those texts of philosophy (and of Genesis) that relegate "the animal" to singular categorization. In an effort to displace this multiplicity erasing singularity, Derrida coins the term *l'animot*. He further elaborates a link between redemption discourse and "what is proper to," and therefore superior in "man'" (ibid., 388–90, 409).

62. This transposition resonates with ecological emphases in Spivak's work, however discordant with her skepticism of a theopolitical rehabilitation of "the so-called great religions." Spivak, *A Critique of Postcolonial Reason*, 382.

63. Gayatri Chakravorty Spivak, "Can the Subaltern Speak?" in *Marxism and the Interpretation of Culture*, ed. Cary Nelson and Lawrence Grossberg (Urbana: University of Illinois Press, 1988), 288–89.

64. Gayatri Spivak, "Practical Politics of the Open End," in *The Post-Colonial Critic*, ed. Harasym, 109.

65. For Spivak, the radical vulnerability that is deconstruction serves as "reminder of the fact that" critique and loving practices necessarily inform and undo one another. Ibid., 111.

66. Elisabeth Schüssler Fiorenza, *The Power of the Word: Scripture and the Rhetoric of Empire* (Minneapolis: Fortress Press, 2007), 26.

67. John B. Cobb Jr., "Commonwealth and Empire," in *The American Empire and the Commonwealth of God*, ed. David Ray Griffin, John B. Cobb Jr., Richard A. Falk, and Catherine Keller (Louisville, Ky.: Westminster John Knox Press, 2006), 144.

68. John Milbank, "Liberty versus Liberalism," in *Religion and Political Thought*, ed. Michael Hoelzl and Graham Ward (London: Continuum, 2006), 229, 228, 232–33.

69. The thirteenth book in the series is titled *Kingdom Come: The Final Victory*. For further discussion of the rhetoric of the "axis of evil" see, Griffen et al., *The American Empire and the Commonwealth of God*.

70. Spivak, *A Critique of Postcolonial Reason*, 382–83.

71. Cobb, "Commonwealth and Empire," 142.

72. Former President Bush's not so subtle theospeak is well documented.

73. As the work of Elisabeth Schüssler Fiorenza indicates, it is *ekklesia* and not *basileia*, in the Greek, which—with its meaning tied to "democratic assembly"—addresses issues of membership and citizenship. See Elisabeth Schüssler Fiorenza, *Jesus and the Politics of Interpretation* (New York: Continuum, 2000), 75. Nevertheless, due to the pervasiveness of the image in theological and social imaginaries, this essay will associate the *basileia* with a discussion of citizenship and belonging.

74. Stephen D. Moore, "Mark and Empire: 'Zealot' and 'Postcolonial' Readings," in *Postcolonial Theologies: Divinity and Empire*, ed. Catherine Keller et al. (St. Louis: Chalice Press, 2004), 142. While Moore's analysis of *basileia*/empire concerns the text of Mark, "profound ambivalence" aptly describes the contradictory images portrayed throughout the parables of the kingdom.

75. Immanuel Kant, "End of All Things," in *Immanuel Kant: Perpetual Peace and Other Essays*, 102, 101.

76. "[T]urn of the plough, furrow, line, row," from "Verse," in *The Oxford Dictionary of English Etymology*, ed. C. T. Onions (Oxford: Oxford University Press, 1966), 976.

77. "So then you are no longer strangers and sojourners, but you are fellow citizens with the saints and members of the household [*oikos*] of God, built upon the foundation of the apostles and prophets, Christ Jesus himself being the cornerstone, in whom the whole structure is joined together and grows into a holy temple in the Lord; in whom you also are built into it for a dwelling place of God in the Spirit." For Derrida's analysis of the first two verses of the Ephesians text see his *On Cosmopolitanism and Forgiveness*, trans. Mark Dooley and Michael Hughes (2001; London: Routledge, 2005), 19–20.

78. Distinct from Kant's dream of a perpetual, perhaps too-secure, peace, *Pax Terra* hospitably entertains the displaced and displacing.

CRIP/TOGRAPHY: OF KARMA AND COSMOPOLIS
| SHARON V. BETCHER

1. Ray Bakke, "Urbanization and Evangelism: A Global View," *Word and World* 19, no. 3 (1999): 225.

2. Gayatri Chakravorty Spivak, "Globalicities," *New Centennial Review* 4, no. 1 (2004): 74.

3. Mark Kingwell, *Concrete Reveries: Consciousness and the City* (New York: Viking Press, 2008), 11.

4. Spivak, "Globalicities," 77.

5. Ibid.

6. The terms "global" and/or "world" cities refer to cities that have tended, by virtue of sociological and especially economic processes, to supersede any sense of territorial locale. These cities tend to be referred to on a "first name" basis, e.g., London, New York, Mumbai. While most global cities sport a population exceeding twenty million, other dynamics occasion identification as a global city. These dynamics may include extremely high immigration and therefore the generation of intense multiethnic basins, e.g., Vancouver. Global cities tend, economically speaking, to be "postindustrial" and sell themselves more so as a "cultural" experience; indeed, culture becomes their business. Because of this relation between economics and culture shaping global cities, occasioning something of a landing pad for the economic elite, not all cities exceeding populations of twenty million are grouped into the category of "world" or "global cities." Most world cities have large research universities; but research is notably driven by biotechnology, physics, and so on—not the humanities. Further, even as the elite of such cities prove extremely mobile (moving among the global cities themselves), no global city lives without a migrant underclass; even in or especially in the wealthiest of communities within these cities, the nurturant activities, from nannies to nurses to cleaning services, will be maintained by a migrant populace.

7. Jane M. Jacobs, *Edge of Empire: Postcolonialism and the City* (London and New York: Routledge, 1996), 4.

8. Molly O'Meara Sheehan, Project Director, and Linda Starke, ed., *State of the World 2007: Our Urban Future*; World Watch Institute (New York: W. W. Norton, 2007), 6.

9. Michel Foucault, as cited by Rey Chow, *The Protestant Ethnic and the Spirit of Capitalism* (New York: Columbia University Press, 2002), 11.

10. Don Mitchell, "The Annihilation of Space by Law: Anti-Homeless Laws and the Shrinking Landscape of Rights," in *The Right to the City* (New York: Guilford, 2003).

11. Jacobs, *Edge of Empire*, 4.

12. Leonie Sandercock, *Cosmopolis II: Mongrel Cities in the 21st Century* (New York: Continuum, 2003), 1.

13. David Harvey, *Spaces of Hope* (Berkeley: University of California Press, 2000), 15, 18.

14. Ibid., 16.

15. Jacobs, *Edge of Empire*, 10.

16. Susan Stanford Friedman, *Mappings: Feminism and the Cultural Geographies of Encounter* (Princeton, N.J.: Princeton University Press, 1998), 4, 3. How feminist

theology might proceed is a serious question. Feminist theology—like liberal Protestantism—made use of rationalism to deflate absolute transcendence, thereby also deconstructing male power, and to defend women's agency from serving yet again as the sacrificial site of this economy. Going postmodern, not even "The Future of Christology"—Jesuit theologian Roger Haight's most recent christological proposal—feels the need to make a nod toward feminist and/or postcolonial constructions (*The Future of Christology* [New York and London: Continuum, 2005]). If Haight's recent text shocks by its erasure (Haight, given his postmodern commitments, has been banned from teaching as a Catholic theologian), I might venture that even on my edge of the continent, one of the supposedly fractious dioceses of the Anglican communion in regards to its stand on gay marriage, it appears as if the church's debate over gay lifestyles continues to be a debate primarily over acceptable masculinities. Crip/tography, I hope, begins to take feminist and postcolonial commitments "on location" so as to decouple theology from its inherited imperial axis as well as to exit that rationalist materialism which measures well-being by biosocial pathology and economic productivity standards.

17. Warren Magnusson et al., eds. *A Political Space: Reading the Global through Clayoquot Sound* (Minneapolis: University of Minnesota Press, 2002), 2.

18. Jacobs, *Edge of Empire*, 22. Jacobs cites Paul Carter, *The Road to Botany Bay* (1987) as source of her insight.

19. David M. Halperin, *Saint Foucault: Towards a Gay Hagiography* (Oxford: Oxford University Press, 1995), 62, 66.

20. Ibid., 54.

21. See Seth Mydans, "What Makes a Monk Mad: Karma Power," "Week in Review," *Sunday New York Times* (September 30, 2007): 1, 14. Mydans explains that in Myanmar, which has as many monks as soldiers, "the military rules by force, but the monks retain ultimate moral authority. The lowliest soldier depends on them for spiritual approval" (1), not incidentally because "these young monks remain closer to the lives and concerns of the people whose alms they receive" (14). When the monks inverted their begging bowls, refusing daily donations, they also deprived the soldiers of moral authority and karmic well-being; they rejected the military junta—and it brought with it terror and crucifixion.

22. Yvonne Sherwood, "Passion-Binding-Passion," in *Toward a Theology of Eros: Transfiguring Passion at the Limits of Discipline*, ed. Virginia Burrus and Catherine Keller (New York: Fordham University Press, 2006), 188.

23. Ibid., 178.

24. Holmes Rolston III, "Does Nature Need to be Redeemed?" *Zygon* 29 (June 1994): 220.

25. Donna Haraway, "Ecce Homo, Ain't (Ar'n't) I a Woman, and Inappropriate/ d Others: The Human in a Post-Humanist Landscape," in *Feminists Theorize the Political*, ed. Judith Butler and Joan W. Scott (London and New York: Routledge, 1992), 87.

26. Ibid., 87, 91. Haraway borrows the term "inappropriate/d others" from Trinh T. Minh-ha, ed., "She, the Inappropriate/d Other," *Discourse* 8 (thematic issue, Fall/Winter 1986–87).

27. Sherwood, "Passion-Binding-Passion,"183.

28. Adolf von Harnack, *The Mission and Expansion of Christianity in the First Three Centuries*, trans. James Moffatt (New York: G. P. Putnam's Sons, 1908), 1:109.

29. Zygmunt Bauman, *Liquid Modernity* (Cambridge: Polity Press, 2000). Martha Nussbaum puts this wisdom about humanity's shared incompleteness, its vulnerability, at the heart of the social contract, as a needed correction to "the psychological foundations of liberalism." See her *Hiding from Humanity: Disgust, Shame and the Law* (Princeton, N.J.: Princeton University Press, 2004), 16.

30. Douglas John Hall, *The Cross in Our Context: Jesus and the Suffering World* (Minneapolis: Fortress, 2003), 175.

31. Graham Ward, *Cities of God* (London and New York: Routledge, 2000), 81.

32. Ibid., 96.

33. Stephanie Kallos, *Broken for You* (New York: Grove Press, 2004).

34. James Perkinson explains that "In the first centuries of the church's life . . . , to become a believer . . . meant to enlist. In the Roman imperial order, a *sacramentum* was an oath of loyalty taken by a soldier to Caesar. For Christians living under the imperial regime, celebrating 'sacraments' like the Eucharist was a practice of political resistance in a struggle that engaged war-making as its nonviolent, but combative opposite." See his "Theology and the City: Learning to Cry, Struggling to See," *CrossCurrents* 51, no. 1 (2001). http:// www.crosscurrents.org/perkinson0151.htm.

35. Fustel de Coulanges, *The Ancient City: A Study on the Religion, Laws and Institutions of Greece and Rome*, trans. Willard Small, 12th ed. (Boston: Lothrop, Lee and Shepard, 1901), 193, 205.

36. Andrew Davey, *Urban Christianity and Global Order* (Peabody, Mass.: Hendrickson, 2002), 72.

37. Sharon Zukin, *The Culture of Cities* (Oxford: Blackwell, 1995), 38–39.

38. Michael Hardt and Antonio Negri, *Empire* (Cambridge, Mass.: Harvard University Press, 2000), xii, 142–46.

39. Robert Young, *Colonial Desire: Hybridity in Theory, Culture and Race* (London and New York: Routledge, 1995), 180.

40. Don Mitchell, "The Illusion and Necessity of Order: Toward a Just City," in *The Right to the City* (New York: Guilford, 2003), 227.

41. David D. Yuan, "Disfigurement and Reconstruction in Oliver Wendell Holmes's 'The Human Wheel, Its Spokes and Felloes,'" in *The Body and Physical Difference: Discourses of Disability*, ed. David T. Mitchell and Sharon L. Snyder (Ann Arbor: University of Michigan Press, 1997), 71–88.

42. Brendan Gleeson, "A Place on Earth: Technology, Space and Disability," *Journal of Urban Technology* 5, no. 1 (1998): 96, 90–91.

43. R. Imrie, *Disability and the City: International Perspectives* (London: Paul Chapman, 1996), as cited by Rob Kitchen, "'Out of Place,' 'Knowing One's Place': Space, Power and the Exclusion of Disabled People," *Disability and Society* 13, no. 3 (1998): 346.

44. Harlan Hahn, "Advertising the Acceptably Employable Image," in *The Disability Studies Reader*, ed. Lennard Davis (London and New York: Routledge, 1997), 178–79.

45. Mitchell, "The Annihilation of Space by Law," 163–64.

46. Ibid.,190.

47. Zukin, *The Culture of Cities*, 2.

48. As Vancouver prepares for the 2010 Winter Olympics, the city has consciously sought out the counsel of Rudolph Giuliani in regards to the civic and policing strategies he brought to bear in New York City. Vancouver columnist Geoff Olson analytically observes the results of such legislation in a recent essay, "The Future Isn't What It Used to Be: Measuring Cultural Change": "In the lead-up to 2010's Olympic orgasm for developers, the city council has passed laws to keep street people from sitting on park benches or reclining in parks. Behind this crazy-making effort to create a 'civil city' is a conception of humans as rubbish. It's both a metaphor and a screaming red flag for the world we are creating—or rather, destroying. In many urban centres across North America, this kind of sociopathic civic-mindedness has become the new normal." See *Common Ground* 192 (July 2007): 31. Ironically, Vancouver's "Project Civil City"—the mayoral "anti-crime" initiative, focused on dispersing the homeless from the urban core, reducing panhandling and open drug sales—has been brought forward by Vancouver's wheel-chair riding mayor, Sam Sullivan.

49. "The public geography of a city is civility institutionalized." Richard Sennett, *The Fall of Public Man* (New York: Alfred A. Knopf, 1977), 264.

50. See Wendy Brown's parallel analysis of tolerance, *Regulating Aversion: Tolerance in the Age of Identity and Empire* (Princeton, N.J.: Princeton University Press, 2006).

51. Spivak, "Righting Wrongs," 524.

52. Sennett, *The Fall of Public Man*, 39.

53. Ibid., 264.

54. Spivak, "Righting Wrongs," 533.

55. Perkinson, "Theology and the City."

56. Spivak, "Righting Wrongs," 561, 569 n. 18.

57. Ibid., 531, 524.

58. Ibid., 523–24.

59. Ibid., 533.

60. Ibid.

61. Ibid., 537, 545.

62. Ibid., 545.

63. Zygmunt Bauman, *Wasted Lives: Modernity and Its Outcasts* (Cambridge: Polity Press, 2004).

64. Ibid., 5.

65. Ibid., 6.

66. Richard Sennett, *Flesh and Stone: The Body and City in Western Civilization* (New York: W. W. Norton, 1994), 310.

67. Bauman, *Liquid Modernity*, 119–20.

68. Improvising upon Foucault's sense of modern power as epitomized by the panopticon, Thomas Mathiesen notes a shift in late modern techniques of power to what he calls "the synopticon." Zygmunt Bauman expounds Mathiesen's point: Today "the many watch the few"; and "locals watch the globals. . . . Wherever they come from . . . , celebrities put on display the world of celebrities—a world whose main distinctive feature is precisely the quality of being watched—by many, and in all corners of the globe." See Bauman, *Globalization: The Human Consequences* (New York: Columbia University Press, 1998), 48–54; quotes are from page 53.

69. Bauman, *Liquid Modernity*, 109.

70. Ibid., 109.

71. Janet Jakobsen, "Can Homosexuals End Western Civilization as We Know It? Family Values in a Global Economy," in *Queer Globalizations: Citizenship and the Afterlife of Colonialism*, ed. Arnaldo Cruze-Malave and Martin F. Manalansan (New York: New York University Press, 2002), 59.

72. Kelly Oliver, *Witnessing: Beyond Recognition* (Minneapolis: University of Minnesota Press, 2001), 15.

73. Admittedly, I use the term "karma" casually, as this Vancouver-based, multireligious culture is writing it. In this encounter I was reminded that other religious cultures regard disability as soulful privilege and the disabled then as mature or wise teacher. Or even more simply, for other religious cultures the disabled, the poor, the mendicant may be an opportunity given to build one's own karma.

74. Marcella Althaus-Reid, *Indecent Theology: Theological Perversions in Sex, Gender, and Politics* (New York: Routledge, 2000).

75. Walter Brueggemann, as cited by Davey, *Urban Christianity and Global Order*, 73.

76. Kathryn Tanner, *Theories of Culture: A New Agenda for Theology* (Minneapolis: Fortress, 1997), 113. Tanner argues against thinking Christianity as a culture onto itself. Rather Christian practice, she asserts, has to do with ways of making meaning of the cultural artifacts we find around us.

77. Steve Pile, "Introduction: Opposition, Political identities, and Spaces of Resistance," in *Geographies of Resistance*, ed. Steve Pile and Michael Keith (London and New York: Routledge, 1997), 2–3.

78. Spivak, "Righting Wrongs," 559.

79. Ibid., 534.

80. Sennett, *Fall of Public Man*, 326.

81. Ibid., 333.

82. Ibid., 333–36.

83. Despite the emphatic teachings of the fathers, Christian theology has lived quite comfortably within Roman sensibilities of ownership of property, of the commons, since the fourth century: "[T]he Roman law theory-and-practice of ownership, which the fathers attacked and sought to replace, has retained the ascendancy all through the Christian centuries that have elapsed since their thundering critical voices fell silent." Charles Avila, *Ownership: Early Christian Teaching* (Maryknoll, N.Y.: Orbis Books, 1983), 11.

84. Mitchell, "Annihilation of Space by Law," 166–67.

85. Spivak, "Righting Wrongs," 535.

86. Ibid., 537.

87. Spivak's notion of "collectivity" ironically mimics the ways in which liberalism marks off "primitive" or "less developed" cultures. Her intent seems to be that liberal education needs to assume a cultural axiomatic of being responsible to the other, to assume "that it is natural to be angled toward the other" (ibid., 537).

88. Ward, *Cities of God*, 118, referring to John D. Zizoulas, *Being in Communion: Studies in Personhood and the Church* (London: Darton, Longman and Todd, 1985).

89. Ward, *Cities of God*, 56.

90. Ibid., 61.

91. Ibid., 62.

92. Perhaps not surprisingly, the first theological responses to the emergence of global cities have been developing in the UK, given the history of London as

metropole. In 1985, the Anglican Archbishop launched a commission titled "Faith in the City." Ward's text takes issue with the "old liberal" social politics of that report, criticizing it for its inability to actually take account of the lines of force in the emergent cosmopolis—specifically, the force of desire. To that form of public theology he responds, "new theology needed."

93. Ward, *Cities of God*, 76.

94. Ibid., 74.

95. Ibid., 77.

96. Ibid., 2.

97. Ibid., 82.

98. Graham Ward, "Bodies: The Displaced Body of Jesus," in *Radical Orthodoxy*, ed. John Milbank, Catherine Pickstock, and Graham Ward (London and New York: Routledge, 1999).

99. Graham Ward, "Suffering and Incarnation," in *The Blackwell Companion to Postmodern Theology*, ed. Graham Ward (Oxford: Blackwell, 2001).

100. Ward, *Cities of God*, 83.

101. Ward, "Bodies," 169.

102. Ward, *Cities of God*, 70.

103. Ibid., 84.

104. Ward, "Bodies,"170.

105. Ward, *Cities of God*, 5, 6–7.

106. Ibid., 87.

107. Gary Gardner, *Invoking the Spirit: Religion and Spirituality in the Quest for a Sustainable World*, ed. Jane Peterson, Worldwatch Paper 164 (Danvers, Mass.: Worldwatch Institute, 2002).

108. Wendy Brown, *States of Injury: Power and Freedom in Late Modernity* (Princeton, N.J.: Princeton University Press, 1995), 61.

109. John S. Dunne, *The City of the Gods: A Study in Myth and Morality* (New York: Macmillan, 1965), 135.

110. De Coulanges, *The Ancient City*, 193, 205. Ward cited this passage from de Coulanges in a public lecture on theology and global cities at Vancouver School of Theology, Vancouver, British Columbia, on September 26, 2007.

111. Ward, *Cities of God*, Preface.

112. Spivak, "Righting Wrongs," 567 n. 16.

113. Marcella Althaus-Reid, "'A Saint and a Church for Twenty Dollars': Sending Radical Orthodoxy to Ayacucho," in *Interpreting the Postmodern: Responses to "Radical Orthodoxy,"* ed. Rosemary Radford Ruether and Marion Grau (New York and London: T. & T. Clark, 2006), 110.

114. Ward, *Cities of God*, 92.

115. Spivak, "Righting Wrongs," 568 n. 16.
116. Peter Brown, *Poverty and Leadership in the Late Roman Empire* (Hanover, N.H.: University Press of New England, 2002), 15.
117. Richard Kearney, *The God Who May Be: A Hermeneutics of Religion* (Bloomington and Indianapolis: Indiana University Press, 2001), 18–19.
118. The following benediction, shaped by the reading of the gospel for the day— the "miracle" account of the bent-over woman (Lk 13:10–17)—was given at the end of a worship service held on October 18, 2007, at Epiphany Chapel, Vancouver School of Theology: "Go out to love and serve God's people, not bent, no longer broken, one body in Christ, consecrated by God." Here again, disabled bodies have been liturgically invalidated.
119. Spivak, "Righting Wrongs," 531.
120. Ward celebrates the "translocationality" of body via Eucharist. See his "Bodies," 168.
121. Anita Silvers and Leslie Pickering Francis, "Justice through Trust: Disability and the 'Outlier Problem' in Social Contract Theory," *Ethics* 116 (October 2006): 42.
122. Ibid., 41.
123. Ibid., 62.
124. Spivak gives an intriguing illustration of a noncontractual "nationality" based in responsibility in her essay "Globalicities" (78–80). This leads to her concept of a "para-individual structural responsibility" (79). This appears to resemble the ethics of trust as put forward by disability ethicist Anita Silvers.
125. What happens to humanity's capacity for trust as humans shift that trust toward modern institutions that require trust in abstract systems is at the heart of Anthony Giddens, *The Consequences of Modernity* (Stanford, Calif.: Stanford University Press, 1990).
126. Ward, *Cities of God,* 92.
127. Ibid., 93.
128. Althaus-Reid, *Indecent Theology.*
129. Ward, "Bodies," 168.
130. An analogy may help: When I started practicing Pilates, my instructors ("reformers") would name a muscle, which I was then to try to locate and mobilize. Being well trained in Augustinian prayer practice, I would shut my eyes to locate that which I construed as inward or "internal." The Zen slap, palm on palm, of my instructor would not too patiently remind me that muscles are exercised in relation to a lived world, that closing my eyes shut off 90 percent of my relational interface with the world.
131. Kathleen Sands, *Escape from Paradise: Evil and Tragedy in Feminist Theology* (Minneapolis: Augsburg Fortress, 1994), 63.

132. Paul Newman, in *Spirit Christology* (Lanham, Md.: University Press of America, 1987), explains that "prophecy"—connected with Spirit and in contrast to Wisdom—"is not a discernment of perennial and universal truths about the human condition; rather prophecy is a passionate, concerned insight or action in *particular* crises and situations that call for judgment or action in light of the promises of God" (118).

133. Jessica Schaap, student paper. "Christology and the Songs of the Suffering Servant." Vancouver School of Theology, March 2007.

134. Barbara Ehrenreich in public speech related to the publication of her book *Nickel and Dimed: On (Not) Getting By in America* (New York: Metropolitan Books/Henry Holt, 2001). See http://portland.indymedia.org/en/2002/11/35157.shtml.

135. Warren Carter, "Proclaiming (in/against) Empire Then and Now" *Word and World* 25 (2005): 154.

136. Neil Elliott, "The Anti-Imperial Message of the Cross," in *Paul and Empire: Religion and Power in Roman Imperial Society,* ed. Richard A. Horsley (Harrisburg, Penn.: Trinity Press International, 1997), 167–83.

137. Rowan Williams, *Resurrection: Interpreting the Easter Gospel* (Cleveland, OH: Pilgrim, 2003), 21.

138. Kallos, *Broken for You.* Subsection header is a quotation from 295.

139. Ibid., 313.

140. Halperin, *Saint Foucault,* 82.

141. Adoption does not appear to be unusual to spirit traditions, including Judaism and Christianity; in fact, across many cultures, "spiritual kinship" has been honored as stronger than blood, more enduring than biological filiation. Jesus' question in response to the news that his mother and brothers were looking for him—"Who is my mother? Who are my brothers?"—would appear to evolve from such an orientation (see Mt 12:48ff.). It is possible that even the Annunciation story in Luke, in which God's "holy" name will be given to the illegitimate "son of Mary," could be read as an adoption story—not unlike Paul's sensibilities about the adoption of the humiliated into an alternative "history" to that of Rome (see Rom 8).

142. Ashis Nandy identified the psychopathologies of the West as "the ideologies of progress [cloaking 'the ancient forces of greed and violence'], normality and hyper-masculinity." See his *The Intimate Enemy: Loss and Recovery of Self Under Colonialism* (Delhi: Oxford University Press, 1983), 30, x.

143. Avner Offer, *The Challenge of Affluence: Self-Control and Well-Being in the US and Britain since 1950* (Oxford: Oxford University Press, 2006), 347.

144. Ibid.

145. Ibid., 340.

146. Ibid., 351.

147. Kallos, *Broken for You,* 367.

148. Ibid.

149. Ibid., 348.

150. Spivak, "Righting Wrongs," 536–37.

151. Scott DeShong, unpublished manuscript. See also his "The Nightmare of Health: Metaphysics and Ethics in the Signification of Disability," *Symploke* 15, no.1–2 (2007): 281.

152. Ward, "Suffering and Incarnation," 194.

153. Gilles Deleuze and Felix Guattari, *Anti-Oedipus: Capitalism and Schizophrenia,* trans. Robert Hurley, Mark Seem, and Helen R. Lane, preface by Michel Foucault (Minneapolis: University of Minnesota Press, 1983), 362.

154. Harvey, *Spaces of Hope,* 15, 18.

155. Gordon Lynch, *After Religion? "Generation X" and the Search for Meaning* (London: Darton Longman and Todd, 2002), 3, 120.

156. Gayatri Chakravorty Spivak, *A Critique of Postcolonial Reason: Toward a History of the Vanishing Present* (Cambridge, Mass.: Harvard University Press, 1999), 355 n. 59.

157. Mark Lewis Taylor, "Spirit and Liberation: Achieving Postcolonial Theology in the United States," in *Postcolonial Theologies: Divinity and Empire,* ed. Catherine Keller, Michael Nausner, and Mayra Rivera (St. Louis: Chalice Press, 2004), 40.

158. Mircea Eliade as presented in Tod D. Swanson, "To Prepare a Place: Johannine Christianity and the Collapse of Ethnic Territory," *Journal of the American Academy of Religion* 62, no. 2 (1994): 242.

159. Paula Cooey, *Willing the Good: Jesus, Dissent and Desire* (Minneapolis: Fortress, 2006), 144.

160. To speak of Spirit as "prosthesis"—as an assumed conviction in relation to the world—is a concept that developed in dialogue with my student Beatrice Marovich, within her Directed Readings in "Theologies of Becoming," Vancouver School of Theology, July 2008. But also see Bernard Stiegler, "Derrida and Technology: Fidelity at the Limits of Deconstruction and the Prosthesis of Faith," in *Jacques Derrida and the Humanities,* ed. Tom Cohen (Cambridge: Cambridge University Press, 2001).

161. Pema Chodron, *The Places That Scare You: A Guide to Fearlessness in Difficult Times* (Boston: Shambhala Classics, 2002).

162. Sandercock, *Cosmopolis II,* 4.

163. Marilyn Legge, "Inside Communities, Outside Conventions: What Is at Stake in Doing Theology?" *Studies in Religion* 29, no. 1 (2000): 5.

164. Edward Said, *Culture and Imperialism* (New York: Vintage Books, 1993), 80–97.

165. Ward, *Cities of God*, 21.

166. H. Richard Niebuhr, *Faith on Earth: An Inquiry into the Structure of Human Faith*, ed. Richard R. Niebuhr (New Haven, Conn.: Yale University Press, 1989), 2.

167. Luce Irigaray, *I Love to You: Sketch of a Possible Felicity in History*, trans. Alison Martin (London and New York: Routledge, 1996).

168. Silvers and Francis, "Justice through Trust," 43.

169. Bruce E. Levine, "Mass Society and Mass Depression," *Ecologist* 37, no. 8 (2007): 49.

CONTRIBUTORS

Susan Abraham is Assistant Professor of Ministry Studies at Harvard Divinity School. She is the author of *Identity, Ethics and Nonviolence in Postcolonial Theory: A Rahnerian Theological Assessment* (Palgrave Macmillan, 2007) and coeditor of *Shoulder to Shoulder: Frontiers in Catholic Feminist Theology* (Fortress, 2009). Her current research interests include feminist theory and theology, practical and political theology, and global Christianity between colonialism and postcolonialism.

Ellen T. Armour holds the E. Rhodes and Leona B. Carpenter Chair in Feminist Theology and directs the Carpenter Program in Religion, Gender, and Sexuality at Vanderbilt Divinity School. She is the author of *Deconstruction, Feminist Theology, and the Problem of Difference: Subverting the Race/Gender Divide* (University of Chicago Press, 1999) and coeditor of *Bodily Citations: Judith Butler and Religion* (Columbia University Press, 2006).

Sharon V. Betcher is Associate Professor of Theology at Vancouver School of Theology. A constructive theologian working with pneumatological dimensions, she has authored *Spirit and the Politics of Disablement* (Fortress, 2007) and articles on ecological, postcolonial, and disabilities theologies. Her current manuscript project considers theological responses—worked through the lenses of disabilities studies—to the emergence of global cities.

W. Anne Joh is Associate Professor of Systematic Theology at Garrett-Evangelical Theological Seminary. She is the author of *Heart of the Cross: A*

Postcolonial Christology (Westminster John Knox, 2006). Her current book project proposes a theological and political interpretation of "the crucified Christ" in conversation with postcolonial theory, trauma theory, and Paul's interpretation of the cross along with Jean-Luc Nancy and Giorgio Agamben.

Serene Jones is President of Union Theological Seminary in New York City, prior to which she was Titus Street Professor of Theology at Yale Divinity School and Chair of the Women, Gender, and Sexuality Studies program at Yale University. She is the author of many essays and books, including *Calvin and the Rhetoric of Piety* (Westminster John Knox, 1995) and, most recently, *Trauma + Grace* (Westminster John Knox, 2009).

Namsoon Kang is Associate Professor of World Christianity and Religions at Brite Divinity School, Texas Christian University. She was Director of the Christianity in Asia Project at Cambridge University, and is President of the World Conference of Associations of Theological Institutions. Her publications include *Cosmopolitan Theology* (Westminster John Knox, forthcoming) and a coedited volume, *Handbook of Theological Education in World Christianity* (Regnum, forthcoming).

Catherine Keller is Professor of Constructive Theology in the Graduate Division of Religion at Drew University. She is the author, most recently, of *On the Mystery* (Fortress, 2008); *God and Power* (Fortress, 2005); and *Face of the Deep: A Theology of Becoming* (Fortress, 2003). She has coedited several volumes in the Transdisciplinary Theological Colloquia series, the most recent being *Apophatic Bodies: Negative Theology, Incarnation, and Relationality* (Fordham University Press, 2009).

Kwok Pui-lan is William F. Cole Professor of Christian Theology and Spirituality at Episcopal Divinity School, Cambridge, Massachusetts. She is the author of *Postcolonial Imagination and Feminist Theology* (Westminster John Knox, 2005) and editor of *Women and Christianity* (4 vols.; Routledge, 2010) and *Abundant Hope: Third World and Indigenous Women's Theology* (Orbis Books, 2010).

Tat-siong Benny Liew is Professor of New Testament at the Pacific School of Religion. He is the author of *Politics of Parousia: Reading Mark Inter(con)textually* (Brill, 1999) and *What Is Asian American Biblical Hermeneutics? Reading the*

New Testament (University of Hawaii Press, 2008). He also edited *The Bible in Asian America* with Gale A. Yee (Society of Biblical Literature, 2002); *They Were All Together in One Place? Toward Minority Biblical Criticism* with Randall C. Bailey and Fernando F. Segovia (Society of Biblical Literature, 2009); and *Postcolonial Interventions: Essays in Honor of R. S. Sugirtharajah* (Sheffield Phoenix, 2009).

Dhawn B. Martin received an MDiv from Austin Presbyterian Theological Seminary in Austin, Texas, and is currently working on a PhD in Theological and Philosophical Studies at Drew University. Her research interests include constructive and political theologies, cosmopolitanism, and American philosophical pragmatism.

Stephen D. Moore is Professor of New Testament at Drew Theological School. His many books include *Empire and Apocalypse: Postcolonialism and the New Testament* (Sheffield Phoenix, 2006); *Postcolonial Biblical Criticism: Interdisciplinary Intersections* (Continuum, 2005), which he coedited with Fernando F. Segovia; and *The Bible in Theory: Critical and Postcritical Essays* (Society of Biblical Literature, forthcoming).

Mayra Rivera is Assistant Professor of Theology and Latina/o Studies at Harvard Divinity School. She is author of *The Touch of Transcendence: A Postcolonial Theology of God* (Westminster John Knox, 2007) and coeditor of *Postcolonial Theologies: Divinity and Empire* (Chalice, 2004).

Erin Runions is Assistant Professor in the Department of Religious Studies at Pomona College. Her work brings together politics, culture, and the reading of biblical texts. She is the author of *Changing Subjects: Gender, Nation and Future in Micah* (Sheffield Academic Press, 2001) and *How Hysterical: Identification and Resistance in the Bible and Film* (Palgrave Macmillan, 2003).

Laurel C. Schneider is Professor of Theology, Ethics, and Culture at Chicago Theological Seminary. She received her MDiv from Harvard Divinity School (1990) and her PhD in theology from Vanderbilt University (1997). In addition to a range of articles, she is the author of two books, *Beyond Monotheism: A Theology of Multiplicity* (Routledge, 2007) and *Re-Imagining the Divine* (Pilgrim, 1999).

Gayatri Chakravorty Spivak, University Professor in the Humanities, Columbia University, holds honorary degrees from the Universities of Toronto and London and Oberlin College. She translated Jacques Derrida's *Of Grammatology* (Johns Hopkins University Press, 1974) and provided a critical introduction to it. Her many books include *In Other Worlds* (Routledge, 1987); *Outside in the Teaching Machine* (Routledge, 1993); *Thinking Academic Freedom in Gendered Post-Coloniality* (University of Cape Town Press, 1993); *A Critique of Postcolonial Reason* (Harvard University Press, 1999); *Death of a Discipline* (Columbia University Press, 2003); and *Other Asias* (Blackwell, 2007).

John J. Thatamanil is Assistant Professor of Theology at Vanderbilt Divinity School. He is the author of *The Immanent Divine: God, Creation, and the Human Predicament* (Fortress, 2006). He is currently at work on *Religious Diversity after Religion*, which interrogates how theologies of religious pluralism and comparative theology are compromised by prevailing constructions of the category "religion."

Jenna Tiitsman is a PhD candidate in Religious Studies at the University of North Carolina at Chapel Hill. Her research focuses on American engagement with advances in communications technology—from the telegraph to the internet—with particular attention to religious imaginations of the world and theories of the public. She is a Senior Research Fellow at Auburn Media, an initiative of Auburn Theological Seminary.

Lydia York is a PhD candidate in Theological and Philosophical Studies at Drew University. She is currently using postcolonial critique, object relations theory, and process theology to investigate the divine attribute of benevolence. She is a trained facilitator of the *Doing Our Own Work Seminar for Anti-Racist White People.*

INDEX OF NAMES